LEARNING DISABILITIES: A TO Z

A Complete Guide to Learning Disabilities from Preschool to Adulthood

REVISED AND UPDATED

CORINNE SMITH, PH.D., AND LISA STRICK

Free Press
New York London Toronto Sydney

*f*P

Free Press
A Division of Simon & Schuster, Inc.
1230 Avenue of the Americas
New York, NY 10020

First Free Press trade paperback edition September 2010

FREE PRESS and colophon are trademarks of Simon & Schuster, Inc.

For information about special discounts for bulk purchases, please contact Simon & Schuster Special Sales at 1-866-506-1949 or business@simonandschuster.com

The Simon & Schuster Speakers Bureau can bring authors to your live event. For more information or to book an event contact the Simon & Schuster Speakers Bureau at 1-866-248-3049 or visit our website at www.simonspeakers.com

Designed by Jill Putorti

Manufactured in the United States of America

10 9 8 7 6 5 4 3 2 1

Library of Congress Cataloging-in-Publication Data
Smith, Corinne Roth.
    Learning disabilities, A to Z : a complete guide to learning disabilities from preschool to adulthood / Corinne Smith, Lisa Strick.
    —Revised and Updated.
      p. cm.
    Includes index.
1. Learning disabilities—United States. 2. Learning disabled children—Education—United States. I. Strick, Lisa. II. Title.
    LC4705.S62 2010
    371.9—dc22   2010011900

ISBN 978-0-684-82738-4
ISBN 978-1-4391-5869-2 (pbk)

To our children and grandchildren:
Benjamin, Eli, and Rachel
Juli and Justin, Rachael and Brian
Ariel, Leora, Jed, Caleb, and Lincoln

Contents

PART I: UNDERSTANDING LEARNING DISABILITIES

Chapter 1 **What Are Learning Disabilities?** — 3

Chapter 2 **What Causes Learning Disabilities?** — 13

Brain Injury — 16

Errors in Brain Development — 20

Chemical Imbalances — 25

Heredity — 28

Environmental Influences — 30

Chapter 3 **Basic Types of Learning Disability** — 39

Attention-Deficit/Hyperactivity Disorder — 42

Visual-Perception Disabilities — 49

Language-Processing Disabilities — 59

Fine-Motor Disabilities — 70

PART II: HOW ARE LEARNING DISABILITIES IDENTIFIED?

Chapter 4 **Warning Signs at Home and at School** — 79

Developmental Delays — 80

Inconsistent Performance — 85

Loss of Interest in Learning — 88

Unexpected Underachievement — 92

Persistent Behavioral or Emotional Problems — 96

Declining Confidence and Self-Esteem — 100

Chapter 5 **The Learning Disabilities Evaluation** — 104

Become Informed About Federal
and Local Regulations — 109

Investigate the Investigators — 111

Ask About Tests   113
Find Out What Other Kinds of
   Information Will Be Collected   118
Prepare Your Child for the Evaluation   121
Start Keeping Records *Now*   122
Give Yourself Time to Deal with Evaluation Results   125
When in Doubt, Get a Second Opinion   130

Chapter 6 Becoming an Expert on Your Child   134
Are There Physical or Health Concerns
   We Have to Address?   136
What Is My Child's Overall Learning Potential?   137
Exactly Where Are the Areas of Disability?   140
What Are My Child's Strengths?   143
What Kind of Academic Support Does My
   Child Need?   146
What Kind of Social Support Does My Child Need? 151
What Kind of Emotional Support Does My
   Child Need?   153

PART III: AN APPROPRIATE EDUCATION

Chapter 7 Becoming an Education Activist   163
Preparing Individualized Education Programs   175
Monitoring Student Progress   177
Providing Appropriate Support at Home   181

Chapter 8 Developing an Effective Educational Program   188
The Program Must Teach and Reinforce
   Basic Skills   190
The Program Must Enable the Student to Keep Up
   with Class Content   192
The Program Must Help the Student Learn
   Appropriate Educational Strategies   194
The Program Must Help the Student Address
   Problem Behaviors   201

Chapter 9 The ABCs of Success in School   229
Get Organized   231
Help Children Find Their Preferred Learning Styles 238

Keep on Top of the Curriculum 245
Pay Attention to Basic Skills 254
Take Advantage of Technology 264
Avoid Homework Traps 275
Give Yourselves a Break 284

PART IV: A QUALITY LIFE

Chapter 10 **Social and Emotional Growth** 289
Learning Disabilities and Child Development 292
The Preschool Child 295
The Elementary School Student 302
The Adolescent 306
The Young Adult 314

Chapter 11 **Strategies for Promoting Personal Success** 320
Believe in Your Child 322
Establish Realistic Expectations 328
Give the Child Responsibility 339
Improve Social Skills and Opportunities 349
Be Consistent About Rules and Limits 363
Tune in to Family Dynamics 372
Look For Outside Support When You Need It 388

Chapter 12 **Looking Forward to the Future** 397
Does the Student Have a Plan for Continuing
    Education or Specific Job Training After
    High School? 401
Does the Young Adult Understand His Legal
    Rights and Advocate for Himself Appropriately? 422
Is the Young Adult Ready to Leave Home? 430

Appendix A Common Assessment Measures 447
Appendix B The Development of Reading, Writing,
    Mathematics, and Learning Strategies 465
Appendix C Using Assistive Technologies 477
Appendix D Resource List 487

Index 495
Acknowledgments 509

LEARNING DISABILITIES: A TO Z

Part I

UNDERSTANDING LEARNING DISABILITIES

1

What Are Learning Disabilities?

• Brian's first-grade teacher describes him as "a human pinball machine." He never walks; he bolts. He leaves his desk every few minutes to sharpen his pencil, get more paper, check on the class gerbils. He comments loudly on everything he sees. Brian's classmates find his restlessness and interruptions annoying, but neither punishments nor rewards have produced lasting change in his behavior. On his midterm report, Brian's teacher writes: "Brian is bright and enthusiastic, but he needs to settle down. He is falling behind because he doesn't pay attention."

• Eleven-year-old Aisha is quiet and shy. She works hard, but her progress in school has always been slow. Now in fifth grade, she is more than a year behind her peers in both math and reading. Her teachers do not believe Aisha is smart enough to keep up with the class, and they have reduced their expectations of her. Aisha's parents say she grasps ideas rapidly at home, and they are puzzled by her slow academic progress. They are also worried about the fact that Aisha is becoming increasingly withdrawn. She has no friends, and spends most of her free time watching television.

- Frank has been put on notice that he is failing eighth grade and will have to repeat it if he does not start handing in his assignments and stop cutting classes. He has also been in trouble for other things this year: fighting, vandalism, and (most recently) showing up drunk at a school dance. Frank says he doesn't care if he fails—he plans to quit school at sixteen, so he's just "doing time" until then. All but one of Frank's teachers find him hostile and uncooperative. The teacher who runs the computer lab says Frank is attentive and capable; he even helps others who don't know what to do.

- A popular tenth-grader, Joel has enjoyed sports since he was in elementary school. He has earned places on the high school wrestling, track, and baseball teams. He is also active in student government and sells advertising for the school yearbook. His grades, however, are mostly Cs and Ds. Joel's teachers complain that his homework is careless, sloppy, and incomplete; his handwriting is unreadable. "Maybe if he weren't so involved in extracurricular activities, he'd be able to focus on his work," Joel's history teacher comments. "He'll never get into college if he doesn't start making an effort!"

It can be easy to make assumptions about students like these. Brian is immature and lacks self-control. Aisha is slow intellectually. Frank has a "bad attitude" and needs discipline. Joel has to overcome his lack of academic motivation. If you take a closer look, however, a very different picture emerges:

- Brian's wandering mind and restless drive to keep moving frustrate him and his family even more than they do his teacher, but this behavior is beyond his control. He lacks the ability to "screen out" distractions and plan his actions, so he can't concentrate no matter how hard he tries. Brian also cannot regulate his impulses to investigate anything he notices that is new. At the end of each day he is exhausted from responding to all the sights and sounds that swirl around him, yet he can't "turn himself off" until he falls asleep (which is a struggle in itself).

• A psychologist found that Aisha's intelligence is in the gifted range. She struggles with schoolwork because she has poor visual recall. She cannot remember what words look like and must painfully "sound out" every word she reads. (Aisha also cannot remember maps, charts, or other visual materials, and copying from the blackboard is a nightmare for her.) The psychologist told Aisha's parents that Aisha has become depressed as a result of her school problems. "She sees herself as a total failure," he said.

• Frank started avoiding classes and homework to hide the problems he has understanding verbal directions or remembering much of what he reads. He also has trouble finding words to express himself in speech. Brighter than average, Frank is successful in learning situations that do not call for extensive use of language, but junior high school does not offer him many opportunities of that kind. Frank feels like a misfit and longs to escape the endless failure and criticism that he faces in school.

• Joel's success as an athlete masks very poor fine-motor coordination. Difficulty controlling his hands makes it hard for Joel to manipulate a pen or pencil, or to type on a computer. (He is also "all thumbs" when it comes to chores like washing dishes or setting the table.) Joel is a conscientious student and understands class material, but he finds it virtually impossible to express what he knows when he is required to write it down.

All of these students have *learning disabilities*, neurological handicaps that affect an individual's ability to understand, remember, or communicate information. Once believed to be rare, learning disabilities are now believed to affect at least 5 percent of the American population (or more than 15 million people). Many authorities feel that the number of individuals affected is actually much higher, and experts agree that many children are not doing as well as they could in school because of disabilities that have not been identified. Year after year, these youngsters are erroneously pegged as slow witted, insolent, or lazy. They are constantly being urged to shape up or knuckle down by adults concerned about their academic performance. When the usual tactics of reward and punishment fail, parents and teachers become frustrated—but no one is more frustrated than the students themselves. "The most depressing words in the English language have got to be *Try harder*," says a student whose disabilities were finally identified in high school. "I *was* trying, but because I wasn't *succeeding* nobody believed me."

Although learning disabilities have become the focus of more intense research in recent years, they are still poorly understood by the general public. Information about learning disabilities has been so slow to "trickle down" that misconceptions abound even among teachers and other education professionals. The confusion is not hard to understand. For one thing, the term *learning disability* refers not to a single disorder but to a broad range of handicaps that can affect any area of performance. Only rarely can learning disabilities be traced to a simple cause; many different things can impair brain function, and neurological problems can be significantly complicated by environmental issues, as well as by factors such as temperament and learning style. Disabilities can be divided into general types, but since they often occur in combinations—and also vary tremendously in severity—it can be very hard to see what students grouped under this label have in common.

In fact, learning disabilities can be so subtle that these children often do not seem handicapped at all. Most children with learning disabilities have intelligences in the average to superior range, and what is usually most obvious about them is that they are able (even exceptionally so) in some areas. How can a kid know everything there is to know about dinosaurs at the age of four, but still be unable to learn the alphabet? How can a student who reads three years beyond her grade level turn in written work that is incomprehensible? How can a child read a paragraph aloud flawlessly and not remember its contents five minutes later? No wonder these students get accused of being inattentive, uncooperative, or unmotivated!

This discrepancy between what it seems the child ought to be able to do and what he or she actually can do, however, is the hallmark of this kind of handicap. What children with learning disabilities have in common is *unexpected failure to learn*. Most of the time these students function in a way that is consistent with what would be expected from their intellectual abilities, educational opportunities, and family backgrounds, but on certain types of tasks their brains seem to stall. As a result, their performance in school is inconsistent: on target or even ahead of the class in some areas, but significantly behind in others. While neurological impairments can affect any area of brain function,

Read Aloud What Is Written in the Triangle Below

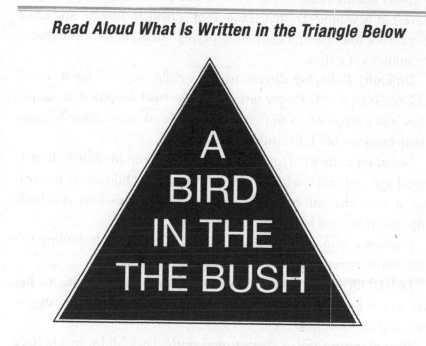

Just as you may have missed an extra *the* in the above sentence, children with learning disabilities often don't correctly process what is in front of their eyes, or information they have heard.

the disabilities most likely to cause academic problems are those affecting *visual perception, language processing, fine-motor skills*, and *the ability to focus attention*. Even minor handicaps in these areas—which may pass completely unnoticed at home—can have a devastating impact as soon as a child enters the classroom.

Many youngsters with learning disabilities also struggle with behaviors that compound their difficulties in school. Notorious among these is hyperactivity, an extreme restlessness that affects about 25 percent of children with learning disabilities (as well as some children who do not have LD). Some other problematic behaviors frequently observed in young people with learning disabilities follow:

Short attention span: The child is easily distracted, rapidly loses interest in new projects, may jump from activity to activity, and often leaves work unfinished; has trouble paying attention for more than a few minutes at a time.

Difficulty following directions: The child may ask for repeated guidance even during simple tasks ("Where was I supposed to put it?" "How was I supposed to do that again?"). Mistakes are made because instructions are not fully understood.

Social immaturity: The child acts younger than his or her chronological age and may prefer to play with younger children; is insensitive to nonverbal information (such as facial expressions and body language indicating how others are feeling).

Problems with conversation: The child has trouble finding the right words, or rambles endlessly.

Inflexibility: The child is stubborn about sticking to his or her own way of doing things, even when it is not working; resists suggestions and offers of help.

Poor planning and organizational skills: The child seems to have no sense of time and is often late or unprepared. Given several tasks (or a complex task with several parts), he or she has no idea where to begin, or how to break down the work into manageable segments.

Absentmindedness: The child frequently loses homework, clothing, and other possessions; forgets to do chores and assignments and/ or has trouble remembering appointments and social engagements.

Clumsiness: The child appears awkward and uncoordinated; often knocks things over, spills things, or fumbles and drops objects; may have atrocious handwriting; is seen as hopeless at sports and games.

Lack of impulse control: The child touches whatever (or whomever) captures his or her interest, blurts out observations without thinking, interrupts or inappropriately changes the subject in conversation, has difficulty waiting or taking turns.

Behaviors such as these can arise from the same neurological conditions that cause problems with learning. Unfortunately, when they are not understood as such, they only help convince adults that the child is not making an effort to cooperate or pay attention. Even students come to see behaviors like these as personality defects: "I was so happy when I found out I had a learning disability," one teenager recalls. "Until then I thought I was just an airheaded klutz."

Although many children with learning disabilities are happy and well adjusted, some (as many as half, according to current studies) do develop related emotional problems. These students become so frustrated trying to do things they cannot do that they give up on learning and start developing strategies to avoid it. They question their own intelligence and begin to see themselves as beyond help. Many become angry and act out; others become anxious and depressed. Either way, these children tend to become socially isolated and often suffer from loneliness as well as low self-esteem. Eventually, the secondary problems associated with a learning disability may become far more obvious—and more serious—than the handicap itself. Studies show that teens with learning disabilities are not only more likely to drop out of school, but are also at increased risk for substance abuse, criminal activity, even suicide. While most students with learning disabilities are not headed for futures this tragic, Casandra's story poignantly describes the frustration and insecurity that can follow these students into adulthood.

Parents of students with learning disabilities often find themselves attempting to cope with a bewildering array of problems. Their children appear to be intelligent but they encounter all kinds of obstacles in school. They have good intentions when it comes to homework

Casandra

I can remember my mother making me wear a letter from the alphabet around my neck to school. I think it was the letter *J*. I knew the letter before I left the house and tried so hard not to forget it all day. Picture a child, five years of age, walking out of her house and knowing that when she comes back through that very same door, she better know the letter.

I walked all the way to school saying the letter *J* over and over again. But do you know over the course of the day I had forgotten that letter? After school was out, I tried so hard—I mean, I looked at that letter, praying that a voice or something would give me the answer before I got home. I love my mother and I know she loves me, and all she wanted was for me to know my alphabet. But I feared her so and hated the fact I couldn't remember what she tried so hard to teach me. I remember crying and being mad at myself because I just couldn't get it. I wanted so much to yell at her, "I'm trying, damn it, I'm trying! Can't you see I'm trying! Just help me, please!"

As I got older, reading and spelling got harder and harder for me. Teachers, my family, and friends all seemed to be picking on me all the time. Teachers blamed me for cutting up in class. So since everyone wanted to laugh or blame me for things, I stopped trying to read either to myself or out loud and became a clown in school and stayed to myself at home.

By the time I reached eleventh grade, I realized the damage that was done. Going to college never entered my mind, or what I wanted out of life, or what kind of job I was going to get. Then I found myself feeling disappointed, not because the people that I cared about or the teachers that were supposed to teach had put me down, but because I had put my own self down. I finally came to realize I was always going to run into people who thought I was stupid, but I knew and really believed I wasn't. I was going to graduate from high school without anyone's help, so I knew I wasn't stupid.

Therefore, why is it to this very day, now twenty-eight, I still fear reading and speaking to people I meet? I find myself only speaking to those I know won't pick on me. I'll tell you why—it's because my family and teachers have made me think that everyone I talk to is going to pick and pick on me until they can't pick anymore. In other words, every human being on earth is smarter than me. And that is wrong.

No child should ever feel like that. How in hell can someone do that to a child who is trying?

Source: Adapted from C. R. Smith, *Learning Disabilities: The Interaction of Learner, Task, and Setting* (3rd ed.). Boston: Allyn & Bacon.

and chores but halfway through the job they forget the directions—or the objective. Their emotional ups and downs are often intense and can pitch the entire family into turmoil. Lacking a better explanation, these children often blame themselves for their inability to meet their parents' expectations and their own cherished personal goals: "I'm dumb," "I'm hopeless," or "People don't like me" can become an endless, self-defeating refrain. "It's the erosion of self-confidence that really kills you," one mother says. "There can't be much that feels worse than watching your kid give up on himself and his dreams."

This book is about helping children and young adults with learning disabilities hold on to their dreams. It is also about helping their mothers and fathers negotiate the maze of challenges that so often leave them feeling overwhelmed and helpless. The fact is that parents are not helpless—quite the contrary. Research proves that "quality parenting" can enable children to grow into happy, independent citizens even when a child's health and educational opportunities are notably poor. Studies of children with disabilities have found that the environment at home outweighs the quality of school programming or the severity of the handicap itself in importance.

Parents do not need a Ph.D. in psychology or education to guide their children effectively. Among the aspects of parenting researchers cite as most valuable are teaching children to make the most of their strengths, encouraging them to believe they can overcome obstacles, helping them set realistic goals, and encouraging them to take pride in their own competence by giving them responsibility at home and in the community.

Parents of children with learning disabilities do need to learn how to work with teachers and school administrators to develop an appropriate educational program—a prospect many find intimidating. Becoming an activist at the school, however, is the best way to ensure that your child's educational needs will be fully met. Because teacher-education programs until recently included next to nothing about learning disabilities, you cannot assume that your child's teachers will be well informed about them or sympathetic to your child's individual needs. Parents of successful students with learning disabilities say that they often find themselves in the position of "educating the educators" about learning disabilities and the many ways children can be affected by them. Keep in mind that many of the common teaching methods and materials that work for typical students are useless for children with learning disabilities. Careful monitoring and advocacy is the only way to make sure that your child is consistently taught in a way that makes it possible for him or her to learn.

Our goal is to provide you with both the information and the encouragement you need to become an effective advocate for your child. We will examine the causes and types of learning disabilities, and discuss the ways they affect both education and social and emotional growth. We will take you through the process of identifying learning disabilities and show you how to work with professionals to develop an individualized education plan. We will also talk about ways of addressing some of the persistent problems that can upset life at home. Let us begin, however, with the reminder that no "expert" you meet is ever going to know as much as you do about your child. More important, you are the only authority who can be depended upon to look at the whole child. Professionals are paid to concern themselves primarily with a student's problems and weaknesses; it is the *parents* who are most aware of all the ways a young person is strong and wonderful. Your most vital job is to remind your child that he or she is splendid and capable most of the time. Children who know they are mostly able—and entirely loved—do not let disabilities get in their way for long.

10 Myths About Learning Disabilities

2

What Causes
Learning Disabilities?

Even though students with learning disabilities are by far the largest special-needs group in the American school population, parents cannot always get clear answers to their most urgent questions when a learning problem is identified: "How did this happen?" "What went wrong?" "Can children outgrow learning disabilities?" "Is there a cure?"

These questions are difficult to answer because multiple factors can contribute to learning disabilities. In recent years, the relative importance of these causes has become a matter of increasing research and debate. In some of the newest research, investigators are using sophisticated imaging techniques to watch living brains at work. These studies compare structures and activity levels in the brains of normal subjects with those of subjects who have learning problems during the processes of reading, listening, and speaking. Scientists have also autopsied the brains of persons with learning disabilities, looking for anatomical differences, and geneticists have been searching for (and finding) evidence that some kinds of learning disabilities are inherited.

But while this research is producing more and more valuable information about the intricate structures and complex workings of the

10 Myths About Learning Disabilities

Although research has shed a great deal of light on learning disabilities in recent years, they are still widely misunderstood. Many of the myths below have believers even in the professional community.

1. Myth: *Mostly boys get learning disabilities.*

Fact: Boys and girls are both at risk. Boys, however, are more likely to "act out" when bored or frustrated, so they get referred for evaluation and services more often than girls do. Parents of girls (and quiet boys) with learning problems may need to be assertive about getting appropriate help for their children at school.

2. Myth: *Children can outgrow learning disabilities. If a child is having trouble in school, it is best to watch and wait.*

Fact: Learning disabilities are permanent, biologically based conditions. While the skills of students with LD do improve over time with appropriate instruction, some deficits persist into adulthood. These children benefit most from early intervention.

3. Myth: *Children with* dyslexia *(the medical term for "reading disabilities") literally see backward.*

Fact: The vision of these students does not cause their reading delays. Problems like reversing letters (saying or writing **b** for **d**) or reading **saw** for **was** arise from inefficient information processing in different parts of the brain. Since they are not vision problems, learning disabilities cannot be cured by eye exercises or glasses.

4. Myth: *Allergies can cause learning disabilities.*

Fact: Children with LD have no more allergies than children who do not have LD, and the disabilities do not go away when allergies are treated. Although coughing, itching, and sneezing can make it harder for any child to do his best, there is no evidence that allergies alone interfere with the ability to learn basic skills.

5. Myth: *Sugar makes children hyperactive.*

Fact: Research does not support this idea. Well-controlled experiments find that children whose parents claim they become "hyper" after eating sugar show no differences in learning or behavior from when they haven't consumed sugar. The stimulating environments in which sugary treats are offered—birthday parties, for example—probably contribute more to over-exuberant behavior.

6. Myth: *Wearing colored lenses or putting special plastic overlays on the page can improve reading ability and comprehension.*

Fact: There is no scientific evidence to support the claim that these devices produce dramatic or instantaneous improvement in reading results. Before paying for *any* kind of LD treatment, parents should ask what reliable research supports it. Anecdotal evidence (such as stories and quotes from people who swear they have been helped by a product or process) does *not* amount to scientific proof.

7. Myth: *Artificial coloring, flavors, and preservatives in food, or aspirin and salicylates (natural compounds in fruits and vegetables), can cause hyperactivity.*

Fact: While any child can benefit from improved nutrition, only a very small group of hyperactive preschoolers (about 3 percent) are helped by eliminating these substances from their diets. For the great majority, changes of diet have no impact. Vitamins also have no effect on learning disabilities.

8. Myth: *Left-handedness causes learning problems.*

Fact: Left-handedness itself is unrelated to learning. However, if a child becomes left-handed due to a brain impairment that makes it difficult to *use* her right hand, nearby brain areas affecting higher levels of learning may also be affected. When there is no impairment of this kind, left-handers learn as well as right-handers.

9. Myth: *Children who skip the crawling stage will have reading delays.*

Fact: Crawling has nothing to do with reading. Teaching a child to crawl (or perform any other motor activity) will not improve future response to reading instruction.

10. Myth: *Learning disorders arise from problems with language.*

Fact: About 60 percent of children experiencing reading delays have phonological-awareness (sound-processing) or other language weaknesses. The remaining 40 percent are slow to read because of difficulty maintaining attention, visual-perception disabilities, and/or problems with mastering basic learning strategies.

human brain, it is not always easy to apply this information to an individual. In addition, irregularities in brain function tell only part of the story. Children's development is also heavily influenced by their family, school, and community environments. While learning disabilities have a biological basis, it is often the child's environment that determines the severity of the disability's impact. Science has not yet provided much in the way of medical treatment for learning disabilities, but long experience has shown that modifying the environment can make a remarkable difference in a child's intellectual and academic progress.

The biological factors contributing to learning disabilities can be divided into four general categories: *brain injury, errors in brain development, neurochemical imbalances*, and *heredity*. In this chapter we will review each of these separately, and also discuss how environmental factors influence learning and development. Since there are no definitive neurological tests for learning disabilities, determining the cause of a given student's learning problems is now largely a matter of informed clinical judgment. When a child's home and school situations are examined and a detailed history is taken, one or more factors discussed in this chapter often stand out. It must also be admitted, however, that sometimes the only honest answer to the question "Why does my child have a learning disability?" is "We don't know for sure." We trust that ongoing research in this rapidly developing field will eventually provide us with new ways of evaluating these disabilities and pinpointing the source of individual learning problems.

BRAIN INJURY

For many years it was assumed that all students with learning disabilities had experienced some kind of brain damage. Today we know that most of these children have *no* history of brain injury, and even when they do it is not certain that this is the source of their academic difficulties. Research has shown that head injuries are almost as common among typical achievers as they are among children having trouble in school. One investigator estimates that as many as 20 percent of all children suffer significant head injuries by age six, yet most of those injured do not develop learning problems.

Efforts to link learning disabilities to brain damage caused by birth complications have also failed to find a conclusive connection. Birth trauma is associated with some cases of learning disability, but it can also be found in the histories of typical and high achievers. A study of seven- to fifteen-year-olds, for example, found that 23 percent of the students reading a year or two behind grade level had a history of birth injuries. A similar background, though, was found for 19 percent of the students reading a year or more *ahead* of grade level—hardly a convincing correlation!

There is no doubt, however, that some learning disabilities do arise from injury to the brain. Serious head trauma, strokes, high fevers, brain tumors, and diseases such as encephalitis and meningitis can all produce learning disabilities. Malnutrition and exposure to toxic chemicals (such as lead or pesticides) have also been shown to cause brain damage leading to learning problems. Children who receive radiation and chemotherapy treatments for cancer sometimes develop learning disabilities, especially if radiation has been applied to the skull. Events that cause the brain to be deprived of oxygen can result in irreversible brain damage in a relatively short time; incidents involving choking, suffocation, drowning, smoke inhalation, carbon-monoxide poisoning, and some birth complications fall in this category.

Brain injury can also occur before birth. When certain illnesses occur during pregnancy—diabetes, kidney disease, and measles among them—brain damage to the fetus is sometimes the sad result. Prenatal exposure to drugs (alcohol, nicotine, and some prescription medications as well as "street" drugs) has been clearly associated with a variety of learning difficulties, including cognitive delays, attention deficits, hyperactivity, and memory problems. The developing nervous system of a fetus is so fragile that even relatively minor insults can have significant lasting effects. The nervous systems of premature infants are also vulnerable to injury, and there is a significantly higher incidence of prematurity among children who have academic and behavioral problems.

Teddy

Teddy was adored by his parents and four older sisters, and it was not hard to see why. At two years old, he was a handsome, affectionate child who responded to all the attention given him with hugs, smiles, and laughter. He was tall for his age and obviously bright: he learned to talk early, spoke in clear three- and four-word sentences, and already recognized some letters of the alphabet. Teddy loved to watch *Sesame Street* and look at picture books, and he also loved the playground. He was so graceful on the slide and jungle gym that his father boasted that Teddy was certainly slated for athletic stardom.

Teddy's life changed, however, as a result of a severe viral illness. Teddy developed a high fever, had seizures, and was rushed to the local emergency room. He was hospitalized, but it was several days before the fever and seizures abated. By the end of the week it was clear that Teddy's illness had caused brain damage: the little boy could walk only with assistance, and he couldn't speak at all.

Over the next six months Teddy's ability to walk and talk returned, but he wasn't the same child. Instead of sitting quietly absorbed with crayons or a picture book, he became a human tornado. His coordination was poor, and he tried to stomp through things rather than move around them. He was impulsive and easily frustrated. He could not be taken to the supermarket without climbing and grabbing things off the shelves. When his parents tried to restrain him he would kick, bite, and throw tantrums. Even worse, Teddy continued to have seizures, which required frequent trials with different doses of medication.

Teddy's "out of control" behavior caused him to be dismissed by several nursery schools. Teachers complained that he knocked down other children's block towers, spoke out during story time, and splattered paint everywhere. He grabbed other children's toys and helped himself to other children's lunches. The teachers agreed that Teddy was bright enough, but they cautioned that he would have trouble in kindergarten if he could not control himself and learn to stick with tasks. Unfortunately, the teachers' predictions proved correct. Teddy's first years in school were a disaster; he couldn't attend to his lessons for long, and he was the last in his class to master basic skills. By the end of the second grade, it was obvious that reading and writing were both going to be very difficult for him. Teddy's skills always continued to develop, but his progress was so slow that the gap between him and the other students in his class got wider every year. By the time he finished sixth grade, Teddy was reading and writing like a fourth-grader. His seizures were largely under control and he had stopped having temper tantrums, but he remained an active, angry boy who was unpopular with other students and teachers alike.

During junior high school, continued low achievement and social isolation ate away at Teddy's feelings of self-worth. He became so angry and depressed that his parents became truly alarmed. After lengthy discussions, they decided to try placing Teddy in a private boarding school for students with learning disabilities. Teddy left home at the beginning of ninth grade.

Teddy's parents reported that by their first Parents' Day visit, they could see a change in their son. Teddy seemed heartened by the discovery that he was not the only student of his kind. He had made some friends, and he played on the school's soccer team. Teddy's teachers helped him complete tasks by allowing him to work in short sessions that were spread throughout the day. The school stressed learning through doing whenever possible, and Teddy found many of the projects he was assigned enjoyable and interesting. He had discovered that he could be a good student if he was allowed to do things his own way. For the first time since he was two, Teddy was thinking of himself as a success.

In twelfth grade, Teddy passed all of his state competency tests and declared he wanted to go on to college. Initially his parents panicked, afraid that demands at the college level would resurrect old patterns of frustration and failure. Several sessions with the school's guidance counselor, however, produced an ideal solution: following graduation, Teddy enrolled in a two-year culinary arts institute. He excelled in this training, earned an associate's degree, and rapidly found a job as a pastry chef in an exclusive resort. He recently became engaged to a vivacious young woman employed in resort management. Teddy's fiancé does all the driving because of his seizure disorder; Teddy does all the cooking, which his wife-to-be declares is a more-than-acceptable trade-off. Teddy is also designing the cake for his wedding, planned for June.

As Teddy's story demonstrates, the effects of brain injury can be sudden and dramatic, but just as often they are subtle and delayed. Sometimes children recover from an injury well enough to handle challenges at their current developmental or educational levels, but deficits become apparent when life becomes more complex and demanding. For this reason, significant problems in school at any point following a brain injury need prompt evaluation. In general, the earlier a child receives support following a brain injury, the better the chances are that he or she will recover—or learn to compensate for—skills that have been lost.

Brain injuries can cause multiple problems, and children who develop seizure disorders, cerebral palsy, or other physical disabilities as a result of brain damage sometimes have learning disabilities as well. It is important to keep this in mind when seeking services for a child following a brain injury, since subtle handicaps (such as learning disabilities) can be overlooked when there are more obvious or urgent physical challenges to overcome. Appropriate educational programming for a child with brain injuries often involves coordinating several different kinds of support; for example, a child may need physical and speech therapy as well as special education programming. Frequent monitoring may be needed to ensure that all the necessary elements are being provided and kept in reasonable balance.

ERRORS IN BRAIN DEVELOPMENT

Development of the human brain begins at conception and continues through young adulthood. In the nine months before birth, all of the basic structures of the brain are formed. A particularly critical developmental period occurs between the fifth and seventh months of gestation, when cells move into position in the cerebral cortex. The cortex, a multilayered structure that forms the brain's outer shell, is involved in virtually all aspects of conscious activity. Proper functioning of the cerebral cortex is essential for higher-level thinking and learning.

During infancy and childhood, regions of the brain become increasingly specialized to support specific functions. New connections between parts of the brain also form, so that these specialized areas can "cooperate" to varying degrees during different kinds of higher-level thinking. This continuing process of brain maturation explains why children gradually become able to do things they could not do before. Babies learn to walk and talk, for example, not only because eager parents encourage them to do so, but also because the necessary neural connections are made between one and two years of age. Within a few years, the brain develops to a point where a child can take on remarkably sophisticated challenges. The task of reading aloud, for example, involves the coordinated activity of fourteen areas of the cerebral cortex, including those concerned with vision, language processing, listening, and speech.

If this ongoing process of neural "wiring" goes awry at any point, pathways supporting different kinds of cognition may not develop completely. Experts believe that developmental errors of this kind are responsible for many learning disabilities. Support for this belief comes both from anatomical studies (which have found a variety of structural abnormalities in the brains of individuals with learning disabilities) and from research demonstrating that electrical and metabolic activity in the brains of students with learning problems is often different from that of typical learners. Current research has identified more than a dozen regions in the brain that can contribute to learning problems when their size or activity levels are diminished.

The types of problems produced by errors in brain development depend on which regions of the brain have been affected. It is important to understand, however, that since learning and other complex behaviors depend on the activation of "circuits" involving many brain areas, impairment in one brain region can affect growth and performance elsewhere in the system. For this reason, it is unusual for a student with learning disabilities to have a single, isolated weakness; *patterns* of related problems are far more common. Scientists using imaging technology to study activity in the cerebral cortex have identified three patterns that occur particularly often in individuals who have academic difficulties:

1. ***Left hemisphere is underactive/right hemisphere is overactive.*** The left cerebral cortex usually specializes in language functions, and youngsters displaying this pattern can have trouble with any aspect of language processing (reading, writing,

listening, and speaking). They find the task of breaking words down into sounds and syllables particularly hard. Reading skills are often delayed, and comprehension and memory for verbal material may be poor. In addition, these individuals often have difficulty with tasks involving logic and analysis: they grasp the "big picture," but are impatient with details, and may not understand that specific sequences of steps are necessary to arrive at a final product or solution. These children are likely to need some help analyzing tasks and coping with written material throughout their educations.

2. Right hemisphere is underactive/left hemisphere is overactive. The right side of the brain normally organizes and processes nonverbal information. Individuals with deficiencies in the right cerebral cortex can have problems with visual perception and visual memory, spatial orientation, body awareness, and time sense. They often take an overly analytical approach to problem-solving: they are attentive to details but may become so bogged down in trivia that they miss the main point of a lesson. This places them at risk for problems with higher-level tasks like organizing research projects, planning papers, and advanced math reasoning. Since youngsters displaying this pattern do not readily pick up on nonverbal "cues" (such as facial expression and body language) they are sometimes regarded as insensitive and socially inept, which can compound their problems at school.

3. Underactivity in the frontal lobes. The frontal lobes of the cerebral cortex govern motor behavior, and they also include regions involved in planning and judgment, focusing attention, organizing and evaluating information, and moderating emotions. When the frontal regions of the brain are not functioning efficiently, children can have problems with muscle coordination, articulation, impulse control, planning and organization, and maintaining attention. Problems of this kind affect children's readiness for classroom instruction, and they create an overall impression of immaturity even when the children are capable of functioning at a high level intellectually.

Individuals with errors in their cortical "wiring" must develop alternate neural pathways for processing information. Because these pathways are not always as efficient as normal brain circuits would be, students with learning disabilities tend to process information more slowly than typical peers. As a result, these students need more time both to understand tasks and to complete them. While the additional time required is often only a matter of seconds, this handicap can have a significant impact on a student's ability to compete in classrooms. Information-processing delays can be devastating when students face "pressure" situations such as timed tests or math drills. In some cases, simply removing time constraints is enough to help a student with learning disabilities do better at school. More often, however, the need for extra time is only one part of a larger pattern of learning problems.

Not all developmental problems involve irregular anatomy. Experts believe that some individuals develop learning difficulties because parts of their brains simply mature more slowly than usual. Such children are not always ready to take on the tasks and responsibilities that are appropriate for their chronological ages: they act like their peers in some respects, but in other areas their behaviors and needs are more like those of younger children. In such cases of *maturational lag,* delayed regions of the brain may reach normal or near-normal levels of development eventually, but by this time victims are likely to have spent many discouraging years in classrooms where what they were being taught was out of sync with what they were ready to learn. Even after their brains mature, these students may continue to be handicapped because they missed out on acquiring the skills and concepts that are the basic building blocks of a higher education. Too often, these students find that their skills never quite catch up with the increasingly complex demands of the curriculum. If their programs are not modified, they fall further and further behind academically, and their problems compound as feelings of inadequacy sap their emotional energy and their enthusiasm for learning.

Information-Processing Delays and Memory

Nearly all students with learning disabilities experience delays in processing some kinds of information. Although the delays are slight (research indicates, for example, that these children are $\frac{1}{10}$ to $\frac{1}{3}$ of a second behind typical peers in "registering" what they see or hear) they can have a significant impact on how well students retain what they have been taught.

This is because any time we are exposed to new information, we have a very small window of opportunity (only a few seconds) to figure out a way to remember it. If we do not succeed in creating a memory within that period, the information is lost. While this amount of time is ample for learners whose brains are wired efficiently, children with learning disabilities may still be struggling to understand and interpret what they have seen or heard when the memory window slams shut.

Imagine a student who is being taught math facts. The teacher shows her a card stating $1+1=2$, repeats the information, and then moves on to $1+2=3$. If the student has a visual-processing disability, she may not have had enough time to fully register the series of symbols she has seen, let alone understand their relationship to one another and remember them. Her future failure to progress in math is likely to be due more to these problems with recognition and recall than issues of intellectual or reasoning ability.

Research finds that when students with learning disabilities are given the extra time they need to enter correct information into their memory banks, most can retrieve and use the information as well as typical learners. To assist the memory process, it may be necessary to present information in small "chunks," to slow the pace of instruction, and to provide extra practice with new skills. Teachers should also target students' strongest learning channels—for example, a child with visual-processing disabilities might be taught math facts by giving her blocks to manipulate and encouraging her to recite the facts aloud. Parents will need to use similar strategies for helping children remember new information at home.

Why developmental errors and delays occur is not always clear. Events that disturb prenatal brain development are undoubtedly responsible for some abnormalities. In other cases heredity appears to play a role. The good news is that most students with learning disabilities respond positively to a stimulating educational environment and make steady progress given appropriate instruction. Exciting new research suggests that students who receive intensive, timely intervention can actually "rewire" their brains and start to use neural pathways that lead to more efficient processing of information. As our understanding of how the brain responds to different kinds of stimuli grows, more targeted and effective educational interventions should become possible. In the meantime, parents should be aware that research strongly supports the importance of early intervention and intensified instruction for children who are falling behind in any area of development.

It is also important to remember that children whose brains develop unevenly sometimes exhibit strengths and talents that are out of the ordinary. Thomas Edison and Albert Einstein are among the geniuses who had learning problems; the list of celebrities in sports, business, politics, and the arts who had serious difficulties with reading, writing, or math in school is a long one. Parents and special educators note that children with learning problems are sometimes exceptionally creative; because traditional solutions do not always work for them, they become inventive about finding "work-arounds" of their own. Since teachers faced with a student who cannot read or write well will not necessarily get excited about that youngster's leadership qualities, entrepreneurial ability, or musical talent, parents need to be alert about noticing and encouraging emerging strengths in nonacademic areas.

CHEMICAL IMBALANCES

Brain cells communicate with one another by means of chemical "messengers" called neurotransmitters. Any change in the brain's delicately balanced chemical climate can interfere with these neurotransmitters and impair the brain's ability to function properly. People who are intoxicated by alcohol, for example, experience a temporary alteration in brain chemistry. As any police officer can affirm, disturbances in speech, motor coordination, and problem-solving ability are the usual results.

A growing body of evidence suggests that neurochemical imbalances contribute to some learning disorders, particularly those involving difficulty with attention, impulsivity, hyperactivity, organization, and planning. This includes the syndrome known as *attention-deficit/ hyperactivity disorder* (ADHD). Youngsters with ADHD typically appear to be restless, careless, distractible, and disorganized; they may also be overly talkative, poorly coordinated, and so energetic that they wear out their caretakers. They have trouble getting started on tasks, attending to details, staying alert and focused, thinking through solutions, and managing their emotions appropriately. While their behavior may not seem seriously out of line at home or on the playground, these children are easily identified in the classroom by their inability to sit still and concentrate. Although some of these children are no more active than average, their tendency to leave their seats at the wrong times makes a poor impression on teachers and fellow students alike.

Investigators have found a variety of structural and functional irregularities in the brains of people with ADHD. An overview of the research suggests that, in these individuals, brain circuits governing attention, impulsivity, and motor control are underactive, particularly in the frontal lobes. As early as the 1930s, it was observed that stimulant medications—which boost the levels of neurotransmitters regulating these circuits—temporarily normalize the behavior of people who are hyperactive and have problems with concentration. Recent controlled studies suggest that 70 to 80 percent of students with ADHD receive some benefit from stimulants (see box, pages 204–7). In the last twenty years the number of drugs (both stimulant and nonstimulant types) available for the treatment of ADHD has grown tremendously, and so have the numbers of young people using them. It is estimated that more than 2 million children—nearly one in thirty school children—take medication for ADHD, with prescriptions for Ritalin being the most common.

Medication has also been used to regulate brain function in children who are *hypoactive*. These young people are lethargic and easily bogged down by details; they ponder problems at excessive length and have difficulty making decisions. In school they appear dull and unmotivated because they complete their work slowly and ask few questions. Interestingly, these students sometimes "perk up" when given sedatives. Experts theorize that sedative medications regulate overactive neurotransmitter systems that have caused the brain to overfocus, rendering the students oblivious to much that is going on.

Medications can produce undesirable side effects, so the decision to use them needs to be made with care. We will discuss the pros

Effects of Adderall on Handwriting

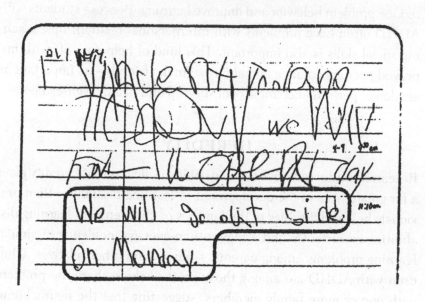

This six-year-old boy copied the top three lines just before taking Adderall (a stimulant medication for ADHD). An hour and a half later he copied the same lines with more success.

Source: C. R. Smith, *Learning Disabilities: The Interaction of Students and Their Environments,* 5th ed. Boston: Allyn & Bacon, 2004. Reproduced by permission of Pearson Education, Inc.

and cons of medication for ADHD more thoroughly in Chapter 8. In the meantime, it is important to remember that medication is not a "cure" for ADHD, and it is rarely a total solution to a child's problems. First of all, medication can only improve a child's ability to take advantage of educational opportunities; it is not a substitute for suitable educational programming and skilled teaching. About a third of children with ADHD have additional learning disabilities that must be addressed, and virtually all of these children need ongoing support both at home and at school to help them develop effective learning strategies and maintain appropriate behavior. Studies have shown that behavior modification programs can enhance the effectiveness of medication, and in situations where medication is ineffective or undesirable, behavioral and educational intervention alone can significantly reduce problem behavior and improve learning. Because students with ADHD often have problems with interpersonal relationships, teaching social skills is also important. This kind of help pays off with improved peer acceptance and ability to make friends—as important as academic performance for school survival and healthy self-esteem.

HEREDITY

Research conducted since the mid-1980s indicates that heredity plays a far greater role in the development of learning disabilities than previously believed. Studies of the families of children with learning disabilities consistently find a higher-than-average incidence of similar learning problems among parents, siblings, and other relatives. Children with ADHD are among those most likely to share the problem with one or more family members, suggesting that the neurochemical imbalances which contribute to this disorder could be genetic in origin. There is also substantial evidence that heredity influences sound-processing ability, visual memory, and the speed at which children absorb new information. Boys are more likely than girls to inherit weaknesses in these areas by a margin of two to one—although not all cases are as dramatic as Jimmy's (pages 30–31).

Recent studies have found that about 40 percent of children with learning disabilities have a parent or sibling with similar learning problems. A study of children with reading disabilities found that 88 percent had relatives who had experienced language-processing problems! Some of the most convincing data in support of the inheritability of learning disabilities comes from research involving twins. While fraternal twins have similar learning problems about half the time, identical twins—who share the same genetic "blueprint"—are found to have similar disabilities about 70 percent of the time. Since both types of twins share the same environment, the higher incidence of similarity among identical twins is likely due to genetic factors.

In a new research focus, *linkage analysis,* scientists are attempting to locate the genes that carry learning disabilities. While evidence implicating a number of specific genes has been collected, this research suggests that there are probably many ways that learning disabilities can be inherited—for example, unusual brain anatomy, uneven patterns of brain maturation, and susceptibility to illnesses that affect brain function all could be passed down genetically. Researchers believe that some genes are linked to one specific skill (such as distinguishing sounds in words), while others influence a broader spectrum of information-processing abilities. How genes combine with environmental triggers also affects their impact. Investigators note that heredity is never likely to be the *only* cause of a learning disability. For example, the authors of some of the best-known twin studies estimate that when identical twins share reading disabilities, 54 percent of each child's deficit is due to genetic problems, 40 percent is due to shared environmental influences, and 6 percent is due to random factors unique to the individual.

Clinicians who test for learning disabilities observe that when results are presented to parents, Mom or Dad frequently remarks, "But I can't do that either!" These parents may also have struggled in school, but since learning disabilities were rarely identified a generation ago, they may have never suspected they have a neurological handicap. While some parents seem grateful that an explanation other than "stupidity" exists for their own histories of learning problems, others find the suggestion that there is something wrong with both them *and* their children more than they want to take on. Parents who feel their own lives have been made harder as a result of educational failures may feel particularly disturbed about the prospect of their children facing similar obstacles. Education about learning disabilities—understanding that they are very different from mental retardation, for example, and that help is available now which did not exist years ago—often is needed to help these parents accept facts and move on to appropriate action. Encouragement is also important; helping a child with tasks that made you feel defeated in school takes a special kind of courage and motivation. When there is a family history of learning disabilities, parents need as much support as children do both from professionals and from other family members.

Jimmy

When Jimmy's mother called a clinic to refer her son for an evaluation, the first hint that Jimmy's learning difficulties might be hereditary came over the phone. Jimmy's mother expressed her deep "flustration" in obtaining adequate services for her son's "dilekia." From a woman with a Ph.D. who was the director of a counseling center, such mispronunciations were unexpected. The mother's worst fear was that Jimmy had inherited "dilekia" from both sides of the family.

Jimmy's mother had two siblings, neither of whom had learned to read until adolescence. One now writes books but remains a terrible speller. One child of the other sibling has been identified as learning disabled, and her younger child, a preschooler, is receiving speech and language therapy.

Jimmy's father has a master's degree in social work, a Ph.D. in philosophy, and now spends all his time back in law school. He is never satisfied with his accomplishments and keeps trying to prove his competence in new ways. Jimmy's father was very late in learning to read and still reads, in his words, "a word an hour." What he reads he remembers, however, and he is an excellent student. His professors have always allowed him to use a spell-checker on exams. Jimmy's father comes from a family of five children, and every one has a reading disability. All but one sibling, who suffers from severe depression, have become vocationally successful. One of his brothers stutters and a sister gets stuck on very simple words when speaking. (Her conversations are punctuated by referring to objects as "thing" and elaborating when recounting an event by adding "or some such thing.") Another brother is described as extremely disorganized; he gets lost in supermarkets and shopping malls and panics at the idea of traveling through a strange city.

ENVIRONMENTAL INFLUENCES

Although learning disabilities are caused by physiological problems, the extent to which children are affected by them is often decided by their environments. Conditions at home and at school can, in fact, make the difference between a mild disability and a truly devastating handicap. In order to understand learning disabilities fully, it is necessary to understand how children's environments affect their intellectual development and learning potential.

Jimmy's mother had reason to believe that her ten-year-old son may not have been lucky enough to escape this genetic history. Take a look at his spelling and judge for yourself the outcome of his assessment.

Transcription

In a race for survival I raised my sharp spear at the great beast. It fought back with its great trunk and just missed him by an inch and even though a spear had hit it doesn't give up yet it can tire you to fight.

Adapted from C. R. Smith, *Learning Disabilities*, © 2004. Reproduced by permission of Pearson Education, Inc.

The Environment at Home

The home environment plays a major role in determining how well or how poorly any child learns. An enormous body of research has shown that a stimulating, encouraging home environment produces adaptable, eager learners, even among children whose health or intelligence has been compromised in some way. A long-term study of orphans who were mentally retarded, for example, found that the IQs of children adopted into families of normal intelligence rose measurably, while the intelligence of those who remained institutionalized actually declined over the years. While the institutionalized group remained undereducated and underemployed, most of the adopted children completed high school (and a third went on to college). Animal studies have shown that an enriched environment not only has an impact on learning, but actually stimulates brain growth and development. Neuroscientists are building an impressive body of evidence that human brains also respond to "mental exercise."

In addition, children who have received affectionate encouragement throughout their lives tend to have positive attitudes, both about learning and about themselves. Their "I can do it" spirit helps them rise to challenges and overcome obstacles. These children look for and find ways around disabilities, even when their handicaps are quite severe.

In contrast, children who have been deprived of a nourishing environment in their early years face discouraging hurdles even when they don't have disabilities. These youngsters are typically slow to acquire basic cognitive skills. They do not use their intellectual abilities to advantage and may show little curiosity or interest in learning. They often lack social skills and self-confidence. Deficiencies like these place children at risk throughout their school years. Studies have repeatedly shown that students who are emotionally and academically "ready" when they begin kindergarten usually remain near the top of their classes right through graduation, while youngsters who enter school with significant social and cognitive delays continue to struggle academically, even with special help.

Not surprisingly, socially and emotionally disadvantaged children also find it hard to marshal the resources needed to overcome neurological handicaps. Students with learning disabilities normally use their areas of strength to help compensate for areas of weakness, but students who have not had adequate levels of stimulation and support have fewer areas of strength to draw upon. In addition, these students are less persistent than other children when they encounter problems. Teachers observe that they often anticipate failure, seeming to "quit before they start."

There are many aspects of a home environment that can under-

What Do Children Need to Learn and Grow?

Psychologist Erik Erikson believed that children's attitudes about themselves and the world around them depend largely on how they are treated by adults as they grow up. Below is a summary of what Erikson believed children need most from their families at different stages of development.

Trust (birth to 1 year): Infants learn to trust when interactions with adults are pleasurable and gratifying. Babies need caregivers who are warm, predictable, and responsive to their needs. If infants regularly have to wait a long time for comfort or are handled harshly, fear and a sense of worthlessness grow.

Autonomy (1 to 3 years): Self-confidence develops as children exercise the exploratory skills of walking, running, climbing, and handling objects. Toddlers need parents who encourage them to choose from a variety of safe activities. If children are overly restricted, or shamed for making mistakes as they explore, self-doubt will grow instead of self-control.

Initiative (3 to 6 years): Children closely observe and imitate adults, but also start making their own choices about such matters as what to wear, what to eat, and what to do. Parents who support responsible decision-making encourage ambition and pride in accomplishment. If parents are overly demanding or controlling, children may become guilty and repressed instead of independent.

Industry (6 years to puberty): Children learn to work with others and start to judge their performance against what others can do. School-aged children need families who encourage competence and mastery by giving them responsibility and opportunities to use and increase their skills. Young people who are frequently criticized or do not have these opportunities may see themselves as inadequate or inferior.

Identity (adolescence): Teens integrate what they have gained from the previous stages into a lasting sense of identity; they develop an understanding of their place in society and form expectations for the future. Adolescents need respect for their emerging adult selves. Children who have not had their needs met at this and earlier stages are likely to be confused about who they are and where they want to go.

mine a child's capacity for learning. Children who do not get enough nourishing food or enough sleep will obviously suffer in their ability to concentrate and absorb information. So will youngsters who are frequently ill due to poor hygiene or substandard medical care. Children who have had limited exposure to the English language before starting school or who watch excessive amounts of television, are likely to be delayed in their English language development; this impacts their ability to express themselves and understand their teachers, and makes it harder for them to learn to read and write. Students whose families cannot provide them with school supplies, a predictable time to do homework, and a relatively quiet place to study, have to be exceptionally motivated in order to achieve—as do children who live with little encouragement and low expectations. Any of these factors can reduce a child's chances of overcoming a learning disability successfully. Emotional stress also compromises children's abilities to learn. Anxiety about money or relocation or family discord or illness not only can be distracting in themselves, but also over time can erode a child's willingness to trust, take chances, and be open to new experiences, all of which are important to success in school. It is a tragic fact that growing numbers of children are not really available for learning because their lives are dominated by fear: dangers in their homes or neighborhoods make it necessary for them to devote most of their mental energy to the urgent issue of personal protection. If the school itself is not safe, the academic prospects of an entire student body can be undermined.

While problems such as these can afflict any child, children raised in poverty encounter more than their share of environmental hazards. Such children—who are also more vulnerable to some kinds of brain injury and developmental problems—are overrepresented in our special-education population. Since even preschool intervention is too late to remedy all the effects of long-term physical or intellectual deprivation, the best hope for many children may lie in making health care and easy-to-obtain, quality education available to *parents* in such key areas as nutrition and infant and toddler stimulation. Social programs designed to reduce the shocking number of children living in poverty (now nearly one in five in the United States) are also critical to improving children's learning potential. The cost of such programs needs to be evaluated in light of the gloomy prospects faced by students who begin school with cognitive deficits: they are less likely to graduate, less likely to find satisfactory employment, and more likely to end up in prison or in need of public assistance than more fortunate youngsters. When these long-term social consequences are taken into account, the failure to prevent learning problems becomes very expensive indeed.

The Environment at School

In order to make intellectual progress, children must not only be ready and able to learn, they must also have appropriate learning *opportunities*. If the educational system fails to provide these, students may never develop their full range of abilities, effectively becoming "disabled" even though they have no neurological issues. Unfortunately, many students must struggle to do their best under less-than-optimum conditions in our nation's schools.

Obviously, overcrowded classrooms, overworked or poorly educated teachers, and inadequate supplies of good teaching materials all compromise students' ability to learn. But so do many widely accepted practices that fail to provide for normal variations in learning style. A student whose orientation is primarily visual and exploratory, for example, needs to see and touch things in order to understand them. This student will not do well with teachers who lecture all the time, no matter how bright and interested in the subjects he may be. Similarly, a child whose approach to learning is basically reflective—who needs time to consider all aspects of a problem thoroughly before attempting a solution—will do miserably in a classroom where students are hustled from assignment to assignment according to the dictates of a rigid curriculum. What about the recent immigrant who does not participate in discussions because she lacks confidence in her English vocabulary, or because her notions of respect forbid her to be "forward" about volunteering information? When students such as these do poorly in school, is it right to say the problem is exclusively theirs?

The truth is that many low achievers are victims of their schools' inability to adjust to individual and cultural differences. Despite the fact that the population in America's schools is becoming increasingly diverse, it is still standard practice in many classrooms to "teach to the middle," using methods and materials designed to reach the average white middle-income student of a generation ago. When children who do not fit the mold fail to progress, school officials sometimes find it easier to blame the students than to examine their own or the programs' shortcomings. Incredibly, there are schools where the failure rate exceeds 50 percent, and teachers are still talking about problem *children*!

Children with learning disabilities cannot adapt to rigidity in the classroom. In order to make progress, these students must be encouraged to work in their own way. If placed with a teacher who is inflexible about assignments and testing, or who uses materials and methods inappropriate for their needs, these students will fail. If they are regularly shamed or penalized for their failures ("Since you haven't finished your work, you're going to have to stay in from recess again, Jimmy; you really must try harder . . ."), these students are unlikely to remain motivated for long. Sadly, loss of interest in education and lack of self-confidence can continue to fetter these children even when they move on to more favorable settings. In this way, the wrong school environment can encourage even the most minor disabilities to blossom into major handicaps.

Parents of students with learning disabilities frequently observe that their children appear to be more "disabled" in some classes than in others. While this can be a reflection of the students' particular types of learning problems, it is also true that disabilities tend to fade or even disappear in classrooms where creative, flexible teachers make an effort to match tasks to their students' readiness levels and learning styles. Since typical learners also flourish in these classrooms, it seems fair to say that at least part of the solution to the growing demand for special education services is to improve curriculum design and teacher preparation across the board. In the meantime, it is important for parents to realize that intervention for children with learning disabilities often calls less for "fixing" the child and more for adjusting the environment in which the child is being educated. The right class, the right curriculum, and the right teacher are critical for these children, and choosing them often makes the difference between solid success and frustrated failure. As Mancele's sad story indicates, schools cannot always be counted upon to program for students appropriately. Parents who thoroughly understand their own child's learning strengths and weaknesses are

Mancele

My disability in reading, writing, and spelling affected me in two ways. First I had no confidents in myself and the second is the fear I had inside of me.

My fear was and still is so grete [great] that if someone asked me to read, spell, or write down directions, I would break out in a sweat. The fear was divercateing [devastating] to me. About school I don't remember my early years because I don't thing I was taught anything to remember anything about school. However, from the sixth or seven grade, I new I had a problem. I was tested and put into what was called an opportunity class, they call it.

They sed that it would be a special class to help me. Most of the "opportunity" class was made up of young black men. We had the "opportunity" of running movies all day for other classes in our school. This was our opportunity for learning. The classes were taught by one teacher. He was subpose to teach us in all subjects, math sceance [science] and Enlish, History, etc. The movies were fun to show, however the only thing I learned was showing movies. So my seventh and eighth grade Education was a lost, too. Most of our tests in class were motobowt [multiple] chosuis [choice]. I got good marks some B, too. I became putty [pretty] good in taking tests. Even on my spelling lists I got 75% or 80% carick [correct]. I could menerize [memorize] anything for a short time, but in two weeks after I forget it all. Because I menorize it. It did not matter what order it was in or giving it to me. I learn the sound of each word, then the letters. But didn't know the words themself. I graduated from High school knowing I could not read or spell afbulb [above] third grade. When I had to write a book reported, the pain in my head would come and I would pannick. I would pick out key words in some books I knew, and picked out key sentence, then put them together for my book report. So now they say I have a learning disability. I say I wasn't taught.

Source: C. R. Smith, *Learning Disabilities*, © 2004. Reproduced by permission of Pearson Education, Inc.

in the best position to evaluate the educational options available from year to year and decide which are the *real* "opportunity" classes.

Often, the question "Why does my child have a learning disability?" translates into "Whom should I blame?" One mother remembers, "My greatest fear was that *I* was somehow responsible. I questioned everything from the anchovy pizza I ate in the second month of pregnancy to my decision to go back to work when my son started school. Meanwhile, my husband was blaming everyone from the obstetrician who delivered our son to the psychologist who did the testing." Reactions like this are normal, but they are not really productive. Anger, anxiety, or guilt over "what went wrong" do nothing to help a child; usually they serve only to exhaust parents' emotional energy and elevate their level of stress. In the end, understanding how a child came to have a learning disability is far less important than knowing how it affects the child's worldview and how to find the right kinds of help.

3

Basic Types of
Learning Disability

Everyone has learning strengths and learning weaknesses. As adults, most of us confess our weaknesses willingly: We were idiots in math, for example, or rotten at foreign languages. We could not draw a straight line in art. We had trouble remembering the dates in history, never got the hang of book reports, had a "tin ear" for music, or tripped over our own feet in gym. We can afford to be cheerful about our shortcomings, because we managed to succeed in spite of them. Our weaknesses were either in areas that did not interfere seriously with our progress through school or not severe enough to prevent us from achieving our most important goals. Along the way we developed some talents we feel pretty good about, and we use those strengths to define ourselves.

Children with learning disabilities, however, suffer an unlucky combination: not only are their weaknesses more pronounced than usual, but they also lie in those areas most likely to interfere with the acquisition of basic skills in reading, writing, or mathematics. As a result, their progress in school is repeatedly blocked. These children are often bright, creative, and even gifted in other spheres, but since they are achieving poorly in the areas most valued by our society, their talents may be judged unimportant or irrelevant. Some of these students come to feel defined by their failures. They do not understand *why* they can't do what other kids seem to find easy, so they see themselves as stupid or generally defective.

In fact, children with learning disabilities are generally found to be struggling in one or more of four basic areas that prevent smooth processing of information: *attention, visual perception, language processing,* or *fine motor coordination.* Even minor weaknesses in these areas can create formidable obstacles to learning and communication in traditional classrooms.

In order to overcome learning disabilities, it is vitally important for both parents and students to understand exactly in which of these areas deficits lie. This information is essential for evaluating a child's educational program and determining what kind of changes need to be made. It is needed to establish reasonable goals both at school and at home. Most important, this knowledge will ultimately make it possible for the child to become a confident, independent learner. In general, the more youngsters with learning disabilities know about their own patterns of strengths and weaknesses, the more likely they are to accept themselves, advocate for themselves, and plan strategies that minimize their disabilities and make the most of their skills and talents.

Precise identification of a child's learning problems requires a comprehensive evaluation, which we will discuss in detail in Part II. Our goal here is to introduce the four basic types of disability, and describe how each can affect a child's school performance and development. Before we do that, however, any adult concerned with children who have learning disabilities must understand the following three points:

1. *Children with learning disabilities frequently have problems in more than one area.* For example, a child's primary disability (the one causing the most trouble in school) may involve problems with language comprehension, but he may also have trouble concentrating and be somewhat delayed in his fine-motor development. In cases of this kind it is necessary to understand not only each of the disabilities, but also how they can complicate one another. To maximize chances for improvement, all the disabilities have to be addressed.

2. *Learning disabilities do not vanish when a child leaves school for the day.* These conditions affect the way a child perceives the *world*, so they influence conduct at home and social and family relationships as well as academic performance. A lot of behavior that seems careless or even willfully obstructive (such as difficulty being on time, losing possessions, or chronic failure to complete chores) may at least in part be related to a child's learning problems. Parents who understand the nature of their children's disabilities are in the best position to develop realistic expectations—and they will also spare themselves fruitless nagging and aggravation.

3. *Learning disabilities can produce emotional consequences.* The reason is no mystery. How would you feel if you faced a daily requirement to do something you could not do: read a book in Sanskrit, for example? Day in and day out, you earnestly plug away at it without success. Would you become frustrated? Anxious? Angry? Now suppose you are the only one in a group of twenty-five who cannot accomplish this task. All your peers are moving on to intermediate Sanskrit, and you can't get off page one. Your teachers and loved ones are becoming impatient with you. Of *course* you can do it, they insist—all you have to do is try!

Nearly every child with a learning disability has experienced this scenario, and some children live it for years. Without the right kind of encouragement and support, these youngsters rapidly stop believing in themselves and their ability to succeed. Convinced they will fail no matter what they do, they simply stop trying. Eventually, resistance to learning may become the biggest part of a child's problems in school—far more of a handicap than the original learning disability, and far harder to overcome.

Let us begin our exploration of the different types of learning disabilities, then, with a reminder that however many problems a student may encounter in school, a parent's primary concern must always be the child's emotional well-being. If you focus on protecting your child's self-esteem, you can avoid the most "disabling" aspect of learning disabilities: the desire to give up. As one special educator puts it, "It takes a lot of courage for these children to face all the problems they have in school. The kids whose parents understand and believe in them are the ones who have it. Even when it's all uphill, those kids keep setting goals and finding ways to get where they want to go."

ATTENTION-DEFICIT/HYPERACTIVITY DISORDER

Children with ADHD make up 3 to 5 percent of the school population, but they generate a disproportionate amount of concern. Challenging to parent and to teach, they are among the children most likely to be referred for academic assistance, disciplinary action, and mental health services. At one time it was believed that far more boys than girls were affected by ADHD, but many experts now believe that girls and boys are equally at risk. Because boys with the disorder are more likely to exhibit aggressive or disruptive behavior, however, they get noticed and referred for evaluation and special help more often than girls do. One authority calls girls with ADHD "the silent minority": they share the risk for developing academic and social problems, but because they do not call attention to themselves, they are at additional risk for not getting the support they need. When boys have attention deficits without hyperactivity, they too are less likely to be referred for evaluation and services.

Although many symptoms of ADHD are observable from early childhood, they are most obvious in situations that call for sustained mental activity (see checklist, pages 44–45). For this reason, many cases of ADHD go unnoticed until the child starts school—at which point problems seem to multiply on a daily basis. Teachers complain that the child interrupts, can't sit still, doesn't pay attention, doesn't finish work, or won't listen. Unable to plan or stick to a course of action, the youngster soon begins to flounder academically. Perhaps even more painful, the child is left behind socially as well. Children with ADHD have difficulty learning the rules of games and are impatient about taking turns; they impulsively blurt out whatever is on their minds without considering the effect of their words. They can't manage their emotions, which often brings them the wrong kind of attention. Peers tend to regard them as rude, pushy, and inconsiderate. When birthday party invitations go out and valentines are exchanged, the child with ADHD is left with little doubt about how his or her classmates feel. Social rejection plus academic underachievement is a good recipe for loss of self-esteem. Many of these children begin to see themselves as losers at an early age.

Unfortunately, children with ADHD also have a gift for alienating adults. Many were irritable and hard to handle even as infants; they cried often and did not calm down when cuddled or held. Their "terrible twos" were more terrible than most. They were difficult to toilet train. Because youngsters with ADHD have difficulty considering alternatives, they seem stubborn and headstrong and do not respond to ordinary means of discipline. They make scenes and embarrass Mom and Dad in public. In short, these youngsters not only exhaust parents but also make them feel rejected and inadequate. Studies show that mothers of children with ADHD experience unusual amounts of stress and feel less attached to these boys and girls than to their other children. If parents blame themselves or each other for the child's problems ("You should stop acting like such a pushover and discipline him more!" "Well, maybe he'd settle down if you spent more time with him!"), stress factors multiply. Since siblings also experience negative feelings about children with ADHD, youngsters with this disorder sometimes find themselves coming home to atmospheres not much more welcoming than the ones they left in school.

Not surprisingly, if their problems are not recognized and appropriately addressed, these children often grow into angry teenagers. Studies find disproportionately high numbers of young men with ADHD among juvenile offenders, and research indicates that teens with ADHD are also more likely to indulge in thrill-seeking behavior and to abuse drugs and alcohol than their typical peers. Students with ADHD are also at risk for mental health complications such as anxiety and depression. Conduct problems, low self-esteem, and poor academic performance all reduce the chances that these students will finish school, pursue higher education, and find satisfactory employment.

Attention-Deficit/Hyperactivity Disorder Checklist

Three types of ADHD have been identified. In the **predominantly inattentive** type there is little or no hyperactivity. In the **predominantly hyperactive/impulsive** type there are few if any attention problems. In the **combined type** the child shows characteristics from all the lists below. Hyperactive students are usually identified quickly in school. Children who have attention problems without hyperactivity call less attention to themselves and often struggle longer before receiving help.

According to the manual most frequently used by professionals to identify ADHD, six or more symptoms from the following lists suggest presence of the disorder.

Inattention

- often fails to give close attention to details; makes careless mistakes in schoolwork or other activities
- frequently has difficulty sustaining attention in tasks or play
- often does not seem to listen when spoken to
- often does not follow through on instructions and fails to finish schoolwork and chores
- has great difficulty getting organized
- dislikes and avoids tasks that require sustained mental effort (such as schoolwork or homework)
- frequently loses things (such as toys, assignments, books, and pencils)

As we discussed in the last chapter, problems with attention, impulse control, hyperactivity, planning, and organization arise from abnormal activity in the frontal regions of the brain. Neurological indicators show that these youngsters must put enormous effort into organizing and getting started on tasks, attending to details, staying alert and focused, and managing emotions. Deficits of this kind do not impair intellectual ability (ADHD can be found among gifted children as well as among children of average and below-average intelligence), but they make it hard for youngsters to sustain attention long enough to learn important skills and concepts. As a result, children with ADHD often fall behind in elementary school, and if intervention is delayed, they may fail to build the solid academic foundation they need to succeed at higher grade levels.

- is easily distracted by irrelevant sights and sounds
- is often forgetful in daily activities

Hyperactivity

- often fidgets with hands and feet and squirms in seat
- often leaves seat in classroom or other situations where remaining seated is expected (such as at the dinner table)
- often runs about or climbs excessively in situations in which it is inappropriate (adolescents and adults are very restless)
- often has great difficulty playing quietly
- is often "on the go" or acts as if "driven by a motor"
- talks excessively

Impulsivity

- frequently blurts out answers before questions have been completed
- often has trouble waiting turns
- often interrupts or intrudes on others (butts into conversations or games)

Adapted with permission from the *Diagnostic and Statistical Manual of Mental Disorders*, Text Revision Fourth Edition, American Psychiatric Association (copyright 2000).

Parents of "itchy" underachievers must be very cautious about jumping to the conclusion, however, that ADHD is to blame. There are many other causes of chronic inattentiveness in the classroom. For example, children who suffer from frequent illnesses or allergies sometimes have trouble focusing their attention, either because of their health conditions or because of side effects of their medications. Inattention can also be a sign of undetected problems with hearing or vision: if children cannot see or hear well, they may not even be fully aware there is something they are supposed to pay attention *to*. Students who are not eating enough are often restless and inattentive (this applies to teens on crash diets as well as children who have empty cupboards at home). Young people living with high levels of stress— because of a parent's substance abuse or a sibling's serious illness, for example—also find it hard to concentrate; their situations give them more pressing things to think about than math facts or spelling words.

Inappropriate educational placement can also produce inattentive behavior. An intellectually gifted student "stuck" with a curriculum geared to average peers may stop paying attention and start clowning around out of sheer boredom. Similarly, students who are immature or otherwise behind in their intellectual development may become bored and inattentive because they don't fully understand what is going on. Sometimes students have trouble maintaining attention because their learning styles are poorly matched with the way information is being presented to them. A child who is easily distracted, for example, will find it almost impossible to concentrate in a room where the teacher has decorated every square inch of wall space with maps, charts, posters, and other "helpful" visual aids. In contrast, students whose preferred learning style is interactive are likely to find their attention wandering during lectures or long periods of reading. Children who learn best through listening can also find it hard to maintain their focus while reading unless they read aloud—which, of course, is not permitted in most classrooms. These are only a few of many cognitive incompatibilities that can produce problems with attention.

All the youngsters mentioned in the two preceding paragraphs need support in order to do their best in school, but they probably do not have attention-deficit/hyperactivity disorder. Parents should never accept a diagnosis of ADHD or consider the use of medication until they are sure their children are being given appropriate work in school, and that other causes of attention problems have been explored and ruled out. To be sure of a diagnosis of ADHD, a thorough assessment is necessary. The American Psychiatric Association recommends that all of the following conditions be met before a diagnosis of ADHD can be confirmed:

- Many symptoms of the disorder are present.
- The symptoms are severe enough to impair academic and/or social functioning.
- The symptoms are not consistent with the child's age and developmental level.

- The symptoms have persisted six months or more.
- The symptoms were observed before seven years of age.
- The symptoms are observed both at school and at home.
- There is no evidence of a health condition or mental illness that could cause the behavior.

The majority of children with ADHD do not need special education services. Unless their problems are very severe, these students can function successfully in general education classrooms with the help of good classroom-management techniques, and sometimes medication. About a third of students with ADHD, however, have additional learning disabilities. Since ADHD makes remediating the disabilities harder, these children usually do need special education services.

Research indicates that what youngsters with ADHD usually need most is extra time and guidance to *master* information: once they have learned something, students with ADHD remember and use it as well as anyone else. Special services for children with ADHD therefore usually involve reinforcing lessons taught in the classroom and practicing new skills. These students can also be taught to monitor their own attention, and to bring themselves back "on task" when their minds start to wander. It is very important to teach these youngsters good study habits and memory strategies such as rhymes, mnemonic tricks, and visual imagery. (Children with learning disabilities almost never think of "gimmicks" like these on their own.) Assistive technology also offers a range of increasingly sophisticated tools for helping children with ADHD manage their work. Students can learn to use computerized agendas and schedules to stay on track, for example, while gamelike skill-building programs may hold attention longer than traditional practice methods. When assistive technology is not available in the classroom, special education can often provide it.

Parent support and education is another key ingredient in helping the child with ADHD succeed. Many mothers state that both their sanity and their own self-esteem have been saved by support groups, publications, and websites designed for parents of children with

ADHD (see Appendix D for some suggestions). Family counseling is also often helpful: therapy may be of critical importance if a child appears to be depressed or angry, or if a lot of negativity has built up inside a family. Parenting classes and publications can help parents learn how to use positive reinforcement to reward desirable behavior, how to strategically ignore unwelcome behavior, and how to develop appropriate and effective methods of discipline. Rest and recreation for Mom and Dad are also important! Caring for children with ADHD is a demanding and often exhausting job; most parents find they can handle it better if they give themselves a break now and then.

Children with ADHD often show significant improvement by the time they reach their teens. They tend to remain energetic people, but they are no longer "out of control." If taught appropriate learning strategies and social skills, they can do well in school and on the job. Some individuals who have used medication are able to discontinue it. Many who benefit from medication as children, however, continue to need it in order to do their best as adults. "Hey, I figure I'm no worse off than the guy who needs glasses," says a college senior who takes Ritalin every day. "Nobody likes taking medication, but without it I wouldn't have gotten through fourth grade, let alone through high school and four years of college."

Early identification and intervention are critical for children with ADHD. The earlier the problem is recognized, the less likely it is that antisocial behavior or emotional problems will develop. It is also less likely that parents will blame themselves for the child's difficult behavior. As one mother remembers:

For seven years it seemed like everybody was looking to me to control this kid. My husband, my mom, my friends all seemed to think I should be able to manage him, because I was the mother. People made "helpful" suggestions hinting at where they thought I was going wrong: "Do you feed him a lot of processed food? Does he get enough sleep? Maybe if you weren't working and could spend more time with him . . ." I felt like wearing a sign: "I'm a good mother! I breast-fed him! I read to him every day!" But the bottom line was I did feel responsible. Scott was repeat-

ing first grade when we learned he had ADHD. The first thing I thought when they told me was, "Thank God! It's not all my fault!" ADHD isn't the easiest thing to live with, but I find I can deal with it a lot more effectively since I've educated myself about it and let myself off the hook.

VISUAL-PERCEPTION DISABILITIES

Students with visual-perception disabilities have trouble making sense out of what they see. The problem is not with their eyesight, but with the way their brains process visual images. These children have difficulty understanding, interpreting, organizing, and/or remembering all sorts of nonverbal information. In school, the whole world of written symbols—not only letters and words, but also numbers and math symbols, diagrams, maps, charts, graphs, and pictures—can become a minefield for them.

Because they are often very subtle, visual-perception disabilities

---

How many Fs are in the sentence below?

> FINISHED FILES ARE THE RESULT OF YEARS OF SCIENTIFIC STUDY COMBINED WITH THE EXPERIENCE OF YEARS

Did you see three? Count again.

There are *six* Fs in the sentence. Most people overlook Fs that make a *V* sound (as in the word *of*). This is an example of how your language-processing system (which was searching for letters sounding like *f*) can overpower your visual-processing system, making you "blind" to what is right before your eyes. It is this kind of imbalance in brain activity that children who have perceptual disabilities struggle with every day.

Source: available at http://wiki.answers.com and many other websites.

---

are rarely suspected until a child starts having problems in school. Even then, the source of the trouble can seem baffling. As one mother remembers:

All through nursery school, Seth's teachers told me he was extraordinarily bright. That was obvious at home, too. Seth learned to talk early, and by five he had a near adult vocabulary. He was relentlessly curious and loved being read to. He became a walking encyclopedia on all his enthusiasms: birds, dinosaurs, Greek mythology. He couldn't wait to start school. He was so excited about learning to read for himself!

Seth loved kindergarten, but his attitude toward school changed completely in first grade. He started complaining about the work, the teacher, and the other children. By the end of October he was saying he hated school and didn't want to go anymore. Alarmed, I made an appointment with his teacher to see what was going on. She said Seth got along well with the other students, but he was falling behind in every subject. He couldn't keep up with even the slowest group in reading. I was stunned! Were we talking about the same kid? All through this conference I kept having the feeling some mistake had been made, and the teacher thought I was some other child's mother. When she suggested that I work with Seth at home to help him catch up, I agreed eagerly. I figured this problem had to be the teacher's fault. I could straighten Seth out; all he needed was a little extra encouragement and attention.

The teacher gave me flash cards for thirty sight words she wanted Seth to learn so he could get started in the first-grade reading primer. I chose three to start with—I think they were boy, the, and cat. We drilled those words for a week. Relaxed atmosphere, lots of encouragement, lots of praise. At the end of the week, Seth couldn't recognize a single word. He didn't recognize any at the end of the second week either, and the third week he refused to play this game anymore. He also started saying he didn't want me to read to him. It seemed like he didn't want to have anything to do with books or print at all.

By Thanksgiving Seth had made almost no headway in either reading or arithmetic, and he started complaining of stomachaches: almost every morning he cried and begged to be allowed to stay home from school. We made several visits to our pediatrician, but tests found nothing wrong. Seth's deteriorating emotional state worried me even more than his lack of academic progress—three months of first grade had turned my happy, outgoing six-year-old into a basket case! Finally, because I didn't know what else to do, I asked the school to test Seth for anything they could think of that might be contributing to all these problems.

By the end of the semester we had an explanation: Seth had a gifted IQ and a learning disability. His main problem was visual memory; he understood things just fine when he was looking at them, but he couldn't seem to hold on to any kind of mental picture. Practically the whole first-grade curriculum involved memorizing visual images—letters, words, and numbers. No wonder Seth wasn't going anywhere!

While it is unusual for a learning disability to be identified this early, visual-perception handicaps do start causing problems in the early grades of elementary school, where they can interfere with progress in almost every subject. To understand why, let's look at the types of information processing this category includes. Visual-perception skills include the ability to recognize images we have seen before and attach meaning to them (the way a preschooler will recognize a McDonald's sign and announce he is hungry); to discriminate among similar images (such as the letters *b* and *d*, or the words *skate* and *stake*); to separate significant figures from background details (pick out one's own name on a printed page, for instance); and to recognize the same symbol in different forms (understanding that an *A* is an *A*, even when it appears in different sizes, colors, or typefaces). Recognizing sequences is another important visual-perception skill: people with visual-sequencing problems ignore the order of information, so they may not recognize the difference between the words *was* and *saw* and have trouble copying even a short series of letters or numbers

Visual-Perception Disability Checklist

It is normal for children to display a few of the symptoms on this list. A learning disability may be responsible if many of these behaviors are present, and if they persist beyond the age where such errors are typical.

Writing

- dislikes and avoids writing
- slow and sloppy writing
- delays in learning to write
- messy and incomplete papers, with many cross-outs and erasures
- difficulty remembering shapes of letters and numbers
- frequently reverses letters and numbers
- uneven spacing between letters and words
- omits letters from words and words from sentences
- inaccurately copies designs or words
- cannot remember how words look and spells poorly (phonetically)
- cannot spot errors in own work
- has difficulty preparing outlines and organizing written work
- is oblivious to capitalization and punctuation rules
- poor planning of space on written tasks or drawings

Reading

- confuses similar-looking letters (*b* and *d, m* and *w, h* and *n, p* and q)
- has difficulty recognizing and remembering "sight" words (but can sound out words phonetically)
- frequently loses place when reading
- confuses similar-looking words (*bread* and *beard*)
- reverses words (reads *was* for *saw, no for on*)
- has trouble finding letters in words or words in sentences; cannot skim for key words
- poor memory for printed words (also number sequences, diagrams, illustrations, and so on)

- poor comprehension of main ideas and themes; may be unable to explain what a paragraph or story is about

Math

- poorly aligns figures in problems, resulting in computation errors
- difficulty memorizing math facts, multiplication tables, formulas, and equations
- has trouble interpreting graphs, charts, and diagrams
- difficulty with higher-level math concepts

Related Problems

- confuses left and right
- shows poor spatial judgment (Is the parking space big enough for my car?)
- difficulty estimating time, being on time
- poor sense of direction; is slow to learn his or her way around a new place
- difficulty judging speed and distance interferes with sports; may be a problem when driving a car
- trouble interpreting maps, doing puzzles
- has poor visual imagery (cannot imagine how a completed puzzle or finished project might look); finds it difficult to detect objects in a pile (i.e., the markers versus the pens) or identify a person in a crowd
- has trouble "getting to the point"; becomes bogged down in details
- does not pick up on other people's moods and feelings (results in saying the wrong things at the wrong time)
- has trouble perceiving the body language and subtleties in social communication
- lacks effective planning and organizational skills
- often loses things; cannot spot objects "in plain sight"
- has difficulty perceiving strategies for being successful in games (may not understand the objective)
- is clumsy due to poor spatial judgment (bumps into furniture and doorways)
- is slow to react to visual information (yells "Bingo" too late; is late to recognize and hail a cab)

correctly. Students with this kind of handicap, of course, struggle with learning their letters and numbers. Their workbooks and papers are full of reversals, omissions, and other errors that are often blamed on carelessness (see illustration below).

Most students with visual-processing weaknesses also experience some problems with *visual memory*. Recall of any information pre-

Cursive Copying and Mathematical Calculation of an Eight-Year-Old Boy with Average Intelligence Who Has Visual-Perception Disabilities

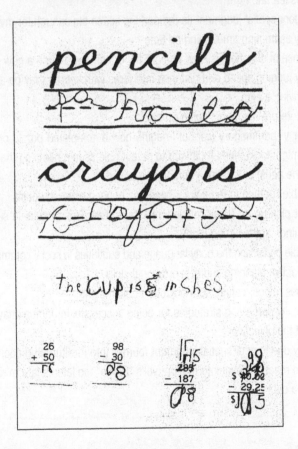

sented primarily in visual form is likely to be inconsistent at best. These children are typically slow beginning readers because they can't easily recall words they have seen before and must "sound out" as they go along. They don't remember how to spell irregular words (*yacht, pneumonia*), although they can spell phonetically (see illustration on page 56). Routine tasks like copying from the blackboard may be impossible: in the time it takes to look from the board to their papers, these youngsters lose parts of the image, or lose the image completely. They have trouble checking or proofreading their own work because they can't remember what the correct form is supposed to look like when they are looking at their mistakes. "Do as I do" demonstrations may leave them completely at sea—they can't remember what they have been shown (unless they are helped to "encode" the information verbally). Despite such problems, these children often have very good spoken-language skills and their memories for what they hear (the lyrics of popular songs, for example) may be excellent. Sometimes their strengths in these areas only help to convince adults that their sloppy and incomplete homework is due to inattention or lack of motivation.

Visual-processing disabilities usually originate in the right cerebral cortex, and it has been noted that children with visual-processing problems often exhibit additional "right brain" deficits (sometimes called nonverbal learning disabilities). These impairments include the following:

- **Problems with spatial awareness.** These students find it hard to deal with concepts of shape, size, speed, and distance, and to understand how related parts fit together to form a whole. As a result, they may have trouble interpreting maps, graphs, charts, and diagrams. This can interfere with learning in any subject, but these students are especially poorly equipped to handle advanced levels of mathematics. Many of these children have difficulty discriminating left from right, and they often have a poor sense of direction (they do not create "mental maps" and must learn to use verbal cues to avoid getting lost). Spatial weaknesses also show up in social behavior. Teachers observe that students with this type of disability

Phonetic Spelling of a Bright Thirteen-Year-Old Boy with Visual-Perception Disabilities

Known Words	Unknown Words
apstract	destuted
misconduct	rumedeul (remedial)
optumistic	insinuate
sublime	cunedic (kinetic)
verify	orthadocs
gyshur (geyser)	odor o caos
garitey (guarantee)	oncore
norishing	ismis (isthmus)
pursowt (pursuit)	busum
cutasturfey (catastrophe)	shampane (champagne)

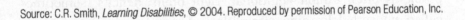

are always "in your face," talking from only a few inches away. These children may be left out on the playground, because their inability to estimate speed and distance accurately makes them inept at pretty much anything involving a ball.

• **Problems with time.** These children are notorious for their inability to estimate time accurately. They are chronically late, and their parents complain that they are never ready to go anywhere, even when they have been given frequent warnings. In school, poor time sense manifests as failure to finish work and tests on time, and difficulty estimating how long homework assignments or other projects will take. Tardiness and unfinished work contribute to the impression that the student is careless and unmotivated.

• **Problems with planning and organization.** Working out strategies for approaching tasks efficiently can be a major stumbling block for these youngsters—one that becomes increasingly obvious as they progress in school and the work they are expected to do independently becomes more and more difficult. Given a complex assignment (like preparing a research paper or designing a science fair experiment), these students often have no idea how to break it down into a series of manageable steps. As a result, the task may seem so overwhelming that they abandon hope before they start. Throughout their educations, these youngsters are likely to need some help organizing their time and structuring their assignments.

• **Problems with grasping the main idea.** These children often have trouble seeing the "big picture"; they may be so detail oriented that they cannot distinguish important information from trivia. (Listening to one of these kids describe a movie often involves sitting through a long, rambling monologue in which every scene is recounted, but the point of the plot is never made clear.) Many are literal thinkers who have difficulty reasoning beyond the information that is right in front of them. These children benefit from direct teaching of facts and concepts, and need help learning to identify the most important information in their lessons. Clearly spelling out expectations and directions also helps them do their best.

• **Issues of social perception.** These youngsters do not "tune in" to nonverbal information. They are often oblivious to their surroundings (told to "Clean up that mess," they may cluelessly reply, "What mess?"). Many do not register changes in facial expression or body language that signal how others are thinking or feeling; as a result they may be perceived as insensitive or rude. "In general, these kids strike the observer as rather self-absorbed and out of it," says a special education teacher; "They are usually the last to catch on to a fad or a fashion trend at school. By the time they catch on that stripes are in, everybody else has moved on to polka dots. This doesn't hurt their grades, but it can really cost them socially. What you have to do is *teach* these kids social awareness—how to pay attention to what the other kids wear, what they like to do. Don't assume they'll pick up on that stuff by themselves. They don't."

The kind of academic support needed by students with visual-perception disabilities varies, depending on the severity of their handicaps. Most of these students learn to read best with their ears—they need reading instruction solidly based on phonics, and if this is not available in the regular reading curriculum, special education programming must provide it. Children with visual-memory deficits need to be provided with ready access to materials they have trouble memorizing, such as multiplication tables, math formulas, and maps. Other than that, what many of these students seem to need most is extra time. Although these children's brains process visual information unusually slowly, many can handle visual tasks competently if allowed to work at their own pace. Some children, however, cannot perform tasks involving visual perception, no matter how hard they try; it is simply too hard for them to assemble visual elements into a meaningful pattern. Intervention is important in either case: special education programming can provide both for extra time and for alternative methods of teaching and evaluation when they are necessary.

These students also benefit hugely from supportive technology. "I can't believe the difference a computer has made in my life," says a ninth-grader. "It points all my letters in the right direction, straightens up my margins—even corrects my spelling. I still make mistakes, but when I correct them I don't have to copy over the whole assignment. I used to hate writing; it was so hard to get everything looking right on the paper that I just wanted to make everything short and get it over with. Now I'm getting my highest grades in English and writing stories and poems on my own time."

Students with visual-perception disabilities usually need the most support in elementary school, when the demand to master systems of visual symbols is greatest. They often need less help as they get older and start to use different areas of strength to compensate for their visual-processing weaknesses. Quite often they blossom in high school, where their performance is sometimes spectacular. Studies find that "left-brain" skills involving language, logic, and analysis are the ones most closely associated with achievement in secondary school. Students with visual-processing disabilities who have strengths in these areas generally become solid academic performers in most subjects (though upper-level math may remain a problem).

LANGUAGE-PROCESSING DISABILITIES

By far the largest number of students identified as having learning disabilities are those with language-processing problems. These youngsters can have trouble with any aspect of language: hearing individual sounds and words correctly, understanding their meaning, remembering verbal material, and communicating clearly. These children's difficulties begin with the spoken word, and they typically interfere with reading and/or writing when the child enters school. The severity of these handicaps ranges from mild to so profound that the most affected individuals find coping with English almost as hard as the rest of us might find learning a language like Russian or Japanese.

Parents are often aware that their children have some problems with language before they start school (see checklist on pages 60–61). Youngsters with language-processing disabilities may be slow in learning to speak, and may use shorter sentences, smaller vocabularies, and poorer grammar than their brothers and sisters did at similar ages. There may be signs that they do not always understand what is being said to them. Their responses to questions may be inappropriate, or they may not be able to follow directions reliably. Their memory for verbal instructions may also be poor, and this can be a source of constant irritation ("Didn't I already ask you twice to put those paints away? Why do I have to nag you about everything?"). Comprehension problems are likely to get worse when the language being used is complex: a child who can handle "Bring me the cake mix" with no difficulty may be completely at sea when asked, "Please unpack the grocery bag, and bring me the cake mix after you put the milk in the refrigerator." Problems may be especially obvious when directions are called out to a child who is in another room. Many children who have

Language-Processing Disability Checklist

It is normal for children to display a few behaviors on this list. A persistent pattern of many of these symptoms, however, may indicate a learning disability.

Speech and Language Comprehension
- delays in learning to speak
- does not modulate tone of voice appropriately; speaks in monotone, or too loud
- has problems retrieving names of familiar objects or people
- uses vague, imprecise language; has a small vocabulary
- has slow or halting speech; uses verbal "stalling" mechanisms ("uh," "um," "you know")
- uses poor grammar and simple sentences
- frequently mispronounces words
- confuses words with similar sounds (such as *frustrate* and *fluctuate;* may produce hybrids, such as *flustrate*)
- often uses hand gestures and body language to help convey message
- avoids talking (especially in front of strangers, authority figures, or groups)
- is insensitive to rhymes; cannot single out words beginning or ending with the same sounds
- shows little interest in books or stories
- retells stories in a disorganized way (plot may be out of sequence)
- does not respond appropriately to questions (replies "Monday" when asked "Where do you go to school?")
- frequently does not understand or remember words, sentences, instructions
- has difficulty discriminating the speaker's words in a noisy background
- has difficulty with articulation

Reading
- significant delays in learning to read
- difficulty naming letters
- problems associating letters with sounds, discriminating between sounds in words, blending sounds into words
- difficulty analyzing sound sequences in words; makes frequent sequencing errors (such as reading *snug* for *sung*)
- guessing at unfamiliar words rather than using word analysis skills
- reading very slowly; oral reading deteriorates within a few sentences (due to declining ability to retrieve sounds rapidly from memory)

- comprehension of what has been read is consistently poor, or deteriorates when sentences become longer and more complex
- poor retention of new vocabulary words
- dislike and avoidance of reading

Writing

- written assignments are short or incomplete; often characterized by brief sentences, limited vocabulary
- problems with grammar persist
- bizarre spelling errors (not phonetic); student may be unable to decipher own spelling
- ideas in written assignments are poorly organized, not logically presented
- little theme development; student is more likely to write bare lists of points or events than to provide details or develop ideas, characters, or plot
- on tests, student consistently does better with multiple-choice questions than essays or filling in blanks

Math

- slow response during math-fact drills due to problems with number retrieval
- difficulty with word problems due to poor language comprehension
- problems with higher-level math due to difficulties with analysis and logical reasoning

Related Problems

- student "garbles" telephone messages; misunderstands what is heard on radio or TV
- difficulty with verbal reasoning; may understand all the words in the proverb "A rolling stone gathers no moss" but be unable to explain what it means; may find it hard to draw logical conclusions
- lack of understanding of puns and jokes; may not detect teasing
- difficulty making comparisons and classifying objects or ideas
- difficulty remembering information or producing facts or ideas on demand
- difficulty presenting a story or directions in logical order
- likely to repeat types of problems encountered learning English when studying a foreign language
- difficulty joining or maintaining conversations
- student doesn't make use of a speaker's stress, pitch, or pauses to aid comprehension

trouble understanding words use visual cues to help compensate for their disabilities; they look for meaning in body language and facial expression, and sometimes they become accomplished lip-readers.

Many youngsters with language-processing disabilities also talk in "mixed-up" ways. Sometimes their brains have trouble sorting out sequences in the sounds they hear, so they mispronounce words— saying "pisketti" for *spaghetti,* or "efelent" for *elephant* long beyond the age where such mistakes are normal. These children also are weak in grammatical awareness and have problems with word sequencing; for example, they may not understand there is a difference between the phrases *blocking a punch* and *punching a block*. It is common for these youngsters to confuse words that sound alike: they may say that an answer is "oblivious" when *obvious* is what they mean, or state that their sick cat had to be rushed to the "vegetarian." Errors like these—which are likely to get worse under the pressure of speaking before groups or authority figures—leave these students painfully open to ridicule, and some sensitive young people will go to almost any lengths to avoid talking in front of others.

There are also children who understand and use words correctly but experience great difficulty producing the words they want from their memories. Ask them to single out the picture of the horse and these youngsters will do it without hesitation, but show them the picture and ask them to name the animal, and their minds go blank. Word-finding problems frustrate some students into silence, but others launch barrages of language in an effort to find the word they are looking for. These are the kids who jabber, "Hey, you know who I saw in school, it was, you know, the guy with the hat, he wears that shirt with his name on it, he's tall and he has that thing, it's long and skinny and he sticks it in the engine. . . ." Finally you gather enough clues to guess "Joe from the gas station?" and the child replies with relief, "Yeah, him." Youngsters with naming difficulties also use verbal stalling mechanisms to give themselves extra time to find words; "Sally lost her, um, you know, thing . . ." is a typical communication from a child with a disability of this kind.

In school, many youngsters with language-processing disabilities continue to have trouble understanding and following verbal directions, a problem that is often blamed on inattention, laziness, or disobedience ("How many times have I told you to line up alphabetically by last name, Johnny? Maybe if you stay in for recess today, you'll learn to listen"). Efforts to use visual skills to improve understanding are also frequently misunderstood ("Keep your eyes on your own paper, Johnny! It's cheating to look at Susie's work!"). Problematic speech patterns may not be considered a handicap in the classroom, where students are usually expected to be quiet, but the difficulties these youngsters have learning to read and write eventually do get attention. The problems students experience with these skills reflect the problems they have processing spoken language. For example:

- Students with phonological-awareness (sound-processing) weaknesses have trouble learning to associate sounds with letters, and they find it hard to sort out the sequences of sounds they hear in words. Even if they learn, in time, to tell you what a *t* sounds like, they may still be unable to tell you if that sound occurs at the beginning or the end of the word *cast*—or even if it occurs in the word at all. These students have trouble mastering the process of "sounding out" words, and they make bizarre spelling errors that reflect the scrambled way their brains interpret what they hear (see illustration on page 65).

- Students with comprehension problems may learn to decode words satisfactorily, but the words they read make no more sense to them than the words they hear. These children may have difficulty associating words with their correct meanings, or have such problems with the rules or structure of language that even simple combinations of words confuse them. Most often, these students can manage language in small chunks, but they become overwhelmed when the material they are expected to handle gets longer and more complex. Such youngsters typically have small vocabularies, have trouble mastering the basics of grammar, and frequently use inappropriate words when writing. Memory for what has been read (but not really understood) is also likely to be poor.

- Students who have trouble finding words to express them-selves in speech do no better with pencil and paper. Produc-ing the words they need to describe what they know can be a problem even when students' vocabularies are vast and their knowledge of the subject at hand is comprehensive. Even when these students read well, they may find their difficul-ties speaking and writing a severe handicap in classes where student efforts are judged primarily by discussions and papers. (Not surprisingly, these young people much prefer tests with multiple-choice questions.)

Like all students with learning disabilities, children with language deficits tend to process information more slowly than usual. Their problems are likely to be magnified in the classroom, where prompt answers are usually demanded. Many times these students will know an answer to a question but hesitate when called upon because they need time to find and arrange the words they need to frame a coher-ent reply. Not hearing an immediate answer, however, the teacher is likely to assume that our student has not done his homework and move on to another child. These children are among those most likely to be accused of low motivation. Too often, this accusation becomes reality as mounting school problems eat away at these youngsters' self-esteem and natural zest for learning.

In addition to creating problems with reading and writing, lan-guage-processing disabilities have an impact on how students think. Much of our ability to remember and organize information depends on our skill at naming and describing things, and we need language to do this. For example, our new neighbor may start out as no more than a vague visual impression, but over time we use words to build a "file" on him in our minds: his name is Bob, he has an attractive wife named Phyllis and two small children, he drives a red truck, he works for the phone company, he likes to barbecue in his backyard, and so on. We may make associations with other "files" we have created in the past—perhaps our neighbor wears a cowboy hat like country star Kenny Chesney's, and his enthusiasm for baseball makes us think of another neighbor who is also a fan. The bigger our file gets, the better

Spelling Patterns of a Gifted Seventh-Grade Boy with Language-Processing Disabilities

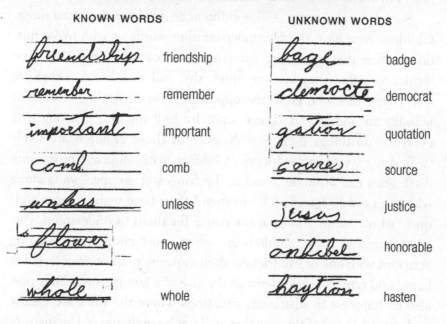

KNOWN WORDS

friendship	friendship
remember	remember
important	important
comb	comb
unless	unless
flower	flower
whole	whole

UNKNOWN WORDS

bage	badge
democte	democrat
gation	quotation
sowre	source
jusus	justice
onlibl	honorable
haytion	hasten

He remembers "known" words by how they look but has difficulty approximating phonetically the spellings of "unknown" words that he has not yet learned to read.

Source: C. R. Smith, *Learning Disabilities*, © 2004. Reproduced by permission of Pearson Education, Inc.

we can say we "know" our neighbor, and the more certain we would be of recognizing him if we saw him in an unexpected place. So it is with everything we learn. We use words to nail down information and store it in a way that makes it easy for us to use it later.

Research shows that the greater command students have of language, the better they are at remembering information, organizing their ideas, making associations between facts and concepts, and handling abstractions. Students with language disabilities often find themselves struggling in all of these areas. One teacher observes, "These kids' minds are like drawers stuffed full of file folders with no labels. There may be a lot of information there, but it's so disorganized that it isn't much use to them." When language-processing handicaps are mild, poor memory and lack of organization may actually be the most obvious aspects of the disability.

Social development is also influenced by language disabilities. Children who have trouble understanding words or who make mistakes when they speak are sometimes so fearful of exposing their weaknesses that they become quiet, shy, and withdrawn. There are also youngsters who go to the opposite extreme, dealing with their inability to understand others' input by bullying and insisting that everyone do things their way! Neither of these children are likely to find it easy to make friends. Children with language-processing disabilities can often be found at the fringes of groups, "going along with the crowd." Some prefer to spend their time with younger children, whose simpler language is easier for them to understand. Parents note that these children are often most comfortable sharing activities with one or two friends: their capacity to understand what is being said rapidly breaks down as the size of a group grows. They may also be happiest in structured situations where the rules are clearly understood ahead of time, so they will not be embarrassed by instructions that may be hard for them to follow.

Many areas of the brain must work together to process language successfully, and disabilities can result from breakdowns at several different points in the system. Difficulty with word usage and comprehension is generally linked to underfunctioning areas in the left cerebral cortex, and students with severe comprehension problems sometimes show evidence of other "left-brain" weaknesses, such as difficulty with arranging facts or ideas in logical sequences. Language-processing disabilities can also arise from inefficient neural "networking": different parts of the brain simply do not cooperate as well as they might. As a result, some brain regions are underactive while others are overworked. Poorly "wired" individuals often end up trying to read using brain areas poorly adapted to the task. Complex processes like extracting information from language, evaluating and categorizing that information, and coding verbal information into memory are also difficult for them to execute smoothly.

In other areas of research, geneticists have been busy attempting to determine why language-processing disorders so often run in families. One day it may be possible to test for "dyslexia genes" and identify at-risk children who should get extra help long before they enter school. For the time being, however, the best hope for children with language-processing disabilities is early recognition and intervention. There is evidence that with appropriate and intense instruction, brain patterns begin to normalize and learning improves.

Special education support is essential. Many students with language-processing disabilities cannot learn to read and write by conventional methods; to master these skills, they need special materials and teachers experienced in working with language problems. Progress in reading can be slow, and alternate means of getting information (such as recorded books) may have to be provided in order to help these children keep up with the curriculum. Because students often do best when instructional materials are broken down into smaller, more manageable chunks of language, it is sometimes necessary to rewrite their basic texts in simpler English, and extra time is usually needed for them to complete tests and assignments. If students read and write very poorly, they may need to have test questions read to them and be permitted to answer orally. Many students with language disorders also need to be taught specific strategies for organizing and remembering written and verbal material. In addition, teachers may need to be informed of the importance of speaking to these students slowly and clearly, and to be made aware of how difficult it is for these children to process words if there is other "sound confusion." Telling students that there will be a math test on Tuesday just as the bell rings amid a general shuffling of papers and scraping of chairs, for example, puts the child with a language disability at a disadvantage. So would "burying" that information in a long list of other announcements. Parents find that simple language is often the key to improving kids' memories at home, too: "Please take out the garbage tonight," clearly articulated face-to-face, is far more likely to get results than "Honey, don't forget I want you to take out the trash after you walk the dog and do your spelling homework" tossed over your shoulder as you leave the room.

Given appropriate support, students with language-processing disabilities can become successful academically. Young people whose disabilities are very severe, however, may never progress much beyond "survival level" in reading and writing. It is most important for these students to find alternative ways to learn and to communicate so that they can develop their other strengths and talents. If they remain motivated, difficulty with reading and writing will not stop them from meeting their goals. Many virtual nonreaders not only have made it to college but also have been outstanding achievers there. (Support for students with learning disabilities is available at all colleges and universities.) People with learning disabilities have made it in nearly every kind of business and profession. As Jason's story demonstrates, energetic and intelligent nonreaders can also become successful operating their own businesses—one method of guaranteeing yourself the flexibility to do things your own way! These students sometimes deliver exceptional performances in career areas that do not rely heavily on advanced language skills: medical technology, architecture, finance, photography, engineering, mechanics, television production, fine arts, and computer programming, just to mention a few. Most parents' greatest fear—that lack of reading ability will make it impossible for children to complete their educations and become independent and self-supporting—is therefore without real foundation. These children, however, do need an extra measure of understanding and encouragement in order to maintain their self-confidence and some enthusiasm for education. It is very important for them to get plenty of opportunities to do the things they do well in order to balance the uphill struggle they face with paperwork in school.

A tremendous amount of technological support has become available in recent years for individuals with language handicaps. For example, computers can now scan printed materials and "read" them aloud; some are programmed to highlight words as they go along. (Even internet pages can be listened to!) Students can also "write" by dictating into voice-activated word processors, and software is available to help with grammar, usage, and spelling. A more thorough discussion of how computers and other assistive technology devices can facilitate learning can be found in Chapter 9, and at the end of this book in Appendix C. Parents should understand, however, that even the most sophisticated technology will not eliminate the need

Jason

Jason, an engineering college graduate who owns his own heating-repair business, explains how his word-finding difficulties have affected his life. Jason always did well at remembering concepts but could never recall names, places, dates, baseball batting averages, and so forth. Early on, he came to believe that he could contribute little to conversations. In elementary school, he became socially withdrawn because he found other children could "outargue" him on any topic. He remained quiet and shy in high school—when he went to his high school reunion, he was not really surprised that no one remembered him. Jason says that today he enters conversations "from the perimeter"; he waits for people to get beyond "small talk" and the exchange of facts to discussions on the idea level.

Jason had reading and writing difficulties throughout school, and they have continued into adulthood. He has read only one novel in his entire life and never reads the newspaper. TV is his primary source of information. When writing, Jason can only catch his misspellings after he finishes a word and inspects whether it "looks right." Number reversals occur continually on his order sheets, but he catches these when sums don't make sense or order numbers don't match those in the catalog. Jason has learned to check and double-check any written work.

Jason is a tall, athletic, sympathetic fellow who has used his strengths in math and engineering to become vocationally successful. He has always sought business partners who could be the upfront salespeople, good at making small talk with customers. Jason, on the other hand, is the mechanical genius on whose skills everyone relies. He describes himself as an accommodating, honest, dependable person who is always on time and always helping others out. "Since I can't teach people anything new besides engineering, I've become the nice guy. When I was sixteen, I was the first person to get my license, so I drove everyone around. What else can I do? I want to be liked."

Adapted from C. R. Smith, *Learning Disabilities,* © 2004. Reproduced by permission of Pearson Education, Inc.

for competent instruction. Kids can get by without computers, but they cannot succeed without qualified, experienced teachers; locating those teachers should be a parent's primary concern.

Although language-processing disabilities are permanent handicaps, children occasionally do have late developmental spurts that bring marked improvement. The brain continues to form new connections into early adulthood, and there are cases where the "circuits" necessary for reading have finally become complete in adolescence or even later. The motto for teaching reading skills, then, is "Never give up." It is necessary to leave educational doors open as long as possible so that late bloomers have the opportunity to reach their full potentials.

FINE-MOTOR DISABILITIES

To get an idea of what it feels like to have a fine-motor disability, try positioning a mirror and a plain piece of paper on a table in such a way that you can see the paper in the mirror. Now try writing your name on the paper while looking only at the mirror image. Do you find it difficult? Confused by the mirror image, your brain has "forgotten" how to guide your hand. If you found writing your name hard, try imagining that the teacher just handed you twenty-five new vocabulary words to copy!

Individuals with fine-motor handicaps cannot fully control groups of small muscles in their hands. This disability has no impact on intellectual capacity, but it interferes with school performance because it impairs the ability to communicate in writing. Children with this type of disability cannot write neatly, no matter how hard they try. Their letters are poorly formed, and their sentences stray from the lines. Their handwriting may be so illegible that it is impossible even to guess whether words are spelled correctly. It takes intense concentration for these students to produce even marginally acceptable written work; when they are striving for legibility, they work slowly and have little energy left over for considerations of content or style. Not surprisingly, many of these students hate to write, and they avoid it as much as possible. Because short, sloppy papers seldom impress teachers, these children don't collect many gold stars. In classes where student efforts are judged primarily by written work, it is often assumed that these students are slow-witted, lazy, or both.

Students with fine-motor handicaps experience difficulties with a surprising variety of tasks in school. Anything involving drawing or writing is a trial, from copying diagrams from the blackboard to taking

Fine-Motor Disability Checklist

It is not unusual for young children to display many behaviors on this list. If symptoms persist into the school years, however, a disability may be responsible.

At Home

- appears awkward and clumsy; often drops things, spills things, knocks things over
- has difficulty picking up and using small objects such as puzzle pieces or Legos
- has trouble with buttons, hooks, and zippers when dressing; finds it very difficult to tie shoes
- is unsuccessful in games and activities that involve hand skills (cat's cradle, piano lessons, basketball)
- has poor coloring ability; cannot keep within lines
- produces artwork that looks immature for age (drawings from imagination are usually better than efforts at copying designs)
- has difficulty using scissors
- has an awkward pencil grip (may hold pencil too loosely or too tightly)
- delays in learning to write; writing is large and immature, letters and numbers are poorly formed
- may have articulation problems

At School

- has poor handwriting (sloppy, illegible, poor spacing, inconsistent letter size, no consistent style, strays from lines on paper)
- turns in messy papers (torn and crumpled with many cross-outs, smudges, and incomplete erasures)
- shows marked slowness, exceptional effort, and frustration during writing tasks
- dislikes and avoids writing or drawing
- written efforts are short and often incomplete
- content/style of written assignments is poor (primary focus is on achieving legibility)
- computation errors are common due to illegible, crowded, and poorly aligned numerals
- in severe cases, has difficulty learning keyboard skills

lecture notes. Mistakes are made in computation because numbers are illegible or not aligned properly. In science lab, these students mangle dissections and splatter acid on their clothes. Efforts in art—like their handwriting—sometimes look embarrassingly immature. These youngsters are also humiliated by their clumsiness in nonacademic settings: they spill their milk at lunch, fumble the balls in gym class, and knock other students' books and backpacks to the floor. While other kids can hide their weaknesses, fine-motor problems are always on display, with predictable consequences to social acceptance and self-esteem. The anger these children feel about their inability to "do it right" can be intense and is often directed at themselves. Anger is plainly evident in Nathan's coloring, and his mother's touching observations record how exhausting trying to manage your own hands can be.

Brain areas controlling hand and mouth movements lie relatively close together in the cerebral cortex, and children who have trouble with hand coordination sometimes have articulation problems as well. These young people are doubly frustrated in their efforts to communicate, and at double the risk for being underestimated intellectually. Students with fine-motor disabilities, however, often find that their large-motor systems are completely unaffected. Activities like dancing, running, throwing, and jumping are usually not a problem, and these youngsters may even be talented athletes in events that do not require hand skills.

Students sometimes do show improvement in motor skills over time, although they may be well advanced in school before significant progress is noted. Support for children with fine-motor disabilities is usually directed at improving handwriting (guidance and practice can make a difference). Special pencil grippers and raised-line paper can be lifesavers. There are some students who have such difficulty with written tasks, however, that they must be provided with alternate means of recording information and expressing themselves. Students can be allowed to dictate reports or give them orally; they can tape-record homework assignments and be provided with copies of notes by teachers or other students. Care must also be taken that these students are not penalized for their handicaps on tests—they understandably do much better on oral or short-answer questions than

When Nathan Colors

When Nathan colors, his crayon
becomes a weapon against the white paper.
It is his mission to color in every bit of
available background.
His coloring brain comes from his toes
and grips his entire body driving its power
down into his he-man fingers.
He sucks in drool as his concentration grows.

When Nathan colors, his crayons
make a popping sound as weapon after weapon
is broken by the paper enemy.
On December 26th, Nathan's coloring can
is filled with new, smooth shiny soldiers.
By January, his army is broken into small
midget fighters.
His mother watches as he pushes 1/4" nubs
into the paper with his he-man thumb ends.

When Nathan colors, his world is
lost in the mission of wiping out white.
This is no calming, passive playtime
like it might be for other children.
Coloring is exhausting and sometimes,
it must be followed by a snack break
or, on rainy days,
a doze on the couch.

Source: Debra Morse-Little, Penn Yan, NY (1996)

on handwritten essays. Typing is a real survival skill for these young people, and word processors can be a blessing, especially for students attempting to cope with the increased communication demands of secondary school. Special keyboards with larger, colorful keys can be helpful, as can portable keyboards for note taking and writing in class.

Children with fine-motor disabilities may also need help with making a neat appearance (without it, they are likely to show up at school unbuttoned, unzipped, and untied)—slip-on shoes and pullover shirts can make life a lot easier. Given these kinds of support, youngsters with uncomplicated fine-motor problems can usually be expected to make good progress, both academically and in their social standings.

It is important to keep in mind that all types of learning disabilities can vary tremendously in severity. While some have a fairly global impact on school achievement, many handicaps are so subtle and specific that they interfere with only a quite narrow range of activities. It is also important to remember that learning disabilities frequently overlap and occur in almost endless combinations: a student with a language-processing disability (comprehension) complicated by ADHD will appear to have little in common with a student who has a language-processing disability (word retrieval) complicated by fine-motor deficits. In fact, each student with learning disabilities is virtually unique—a reality that can make identification and intervention a challenge.

Still, it is possible to make some general comments about the long-term effects of the different types of learning disabilities. First, all learning disabilities are permanent handicaps; while they may show considerable improvement over time, they cannot be entirely outgrown or "cured." They have a discouraging way of presenting themselves in different forms as a student progresses through school. For example, Susie's parents may heave a sigh of relief that she has finally learned to read, only to notice that her spelling is pretty awful. When her spelling improves, Susie's eighth-grade English teacher expresses despair over her incoherent book reports. And no sooner will Susie learn to write a decent paper than she will be expected to do it in Spanish. Students with learning disabilities thus usually need some kind of support throughout their school years, though the level and type of help required may change.

During elementary school, support usually focuses on providing the extra time and instruction needed to master the basic skills of reading, writing, and mathematics. Students with mild language problems or uncomplicated visual-perception or fine-motor disabilities can usually be expected to attain passable basic-skill levels during this time. Research shows, for example, that the visual-perception skills of a ten-year-old are good enough to handle most of life's challenges. If children with visual-perception disabilities can reach this skill level, their handicaps are likely to amount to not much more than a moderate annoyance in secondary school and after graduation. If they have been able to maintain their motivation and self-confidence, these students rapidly learn to compensate for what is left of their handicaps, and the help they need in secondary school is often minimal.

Students with more extensive language-processing handicaps, severe ADHD, or multiple disabilities are less likely to reach satisfactory basic-skills levels in elementary school. While efforts to teach basic skills may continue, support strategies in secondary school usually shift to teaching compensatory skills and providing students with alternate means of communicating and keeping up with the curriculum. It is of critical importance that students who have difficulty learning to read and/or write be helped to develop other strengths and talents to the fullest extent possible, and that they be encouraged to let these areas of ability guide their postsecondary-school planning. Persistent advocacy may be needed to make sure that these students do not become "opportunity impaired" as a result of their basic-skills deficits.

Severe language and attention problems are also more likely to have an impact on the lives of adults than do the other disabilities. Individuals with visual-perception or fine-motor disabilities will face some lifelong reminders of their handicaps (they may continue to drop things, misplace their possessions, turn right when they are told to turn left, and have atrocious handwriting, for example), but these problems will not isolate them socially or interfere substantially with their ability to produce on the job. In contrast, difficulties with comprehension, speaking, and maintaining concentration can present enduring obstacles to social and vocational growth, even when an individual's life has been arranged so that reading and writing are not major issues.

Even those most profoundly affected by learning disabilities, however, can look forward to productive and fulfilling lives if they feel loved and accepted in spite of their handicaps, and if they are encouraged to make the most of their positive qualities and invest time in activities they enjoy. This may require parents to adjust their expectations. As a mother who is a successful attorney recalls:

> *Initially I was bitterly disappointed that my son was not going to college, although after all the frustrating years he spent floundering in school, I had no trouble understanding his choice. Even I could see that his comprehension for verbal material is so poor that college was not a realistic option. Andy loves cars and he found steady work at a body shop, where he's learning on the job. He plays regularly in a softball league, and through that activity he has made a lot of friends. He also has found immense satisfaction volunteering as a "big brother" to an eleven-year-old boy with Down syndrome; they do all kinds of things together—camping, ball games, trips to the zoo. Is this the life I would have chosen for Andy? No. But my plan would have made him miserable, and today he is so happy that I can't help but be grateful for the way things have worked out.*

Part II

HOW ARE LEARNING DISABILITIES IDENTIFIED?

4

Warning Signs at Home and at School

Because learning disabilities are defined as handicaps that interfere with the mastery of academic skills, they cannot be formally identified until a child starts experiencing problems in school. Many schools will not consider an evaluation for learning disabilities until a student has fallen a year or more behind his or her grade level in one or more subjects. This kind of policy makes sense from the school's point of view. Identifying learning disabilities involves hours of observation, interviews, and one-on-one assessments. It is a time-consuming, labor-intensive, and therefore costly process. School districts with limited resources—in other words, most school districts today—do not wish to waste time and money evaluating students who are unlikely to qualify for special education services. Therefore, when a student starts to fall behind, schools often recommend a "wait-and-see" approach, trying traditional means of "extra help" for a year or two before deciding on further action.

What this practice means in reality, however, is that children with learning disabilities sometimes flounder for years before an intensive effort is made to find out how best to help them. Unfortunately, the longer a learning disability remains unrecognized, the more likely it is that a student's problems will begin to compound. The gap between the child's achievements and those of his or her peers' typically grows with every passing year—the curriculum moves on so rapidly that the student with information-processing problems never quite catches up. Frustration and embarrassment about poor performance start to eat away at the child's motivation and self-confidence. Expectations are reduced and enthusiasm for education is lost. It is therefore critically important for parents to investigate promptly whenever they develop concerns about a child's progress in school.

Fortunately, parents need not wait for school personnel to recommend evaluations for learning disabilities: school districts are required to respond when parents request evaluation or educational intervention (see box, pages 86–89). As taxpayers, parents of children enrolled in private or parochial schools may request evaluations without charge from their public school districts. It is also possible to have a child's learning problems assessed privately. In the next chapter we will discuss how to obtain an evaluation, and what it should include.

Our purpose here is to describe the earliest warning signs of learning disabilities so that you will know when an evaluation is necessary. Some problems in the areas described below will be observable well before a child starts school, while others are more likely to become apparent after the child enters the classroom. Sometimes these behaviors indicate a problem other than a learning disability. All should be regarded as red flags that something may be wrong, however—and if there are problems in several of the areas discussed here, an evaluation for learning disabilities should not be delayed.

DEVELOPMENTAL DELAYS

As we discussed in Chapter 2, learning disabilities can be caused by uneven brain development. When this is the case, a child is almost always going to be delayed in reaching some developmental milestones. Parents may note that a baby understands words or talks significantly later than other children of the same age, for example, or is very late to roll over, stand, and walk. It may be observed that a preschool child has an unusual amount of difficulty understanding directions, pronouncing words, doing puzzles, handling tableware, recognizing shapes and letters, or counting. During physical examinations, the child's pediatrician may note other subtle signs of a delay in neurological development, such as poor coordination. Children with learning disabilities are typically delayed only in some areas; in others their development will be normal or even advanced. (Delay in all areas of development is generally a sign of a more serious handicap.)

It is important to remember that a delay does not always indicate a disability. Children do not develop according to rigid timetables, and in most areas of development there is a wide range of behaviors that are normal. Most children start speaking words between the ages of one and two, for example, and a small percentage of normal youngsters begin to talk even later. Development can also be affected by outside factors. Children who are placed in substandard day-care situations or raised by caretakers who do not speak English are likely to be delayed in their English language development, for example, but they are not disabled. Similarly, youngsters who do not have access to play materials such as construction toys, crayons, puzzles, and scissors may be late developing fine-motor skills and eye-hand coordination, but they will catch up given the opportunity. If there are no environmental concerns of this kind, however, significant delays may signal irregularities in the brain. In general, the longer a youngster is delayed in reaching developmental milestones, the more a parent needs to be concerned.

Parents need to be especially alert to developmental delays as a child approaches school age. Research demonstrates that children who begin school with developmental delays often progress at a slower rate than usual; as a result, the gap between them and their average peers tends to grow over time. Studies that have tracked such students over lengthy periods find that they tend to remain low achievers throughout their school years, and they have an unusually high rate of retention and failure to complete school. It is therefore important to address developmental delays well before children begin kindergarten, through enriched preschool programming. School districts are required to provide such programming without charge to children who have been identified as developmentally delayed, starting at the age of three. Free services to support infants and younger children with

Is Your Child Ready for School?

If your child can do many of the tasks on this checklist *before* beginning kindergarten, he or she is well on the way toward school success. The remaining skills will need to be developed during the kindergarten year in order to promote success in first grade.

- sings the alphabet song
- recognizes and names alphabet letters
- identifies words that rhyme, adds a rhyming word where appropriate in a story
- identifies whether dictated words begin with the same or different sounds
- claps to the number of syllables heard in a word
- blends dictated syllables into words (pop-corn; e-le-phant)
- substitutes initial and final sounds in words (say "man," say it again, but instead of the "mmmm" sound, say the "ffff" sound—*fan*)
- recognizes and names common colors, objects, shapes, and body parts
- tells full name, age, address, telephone number, and birthday
- comprehends age-appropriate stories
- uses vocabulary similar to other five-year-olds
- recites familiar nursery rhymes
- completes sequences (e.g., breakfast, lunch, ___; yesterday, today, ___)
- completes analogies (e.g., in daytime it is light, at night it is ___; birds fly, fish ___)
- can respond to various question forms, such as **how many** ("How many eyes do you have?"), **which** ("Which is slower [longer, more]?"), **where** ("Where do people buy gas?"), **whom** ("Whom do you go to when you are sick?"), **what** ("What do you do when you are hungry?" "What is a house made of?"), **why** ("Why do we have stoves?"), and **what if** ("What happens if your ice cream gets hot?")
- expresses opposite relationships ("How are a spoon and a glass different?")
- tells simple stories that contain several characters interacting
- follows two- and three-step simple directions, such as "Put on your boots, get your jacket, and get in the car"

delays are also available in most states. Your pediatrician or the special education department of your local school district can refer you to a screening program that identifies children in need of these services.

What skills are most important for a successful start in school? The checklist above lists some basic indicators of school readiness.

- succeeds at simple concentration-type games requiring matching pictures from memory
- recognizes own name in writing
- recognizes some common signs or labels by their shapes (McDonald's, Coca-Cola)
- sorts and names objects by category: food, clothing, animals
- recites and recognizes numbers up to ten
- counts groups of objects, to ten or more
- matches equal sets of objects, such as three triangles being the same amount as three circles
- points to positions in a series: beginning, middle, end; first, second, last
- recognizes and names common shapes, such as circles, squares, and triangles
- copies designs: circle, cross, square, X, triangle
- copies letters and simple words
- prints his or her name
- draws recognizable house, person, tree
- cuts out picture fairly close to edge
- completes age-appropriate puzzles
- constructs complex "buildings" or designs with blocks
- attends to a task for a reasonable period of time until done (coloring a picture, singing a song, playing a game of checkers)
- dresses self fairly independently
- ties shoes
- uses fork and spoon appropriately; cuts soft food with a knife
- usually finishes age-appropriate activities (such as a puzzle, listening to a short story, making an object out of clay) rather than abandoning activities in the middle
- develops friendships and plays cooperatively with other children

Children who are not comfortable with a majority of these skills by the age of four and a half years will almost certainly benefit from a year of preschool programming before starting kindergarten. Even when children do have these skills, it may be unwise to start them in school before the age of five (for girls) or five and a half (for boys, who mature later than girls do). Many of today's kindergarten classes present information at a very rapid pace, and children who begin school at younger ages often have problems keeping up even when they do not have developmental delays or learning disabilities. Research suggests that starting a child in school at age four is advisable only when the child has mastered most of the skills on the checklist, *and* flexible, individualized kindergarten and first-grade programming is available.

If delays persist beyond school entry, parents should not hesitate to request intervention. The first step is to help the child's teacher identify the skills that are delayed. Arrange to talk to the teacher at the earliest opportunity—before the beginning of school, if possible. Describe your concerns, and ask what can be done to help your child catch up in problem areas. Basically, the teacher has three options:

Intensify instruction. The teacher can arrange for additional instruction in areas where the child is behind. The extra help may be provided by a teacher, a classroom aide, a parent volunteer, or a student tutor—even a computer, in some cases.

Try different instructional methods and materials. The teacher can see if the student responds to activities or materials different from those being used by the rest of the class. A student who has been unsuccessful learning to recognize letters and numbers in a workbook, for example, might succeed when asked to cut these figures out and paste them on sheets of paper.

Reduce the academic load. If the child appears overwhelmed by demands to absorb too much too soon, the teacher can slow the rate of instruction and focus on the skills that are most important for success in first grade (usually prereading, counting, and writing skills). Instead of learning to count ten numbers at a time, for example, a student might concentrate on recognizing only one or two. This kind of intervention gives students room to build a solid academic foundation at their own pace.

If necessary, these strategies can be continued in first grade. If the student has not responded to intervention by the middle of the first-grade year, however, special education support may be needed.

Any discussion of retention should take place with the results of an evaluation on the table. A child who has information-processing problems will usually not benefit from repeating lessons that did not work before. Individualized programming is needed to address the child's specific disabilities while he or she moves on with classmates to the next grade. (For more information on retention, see Chapter 9.)

INCONSISTENT PERFORMANCE

One of the most confounding (and sometimes maddening) aspects of living with children who have learning disabilities is that their behavior is erratic. They are competent—even exceptionally able—sometimes, but other times they appear totally lost. Memory is an area where inconsistency is often most obvious; children with learning disabilities typically remember some kinds of information much better than others. This is easy enough to understand once you know your child has a learning disability, but before then parents go crazy trying to figure out how a kid can remember every gift he got for his fourth birthday but not where he left his new jacket, or how a student who remembered to do a homework assignment (and spent three hours on it) can then forget to hand in the paper!

Inconsistency can show up in any aspect of a child's activities. A child with learning disabilities may be able to draw well but not write clearly, for example, or he might be terrific at running, jumping, and climbing but unable to bounce a ball. A child who teaches herself to read before starting school may have problems counting up four forks or spoons, or she might speak brilliantly but find it impossible to put words on paper. Discrepancies of this kind puzzle parents and sometimes convince them that children are being inattentive or uncooperative. This type of behavior is typical of children who have information-processing weaknesses, however.

When a child with learning disabilities starts school, the baffling pattern of erratic performance continues. While many children are better in math than in language skills (or vice versa), the child with learning disabilities may be good in math on Tuesday and unable to

What Is Response-to-Intervention (RTI)?

Until 2004, the only way to legally identify a learning disability was to demonstrate that a "severe discrepancy" existed between a student's intellectual potential (as measured by an IQ test) and his or her academic performance. There were two major problems with this method of identification. First, students with disabilities often had to endure years of struggle with unsuitable methods and materials before falling far enough behind to meet the discrepancy criteria. As a result, many developed secondary problems that made addressing their disabilities harder. Second, some students met the criteria who were *not* disabled: their poor performance was primarily because they had not received adequate teaching. These children (many of whom were raised in poverty) needed help, but referral to special education was not really appropriate.

Federal lawmakers were concerned that both groups of children were floundering too long before getting the attention they needed. As a result, in 2004 new language was added to the Individuals with Disabilities Education Act (a large package of federal legislation that regulates the rights of students with all kinds of disabilities). The law now specifies that "a local educational agency *may use a process that determines if the child responds to scientific, research-based intervention*" (italics added) as a means of determining whether or not special education services are needed.

What the law now proposes is that students who are achieving poorly in school *for any reason* be quickly identified and offered intensified instructional support based on

comprehend math at all on Thursday (quite likely if the child has a language-processing handicap and the teacher has just introduced word problems). These children may love history one week and hate it the next because an essay has been assigned, or find that their best subject in third grade becomes their worst nightmare in fourth because there is more material to memorize. Performance may be inconsistent even within a given assignment or activity. A student may read a word correctly in the title of a chapter but fail to recognize the same word in the first paragraph—or she might write beautifully for two lines, after which her handwriting deteriorates into illegibility. Sometimes parents blame teachers for these problems, while teachers (who may be equally bewildered by this erratic behavior) start materials and methods that research has proven to be effective, with competent teachers who are experienced in the use of these materials. While there is no single model for delivering these services, many states have adopted a tiered approach to bringing low-achieving children up to speed. For example:

Tier 1: Large-Group Instruction.

High-quality programs in reading and other skills are administered to large groups—often the entire class. Individual progress in learning the school curriculum is monitored several times a year. Students who fall behind move to Tier 2.

Tier 2: Targeted Small-Group Instruction.

Students who are struggling to keep up are given small-group instruction in key skills areas in addition to their regular lessons. Individual progress is monitored to see if students begin to make more rapid progress. If students do not respond to the more intensive instruction in Tier 2 in a timely manner, they move to Tier 3.

Tier 3: Individual Instruction.

Student is given more intense instruction using methods and materials that target the child's particular skill deficits. Teaching efforts are specifically adapted to each child's individual pattern of learning strengths and weaknesses. Children's progress is measured frequently, and

continued

using phrases like "lacks motivation" and "needs to try harder." All sorts of incentives, punishments, and rewards may be employed to make performance more consistent. Since they do not address the underlying cause of the problem, these strategies are rarely successful for long.

It is sometimes noted that children with learning disabilities work better at home than at school. This is likely to be the case with children who need extra time to process information (Mom and Dad don't usually ring a bell and force a child to move on to a new activity) or who benefit from one-on-one instruction. If a child is consistently having trouble completing class work or tests in the time allotted, frequently needs instructions to be rephrased or repeated, those who do not respond satisfactorily to this level of intervention are referred to a multi-disciplinary evaluation team to determine the child's eligibility for special education services.

Children who do not have disabilities can be expected to improve given intensive intervention. But children who fail to respond—or who respond unusually slowly—probably need a type or intensity of instruction that can best be provided by special education. They require additional evaluation to pinpoint the specific nature of their learning problems, but the law now states that documenting their "response-to-intervention" can be a major part of the diagnostic process (it essentially rules out poor teaching as a source of the student's academic issues). Federal law no longer requires an evaluation to find a "severe discrepancy" between intellectual performance and academic potential to identify a learning disability (although many states continue to use discrepancy formulas).

RTI can improve instruction in the general education program, prevent failure, and streamline the process for identifying disabilities—a win/win situation. Implementing RTI is a complex process, however. Local education authorities must establish methods of identifying children in need of help. They must select "scientifically proven" curricula for teaching basic skills to these children and educate teachers in the use of these curricula. Student progress must be carefully documented using evaluation methods that are research-based and reliable. Some states have made more progress developing RTI programs than others.

or often has difficulty explaining what he or she knows to you, these are also clues that a learning disability may exist, and that it is time to ask for an evaluation.

LOSS OF INTEREST IN LEARNING

Most small children, including those with learning disabilities, love to learn (of course, they think of it as exploring rather than learning). It is wonderful to watch the determined optimism of babies who are learning to climb stairs or to walk: repeated failure hardly discourages them at all. Some of us can't resist spoiling our toddlers with too many toys, because we love that gleam they get in their eyes when they discover something new. How many of us have at some point fallen into bed exhausted from trying to answer questions for a child with

Any parent with an underperforming child should find out what RTI programs are in place. Following are ten questions about RTI to ask your school principal, district superintendent, or director of special education services:

1. Is the school district currently using an RTI process to support struggling students? If not, are they developing one?
2. What screening procedures are used to identify students who need help?
3. What interventions and instructional programs are being used? What research supports their effectiveness?
4. What process is used to select the interventions that will be provided?
5. What length of time is allowed for an intervention before determining if a student is "responding to intervention"?
6. What strategy is used to monitor progress? What types of data will be collected?
7. Is a written intervention plan provided to parents as part of the RTI process?
8. Are the teachers providing the interventions trained in using them?
9. How will information about a student's progress be provided to parents?
10. At what point in the RTI process are students suspected of having a learning disability referred for further evaluation?

Ten Questions adapted with permission from *A Parent's Guide to Response to Intervention* by Candace Cortiella, National Center for Learning Disabilities, © 2010.

a serious case of the "Why?"s. (One father we know remembers that his five-year-old son—a very bright lad who was later discovered to have learning disabilities—was in bed and half asleep when he asked his hundredth question of the day: Why did America fight World War II?) While it can be hard to keep up with children's relentless curiosity, most parents find this open delight in learning one of the most appealing aspects of childhood.

Conversely, there is nothing much sadder than watching the erosion of enthusiasm for learning that can take place after a child with learning disabilities starts school. Some parents recall that this process occurred almost overnight—that their children went from happy, eager-to-tackle-anything preschoolers to declaring, "I hate school and everything connected with it" in a matter of weeks. Other students gradually become disenchanted with subjects that once interested

Children with Learning Disabilities Often Have Problems with Memory

NANCY reprinted by permission of United Feature Syndicate, Inc.

them. For example, a student who has difficulties with reading comprehension may enjoy science in elementary school (when the curriculum includes many hands-on activities) but starts to lose interest in secondary school when science reading requirements increase. It is very common for students with learning disabilities to develop a distaste for subjects that demand research and writing, which are problem areas for most students with information-processing weaknesses. Students with relatively mild disabilities who are successful in elementary school may become discouraged and uninterested in secondary school, when they are faced with the challenge of organizing and remembering larger amounts of information and expectations to complete work independently.

If students' learning disabilities are not identified and appropriate help is not provided, disinterest in learning usually progresses to outright avoidance. Children start developing strategies to spare themselves the frustration of trying to accomplish tasks that are painfully difficult or impossible for them. These kids become expert procrastinators; it takes them forever to get around to doing their homework. Often they rush through it, leave it unfinished, or claim "I did the homework in school." Some children complain chronically of fatigue, stomachaches, or other afflictions and beg to be allowed to abandon schoolwork or stay home from school entirely—and they are not necessarily faking it, since stress-related discomforts can be very real. If the situation is allowed to deteriorate into junior high and high school, teens may start cutting classes, become truant, or even drop out of school entirely.

There are causes other than learning disabilities for a loss of interest in learning. Family problems, health concerns, an ineffective teacher, or a poor match between student and curriculum can all undermine enthusiasm for education. And of course around puberty, the whole school population has a hard time keeping its mind on learning, as any middle school teacher knows. In general, however, an unexpected loss of interest in learning—whether sudden or gradual—is a sign that *some* kind of intervention is needed. A "wait-and-see" approach can have serious consequences here: once a student has stopped enjoying learning and started to avoid it, it can be very difficult to restore motivation.

Listed below are a few common early signs that a student's interest in learning is declining:

- *General complaints about school.* Sometimes a student in academic trouble will issue a barrage of complaints that appear to have nothing to do with learning: the teacher is unfair, the other students are stuck-up, the playground is too crowded, the cafeteria food is disgusting. When children repeatedly claim to hate school, parents would be wise to check with teachers about how things are going academically.

- *Persistent complaints that work is too hard.* Children with learning disabilities frequently feel "over their heads" in some classes or subjects. This kind of complaint needs to be investigated promptly, as students who cannot do the work assigned to them rapidly lose confidence in themselves and quit trying.

- *Complaints of boredom.* Children having trouble understanding schoolwork are as likely to complain that the work is "dumb" or boring as to say it is difficult or hard to understand. Persistent complaints of boredom may also indicate that students are not being given work appropriate for their intellectual levels (a common problem for students with superior intelligence).

- **Refusal to talk about school.** When young children who previously bubbled over with reports on their school days start giving you one-word answers ("What happened in school today?" "Nothing." "How was the spelling test?" "Okay."), it's a good idea to find out what has undermined their enthusiasm. This sort of response is, of course, more or less normal for adolescents.

- **Loss of pride in schoolwork.** Children with learning problems often become ashamed of their written work, which tends to be messy, incomplete, and liberally overwritten with the teacher's red pencil. Parents should be concerned if children stop showing them schoolwork or stop bringing it home.

UNEXPECTED UNDERACHIEVEMENT

The definitive characteristic of a learning disability is an unexpected failure to learn—the student is simply not doing as well in school as expected, given that student's intelligence, health, and opportunities. Taken by itself, however, underachievement is not a particularly strong indicator. As Alexander's story demonstrates, a great many factors can influence school performance. Most students who are having trouble working up to potential do *not* have learning disabilities, although, like Alexander, they may be in need of some form of help in order to do better.

Parents do need to be concerned, however, when elementary-aged youngsters have a hard time learning to read, write, perform elementary calculations, or sustain attention long enough to absorb an average lesson. Research suggests that the longer children struggle in these basic areas without appropriate help, the poorer their chances of catching up with typical peers, regardless of the source of the problem. It is therefore important for parents to monitor basic-skills development carefully and request intervention if children fall behind in any basic subject. Note that, according to federal law, school districts may provide special education services to *any* child aged three to nine who is experiencing significant delays in communication skills (or with physical, cognitive, adaptive, emotional, or social development) without identifying a specific disability. (The student will be temporarily identified as having a "developmental delay.") If a child does not respond promptly to educational intervention—or is likely to require continued services after the age of nine—a special education evaluation for the purpose of determining a specific handicapping condition is the next step.

There are times when parents need to be concerned, even when youngsters are achieving at average levels. The expected achievement level for children who have superior intelligence is better than average: a nine-year-old fourth-grader with an intelligence in the top 2 or 3 percent of her age group ought to be able to read fifth- and sixth-grade books, for example. Average school performance merits investigation when a child speaks, draws, or understands concepts exceptionally well or is doing advanced work in other academic areas. Average academic work should also be investigated when it is accompanied by marked slowness or extraordinary effort—particularly if other warning signs discussed in this chapter are present.

Parents should also be concerned about unexpected *drops* in achievement. Learning disabilities often assert themselves at fairly predictable "stress points" in the educational process. Children with mild information-processing problems may learn to read satisfactorily, for example, but develop academic difficulties around fourth grade when demands on reading comprehension typically increase dramatically. The need to organize schedules and larger amounts of information in junior high and new expectations concerning writing, research, and ability to work independently in high school may also cause students with learning problems to stumble. Typical students also frequently experience temporary setbacks at these educational junctions, but if a child does not "bounce back" within one school year, parents should investigate without further delay.

Alexander

Alexander's mother and school psychologist referred him to a university clinic for evaluation. Because the ten-year-old fourth-grader had persistent written-language difficulties, they wondered if it would be appropriate to identify him as "learning disabled."

Alexander's background revealed a great deal of turmoil. He had moved seventeen times and attended four different schools. His parents divorced when he was three years old. His mother had recently remarried, and Alexander was having trouble accepting a new authority figure in the house. To complicate family matters, it was apparent that Alexander's biological father disliked and avoided Alexander, while showering affection on his younger sister. Alexander claimed to have no close friends among his peers. He appeared to be a rather lonely and isolated little boy.

Testing showed that Alexander was an incredibly gifted child. His vocabulary and reasoning ability were equal to those of most adults. He scored at a high school level in all areas of achievement with the exception of written expression, where his achievement was average for his age and grade. Alexander's spelling, sentence structure, and punctuation were perfect, but he took an unduly long time getting words down on paper. He also developed his ideas in such a detail-oriented way that it was impossible to guess the main thought he was trying to convey. In conversation as well, Alexander included many unnecessary details and had trouble getting to the point.

The evaluation revealed a captivating youngster struggling with many personal issues. Alexander's writing difficulties were found to be primarily due to very poor motor planning. He could not write a word without actually thinking about telling his hand how to move. It was also difficult for him to touch his thumb to each successive finger, figure out how to skip, or walk through a doorway without bumping into the frame. His mother reported that Alexander often dropped tableware when setting the table, and that getting a coin into a vending-machine slot was very difficult for him. Given a little extra time to think, however, Alexander could perform these tasks successfully.

Alexander's overly analytical personal style complicated his writing difficulties. The boy typically became so concerned with keeping track of minor points and details that he forgot his main ideas. When he was shown how to plan and outline, instructed to begin each paragraph with a topic sentence, and encouraged to dictate or tape-record his assignments rather than write them out in longhand, however, Alexander quickly began to produce work that was very superior for his age and grade.

Alexander's school psychologist and his parents thought he should be identified as having a learning disability. Without this label, they feared they would be unable to convince Alexander's teachers to give him extra time to do written work or allow him to record his assignments. Alexander objected, however, saying he thought he could meet the expectations and requirements of his classroom teachers with minimal help. He pointed out that he could tape most of his assignments at home and transcribe them before handing them in.

Alexander was right. The child who is truly "learning disabled" requires a quality or intensity of instruction beyond what can be provided in an ordinary classroom. Although Alexander had some significant weaknesses, simple adjustments in his educational program were all that would be needed to promote success. In their report, the evaluation team recommended that these minor modifications be made in Alexander's program. They also suggested weekly counseling for emotional issues, and they strongly encouraged Alexander's parents to seek out and involve their son in programs for gifted children. In addition, the team explained Alexander's weaknesses to him and described how he could work around them.

Fortunately, Alexander's teachers proved cooperative and implemented the evaluation team's recommendations. If they had not, however, assigning Alexander a "handicapped" label might have been the only way to get support for him. This is how rigid educational systems can *create* disabilities instead of minimizing them. There are always fewer "disabled" students in classrooms where teachers are flexible and skilled at individualizing instruction.

Adapted from C. R. Smith, *Learning Disabilities,* © 2004. Reproduced by permission of Pearson Education, Inc.

PERSISTENT BEHAVIORAL OR EMOTIONAL PROBLEMS

Children with learning disabilities have been observed to have a wide variety of behavioral problems. In some cases, these will be evident early. Children with attention-deficit/hyperactivity disorder, for example, are often cranky and irritable even as infants and they are notoriously difficult to live with as preschoolers (studies show that the stress experienced by parents of children with ADHD peaks when the children are between three and six years old). The problems youngsters with visual-perception and language-processing disabilities have understanding and remembering information can also create an impression that the children are disobedient or rude, although these behaviors have more to do with neurology than with choices made by the child.

When children with learning disabilities start school, behavior problems start multiplying. As Joe's story poignantly illustrates, frustration and anxiety over schoolwork, combined with a painful lack of success in social relationships, can have a powerful impact on a student's emotional state. How children react to this stress depends on precise circumstances and the child's temperament. While some are able to bounce back from academic disappointment, others become angry, hostile, withdrawn, or depressed. Emotional upheaval is not always obvious at school, but it is usually apparent at home. One mother remembers: "When my daughter began school, it seemed like she developed a split personality. She tried very hard to be good in the classroom and got glowing behavior reports from her teachers. Then she came home and kicked furniture and yelled at everybody in the family for the rest of the day."

Behavior problems in the classroom or a change of mood at home can be the first sign of a learning problem. Sadly, they are not always recognized as such; instead, they may be perceived as defects in the child's character or personality. The unfortunate outcome is that adults—teachers and parents alike—may see academic problems as resulting from undesirable behavior, instead of the other way around. Young people with learning disabilities are forever being accused of being stubborn, insensitive, irresponsible, careless, uncooperative, and lazy. Their low achievement is blamed on indifference to their parents' and their teachers' wishes and their own unwillingness to apply themselves. Such misperceptions can have sad consequences— not only do conflicts with adults over these issues add to children's stress levels, but also in the absence of any other explanation, students all too quickly come to accept these negative views of themselves as correct. Since youngsters who have decided that they are "no good" generally find it easier to conform to negative expectations than to rise above them, a vicious downward spiral can be created.

To avoid this kind of self-perpetuating defeat, parents need to recognize behavior problems for what they usually are—cries for help. Persistent misbehavior generally indicates that children's needs are out of sync with their environments in some important respect (a learning disability is only one possibility). Emotional problems such as excessive fear or anger also suggest that a child is under some kind of stress and intervention is needed. It is seldom wise to delay addressing emotional or behavioral issues in the hope that the child is "going through a phase" and will outgrow them. Problems in the areas described below seldom resolve on their own, and most often get worse with time. Children who have developed behavior or emotional problems may need a program that combines professional counseling with intervention at school.

Persistent problems in the areas listed below, combined with underachievement, should be addressed by a psychological *and* an educational evaluation:

- *Excessive anger or hostility.* This may be expressed verbally (sarcasm, cursing, and name-calling) or physically (destroying property, bullying, fighting, tantrums, and rages).

- *Excessive anxiety.* Fears may not appear connected with school: a child might develop excessive anxiety about strangers or separation from parents, for example.

- *Depression.* Symptoms include isolation; feelings of sadness and emptiness; loss of interest in activities once enjoyed; changes in sleep patterns; changes in appetite; feelings of guilt

Joe

I always would end up in the boneheaded reading section. All of my friends were over on the other side, and I was over with those "others." I hated being over with the other kids. They were the ones the "cool" kids picked on. It was a pain to be with them. I was really scared about something rubbing off on me. And I am sure now that they felt the same about me.

It was funny, I always knew I have a problem learning like everybody else, but I always knew I wasn't dumb. I was scared all the time of being thought dumb, but in my heart I knew I wasn't. I hated being set apart. It made everything so tense for me.

So, like a lot of learning-disabled kids I was beginning my career of sticking out, being different. I was noisy, not because I wanted the negative attention it got me, but because I needed and wanted acceptance from my peers and couldn't figure out how to be one of them.

I felt different enough from my classmates that stress began piling upon stress. Soon I couldn't trust anything. If a teacher were to ask me what county I lived in, I could be thinking "Gallatin County" and out would pop "America." This would happen often. The classroom would be disrupted and the teacher would be mad. I didn't want to be a smart Alec, but the teacher thought I did and my classmates thought I did. If the principal became involved he thought I did, and heck, even my parents began to think I did.

There were times I would do or say something and my friends would look at me like I was from another planet. It would mostly happen to me when I would come upon a group of my friends somewhere and try to join the conversation. I would listen in a group and then give the group my ideas. When I did that, the conversation would die and they would all look at me. I'd die a thousand deaths. I thought people were starting to laugh at me, and maybe even call me dumb, stupid, or retarded. I was never sure, but to me it

or worthlessness; fatigue; restlessness and irritability; difficulty concentrating or making decisions; and thoughts of suicide. In teens, warning signs also include apathy, a sudden drop in grades, rebellious behavior, and/or use of alcohol and drugs. *Not getting help for depression can be life threatening.*

- *Escapist behavior.* This may include excessive fantasizing and daydreaming, or obsessive involvement with television or felt that way, and I started to react to these feelings. What I started to do was go totally nuts every time the word *dumb* or a synonym of it was associated with me. I beat up people for even thinking I was dumb.

A close friend took me aside one day and talked to me about how many people were scared of me and asked if that was what I wanted. The answer was easy: "No, I don't want anyone scared of me." So I came up with another answer, and that was the one I stayed with for a long time. I just went quiet, and just didn't join things as much. I hated that part of me that I couldn't seem to control.

I was totally lost. I was going farther and farther down a road I didn't like, and I was getting into more and more trouble. I was starting to get caught skipping classes, and my parents weren't happy with me. I was feeling angrier and I wasn't having much luck expressing it. I would be in class, trying to listen to the teacher and not be a nuisance, and something—anything—would happen and I'd get mad. I would be in the hall walking just after class, and rage would just start welling up in me. I would reach over and smack a locker and bust up my knuckles.

The people around me would look at me like I was a totally freaked out person. The sad fact was that I was feeling freaked out. I was pulling farther away from everybody around me, and I wasn't talking to people anymore. Not talking was driving me crazy, but I was scared to open up.

There were people who were reaching out to me and trying to help me, but I'd just blow them off as fast as I could.

Adapted with permission from *Cookie and I*, by Joe Lair, Bozeman, MT, 1996.

video and adventure games; it can later include withdrawal into drug and alcohol abuse and promiscuous sexual activity.

- *Thrill-seeking behavior.* Such children enjoy placing themselves in danger and "living on the edge." They may be attracted to heights, speed, violence, or illegal activity.

- *Antisocial/oppositional behavior.* This is a willful refusal to obey rules or comply with authority (which is not to be confused with *inability* to comply or to understand what authorities want). It typically involves repeated conflicts with adults and truancy; it may also include substance abuse and such criminal activities as setting fires, theft, and vandalism.

DECLINING CONFIDENCE AND SELF-ESTEEM

Loss of confidence and self-esteem is perhaps the most common "side effect" of a learning disability. All too often, children blame themselves for the problems associated with these handicaps (low achievement in school, failure to live up to parental expectations, lack of acceptance by peers). They assume they are stupid because they do not do well in school, and are unlikable because they do not have hordes of friends. It can be heartbreaking to hear how mercilessly these kids regard themselves. One mother remembers her first-grader concluding, "Mommy, even the dumb kids in the class can do this stuff, so I must be *dumber* than dumb, whatever that is." Even after learning problems have been identified, youngsters may continue to berate themselves for needing extra help and being "different." There is probably no society that values conformity as much as a classroom does. Children all too easily define being different as being a misfit and a loser.

If these negative self-impressions are not addressed, a child's emotional well-being is likely to be affected, as described in the preceding section. Low self-esteem also rapidly undermines academic motivation. Youngsters with learning disabilities are exceedingly vulnerable to *learned helplessness*. This term was coined by well-known psychologist Martin Seligman. In studies with animals, Seligman demonstrated that when experience teaches a creature that its efforts have little impact on its circumstances, the creature becomes passive and stops trying to influence events. In one experiment, dogs were trained to avoid an uncomfortable electric shock by jumping over a barrier. Most learned to escape the shock promptly, but dogs who had previously been given shocks they could not escape proved unable to learn this task. Convinced that they were helpless, these animals made little effort to save themselves, even when provided with the opportunity.

Studies examining student attitudes reveal that the same phenomenon applies in the classroom. Long-term low achievers come to see themselves as *unable* to learn; they anticipate failure and are far less persistent than students who believe there is a relationship between effort and success. Once a student stops trying, of course, continued failure is pretty much guaranteed. Belief in one's ability to succeed is therefore essential for any kind of achievement. One study of students with learning disabilities found that self-concept and motivation were more powerful predictors of academic progress than intelligence!

Parents need to be concerned, then, when they hear negative self-talk: "I'm dumb," "I'm hopeless," "Nobody likes me," "I can't do anything right," and so on. Alarms should also go off if a child makes frequent use of "I can't," whether in regard to his or her ability to add, dance, play sports, or talk to the opposite sex. (One wise teacher we know encourages students who say "I can't" to add "yet" to the end of the sentence.) If students seem to have become discouraged about schoolwork, it is important to draw teachers' attention to the problem as early as possible, and to see what can be done about restructuring tasks so that students can start experiencing success. In the long run, showing students what kind of *effort* produces results ("See? You practiced on the computer, and you went up to a B in math!") is a more effective motivator than external incentives and rewards ("Okay, five dollars if you bring your grade up to a B, and for an A you get ten"). Once students start achieving, success becomes its own reward, and external inducements may be unnecessary.

It is also important to remember that parental attitudes have a major impact on the way children approach learning. Some parents help promote helplessness by conveying low expectations. Studies find that such parents often regard success as resulting primarily from luck and other factors beyond personal control. If a student comes home with an A on a test, for example, these parents might say, "You must have made some good guesses," or "I guess the teacher was in a specially good mood." Children exposed to these views see little relationship between effort and achievement. Working to solve problems therefore makes no sense to them.

Positive parents, on the other hand, see their children as essentially capable and competent—even when they are having problems in school. Presented with an F, they might say, "You did not get a good night's sleep before that exam" or "I bet you do better if you review a little every day instead of trying to cram at the last minute." Children exposed to this outlook understand that there are things they can do to influence events and bring about change. These children can usually be counted on to apply themselves to problems and derive personal satisfaction from overcoming them.

It is therefore extremely important for parents of children with learning problems to maintain a positive and encouraging attitude. Your most important job as a parent is to convey to your children that they *can* succeed; helping them find the means to do so comes second. The fact is, the most skillful teaching in the world will not do much for a child who lacks the will to try. "Self-confidence is the magic ingredient that we can't always provide," one teacher says; "The kids who have it usually learn it at home—and they always rise to the top."

There is one final warning signal that should not be ignored: *parental instinct*. Very often, when students with learning disabilities are identified, we hear parents (most often a child's mother) say, "I *knew* something was wrong; I was sure there was more to it than immaturity" (or "getting used to the new teacher," "paying more attention," or "trying harder"). Parents frequently allow themselves to be talked out of these gut feelings, however, by professionals who are supposed to know more about child development or education. Our natural, human desire to believe our children are perfect (or at least normal) sometimes contributes to this process. When a teacher says a student who is falling behind may outgrow the difficulty, or that there's nothing wrong that can't be overcome with a little extra effort, who wouldn't prefer to believe that rather than accept the possibility that the child may have a disability or other serious problem?

Our experience, however, is that "gut instinct" is trustworthy. Your knowledge of your child, your sense of your child's happiness and well-being, and your feelings about what the child ought to be able to do are as valuable as any of the other types of information discussed in this chapter. What this means in practical terms is that if the school's explanations for your child's lack of progress don't make sense to you—or if you lack confidence in the solutions being proposed—you should trust your judgment and keep looking for other answers. To do so, you may have to learn to be assertive with professionals who think you are overreacting, overprotective, overly emotional, or over-involved. We find that the best way to counter those opinions is to become well-informed and to be persistent—this is a virtually irresistible combination.

If your gut is telling you that your son or daughter needs more help than he or she is getting in a typical classroom, don't wait to address the problem. Research consistently shows that children with disabilities benefit from the earliest possible intervention, and federal law is also on your side: in recent years, lawmakers have placed increasing emphasis on *preventing* children from experiencing prolonged periods of failure. Whether or not a learning disability is eventually identified, prompt attention to academic setbacks can establish the methods and materials that help your child learn best, and enable your child to face the future with real confidence and enthusiasm.

5

The Learning Disabilities Evaluation

In order to succeed in school, most children with learning disabilities will need some special education services and accommodations. To obtain these services, a formal evaluation must demonstrate that a child's learning problems match those described in the Individuals with Disabilities Education Improvement Act (IDEA 2004). This complex package of federal legislation specifies the types of disabilities for which special education may be provided, regulates the methods used to identify these disabilities, and outlines the rights of children with disabilities and their families in considerable detail.

IDEA recognizes thirteen categories of disability: developmental delay, mental retardation, autism, deafness/hearing impairment, visual impairment (including blindness), orthopedic impairment, speech or language impairment, deaf/blindness, emotional disturbance, traumatic brain injury, specific learning disability, multiple disabilities, and other health impairment (which includes ADHD). *Specific learning disability* is defined as follows:

A disorder in one or more of the basic psychological processes involved in understanding or in using language, spoken or written, that may manifest itself in an imperfect ability to listen, think, speak, read,

write, spell, or to do mathematical calculations, including such con-
ditions as perceptual disabilities, brain injury, minimal brain dysfunc-
tion, dyslexia, and developmental aphasia. Specific learning disability
does not include learning problems that are primarily the result of
visual, hearing, or motor disabilities; mental retardation; emotional
disturbance; or environmental, cultural, or economic disadvantage.

In addition to defining *learning disability*, IDEA specifies how evaluations for learning disabilities are to be conducted. In general, the
law requires evaluations for learning disabilities to be comprehensive
enough to meet four standards:

- The evaluation must document that a child is achieving well
  below potential in one or more academic subjects *or* that the
  student has shown a very poor response to educational intervention (for more on Response-to-Intervention, see Chapter 4).

- The evaluation must show that the child's disabilities are severe enough to require special education services. (Services may
  not be offered if a child's disability is deemed mild enough to be
  addressed by general education teachers in a typical classroom.)

- The evaluation must demonstrate that the child has had adequate and appropriate learning opportunities.

- The evaluation must rule out other causes of underachievement, such as health issues, emotional problems, cultural concerns, and other types of impairment.

Clearly, no one test—and no one individual—can possibly be
expected to provide all this information. The law therefore requires
public school districts to use *multidisciplinary teams* of professionals
in the identification process. Furthermore, these teams must use a
variety of assessment strategies to gather information about a student
(interviews and classroom observation, for example, as well as tests).
Evaluations must also be provided in a timely manner. Federal law
requires that an evaluation for learning disabilities take place within

sixty days of parental consent for one (unless a different timetable is specified by the state). If the school requests an evaluation and parents do not consent, the school is absolved of responsibility for offering special education and related services to the child.

Members of assessment teams have a wide range of tools and techniques available to them for gathering information. The goal is to use as many methods as needed to develop a well-rounded view of the student. A comprehensive evaluation goes far beyond pinpointing a child's learning weaknesses; it should also identify the student's strengths and determine how his or her performance is affected by different teaching approaches and environments. While the selection of evaluation methods will vary according to the nature of a student's problems, a thorough learning-disabilities evaluation ought to include the following:

- a review of school records and an examination of the student's work;
- preparation of a medical and social history covering major aspects of the student's growth and development;
- observation of the student in the classroom (in some cases, it might also be desirable to observe the child at home);
- interviews with the student and important adults in the student's life (parents, teachers, others who spend significant amounts of time with the student);
- tests and other assessment measures to establish learning potential, academic-achievement levels, and information-processing abilities; and
- an examination of the curriculum and the student's classroom environment, and a review of the teaching methods and materials that have been used with the child so far.

This work is usually done by learning specialists, psychologists, and social workers employed by the school system. When you consider that evaluating a child for learning disabilities can occupy four or more professionals and is typically spread out over several weeks, it becomes easier to understand why school districts are reluctant to undertake evaluations without clear cause. It has been estimated that as much as 40 percent of the cost of educating students with learning disabilities is related to the painstaking procedures that must be followed both to identify these students and to monitor their progress.

If a comprehensive, multidisciplinary approach to evaluation is not taken, however, students' learning problems may be misunderstood. Consider the students whose stories appear in this chapter. Jessica and Maria were both incorrectly identified until home visits and interviews with their parents placed their learning difficulties in perspective. Rachel's baffling writing habits would never have been explained by testing (oddly, adults often forget to *ask* students why they do what they do; this step yielded key information in Rachel's case). In contrast, Casey's ability to compensate for his disability on tests masked visual-perception problems that were actually quite severe. As student populations around the country become more and more diverse, it is increasingly important for evaluation teams to understand how social and economic circumstances affect learning, and be sensitive to cultural differences. Many assessment tools are keyed to the traditional majority culture; teams must be knowledgeable enough to choose alternative strategies when these tools are not appropriate.

The most important factors affecting the quality of a learning disabilities evaluation, then, are

- the experience and skill of the members of the evaluation team,
- the variety and relevance of approaches they employ, and
- the quality of the specific tests and other assessment tools they select.

An evaluation's outcome is also influenced by the way different localities interpret federal law. For example, IDEA specifies that either documenting a poor response to intervention or establishing a severe discrepancy between intellectual potential and academic achievement (or a combination of the two) may be used to identify a learning disability, but each state is left to define for itself what the terms *severe discrepancy* and *response to intervention* mean. Some states do so in a way that seems intended to include the greatest numbers of students with learning problems, while others seem determined to

Jessica

Jessica was brought to a university teaching clinic by her mother, who refused to accept the results of a school assessment that had determined Jessica was mentally retarded. The seven-year-old had made almost no progress in first grade, and she had performed very poorly on a standard IQ test. In addition, the psychologist who had administered the test indicated that Jessica's responses seemed random on many tasks. It was as if she did not even understand what she was expected to do.

Jessica's mother told the clinic staff that the child's father had died five months ago. He had battled cancer for five years, and during that time the family's activities had revolved around his needs. The family was supported by public assistance. There was barely enough income to cover the most basic necessities; there was nothing left over for "extras" for Jessica or her two younger brothers. None of the children had received regular dental and medical care or attended preschool programs.

A visit to Jessica's home found it barren of books, children's games, or toys. Jessica's brothers were amusing themselves by throwing themselves at a wall and seeing who rebounded farthest. Jessica's mother confirmed that the children had never owned blocks, puzzles, picture books, or crayons. It seemed possible that Jessica's poor performance on the IQ test was at least in part because she was unfamiliar with the tasks that the test asked her to perform.

Clinic staff decided to administer another intelligence test. Before doing so, they spent some time playing with Jessica, using "games" that were similar to the tasks on the test. For example, Jessica was encouraged to point out similarities between objects, copy designs, and create sequences from pictured events. Before taking the test, Jessica was reminded to approach the questions in the same way she had when playing. This time she scored well within the normal range. The first test had tapped Jessica's relatively empty experience, not her cognitive abilities.

The clinic began to look for other explanations for Jessica's poor performance in school. Eventually she was found to have language-processing disabilities that required special services from the speech pathologist and a learning disabilities specialist. When these were provided, her schoolwork began to improve. The clinic staff also helped Jessica's mother find free preschool programs for her two boys and guided her to a parenting workshop where she could learn more about her children's needs and develop her own parenting skills.

Adapted from C. R. Smith, *Learning Disabilities*, © 2004. Reproduced by permission of Pearson Education, Inc.

provide special education services to only the most severely affected. This helps explain why in recent years more than 9 percent of the students in Massachusetts have been identified as having learning disabilities, while Kentucky has identified 2 percent.

Are local special education policies sometimes motivated by economic concerns as much as by concerns for student welfare? Some experts think so. It costs significantly more to educate students with disabilities, and federal reimbursements offset only a small portion of the increased expense. Restricting the number of students who get special education help (or limiting the kinds of help these students get) can therefore serve as a cost-containment measure. It has been argued that a student's chances of getting help for a learning disability are greater in relatively "wealthy" states than in states where the average family income is lower and school districts have fewer resources. Whether or not this is true, local special education policies do have a major impact on determining who becomes eligible for services.

Given all these considerations, what can a parent do to ensure that an evaluation for learning disabilities is thorough and fair? Taking the following steps will help you get the most out of the assessment process.

BECOME INFORMED ABOUT FEDERAL AND LOCAL REGULATIONS

Information about eligibility for special education services is available from your public school district (request it from the department of special education) or from your state department of education. The publication you receive should explain what guidelines your state uses to document the existence of a learning disability. Must a child be functioning a year or more below grade level in some subject to qualify for special education help? Does the state use a "discrepancy formula" that compares achievement and intelligence test scores and mandates a specific gap? (The box on page 110 explains the use of standard deviations to determine discrepancy—the most common method.) Are Response-to-Intervention (RTI) programs in place and used as part of the diagnostic process? While all equations for establishing a learning disability are arbitrary, imperfect, and to some

Calculating Severe Discrepancies

One way of identifying a learning disability is to establish that there is a "severe discrepancy" between a student's ability (as judged by an IQ test) and performance (as judged by one or more achievement tests). States using discrepancy formulas usually require that IQ and achievement be 1½ to 2 *standard deviations* apart for a discrepancy to be considered severe. Each section on the chart above represents one standard deviation. For example:

Ryan has an IQ of 100 and a reading score of 70. These scores are two standard deviations apart—enough to identify a learning disability in many states.

Vanessa has an IQ of 100 and a math score of 85. Although she is behind, one standard deviation is considered within the normal range. She will need extra help in the classroom but will probably not be identified as "learning disabled."

Darryl has an IQ of 130. His writing score is 105. Even though his achievement is average, it does not reflect his very superior intelligence. Darryl's discrepancy of 1½ standard deviations will identify a learning disability in some states.

Alana's IQ of 70 is considered retarded. Her reading comprehension score is 40, which suggests that she also has a specific learning disability. While not all states will recognize a student with mental retardation as also "learning disabled," it should be recognized that Alana will need unusually intense instruction in reading comprehension in addition to other special education services.

degree unfair, these are nevertheless the rules you are going to have to work with, so make sure you understand them.

It is also essential to understand that during every stage of the evaluation and special education process, children with disabilities and their parents have important rights and protections under the law. Many of these are summarized in a document called the *Parent's Notice of Procedural Safeguards*. This document is available in six languages, including Spanish, Russian, Chinese, Vietnamese, and Arabic. Your child's school is required to give you a copy of this notice as soon as an evaluation is requested. The rights described in this document (which vary from state to state but must comply with federal standards set forth in IDEA) offer parents a powerful role in planning the education of a child who needs special services. It is up to you, however, to learn about your options and to exercise this role.

INVESTIGATE THE INVESTIGATORS

When seeking an assessment for learning disabilities, you have two choices: ask for a free evaluation from your school district (this request should be made in writing, and directed to the special education department or to the principal of your child's school) or pay for an independent assessment. Either way, find out exactly who your child will see over the course of the evaluation. What are their qualifications and areas of expertise? Do they have specific experience in the suspected area of disability? Are team members sensitive to any cultural issues that you feel are important, and to social or emotional issues that could be affecting your child's performance? Who will coordinate the activities of different team members, keep track of the information collected, and make final recommendations? Whom should you contact if you have questions?

If you are seeking a free evaluation from your public school district, you may not have much choice about who is assigned to your child's evaluation team. Experienced parents note, however, that it can pay to "ask around" among parents of students who have learning disabilities to see if any school district personnel are known to be particularly sensitive and skilled with evaluations. A psychologist at a different school might have a good reputation for working with children from particular minority groups, for example, or there may be one special education teacher who has a great deal of experience sorting out reading problems. If this is the case, you can request that a certain professional be assigned to your child's evaluation. Your school district's special education department should be able to direct you to support organizations for families of students with disabilities in your area. These organizations are an excellent place to start when looking for public evaluation information.

Is a private evaluation likely to be better than those done by the public school district? Not necessarily. Federal guidelines concerning evaluations apply only to agencies receiving public funds. Private agencies can (and sometimes do) get away with "quickie" evaluations that could overlook significant factors contributing to a student's learning problems. If the evaluation is thorough, it is probably also going to be expensive: fees for private assessments can run into the thousands of dollars, depending on how many specialists are involved. (Health insurance may cover part of these costs, and some agencies do offer sliding fees based on income.) In addition, school district policies on outside evaluations vary: your district may accept a private assessment in place of its own, or it may insist on doing its own evaluation as well before providing services. For all of these reasons, most parents prefer to start with a school district evaluation, reserving the right to follow up with a private evaluation if they disagree with the school district's findings.

A private evaluation, however, does give you more control of the assessment process. You can not only select the professionals who will be involved, but also choose whether or not to share the information they obtain with your school district. Beginning with a private evaluation might make sense if you have reason to lack confidence in your school district's special education department, or if you are considering seeking private help for the child rather than obtaining special education services in school. Professionals who conduct evaluations can be found in private practice, as well as connected with colleges and universities, hospitals, and mental health clinics. Your school district's department of special education can provide you with a list of people in your community who do this sort of work (they are also required to provide this information to parents seeking second opinions). Parent support groups are another good source of information about independent evaluations.

ASK ABOUT TESTS

Federal law provides very clear guidelines in the matter of testing for learning disabilities. Tests must be conducted on a one-to-one basis (previously taken group tests are not acceptable for assessment purposes). Several measures must be administered, and four domains must be assessed: cognitive, behavioral, physical, and developmental. Tests must be given in the student's native language. The evaluation team is also required to use tests that are free of "cultural bias," meaning they must not put children from racial or culturally underrepresented groups at a disadvantage (much easier said than done, as we will see below). Within these guidelines, however, evaluation teams have a vast array of different assessment instruments to choose from.

It is important to understand that every test comes with its own set of strengths and weaknesses—there is no test or set of tests that work well for all students all the time. Tests must therefore be selected on a case-by-case basis. The evaluation team coordinator ought to be able to answer these questions about the testing proposed for your child:

- *Which tests do you plan to use, and what are they intended to measure?* Evaluation teams often administer IQ tests to estimate learning potential, as well as tests to establish achievement levels in reading, writing, and/or mathematics. If RTI is part of the evaluation process, measures drawn from the curriculum will be needed to document how the student responds to intensified instruction. The team should then follow up with measures designed to pinpoint what tasks give the student the most trouble in areas of weakness. In a careful evaluation, a variety of strategies will be used to assess a student's capabilities. (Paper-and-pencil tasks alone, for example, would not identify problems a student might have producing or understanding speech.) In Appendix A you will find a summary of some assessment measures frequently used in evaluations for learning disabilities. If the evaluation team proposes tests other than those on our list (there are literally hundreds of measures to choose from, and we could not describe them all), ask how the test works and what sort of information it is expected to provide.

• *Why have these particular tests been selected?* "We always use these tests" or "These are the tests our people are trained to use" are not satisfactory answers to this question. The evaluation team should be able to explain why the test's content or design is appropriate for your child's age, experience, background, and/or learning patterns. In addition, the team should use tests that are known to be *reliable* (meaning the test offers consistent results when it is taken at different times or given by different evaluators) and *valid* (meaning it has been demonstrated that the test actually measures what its authors say it will measure).

• *Will my child's learning problems interfere with taking any of the tests?* A written test would put a student with poor handwriting skills at a disadvantage in all areas being tested, and the results of such a test could not be considered valid or fair. Similarly, a heavily verbal intelligence test would not reflect the true thinking power of a student who has problems with vocabulary or finding words. Evaluation teams need to be skilled and flexible enough to find measures that do not depend on weak information-processing areas, in order to get a true picture of a student's abilities and knowledge.

• *Are test contents appropriate for my child's cultural background?* Many experts feel that overdependence on culturally biased standardized tests is largely responsible for the fact that children from racial and cultural minority groups are overrepresented in the special education population. Since there are few reliable tests keyed to minority cultures, the use of alternative information-gathering methods is very important when evaluating minority students. It is important that the team include professionals who are familiar with such alternative techniques, and with the culture of the child being evaluated. If English is not the student's first language, testing should be conducted in the language in which the student is most fluent. (Note that immigrants to the United States typically need five to seven years to fully absorb American cultural and language nuances.) State education departments usually maintain lists of professionals who are qualified to test in languages other than English and can supply this information to local school districts.

• *If a test compares my child's work with that of a larger group of students, what does the larger group look like?* Tests often rate a child's performance according to how it compares with that of same-aged children in a larger group. For many standardized tests, the comparison group is composed primarily of middle-income white students. If the child being tested is a white, middle-income student who has had average educational opportunities, the test may provide useful information. If the child comes from a different background, however, test results might not be accurate. A homeschooled student raised on a rural ranch, for example, could have knowledge and skills quite different from those tested on many standardized exams. Whenever possible, a child's performance should be compared to that of students from similar backgrounds. At the very least, the disparity in background experiences of the child and the comparison group needs to be taken into account.

• *How similar are the problems in the test to problems encountered in the classroom?* The most useful tests relate closely to what students have been taught. Unfortunately, students are sometimes given standardized tests that have little or nothing to do with the school's curriculum. A test might evaluate spelling by asking students to identify the correctly spelled words on a list, for example, when in class students write spelling words from dictation (a task that involves a very different set of skills). When the test relates poorly to the curriculum,

Maria

Five-year-old Maria had failed her kindergarten screening test and been referred for additional testing. A school-administered IQ test found that she performed within the mentally retarded range. A self-contained class for children with intellectual disabilities was recommended. Very upset, Maria's father insisted on a second opinion.

A home visit found that Maria's mother spoke only Italian. Her father, an Italian-American, spoke Italian at home until a year before, when he realized that Maria needed to start learning English. One year of English was not enough, however, to allow Maria to perform well on the highly verbal intelligence test she had been given. In addition, the child's mother—admitting that she was somewhat overprotective—explained that Maria had led a very sheltered existence. The child had never used scissors or a knife, played unsupervised, or helped with cooking or other chores. Maria's mother was proud of her management of the household and boasted that Maria did not have to do any-thing—even dress herself! Television was not allowed in the home because of fears that it would warp Maria's mind. As a result, Maria's understanding of American culture was limited; she did not have the same fund of general information as other children her age. She could identify the characters of Italian fairy tales, for example, but not George Washington, Cinderella, or Bert and Ernie.

It was obvious that the IQ test given to Maria had been culturally inappropriate. It was suggested that Maria continue with kindergarten and also be allowed to watch some quality children's television programs at home to help her develop her language skills. Her parents were urged to read to her from English-language children's books and also to involve her in out-of-home activities (trips to museums, children's theater, or the zoo) to increase her exposure to American culture. These measures brought some improvement in her English, but by the end of first grade, Maria's language skills were still sufficiently delayed that language therapy was recommended. Maria is now in third grade and doing average work; her language therapy will be discontinued next year. Maria's parents continue to support her, and thanks largely to their love and encourage-ment, she is a happy, well-adjusted, and charming little girl.

Adapted from C. R. Smith, *Learning Disabilities*, © 2004. Reproduced by permission of Pearson Education, Inc.

"problems" identified by the test may simply indicate that the student has had no experience with the area being tested. To avoid this pitfall, some teams use *curriculum-based measurement* (CBM), which evaluates achievement on the basis of how well a student has mastered actual class content compared with other students in the same class or grade. Since CBM measures how well a child has learned what he or she has actually been taught (as opposed to some test maker's idea of what students of a certain age should know) and compares his or her performance with that of other students who have been taught the same thing, its results can be more accurate and of greater value in identifying learning disabilities than those of standardized tests. (Curriculum-based measurement is also useful for keeping tabs on a child's progress in school at weekly intervals. For more on CBM, see Chapter 8.)

• **Is special training needed to administer, score, or interpret any of these tests?** If so, do members of the evaluation team have the required training? It is important to understand that interpreting the scores of *any* test requires experience and judgment. Professionals responsible for interpreting test scores need to have a thorough understanding of each test's advantages and disadvantages. In addition, examiners must have the skill and sensitivity to interpret scores in light of each student's educational experience, cultural heritage, family background, emotional state, and level of motivation. Conclusions based on numbers alone are seldom valid.

• **Where, when, and how will the tests be given?** Will the child be tested at school or taken to another facility? Will most of the tests be given by the same individual, or will many different people be involved? Will the tests be scheduled over a reasonable period of time so that the child will not become tired? Children need time to become accustomed to new surroundings and new people; they cannot be expected to do their best when they are unfamiliar with the person testing them, the test environment, or if tested for four or five hours straight.

Whenever possible, arrange for the child to meet the people who will conduct the evaluation and visit the test site(s) in advance. And while everyone may be anxious to know the outcome of the evaluation, it is usually best to spread testing out over a period of several weeks.

Testing is a complex and controversial subject—one on which authorities often disagree. It is worthwhile from the beginning, however, to sort out how tests are selected and used. Tests are not only an important part of the identification process, but also help guide educational planning. If a child is found to have a disability, retesting will be required every three years to evaluate progress (unless parents and the school district agree that reevaluation is unnecessary). Discovering how your child reacts to different testing situations and which tests most accurately reflect his or her strengths and weaknesses therefore has long-term benefits.

FIND OUT WHAT OTHER KINDS OF INFORMATION WILL BE COLLECTED

Tests can never be relied upon to provide the whole picture in a learning-disabilities evaluation. Tests cannot establish, for example, whether illness or other problems have compromised a child's learning opportunities, determine whether materials or methods used by a particular teacher are contributing to a child's problems, or evaluate what role emotional issues might be playing in preventing a child from working up to potential. Evaluation teams typically use interviews with students, parents, and teachers; observation of the child at work and play; and reviews of school and medical records to address these concerns. The team may also use informal methods such as trial teaching (a process of systematically trying out different instructional techniques) to shed additional light on how a child thinks and approaches academic tasks.

An understanding of a child's family background and home environment is also important for interpreting learning patterns. For this, the team will need your cooperation; share as much information as

Rachel

Rachel turned five just before entering kindergarten. At the beginning of the year she could write her name in capitals, but she sometimes reversed letters—fairly common in this age group. Rachel's teacher noted that the child's drawing ability was far beyond age expectations: it showed excellent attention to detail and appreciation of spatial relationships. Rachel was also well coordinated and had good fine-motor skills.

After about two months of school, Rachel began to write her name from right to left, reversing all the letters. When her teacher corrected her, Rachel would respond irritably, "I know." The next day she would write her name correctly on one paper and in reverse on another. The teacher was confused and began to wonder if Rachel might have a learning disability. Yet the fact that Rachel *could* write her name correctly—combined with her excellent drawing skills—led the teacher to believe there was nothing wrong with Rachel's visual-perception abilities. Rachel also knew the difference between right and left and could indicate each direction correctly. Baffled, the teacher continued to monitor the situation and to remind Rachel that she should write from left to right.

Soon Rachel began to write other words in mirror-style writing. Exasperated, the teacher finally asked the little girl why she chose to write this way. Rachel responded, "This is the way I'm *supposed* to write in Hebrew!"

A call to Rachel's parents cleared up the issue. Rachel had begun Hebrew instruction in religious school about the same time she started kindergarten. Apparently she had decided to make the English language conform to Hebrew rules (Hebrew is written from right to left). Because Rachel had excellent visual-perception skills and a keen sense of direction, it made sense to her that if you were going to reverse the direction of a word, you should reverse the direction of all the letters, too!

The possibility of delaying further instruction in Hebrew until Rachel had mastered the basics of writing in English was discussed, but in the end all this bright child needed was an explanation that different languages had different rules. By January, Rachel's writing (in both English and Hebrew) was perfect.

Adapted from C. R. Smith, *Learning Disabilities,* © 2004. Reproduced by permission of Pearson Education, Inc.

you can about your child's growth and behavior. If you have any concerns about the child's physical, social, or emotional development, alert the team promptly. The team will also want to know if there are any current health concerns, or if there are family circumstances (such as a move, sibling conflicts, or the loss of a loved one) that might be affecting school performance. They may ask questions about your family in general: what you like to do for fun and recreation, for instance, or how you divide household responsibilities and handle discipline. They will likely be interested in whether other family members have experienced any difficulties in school. While such inquiries may seem nosy, the team is not trying to violate your privacy or blame you for your child's school difficulties. Remember that the process of identifying learning disabilities includes *ruling out* other possible causes of learning problems. Investigating the home environment is standard procedure.

The team should be equally thorough about investigating the child's environment at school. Sadly, this is not always the case. Some evaluation teams operate under the assumption that since there is "something wrong" with the student, he or she should be the exclusive focus of the evaluation. As we explained earlier, however, the school's environment and educational practices can contribute significantly to learning problems. If the evaluation team does not seem aware of this, ask how they intend to determine whether making the following adjustments would have an impact on your child's school performance:

Changing the setting: Does the student's performance improve in a classroom that is quieter, or one that has fewer visual distractions? Does the child do better if seated closer to the teacher, or to the blackboard?

Changing methods of presentation: Does the student do better if given more visual cues, or if the teacher uses simpler language?

Changing the curriculum: Will reading improve if the student is switched to a book that places greater emphasis on phonics? Will a program that encourages counting actual objects make it easier to learn number facts?

Changing the task: Does the child do better work if complex assignments are broken down into stages? If allowed to present information orally instead of in writing? If encouraged to work with a study partner?

Changing motivational techniques: Does it help to offer the student feedback throughout a task, rather than wait until a finished assignment is handed in? Does an ungraded approach reduce anxiety and help the student focus better on the work?

Changing the time constraints: Can the child do the work satisfactorily if allowed additional time?

If making adjustments like these significantly improves a child's achievement, special education services may be unnecessary. Children should not be described as "learning disabled" if their needs can be met by making reasonable changes in the general education program.

You will also want to find out if the team anticipates referring your child to any specialists for additional information. Does your child's eyesight, hearing, or speech need to be screened? Is physical, occupational, or speech therapy suggested? Is a psychological examination recommended? If this kind of information is considered essential to the evaluation, these services will be performed at no cost to you. A team may also suggest that you consult specialists such as an audiologist, an ophthalmologist, a pediatrician, a neurologist, or an allergist, at the conclusion of the evaluation. In those cases, following through on the recommendations is your responsibility, and the work is done at your expense.

PREPARE YOUR CHILD FOR THE EVALUATION

Do give your child as much information as you can about what is going to happen before the evaluation; failure to do so only invites stress, confusion, and anxiety (all of which can affect evaluation results). The straightforward approach usually works best. Tell children that an effort is going to be made to find out why they are experiencing difficulties in school, and that some people are going to want to talk to them, engage them in some different educational activities, and give them some tests.

Explain that these are *not* like tests at school—the child cannot pass or fail, because the tests are only intended to provide information on how the child learns. Encourage the child to give adults feedback throughout the assessment process: evaluators will want to know which tasks the child finds easy or hard, and they will appreciate any information they can get on how he or she approaches and solves problems. It may help to assure the child that if any test becomes too hard or frustrating, the evaluators will stop and move on to something else.

Also tell children as much as you can about where and when different stages of the evaluation will take place, and about the professionals who will be involved. Young children may need reassurance that the adults involved in the evaluation will be friendly and kind. Avoid explanations that blame or shame the child, such as "We want to find out why you're failing" or "We're going to figure out what's wrong with you." A better explanation would be "These tests will help the school find the best ways of teaching you."

Older children and adolescents may want to know much more about the evaluation process. We feel it is best to be as honest and open as possible in answering their questions; in general, the better youngsters understand why something is being done, the more cooperative they tend to be. The best approach is to arrange a pre-evaluation meeting with the team coordinator so the child can ask questions directly. *Never* try to trick a child into participating in an evaluation, or lie about what is going to take place—even if it might be unpleasant. Doing so will not protect the child in any way, and may very well result in undermining the trust your child places in you.

START KEEPING RECORDS *NOW*

Learning-disabilities evaluations generate enormous amounts of paper, much of which will be passed on to you. There will be papers requesting permission to evaluate your child; papers notifying you of appointments and explaining your rights; test results and reports from the various professionals who see the child (request copies of these if they are not given to you); and a final report with recommendations. Since every stage of identifying and educating a child with disabilities is governed by federal and state law, some of these papers are actually legal documents; they are designed not only to give you information but also to protect your rights and demonstrate that the school district is operating in compliance with regulations. Special education communications therefore need to be preserved with the same care you would give any other important legal records. Some parents like to use a loose-leaf notebook to collect their papers, while others use folders or accordion files. Patricia McGill Smith, a former head of the National Parent Network on Disabilities (and the parent of a child with disabilities), suggests, "If you are not a naturally organized person, just get a box and throw all the paperwork in it. Then when you really need it, it will be there."

When might you need it? Documentation will be important in the event of any kind of dispute with the school district—if you feel an evaluation has been inadequate, for example, you will have to document your concerns (this may involve collecting even more paper from outside specialists). Documentation may also be needed to enforce programming. (If the special education department determines that your child is entitled to have test questions read aloud, for example, this decision is binding on *all* of the child's teachers—a fact that may have to be explained to the high school chemistry teacher a few years down the road.) You will also have to document the presence of a learning disability to qualify your child for special accommodations (extension of time limits, for instance) on national tests such as college entrance examinations, and to prove that the child is entitled to services beyond high school (individuals with disabilities are eligible for special vocational programs, reasonable accommodations at their jobs, and educational assistance in college). If you move, you will need records to show that your child is entitled to services in his or her new school.

An equally important reason for keeping these records is that they will be the foundation of your own efforts to understand how your child learns. Reports and other documents are the starting point for asking questions of educators, psychologists, and specialists. They can also help with problem-solving and serve as the inspiration for new ideas. (Does the psychologist's report say that your daughter suf-

Casey

Casey's mother insisted he did not know his addition and subtraction facts. His second-grade teacher was surprised to hear this. Casey had been slow to learn to read and was a poor speller, but he had always done quite well in arithmetic. Even on pop quizzes he usually got at least 80 percent of the problems right.

Alerted by his mother's concerns, however, the teacher observed Casey during the next two weekly math tests. She noticed that Casey attacked the tests in an unusual manner. He answered questions out of order, starting in the middle and then jumping around until all the problems were done. As usual, his scores were in the B to B+ range.

Intrigued, the teacher took Casey aside and asked him why he did his tests this way. Somewhat embarrassed, Casey admitted that he had not succeeded in memorizing addition and subtraction facts like the other children in the class, but he had worked out a system for timed math quizzes. "First I find the easiest problem," he explained. "Like here, it's 7 + 1, which is easy to figure out: 8. Then I know that 7 + 2 has to be one more than 8, so I look for 7 + 2 and write 9. Then I find 7 + 3 and write 10, and next I look for 7 + 4 and write 11, and I go on like that until the time runs out."

Casey had figured out that subtraction facts also followed a sequence, so he used the same method for subtraction tests. When quizzed orally on math facts, however, it was obvious he had not memorized any of them—although he could add and subtract in his head well enough to produce correct answers if he was given a little time.

Casey was obviously a bright and resourceful lad. The fact that he was not retaining math facts, however, combined with his other academic difficulties, suggested to his teacher that he might have a learning disability. Casey's mother agreed to an evaluation. As it turned out, Casey did have visual-perception deficits that made it hard for him to remember many kinds of information. Casey was unable to picture things in his mind, which made tasks involving rote memorization particularly difficult. He read slowly because he did not carry images of words in his head and so did not easily recognize words that he had seen before. Imagining the spelling of irregular words was also beyond him. Although he used his superior intelligence to compensate for these problems and was passing all his subjects, Casey's evaluation suggested that with special education support he could do much better than the Bs and Cs he was earning.

fers from low self-esteem, while noting elsewhere that her motor skills are exceptional? Perhaps she would benefit from involvement in after-school activities in which she would be likely to excel, such as sports or dance.) So even if the papers you receive sometimes seem dense, repetitive, and so riddled with jargon, you're not even sure what they mean, get in the habit of saving them. You never know which ones you're going to need.

GIVE YOURSELF TIME TO DEAL WITH EVALUATION RESULTS

When the evaluation has been completed, you will be invited to a meeting to discuss the team's findings. If a disability has been documented, recommendations for special education services may also be made at this time. (If a child has been found to have a disability, the law requires services to begin as soon as possible after the specific services have been decided upon. If specific services are not discussed at your first meeting, a second meeting on implementation should be scheduled promptly.) At your initial meeting, a member of the evaluation team should be prepared to share assessment results with you, explain your child's learning strengths and weaknesses, and describe specific disabilities if any have been identified.

Any discussion of educational placement should include an explanation of all the possible options. By law, your child must be educated in "the least restrictive environment" in which his or her needs can be served. As a result, the great majority of children with learning disabilities remain in regular classrooms most of the time, with varying levels of special education support. (For more on educational options, see Part III, where placement and programming are discussed in detail.)

The school district *cannot* initiate services or assign your child to a special education program without your permission (unless they are willing to go to court, an action that is usually reserved for protecting children's welfare in extreme cases). Therefore, before services can begin you will be asked to consent to an Individualized Education Program (IEP) that specifies educational goals for your child, outlines the methods that will be used to reach those goals, determines school placement, and specifies accommodations and special education services to be provided. The IEP is, in fact, a legal contract: once it has been approved, the school district *must* provide all the services described (if services are to be added or changed, the IEP must be formally amended). The IEP therefore needs to be prepared and read with care. Parents sometimes complain, however, that they felt pressed to approve an IEP before they fully understood the nature of their child's disability, the types of special education programs available, or their rights with respect to special education program planning. "At my first meeting I was handed a thick evaluation report, an even thicker handbook of rights and regulations, and a proposed IEP," one mother remembers. "It was a lot of new information, much of it legal and technical. I felt so overwhelmed and intimidated, I figured I'd better just go along with the professionals. I agreed to their recommendations, hoping I could make sense of it all later."

School districts don't usually mean to confuse parents and hustle them into decisions, but professionals sometimes forget that parents are not as familiar with the law and the language of special education as they are. For your child's sake, it is important that you take all the time you need to understand evaluation results and recommendations. If you have already educated yourself about laws governing the identification and education of students with learning disabilities, you will be ahead of the game. It is also reasonable to ask for a copy of the evaluation report in advance so that you can review it, share it with others who are concerned about your child's welfare, and prepare questions before your initial meeting. At the meeting, do not hesitate to ask for plain-English translations of any terms or language you do not understand. If the time allotted for the meeting runs out before all your questions have been answered, then ask for another meeting. The law protects your right to think over recommendations before making a decision, to seek a second opinion, and to participate in all aspects of education planning (including the preparation of the IEP), so there is no reason to feel pressured into premature action. Some parents find it is helpful to take a third party to the school meeting, someone who can listen objectively and ask questions. Your local Learning Disabilities Association of America chapter may have advocates on staff who can accompany you, assist with the interpretation of all the information coming at you, and help you sort out your options and priorities.

You may find you also need time to cope with the emotional impact of an evaluation. Many parents say the news that their child had a disability hit them very hard—even when the handicap was comparatively mild, or when they already strongly suspected something was wrong. The weeks following identification of a learning disability can be an emotional roller-coaster ride in which any or all of the following reactions may be experienced:

Denial: "They've made a mistake! Tests aren't perfect, after all. . . . They just don't realize that she's sensitive/he needs extra encouragement and understanding/all she needs is a little extra help. . . . I'm sure he'll outgrow it if we give him time."

Anger and blame: "These so-called experts don't know what they're talking about! That teacher has always had it in for my kid! It's the school's fault! It's the day care provider's fault! It's the book's fault! He doesn't take after anyone on *my* side of the family!"

Bargaining: "Maybe it will go away if we spend more time with her (help him more with his homework, get her a tutor, send him to a private school). . . . I'll quit work. . . . Let's try another reading program. . . . I'll take him to another specialist."

Guilt: "It's my fault. . . . I didn't take good care of myself when I was pregnant. . . . Maybe that twelve-year-old babysitter dropped him and never told me. . . . I allowed her to eat too much junk food. . . . I deserve this; God is punishing me."

Fear: "Will she be able to go to college? Will he ever be able to support himself? Will a 'normal' person want to date my child? Who will look after her when I'm gone? Can I love him the same way I did when I thought he was 'perfect'?"

Grief and loss: "Our future has been destroyed. . . . All my dreams are shattered. . . . It breaks my heart to think of what might have been. . . . I feel like someone died."

Though often intense and profoundly upsetting, all these reactions are normal. As with other kinds of loss, accepting the reality

Seeking Support

Receiving the news that a child has a disability can have a powerful emotional impact. Here, parents who have been through it share what helped them cope:

Seek assistance from experienced parents. There is nothing like the support of people who have "been there." They can not only offer practical information, but also understand the fear, confusion, and pain that parents of children with disabilities often feel. Many communities have organizations and support groups for parents of children with different kinds of disabilities, and there are also support groups online. Parents involved in these groups are eager to reach out and help.

Share your feelings with significant others in your life. Many people find it easier to share facts than feelings: for example, a mother who is used to being a source of strength for her family may feel uncomfortable about admitting that she feels helpless and lost. While the temptation to keep your pain to yourself may be great, sharing how you feel with your mate, your friends, and others who are close to you can lighten your burden. The worst kind of pain is that suffered alone.

Look for the positive. Sometimes bad news can seem so overwhelming that it overshadows everything; we forget there is still much about our lives—and our children—that is good. The child who cannot yet read may be exceptionally sensitive to others' feelings, for example, or she may display admirable courage and perseverance. If you are not a natural optimist, focusing on the positive can take active effort. It can help to seek the company of positive people, letting them help you see the bright side.

Seek information. Many parents say that the cure for fear is knowledge—the more they knew about their children's disabilities, the less frightening they seemed. Information is available from many sources: your child's teachers, members of your child's evaluation team, parent support organizations, publications, and the internet. "Make people talk to you in English," one mother advises. "Experts have a way of lapsing into

of a disability can require a period of mourning, during which you may find yourself in need of extra understanding and support. In the checklist on these pages parents share advice on what helped them most as they worked through the emotional consequences of discovering that their children had disabilities. There are no quick fixes, however; the acceptance process takes time.

unfamiliar terminology. When they start talking gobbledygook, just stop them and ask what they mean. That way, you'll learn the terminology, too."

Learn to recognize and deal with anger. It is almost impossible to avoid bitterness and anger when you are forced to let go of cherished hopes and dreams. Some parents find themselves lashing out at everyone after discovering that a child has a disability—including the child. You will have to recognize your anger and be honest about it before you can let it go. Both close (and nonjudgmental) friends and professional counselors can be very helpful with this process.

Allow others to have their feelings. For a time your family may seem emotionally "out of sync" as everyone struggles with finding his or her own way to adapt to a new reality. Try to be patient with those whose reactions are different from your own. If there are other children in the family, encourage them to talk about their feelings and fears. Their concerns may surprise you: "My five-year-old wanted to move out of his brother's room because he was afraid dyslexia was contagious," one mother recalls.

Take care of yourself. When you are under stress and concerned about others, it is easy to neglect your own needs. There is no advantage, however, to burning yourself out. Try to get enough rest, eat properly, and make time for recreation (we know it's hard, but try anyway). Reaching out for support is another important part of taking care of yourself. If you feel overwhelmed by depression, anger, or anxiety, don't hesitate to seek the help of a qualified therapist or counselor.

Take it one day at a time. If your seven-year-old has just been found to have a learning disability, you do not have to worry about college and careers today—only about the challenges of second grade (which may be plentiful). If you take on the entire uncertain future, it will deplete the strength you need to handle what's on your plate right now. "Regrets about yesterday and anxiety about tomorrow won't do anything for your child today," one mother says. "Usually, I find that the best way to handle the future is to pay attention to what's right in front of me."

Remember that everyone close to your child—parents, siblings, grandparents—is likely to experience some emotional reaction to the news that the child has a disability. Not everyone, however, will react the same way at the same time. Mom may be swamped with guilt, for example, while Dad is angrily accusing everyone in sight; meanwhile Grandma (who has never heard of learning disabilities and fears the child is retarded) is grieving deeply not only for her grandchild but also for you and the heartache you are experiencing. As a result, communication can be difficult during this time—a fact that can complicate making decisions. The potential for effective teamwork is usually greatly improved when all adults who are regularly responsible for the child's care attend special education meetings, so that everyone starts out with the same information and has ample opportunity to ask questions and voice concerns. If there is continuing disagreement about what should be done for the child, getting a second professional opinion may help resolve the difficulty.

WHEN IN DOUBT, GET A SECOND OPINION

If you disagree with the results of the assessment completed by your public school district, you have the right under federal law to obtain an Independent Educational Evaluation—that is, an evaluation by experts not employed by the school system. You can pay for this evaluation yourself, or you can ask the school district to pay for it. To receive payment from the district you may have to present your case to a mediator, or go before an independent hearing officer (not employed by the school system) who will decide whether or not the original evaluation was adequate. Regardless of who pays for it, the district is obliged to consider the Independent Educational Evaluation in determining eligibility for special education services.

The Independent Evaluation must use the same state and federal criteria to determine whether or not a disability exists, but the assessment team may use different tests and other methods in its investigations. (It is important to tell professionals conducting an Independent Evaluation which tests have already been used, since repeating the same tests in a short time period can undermine the accuracy of results.) If the results from the outside assessment conflict with those of the school district's evaluation, the district has two choices: accept the Independent Evaluation and act on its results or defend its own evaluation. This process usually requires either formal mediation or hearings before an independent hearing officer, who rules on which assessment is valid.

Faced with conflicting evaluations, school districts often prefer to avoid time-consuming mediation. Either they accept the Independent Evaluation outright, or they become willing to negotiate about services. They might suggest providing certain services on a trial basis, for example, and evaluate progress after a specified period of time, after which services may be increased or decreased. It is usually best for children if parents and school officials can cooperate in this way rather than become locked into adversarial roles.

Remember that if a student's learning problems are not considered severe enough to warrant special education services, an assessment can still be used as a basis for requesting other kinds of help at school. Many types of educational assistance—providing tutoring, allowing access to a computer and extra time for some assignments, altering instructional methods, and making modifications in the curriculum, for example—can be negotiated informally with teachers. Parents of children whose test scores "just miss" the criteria for learning disabilities need to be especially assertive about advocating for their children's needs at school. Research suggests that these students are among the most likely to "fall between the cracks" of the public education system.

If you are convinced that your child needs special education services and the school district refuses to provide them—or if you feel strongly that the services being offered are inappropriate—the next step is to request mediation or (if that fails) a *due process hearing*. You have the right to be represented by an attorney during these proceedings, and the school district is required to give you information about finding legal assistance if you need it. If you win your case, the district can be required to pay your legal costs. If your dispute is resolved in the district's favor, though, you will be responsible for your own legal expenses.

What happens if you disagree with the school district's identification? This sometimes happens, and the law leaves the last word about special education with parents: you are free to reject the school district's recommendations in the matter of your child's education. Before rejecting the school's recommendations, however, it may be wise to do some serious soul-searching. Is your decision based on your child's needs, or could denial and wishful thinking be influencing your actions? There are some parents who are so invested in hav-

Welcome to Holland

I am often asked to describe the experience of raising a child with a disability—to try to help people who have not shared that unique experience to understand it, to imagine how it would feel. It's like this. . . .

When you're going to have a baby, it's like planning a fabulous vacation trip—to Italy. You buy a bunch of guidebooks and make your wonderful plans. The Coliseum. The Michelangelo *David*. The gondolas in Venice. You may learn some handy phrases in Italian. It's all very exciting.

After months of eager anticipation, the day finally arrives. You pack your bags and off you go. Several hours later, the plane lands. The stewardess comes in and says, "Welcome to Holland."

"Holland?!" you say. "What do you mean, Holland? I signed up for Italy! I'm supposed to be in Italy! All my life I've dreamed of going to Italy."

But there's been a change in the flight plan. They've landed in Holland and there you must stay.

The important thing is that they haven't taken you to a horrible, disgusting, filthy place, full of pestilence, famine and disease. It's just a different place.

So you must go out and buy new guidebooks. And you must learn a whole new language. And you will meet a whole new group of people you would never have met.

It's just a different place. It's slower-paced than Italy, less flashy than Italy. But after you've been there for a while and you catch your breath, you look around . . . and you begin to notice that Holland has windmills . . . and Holland has tulips. Holland even has Rembrandts.

But everyone you know is busy coming and going from Italy . . . and they're all bragging about what a wonderful time they had there. And for the rest of your life, you will say, "Yes, that's where I was supposed to go. That's what I had planned."

And the pain of that will never, ever, ever, ever go away . . . because the loss of that dream is a very significant loss.

But . . . if you spend your life mourning the fact that you didn't get to Italy, you may never be free to enjoy the very special, very lovely things . . . about Holland.

ing "perfect" children they cannot tolerate the idea of a disability; it's too damaging to their pride. Most special education professionals have also met parents who insist that their children *are* learning disabled because they cannot bear to accept that a child is mentally retarded, emotionally disturbed, autistic, or intellectually incapable of above-average work. Sometimes such parents take their youngsters from specialist to specialist in search of someone who will tell them what they want to hear. Of course, the big losers in such situations are always the children, who get lots of attention but very little in the way of useful educational assistance.

Parents may also resist accepting a special education referral because they fear their children will be stigmatized. These concerns are sometimes fueled by comments from the children, who may vigorously assert that all kids in special education programs at school are regarded as social untouchables. The sensitivity with which children with disabilities are treated by both teachers and other students in local schools certainly is an area of legitimate concern—one that we will discuss at length in future chapters. The disadvantages of a special education label, though, must always be weighed against the hazards of failure to provide appropriate help. As one special educator puts it, "Parents often worry that receiving special education services will identify their children as 'different.' Believe me, kids with learning disabilities already *know* they are different. What they need most is to feel understood for a change, and a chance to succeed. Usually, their best shot at those things is through some kind of special education intervention."

Remember, your child's attitudes about having a learning disability will be strongly influenced by your own. If you are comfortable with intervention and view it as an opportunity for growth, your child will probably approach it positively. Thus one of the most important ways you can take care of your child is to do a thorough job of addressing your own worries and concerns. Never feel embarrassed about asking questions, or apologetic about wanting more information. The more information you have—and the more actively you participate in the evaluation and education-planning processes—the more likely it is that your child is going to get exactly the kind of help he or she needs.

6

Becoming an Expert on Your Child

You don't have to become an authority on education to help a child with learning disabilities. It *is* necessary, however, to become an "expert" on your child, and to develop an in-depth understanding of what he or she needs in order to learn. This is not always an easy matter. The difficulties children with learning disabilities encounter in school are seldom traced to a single, easy-to-understand problem. More often, they arise from clusters of overlapping problems: for example, neurological handicaps, an inflexible educational environment, lack of social skills, and emotional issues may all be contributing to a youngster's struggle to keep up in class.

Children with disabilities need multilevel support that addresses *all* of their varied needs. The problem is that school personnel cannot always be relied upon to look beyond the most urgent academic concerns. If this is the case, the support provided may be only partially helpful, or even harmful to the student's best interests. For example, one mother found that her sixth-grade daughter—a talented artist— was being regularly removed from art class to get extra help in reading. "I guess it made sense from the school's point of view," she says. "They saw art as a nonessential subject. What they didn't understand was that, for Linda, art is the *most* essential subject. Art class is where she gets to shine, win respect, and feel good about herself. What kind of sense does it make to take that away so that she can spend more time doing what she does poorly?" This mother met with the principal, and it was determined that Linda could get her reading help during social studies period, using materials from that class to build her comprehension and writing skills.

Linda has what children with learning disabilities need most: a parent who understands her needs, monitors her educational program, and is willing to speak up for her at school. When a youngster's learning disability is first identified, however, not many parents feel ready to take on this role. Faced with a tangled web of interlocking problems (not to mention an evaluation report full of unfamiliar terms), most feel overwhelmed and unsure of what to do next. Few start out with enough confidence to march into school, evaluate the programming and the classroom environment, and make suggestions for changes. Experienced parents say they developed this confidence though, as they became more aware of how their children perceived and interacted with the world around them. As one mother put it, "The better I understood my son, the easier it was to recognize the conditions that make it possible for him to do his best, and to avoid situations that would only frustrate him and end in failure."

How do you get started on becoming an expert on your child? Below are seven basic questions parents must ask to get a handle on what young people with learning disabilities need in order to succeed in school. The answers will come from several sources: the learning disabilities evaluation, the child's teachers, the child himself or herself, and your own observation. While some of these questions can be answered relatively quickly, others may take some patient investigation. We think you will find, however, that as you become more attuned to these issues, your confidence in your ability to make sound decisions on your child's behalf will grow. By the time you have answered these questions, you should be well on your way to becoming a powerful partner in your child's education.

ARE THERE PHYSICAL OR HEALTH CONCERNS WE HAVE TO ADDRESS?

Learning-disabilities evaluations sometimes raise questions about health issues that may be contributing to a student's problems in school. For example, the student may have problems with fatigue, vision, or hearing that merit investigation. Learning disabilities can also be accompanied by developmental or physical delays that require therapy, and/or seizure disorders that require medication. Students who suffer from frequent illnesses, unmanaged allergies, or chronic health conditions, such as asthma or diabetes, in addition to learning disabilities are at a double disadvantage in the classroom. If the child's health is not stabilized, it is harder to address learning disabilities successfully. Parents and teachers also need to be aware of medication side effects that can affect alertness, memory, and activity level or mood.

A learning disabilities evaluation will usually indicate if physical problems, health issues, or developmental delays are suspected. If problems have been noted, it will be important to determine what therapeutic services (if any) will be provided by the school district in addition to educational services. While public school districts have the resources to provide physical and occupational therapy and can also supply devices to augment vision and hearing, these services are usually offered only if a child's problems are considered severe enough to interfere significantly with performance in the classroom. If you feel your child needs this kind of help, ask the district to consider the total or *cumulative* impact of the child's disabilities. A mild comprehension delay compounded by a slight hearing loss can add up to a very severe obstacle to learning, for example, even when neither problem would be viewed as terribly serious on its own.

It is also important to be aware of the influence that everyday health issues have on academic performance. Youngsters who skip meals, suffer from frequent colds, or try to function with too little sleep rarely do their best in school. The impact of poor health habits on children who are also struggling with disabilities can be devastating. Balanced meals, adequate exercise, enough rest, and regular medical and dental care are therefore a crucial part of treating learning disabilities successfully.

Do not expect, however, that a learning disability will be "cured" by diet, medication, or physical therapy alone. "Quick fixes" for learning disabilities—sugarless and chemical-free diets, vitamin supplements, motion-sickness medications, eye exercises, and special reading lenses, for example—are proposed from time to time, and sometimes they are promoted aggressively (for a price) to parents eager to help their children. So far, none of these methods have proved to be of widespread or lasting value. To date, the most effective treatment for learning disabilities remains appropriate educational programming, planned to fit the child's individual needs.

WHAT IS MY CHILD'S OVERALL LEARNING POTENTIAL?

Most learning-disabilities evaluations attempt to establish the child's capacity to learn, in order to determine if academic expectations are realistic. An intelligence (or IQ) test is typically used to measure intellectual potential. In general, students with high scores on IQ tests can be expected to make faster progress in school than students whose scores are lower. Subscores on different parts of these tests also indicate areas of intellectual strength and weakness. Some types of programming decisions are based largely on IQ test scores (whether a student should participate in programs for gifted children, for example). A very low IQ test score can lead to identifying a child as mentally retarded. A learning disability is suspected when the IQ test suggests a child's academic performance should be much better than it actually is.

A properly administered IQ test can do a good job of measuring verbal problem-solving ability, fund of accumulated knowledge, and skill with tasks involving visual perception, numbers, and logic. Since these are the things that tend to help children get ahead in school, IQ tests are the best predictors we have of a child's ability to handle ordinary schoolwork. It is therefore important to go over the results of IQ tests carefully, preferably with the person who gave the test

More Than One Kind of Intelligence

Most "intelligence tests" measure language ability, visual perception, and aptitude for math and logic. Psychologist Howard Gardner, however, believes that there are eight types of intelligence that contribute significantly to an individual's potential for achievement.

Linguistic Intelligence: Children who are strong in this area are sensitive to the spoken and written word, and they use language to remember information and solve problems. (Memory prompts like "In fourteen-hundred-and-ninety-two, Columbus sailed the ocean blue" were devised by linguistic thinkers.) As students, they are good at reading, writing, storytelling, discussion, and debate—all skills highly valued in the classroom.

Logical-Mathematical Intelligence: These individuals take an orderly, systematic approach to life. They love sorting and categorizing objects; they are intrigued by patterns and relationships; they set up experiments to check their observations and ideas. They are often good at games that call for planning and strategy, like Battleship and chess. As students, they are fascinated by abstract concepts and ask "deep" questions like "Is time real?" Their facility with complex ideas is appreciated more and more as their education progresses.

Spatial Intelligence: People with a high degree of spatial intelligence are good at visualizing and mentally manipulating objects. They have a keen sense of how objects relate to one another to form a whole. Some are fascinated by construction and/or machines; they may design inventions or build complex structures out of whatever is at hand. Others are attracted to fine art or design. Many of these students are better at expressing information visually (drawing, diagramming, or filming their ideas) than at describing their thoughts or writing them down.

Musical Intelligence: Aptitude for music is often obvious when children are very young. Students with strengths in this area are sensitive to sounds and rhythms in their environments and easily remember melodies. Some of these students are strongly motivated to compose music, sing, or play instruments, while others are content to build

---

to your child. Do not settle for being given a number and a quick explanation ("Your son's IQ is 98, which is in the normal range" or "Kim's IQ is 125, which makes her a very bright little girl"). Ask to see subtest scores (that is, scores received on different parts of the test) and to have the types of tasks or problems included in each subtest explained to you. Youngsters who have learning disabilities often do large music collections. Many claim they can't concentrate unless music is playing. (It's true; let them keep the ear buds in.)

Bodily-Kinesthetic Intelligence: Young people with strengths in this area have an unusual ability to control their bodies and express themselves through movement. They may be gifted athletes, actors, or dancers. They also use bodily sensations to process information, learning by touching, manipulating objects, and interacting physically with the world around them. These kids *need* to move: if they can't, they fiddle, tap, and squirm.

Naturalistic Intelligence: These children have a heightened awareness of their natural surroundings, and may be particularly attracted to growing things and working with animals. They are unusually observant of the world around them. Some are very sensitive to weather and other changes in the natural environment. The outdoors is their preferred classroom.

Interpersonal Intelligence: Children with strong interpersonal skills relate exceptionally well to other people. They thrive on social contact. Because they are superaware of the thoughts and feelings of others, these youngsters are often chosen to lead groups or mediate conflicts. Natural-born salespeople, they typically commit time and energy to community projects and extracurricular activities, and they are good at involving others in whatever enterprises they undertake.

Intrapersonal Intelligence: The expression "marching to a different drummer" aptly describes children with a high degree of intrapersonal intelligence. They have a strong sense of who they are, and they are not particularly concerned about what others think about them. Their lives are guided by inner feelings and ideas; they value privacy and often prefer solitary pursuits to group activities. While they may not be "popular" in the conventional sense, these youngsters' self-assurance and sense of purpose are often admired and even envied.

much better on some parts of IQ tests than others. You want to know exactly which tasks gave your child the most trouble, and which tasks he or she performed best. Take your time over this information. The better you understand it, the more accurately you will be able to predict what kinds of activities and assignments will be hard for your child in school, and which will invite success.

Do not make the mistake, however, of thinking that IQ tests measure real intelligence. There are many aspects of intelligence that IQ tests do not address, such as creativity, "street smarts," or ability to relate to people. (How many of us would call a book-smart person with no common sense "intelligent"?). Nor do these tests address a child's aptitudes for achievement in nonacademic areas.

In recent years many authorities have endorsed the concept of *multiple intelligences*, proposed by Harvard psychologist Howard Gardner. Gardner has suggested that there are at least eight different kinds of intelligence that contribute to an individual's potential for success, and that evaluating only a few of these (as most IQ tests do) cannot produce a realistic estimate of an individual's overall ability. Gardner's eight types of intelligence are summarized on pages 138–39. If you believe your child has significant potential in any of these areas, you will want to make sure that school personnel are aware of it and are fully committed to nurturing those talents. In addition, it may be important to provide appropriate opportunities for growth of these talents (such as involvement in sports leagues, volunteer work, or music lessons) outside of school.

EXACTLY WHERE ARE THE AREAS OF DISABILITY?

Quite often, parents are offered only vague descriptions of their children's learning disabilities. You may be told that your child has "a written expression handicap," for example, or that he or she is "moderately dyslexic" (which simply means that the youngster has some trouble reading). The trouble with terms like these is that they give you absolutely no idea what the child actually can and cannot do. *Why* does the child have trouble writing? Is it a matter of penmanship? Difficulty retrieving words from memory? Inability to organize ideas? Is progress in reading blocked by an inability to recognize the shapes of letters and words? Or does the child have problems sorting out sequences of sounds? Is comprehension an issue (that is, the child reads words without understanding them)? Are attention deficits contributing to the problem? Are the disabilities mild or severe?

As we explained in Chapter 3, there are four types of information-processing weakness that can cause a learning disability: those affecting attention, visual perception, language processing, and fine-motor skill. It is of vital importance that you understand the precise nature of your child's disabilities (remember, it is possible to have disabilities in more than one area). It may be obvious that the child has problems remembering verbal instructions, for example, but until you know if the problem is with sound processing, understanding vocabulary, or difficulty concentrating on what is being said (among other possibilities), it will be hard to plan effective intervention strategies.

Ideally, the learning-disabilities evaluation will explore areas of disability in some detail, but this is not always the case. To identify a learning disability, the evaluation must only establish that a student is not performing as well as expected given his or her intelligence and learning opportunities, or that even with intensified, individualized instruction little progress has been made. Some evaluations document that a child is struggling enormously to learn, or is of average or better intelligence but also significantly behind in some skill area, and pretty much leave it at that. If detailed information about your child's disabilities is not provided by the evaluation, you may want to talk to your school district's special education department about additional assessment measures, or invest in having a more thorough assessment done privately.

Your child's teachers may also be able to help pinpoint areas of disability. Experienced special education teachers are particularly good at clarifying learning problems. These teachers also have a gift for explaining learning disabilities understandably, and many parents find that teachers are a rich source of practical advice for commonly encountered problems (such as how to motivate a student who hates homework or help a child who has problems getting organized). Most teachers welcome the opportunity to work with parents. As one teacher puts it, "The parents we consider troublesome are the ones who *don't* get involved with their kids—the ones we never see."

Your own observations can also be an important source of information—in fact, you probably already know more than you think about how your child's brain works. Think about how you communicate with your child when it's *really* important to get the point across (for example, when you have to convey safety information). Do you use fewer words or speak more slowly? Turn off the television and make the child look at your face? Use a lot of body language? Write down the message or draw a diagram? Ask the child to repeat the message back to you several times? Whatever your answer is, it shows that you have instinctively recognized something about how your child learns, and you routinely act on that information. Your child's teacher will have to use similar methods to get through in the classroom.

You can learn even more about how your child thinks if you train yourself to observe him or her systematically. To do this, you have to begin by clearing your mind of assumptions about your child's behavior, which often take the form of judgments ("That girl is so absentminded, she'd lose her head if it weren't screwed on!" "He's a stubborn kid who needs a firm hand, and that's all there is to it!"). Then select one type of behavior to focus on at a time. You might start, for example, by observing what types of activities best hold your child's attention. As objectively as you can, watch your child at work and play for a week. At the end of the period, collect your observations (this is much easier if you take notes) and see how they add up. Was the child glued to the television but restless when Dad tried to read to her? Does she stick with any type of art project but seem bored by music? Does she make mistakes when you explain directions to her but understand when you demonstrate? Taken together, these observations suggest a child who needs to use her eyes to assist her ears. How might that affect her performance in school?

Left to themselves, children with disabilities usually gravitate toward situations that make them feel comfortable and competent, and avoid those they find difficult and frustrating. Try observing the following behaviors, and think about the impact they might have on your child's achievement and adjustment in school:

- How does the child behave in groups of people? In what kind of groups is the child most relaxed and comfortable?

- What type of activities does the child choose given free time (assuming television is not available)? What toys or games does the child avoid or find frustrating?

- How does the child interact with adults? How does he or she respond to guidance or criticism from authority figures?

- In what settings does the child seem most happy and relaxed? Is behavior affected by a change of environment?

Don't forget that your child is a source of information, too. *Ask* why some homework assignments are easy and some are hard, or why certain activities are frustrating and some chores impossible. Sometimes youngsters' explanations are remarkably lucid. "After months of nagging, I finally asked my son why it took him forever to pick up his room," one mother recalls. "He said, 'It's that I don't know where to start, Mom. It looks like a big jumble, and I can't figure out what to do first.' We sat down and made a list of cleaning steps—pick up dirty clothes and put them in the hamper, put trash in the basket, and so on—and posted it on the back of his bedroom door. Referring to the list as he went along, he cleaned his room in a fraction of the time it had taken him before."

Since learning disabilities can be very subtle, it may take time and input from several sources in order to reach a thorough understanding of them. Persistence pays off, however—and there is nothing more important to planning effective educational strategies than knowing exactly how your child thinks and understands the world.

WHAT ARE MY CHILD'S STRENGTHS?

Every child, regardless of his or her intelligence level or degree of handicap, has areas of relative ability. Among children with learning disabilities, achievement in areas of competence usually ranges from average to outstanding. For example, a junior high school student who reads like a second-grader may function at or above grade level when it comes to math calculations. A child whose language-comprehension difficulties interfere with progress in many academic subjects may nevertheless demonstrate exceptional ability with computers or electronics.

A learning-disabilities evaluation identifies academic strengths as well as weaknesses, but all too often it is the weaknesses that take center stage. This is especially likely to be true if a child's disability interferes with reading. Reading skill is perceived as so essential to survival that educators (and often parents) tend to regard everything else as relatively unimportant. The unfortunate result is that students with reading problems may find that their gifts and talents have been either overlooked or devalued.

It is extremely important to identify the strengths of students with learning disabilities for several reasons. First, students with disabilities must rely on areas of strength to compensate for areas of weakness. Although they do this instinctively to some degree, the learning process can be greatly simplified if everyone (especially the student) clearly understands what the areas of strength *are*. (It might quickly become clear, for example, that a student who struggles with writing but speaks well should start dictating first drafts of assignments to a scribe, voice recorder, or computer.) Second, in order to maintain their self-esteem, it is essential that students with disabilities get ample opportunities to do what they can do well. School usually gives them plenty of practice with what they do badly, and without some balance these children are very likely to end up feeling like failures. Finally, students working in the way they find most comfortable are more productive, and far less likely to suffer the stress and loss of motivation experienced by youngsters struggling to perform "out of their element." The parable of *The Animal School* (reproduced on page 145) illustrates how ridiculous it is to ignore individual strengths in education. What's not so funny is that in many real classrooms teachers continue to squeeze children into standard molds, and then blame the kids if they don't fit.

The learning-disabilities assessment should give you a clear idea of your child's scholastic strengths. Don't forget, however, to look beyond the academic subjects. Involvement in athletics and the arts saves the sanity of many students with disabilities. These youngsters can also be uncommonly inventive problem-solvers, and some develop outstanding communication skills, unusual sensitivity to others, and dynamic personalities. "My students have won community-service

The Animal School

Once upon a time, the animals decided they must do something heroic to meet the problems of "a new world." So they organized a school.

They adopted an activity curriculum consisting of running, climbing, swimming, and flying. To make it easier to administer the curriculum, all the animals took all the subjects.

The duck was excellent in swimming, in fact better than his instructor; but he made only passing grades in flying and was very poor in running. Since he was slow in running, he had to stay after school and also drop swimming in order to practice running. This was kept up until his web feet were badly worn and he was only average in swimming. But average was acceptable in school so nobody worried about that except the duck.

The rabbit started at the top of the class in running, but had a nervous breakdown because of so much make-up work in swimming.

The squirrel was excellent in climbing until he developed frustration in the flying class where his teacher made him start from the ground up instead of from the treetop down. He also developed a "charley horse" from overexertion and then got C in climbing and D in running.

The eagle was a problem child and was disciplined severely. In the climbing class he beat all the others to the top of the tree, but insisted on using his own way to get there.

At the end of the year, an abnormal eel that could swim exceedingly well, and also run, climb, and fly a little, had the highest average and was valedictorian.

The prairie dogs stayed out of school and fought the tax levy because the administration would not add digging and burrowing to the curriculum. They apprenticed their children to a badger and later joined the groundhogs and gophers to start a successful private school.

Source: G. H. Reavis, *The Animal School, Educational Forum,* volume 17 no. 2 (1953): p. 141.

awards and prizes in photography, drama, and dance," says a special education teacher. "Many have interests they have explored through jobs and volunteer work, and a few have started successful home businesses. What I'm saying is, if your student has trouble reading but made a 400 percent profit on his lemonade stand, do continue to encourage reading—but back his next business venture also."

WHAT KIND OF ACADEMIC SUPPORT
DOES MY CHILD NEED?

A learning disabilities evaluation documents a student's academic status in considerable detail. It should be clear from the assessment, for example, how your child's achievement in reading, writing, and arithmetic compares with that of other children in the same grade. The evaluation should also indicate the specific skills within these broad areas that present problems: for example, it might indicate that a child understands math concepts but has difficulty with computation because of problems remembering math facts and formulas. What the evaluation report probably will *not* tell you, however, is how much of your child's academic problems have to do with a learning disability as opposed to other factors such as the use of inefficient or inappropriate learning strategies, mismatch with the teacher's instructional style, or failure to master class content at earlier stages of education. In most cases, it is a *combination* of problems like these—not a learning disability alone—that is responsible for a student's falling behind in school. To be successful, educational programming for children with learning disabilities needs to address the learning disability *and* recognize these other academic concerns.

Let's look at the issue of learning strategies. Studies show that children with learning disabilities often approach learning in an inefficient and disorganized way. They do not analyze tasks or approach problems systematically. They seem unaware there are techniques that can be used to assist memory. They do not know how to use outlines or take effective notes. Given a complex task like a report or a research paper, many of these children seem clueless as to how they might even begin. Sometimes poor learning strategies (educators call them *metacognitive skills*) have as great an impact on school performance as a student's learning disability does.

Metacognitive skills can be taught, but in regular classrooms they almost never are, since most children figure out these tricks on their own. Instruction in these skills, however, can be provided through special education. The checklist on pages 148–49 presents some self-help techniques that are frequently overlooked by youngsters with learning disabilities. If your child does not make use of these strategies regularly, ask your special education department about learning-strategy instruction.

Your child's personal learning style may also be contributing to his or her lack of academic progress. Research reveals that some students simply are better suited to traditional methods of education than others. For example, most school systems reward reflective learners (students who consider material thoroughly, pay attention to details, and put a lot of planning into a response). Impulsive learners (who are good at grasping a quick overview of a situation but may respond without thinking things through because they consider details unimportant) get less respect and may even be perceived as careless and unprepared. Similarly, lessons and assignments beyond primary school increasingly favor students who are good at organizing material independently, handling abstractions, making inferences, and figuring out things on their own. Concrete thinkers (who prefer explicit directions, structured tasks, and direct teaching of key facts and concepts) find the deck increasingly stacked against them as they get older. Research suggests that some children identified as "learning disabled" are impulsive, concrete learners whose primary problem is that they are poorly matched with the teaching methods to which they have been exposed. When material is organized and presented to them in a way they can utilize, these children make steady progress.

Students can also be victims of the school's curriculum. Although battles have been waged for decades in the education community over the best ways to teach reading, writing, and arithmetic, the truth is that there is no program for any of these subjects that works for all students all of the time. Even among typical learners, any given reading or math curriculum will work better for some than for others. Children with learning disabilities (who are less adaptable than other students) are likely to have a particularly hard time in classrooms where there is little curricular flexibility. One mother related that her son, who was considered dyslexic until third grade, learned to read almost overnight when given phonics instruction at age nine. He did not have a disability, but his relatively weak

Metacognitive Skills

Metacognitive skills are strategies that good students use to help themselves learn, store, and recall information. Most students figure out these methods on their own, becoming increasingly skillful in their use as they grow older. Students with learning disabilities, however, may not use strategies like those listed below unless they are *specifically taught* how and when to do so.

Organization and Time-Management Skills

- Keep an assignment notebook.
- Record due dates on a calendar.
- Make lists of things to do.
- Estimate the amount of time a project or an assignment will take.
- Set deadlines (What has to be done today, tomorrow, by the end of the week?).
- Establish a work schedule.
- Organize a notebook with pockets and dividers.
- Develop a filing system for items that need to be saved.
- Maintain a clutter-free work space.
- Use tools like watch alarms, "smart phones," and computers to manage schedules, assignments, and other obligations.

Study Skills

- Monitor comprehension (look back through material; when unclear, read slower).
- Read directions.
- Take notes from lectures and books in your own words.
- Paraphrase the main idea of a paragraph or page.
- Preview text (look at introductions, headings, italics, illustrations, and summaries to become familiar with material before reading the entire text).
- Highlight or underline important information.
- Reorganize or regroup information (e.g., put key words or facts on index cards; create charts or lists of related facts and concepts).
- Make an outline.
- Write and revise a rough draft.
- Proofread work for completeness and accuracy.
- Reward oneself for tasks or stages of a task completed.

Test-Taking Skills

- Ask what material will be covered on the test, what format will be used (e.g., true/false, multiple choice, essay).

- Review notes and text on a regular basis (rather than cramming right before an exam).
- Set aside extra time to study the most difficult material.
- Find a study partner or form a study group.
- Look through the test and plan a test-taking strategy (such as leaving the most time for the essays or doing the easiest questions first).
- Read all the answers before choosing an answer; reason through an answer before looking at the options.
- Draw a diagram if it will help organize the response.
- Answer or abandon (don't dwell on difficult questions—come back later).
- Determine when it pays to guess (and when it doesn't).

Memory Skills

- Use verbal rehearsal (repeat "8 times 8 equals 64" until learned; repeat "I will not touch Grandma's piano" quietly or silently throughout visit).
- Invent or use rhymes ("Thirty days has September . . .").
- Study lists of information in categories (U.S. crops, religions, ethnicities) instead of item by item.
- Use acronyms and mnemonic devices (e.g., "HOMES" for the five Great Lakes: Huron, Ontario, Michigan, Erie, Superior).
- Use visualization: associate "picture cues" with important information (picturing Sarah in a toga to remember "The Battle at Saratoga," for example) or make "mental pictures" of charts, diagrams, or previously made outlines.
- Create associations (e.g., for state capitals: People are *tall* in Florida [Tallahassee]; they're *mad* in Wisconsin [Madison]; they're *busy* in North Dakota [Bismarck] . . .).

Problem-Solving and Decision-Making Skills

- Identify the goal to be reached or the main problem to be solved (separate main objectives from less important issues).
- Gather information using different techniques (brainstorming, asking others, internet research).
- Make lists of possible courses of action or solutions.
- Evaluate and eliminate options using such factors as practicality, risk involved, and time required.
- Test solutions to see if they will work.

visual-perception skills made it almost impossible for him to benefit from the school's chosen reading curriculum, which stressed whole-word recognition.

When children are poorly matched with instructional methods or the curriculum—or when they have trouble keeping up with the rate at which teachers present new information—they may not master all the class content necessary to succeed at the next academic level. You cannot expect students to succeed at fractions or algebra, for example, if they have failed to come to grips with the basics of addition and subtraction. For students with learning disabilities, the problem of missed content often compounds their academic difficulties. "When the basics of punctuation and capitalization were taught in third grade, my daughter was still struggling to keep her letters on the lines," one mother recalls. "All that stuff about when to use a comma and when to use upper case went right by her. As a result, Sheena lost points for capitalization and punctuation errors on her written work for years. The problem wasn't that she couldn't understand that material; it was that she had missed the *opportunity* to learn it." This family finally hired a tutor to teach Sheena the rules of written English during the summer before she started high school, and she learned them very quickly.

In the next section of this book we will discuss how compensating for a disability, practicing basic skills, developing better learning strategies, and reviewing class content are blended into a successful educational program. In the meantime, it is important for parents to recognize that it is *general education teachers* (not special educators) who shoulder the bulk of the responsibility for teaching students with learning problems. (Most students with learning disabilities spend at least 80 percent of their school days in regular classrooms, taking their lessons alongside typical learners.) To make sure that their children are being given appropriate lessons at a rate they can tolerate, parents of children with LD need to monitor the classroom environment carefully. At the end of this chapter is a detailed list of qualities that distinguish good teaching. Throughout your child's education, you will want to pay attention to whether or not your child's regular classroom teachers are meeting these standards.

WHAT KIND OF SOCIAL SUPPORT DOES MY CHILD NEED?

There are several characteristics of learning disabilities that can interfere with social success, including problems with verbal communication, difficulty interpreting facial expressions or "body language," failure to understand the rules of games, and impulsive behavior (such as interrupting, making irrelevant comments, or outbursts of inappropriate activity). As a result, youngsters with learning disabilities sometimes have problems entering into and maintaining social relationships. Children with ADHD (who tend to be impulsive) and children with severe visual-perception handicaps (who frequently misjudge the timing and rhythm of social interplay) have the most trouble making friends, but even children with less serious disabilities may find themselves consigned to the social sidelines. Social rejection can have an even bigger impact on children's self-esteem than academic failure. As any fourth-grader will tell you, it's much more important to be popular than to be smart.

Social confidence also affects academic success. Children with good interpersonal skills relate positively to teachers as well as to peers. These students are more likely to show off their accomplishments when they are doing well and ask for help when they are having problems. Not only do these expressive and likable youngsters get more approval and encouragement from teachers, research indicates they get more "strokes" from their parents, too. The support these students receive from adults helps them to aim high when they set goals and keep trying when they suffer setbacks.

Most children pick up social skills by copying the behavior of the people around them. Students with learning disabilities, however, may need to be taught these skills more directly. Some school districts offer social-skills training through special education. These programs use small-group activities to teach and practice such social fundamentals as starting a conversation, responding appropriately to others, and expressing feelings. Typically these lessons are very practical and detailed. The box on page 152, for example, presents instructions for asking for help.

Getting Help

Body Basics
>   Face the person.
>   Make eye contact.
>   Use a serious voice tone.
>   Have a serious facial expression.
>   Keep a straight body posture.

Other Skill Steps
>   Say the person's name.
>   Ask if the person has time to help you.
>   Explain your problem.
>   Ask for advice.
>   Listen carefully to the person's advice.
>   Ask questions if you do not understand.
>   Do the task while the person watches, if needed.
>   Ask for feedback if needed.
>   Thank the person.

Reprinted with permission. J. B. Schumaker, Social performance of individuals with learning disabilities: Through the looking glass of KU-IRLD research. *School Psychology Review* 21 (1992): p. 389.

There is also a lot that parents can do to encourage social growth. For example, research shows that appearance contributes significantly to popularity, so children should be encouraged to pay attention to posture, grooming, and neatness. "We teach our kids that a friendly smile and expressing interest in others can also go a long way toward winning acceptance," a special educator suggests. "The fact is, people tend to like people who they think like *them*." Making an effort to understand your child's temperament and behavior patterns can help you arrange social events that bring out the best in the youngster's personality, and avoid situations that put him or her at a disadvantage. "I was a basket case after my son's seventh birthday party," one mother remembers. "Tony became so frantic and overstimulated that I don't think he enjoyed it much, either. Given his tendency to go off the wall, I don't know what made me think it would be a good idea to invite six energetic little boys for an overnight. For Tony's eighth birthday, I arranged to take him and *one* friend to an amusement park. The rides and the water slide gave them plenty of outlets for their energy, and we were all tired—but happy—at the end of the day."

Children do not need large numbers of friends in order to feel socially successful—young people who have one or two companions to share interests and activities with usually do fine. Children who fail to make meaningful peer connections by about age nine, however, are at increased risk for emotional and behavioral problems. Social isolation is therefore a red flag that should get parents' attention. (In Chapter 11, we have more to say about ways parents can help promote social success.)

WHAT KIND OF EMOTIONAL SUPPORT DOES MY CHILD NEED?

Children with learning disabilities sometimes face a long course of intimidating obstacles once they start school: teachers who don't understand them, books and assignments that make no sense, students who are cruel to anyone who is "different," and sometimes parents who blame or berate them for their failure to measure up to expectations. It should come as no surprise, then, that youngsters who have learning disabilities suffer from more than their fair share of emotional problems. Even students whose disabilities have been identified and whose families are supportive can experience greater-than-normal levels of frustration and stress, as the entry from Nick's journal illustrates with heartbreaking clarity.

At the very least, these youngsters need an extra measure of encouragement and understanding from their families in order to hold on to their courage and self-esteem. Some students, however, need more. Prolonged feelings of anger, anxiety, or helplessness are often best addressed by professional counseling. Professional intervention should be sought without delay if a student has developed destructive (including self-destructive) tendencies or is exhibiting symptoms of depression. Once these patterns have developed, it is unlikely that

Nick

Nick's mother shares the following introduction to his journal: "Nick was in the fifth grade at the time of this journal entry, in complete despair over his inability to make any sense out of the class that he was in. The teacher Nick had during the mainstreamed portion of his school day seemed certain she could handle Nick's slow work pace and misunderstanding of assignments by making him sit on a bench during recess. Nick didn't tell me about the 'benchings' at first, apparently quite sad that the year was beginning so badly."

The hardest thing I ever had to do is get a good grade on my vocabulary test. Because I have a hard time remembering things. I study and study and I can't get it. I try hard but I need *more time*. My mom has been a big help. Now I have to do a poem. I can't do it see I told you now I have to sit on the bench. I wish I could slap myself and get rid of my learning problems, but Mrs. Saunders doesn't understand. My Mom and my Dad will talk to her and my Dad has been a big help too. I've been on the bench for two weeks. This is getting me really mad. My friends understand why doesn't Mrs. Saunders understand. I hope I pass fifth grade. I'm really scared. Somebody help me. Alls Mrs. Saunders does is putting people on the bench. She yells at everybody . . . I'm not having much fun this year. I hate myself. Life isn't fair. I'm not happy. But when I'm around my Dad he makes me feel really good. I love him very much.

I feel like I'm in jail and I will never get out. I want to tell her what I feel like but she will yell at me. I'm to get my guts up and tell her. I'm really sad with a capital S. . . . I'm at the library now. Maybe I will talk to Mrs. Saunders.

Reprinted by permission of Rita Ter Sarkissoff, Sebastopol, CA, 1996.

the student will make significant academic progress until the emotional issues have been resolved.

Professional guidance may also be needed to help family members learn to deal with a child's learning and behavior problems appropriately. Parents, too, develop self-defeating patterns: establishing unrealistic expectations, being inconsistent about rules, becoming overprotective, and helping too much are a few that are very common. A skilled family counselor can help you identify unproductive habits and suggest ways of interacting with your child that are more comfortable and bring better results. Counselors can also help you work through feelings of guilt, anger, or anxiety that may be interfering with your effectiveness as a parent. In Chapter 10 we will talk more about the family dynamics of living with a learning disability, and later we will also discuss how to find a good family therapist.

Parents sometimes wonder how much to tell children about their learning disabilities. Will children be traumatized by discovering that they have a neurological problem? We feel that *not* talking to children about their disabilities presents a greater threat to their emotional health. Remember that children who have learning problems almost always sense that they are different in some way. The explanations they imagine for why they are different, however, are often far worse than the truth. "I couldn't do anything right, and I had such a hard time getting along with everybody, I just figured I was a bad person," says a man whose ADHD was not identified until he was an adult. "As a kid, I spent a lot of time worrying about going to hell. If someone had told me I had a different kind of brain back then, I would have been grateful."

"It's *very* important to get across to these kids that they aren't dumb," a special educator says. "Usually stupidity is the only explanation they can think of for their problems in the classroom. In addition, they need to understand that there is more than one way to solve problems, and that success comes from finding the right approach— not from 'just trying harder,' as they have so often been urged to do."

Experienced parents add that students who understand their handicaps (and how to get around them) are far more motivated and more likely to set challenging goals for themselves than students who are confused about their disabilities or ashamed of them. "It was a sad day for me when my fourth-grade son asked if he'd outgrow his disability and I had to tell him that he wouldn't," a mother remembers, "but he took the news very matter-of-factly. He said 'Well Mom, if I can't outgrow it, I'll have to outlearn it, won't I?'" This student (now on the dean's list at a select college) participated in all special education meetings about his program from the fifth grade on. "In high school, I used to explain to my teachers how they should explain things to me," he says. "Most of the time they appreciated the help."

This young man found that self-confidence came from learning to deal with a disability—not from hiding it, or pretending he didn't have one. When asked how he developed such a positive attitude, he explained it this way:

> *Well, for one thing, I always knew my parents were on my side. I remember one time in elementary school, a teacher refused to put me in the advanced reading group because my writing skills were still pretty bad and the advanced students had to write book reports. My mother was in that classroom the next day, with my reading scores in one hand and a copy of state laws applying to learning disabilities in the other. They had a polite discussion, and I was put in the advanced reading group. I gave my book reports orally.*
>
> *But most of the time, my folks acted like having a learning disability was no big deal. It was something that had to be dealt with, but not something to get upset about, you know? So I guess I just grew up thinking I was basically okay.*

Students with learning disabilities *are* basically okay. If school problems begin to seem overwhelming, it is important to get back in touch with that fact. Take a deep breath, put away the homework, do something fun. On any given day, the most valuable thing you can do as a parent "expert" is to enjoy and appreciate your child as a unique human being. For most children, self-esteem depends largely on how they feel about the person they see reflected in their parents' eyes.

What Should I Expect from my Child's Teacher?

The great majority of students with learning disabilities are included for many of their lessons with typical learners in regular classrooms. While the experience and skill of the classroom teacher affects how well all children in the class learn, children with LD have a greater need for clarity, flexibility, and structure than most.

The following questions focus on qualities that distinguish excellent teaching and classroom management. You can observe many of them during a short (thirty-minute) classroom visit. You will develop a "feel" for others as you interact with your child's teacher over the course of the school year. While parents cannot always choose their child's classroom teacher, you should be aware that when a teacher falls short of meeting many of these standards, students with learning disabilities are likely to need more help than usual (from special education or outside of school) in order to make satisfactory progress.

High Achievement Expectations

- Are the teacher's goals high but attainable? Does the teacher *expect* your child to learn and does he/she very purposefully set about teaching your child?
- Is daily homework assigned to reinforce classroom learning?
- Does the teacher call on children of all ability levels equally, and give equal quality feedback?
- Does the teacher wait up to five seconds for responses, rephrase questions if necessary, provide clues and explanations for students who are slow to respond to questions?

Emphasis on Basic Skills

- Do children spend sufficient time each day reading (aloud or silently) and writing, to promote progress?
- Are basic skills taught to mastery level, in order to build a solid foundation for higher-level skills?
- Is close to 80 percent of the day allocated to the task of academic learning (versus announcements, passing out papers, free time, getting organized, recess, moving between classes, etc.)?

Systematic Monitoring of Student Performance

- Does the teacher use questions, homework, essays, quizzes, performances, and projects to monitor whether children are learning what they are expected to learn?

continued

- Do children get rapid corrective feedback?
- Is student progress graphed, so students have a goal to work toward and feel pleasure in achieving?
- While students are working independently, does the teacher circulate to keep children engaged, check accuracy, answer questions, and give feedback?

Orderly and Positive School Climate

- Is the classroom pleasant, positive, friendly, safe, and orderly?
- Does the teacher convey that all are welcome and valued?
- Are teachers "with it": aware of and responsive to what is going on in their classrooms at all times; able to anticipate and manage problems before they escalate?
- Does the teacher convey enthusiasm by using humor, expressiveness, "hamming it up"?
- Is effort reinforced? ("You tried hard to use more words in your essay; I'm proud of you!")
- Is praise content-related? ("That's right, a triangle has three sides," is better than "You're the best!") Are favored activities (such as time on the computer) used to reinforce academic success, and are exchangeable reinforcers (like points, holes punched in a ticket) used to heighten motivation?
- Is praise used sparingly (not effusively so it loses meaning) and for *real* effort? (Praising easy responses is embarrassing, intrusive, distracting, and a put-down.)
- Does the teacher avoid criticism and sarcasm?
- Does learning include high levels of informal student interaction, as in group projects that are rewarded upon completion?
- Are papers corrected by marking the right answers, and expecting the students to correct those that are incorrect?
- Do teachers incorporate children's ideas and interests into their lessons, thereby conveying that children's ideas are respected?
- Are learning activities creative, varied, and challenging?
- Are students given leadership roles in the classroom (e.g., homework monitor, team captain) to foster responsibility and involvement?
- Is school pride and identification built among students?
- Is parent involvement encouraged?

Organized Instruction

- Are reasonable class rules for conduct and routines established and taught?
- Is the classroom of a reasonable size (low 20s), and children seated in clusters

rather than rows to promote peer learning and socialization? Are activity centers available for group projects?

- Is the classroom composed of a mix of students, with less than one-third struggling learners?
- Does the teacher use small-group and individualized instruction, as well as whole-group instruction?
- Is the pace of instruction rapid enough to sustain student momentum, but slow enough to respond to children's learning needs?
- Is enough time allocated for priority areas of instruction? Important subjects should be taught both in the mornings and afternoons.
- Is my child 90 percent or more successful on tasks before being moved on to something more difficult?
- Are tasks neither too easy nor too hard, so that students stay focused and engaged?
- Does the teacher use different groupings for different subjects (sometimes same levels for basic skills, but most often mixed levels for comprehension and content-area instruction; does the teacher group by interests)? Struggling learners benefit from peer explanations and guidance in heterogeneous learning groups.
- Does the teacher keep group size small? (Children learn more from a teacher in groups of three or four than five to seven.)
- Does the teacher incorporate experiential learning, peer tutoring, cooperative learning? Learning by doing is more instructive than completing independent worksheets, which should never constitute more than 50 percent of the school day.
- Are cubicles available for children who get distracted, and are distractions kept to a minimum (e.g., busy bulletin boards, noise)? Does the child who needs to be redirected to the task at hand sit close to the teacher?
- Do children who need special education assistance get it at times when they are *not* missing essential classroom instruction?

Effective Teaching Strategies

- Does teacher-directed instruction occupy more of the school day than independent work or peer tutoring?

continued

- Does the teacher take an active, direct role in carrying the content to the student, rather than expecting workbooks to teach? Teacher presentations should be followed with questions, student responses, and application opportunities.
- Does the teacher check on understanding of new content at regular intervals through oral or written feedback and reteaching? Redundancy reinforces new learning, often needing as many as fifty repetitions.
- Does the teacher correct student errors immediately, keeping corrections to thirty seconds or less to avoid the class veering off task?
- Does the teacher explicitly teach memory and organizational strategies and guide students to a higher level of reasoning?
- Does the teacher use a variety of teaching and assessment strategies, geared to different modalities so that children with different learning styles and abilities can achieve?
- Do students have choices regarding how to complete an assignment? Are their suggestions heard?
- Is homework begun in class, so the teacher can assist with questions?
- Is new academic content related to a student's own life and previous learning, to make it more meaningful?
- Does the teacher use many different explanations for a concept, including drawing from everyday life examples?
- Does the teacher build reading fluency by providing daily opportunities to read easy material (96 percent accuracy or higher)?
- Except when initially introducing a new concept, is the goal for learning close to 80 percent accuracy (90 percent for homework and seatwork)? Learning should require effort and thought, but not be so hard that the student avoids it and makes errors (then "learns" the errors).
- Does the teacher give clear instructions, demonstrate often, and explain transitions from one idea to another?
- Are student responses actively solicited and discussed?
- Are games and activities with a high-response format used, versus activities that require children to sit, listen, and wait for a turn?
- Does the teacher ask questions every few minutes and call on both volunteers and nonvolunteers? Does the teacher ask lower-level knowledge and comprehension questions as well as questions requiring higher-level application, analysis, and evaluation, so all students may participate?

Part III

AN APPROPRIATE
EDUCATION

7

Becoming an Education Activist

For many parents, identification of a learning disability is accompanied by some element of relief—at last, the cause of all those puzzling problems at school has been discovered! While no one may be thrilled about learning that a child needs special education, at least it is good to know there are specialists who understand learning disabilities and know how to deal with them. Once these experts take over, surely the student will start making progress, and all will be well.

Sometimes things actually work out that way. Other times, however, families find themselves facing scenarios like this one:

- *Nine-year-old Susie has recently been found to have language-processing disabilities that are compromising her efforts in reading. While she does average work in math and most other subjects, she reads at a second-grade level. It is expected that Susie's reading will improve with one hour of special education instruction per day. It is therefore recommended that Susie remain in her regular fourth-grade classroom but go to the school's "resource room" for an hour each afternoon to work on reading skills with a special education teacher.*

  This type of arrangement (which is common for students with learning disabilities, and is consistent with the legal mandate that such students be educated in "the least restrictive environment") seems satisfactory all around. Susie's parents are glad that she is finally going to get the specialized help she needs. Susie is pleased that she will be able to stay with her fourth-grade friends most of the time. School administrators are happy because this system makes efficient use of the special education teacher: working with small groups an hour at a time, one learning specialist can serve twenty or more students in a day. Since Susie's school has identified relatively few students with disabilities, they are getting by with "half a teacher" (one special education teacher serves two schools, one in the morning and one in the afternoon).

Within two months, however, it is obvious that Susie's program is not working. Not only is Susie showing no signs of improvement, but her performance is actually slipping in some areas. She is failing social studies, and her marks in math and science have also dropped. She has a shocking amount of homework—two or three hours' worth every night—and Susie's parents spend most weekday evenings at the kitchen table helping their daughter through her assignments. These sessions are often punctuated by tantrums and tears, as Susie insists she can't do what is expected of her. The level of academic anxiety the little girl is suffering is worse than anything she has experienced before. To make matters even more painful, Susie's workload leaves her little time or energy for recreation. Her friends have stopped including her in after-school activities because she always has too much homework to do.

What went wrong? Susie's father suspects Susie's teachers are incompetent, while Mom worries that Susie's disability may be much more severe than originally thought. The truth, however, is that Susie is a victim of increased curricular demands and poor coordination between her special and regular education programs. Let's take a look at what's actually going on at Susie's elementary school:

- *Susie is pulled out of her regular classroom for reading help between one and two o'clock in the afternoon. During this period her classmates are scheduled for lessons in social studies (Monday, Wednesday, and Friday) and science (Tuesday and Thursday). Although it would make more sense to pull Susie out in the morning during the fourth-grade reading period, this is not possible because the special education teacher does not arrive at Susie's school until after lunch. Susie therefore spends most of her mornings involved in reading activities that are completely inappropriate for her. She misses science and social studies entirely. Math—previously Susie's best subject—is taught in the mornings, but this year math is not making much sense to Susie. Word problems have been introduced, and Susie cannot understand the problems well enough to figure out which of her math skills to apply.*

Mr. Jones, Susie's classroom teacher, is a solid, experienced instructor. He has never received any education about learning disabilities, however, either at the college he attended twenty years ago or since that time. As a result, Mr. Jones knows next to nothing about learning disabilities and the many ways students are affected by them. He has been told that Susie has a learning disability but he hasn't had time to meet with the special education teacher and review Susie's education plan, so he doesn't understand her problems. In any case, Mr. Jones's view is that dealing with Susie's learning disability is the special education teacher's job. He is aware that Susie is struggling, but so are ten other students in his class of twenty-seven. Mr. Jones does not lack for things to do, and he is grateful that somebody else is looking after Susie's problems.

No one has told Mr. Jones that he has to do anything special for Susie, so he assumes she is responsible for the same work as the other fourth-graders. Since Susie misses social studies and science, Mr. Jones sends the classwork in those two subjects home for her to do, in addition to her regular assignments. The science and history texts and worksheets are much longer and more complicated than anything Susie received last year (in most schools, demands on reading comprehension increase dramatically in fourth and fifth grades). In addition, Susie is trying to complete this work without benefit of the instruction and activities—discussions, films, experiments, and the like—that the other fourth-graders received in class.

In effect, Susie must do more work (special instruction in reading has been tacked on to her regular fourth-grade curriculum) with less help than any of her classmates. No wonder she is complaining!

What about the special education teacher? Isn't she supposed to coordinate with Susie's classroom teacher and keep an eye on Susie's program? Technically she is, but let's look at this teacher's day. Ms. Smith has been assigned twenty-five students in the first through sixth grades this year. The law requires her to implement an individualized program for each one of them. Every minute of her time is devoted to direct instruction except for lunch, which she spends commuting from one school to another. Ms. Smith is a competent and caring teacher; she would like to meet with each of her students' classroom teachers (between the two schools, there are more than fifteen of them) and tell them more about her students and their learning disabilities. But when is she to do so? She has no free period. She seldom has time to attend the regular teachers' staff meetings in addition to the special education staff meetings she attends at the school district's central offices. Ms. Smith makes an effort to offer assistance when she becomes aware that one of her students is having a problem in the classroom, but she rarely has time to do more.

Since Susie is new to her as a student, Ms. Smith has spent several weeks investigating which reading materials are likely to help the youngster best. This exploratory process is important to the success of the program, but meanwhile Susie does not appear to have made much progress. Because she sees Ms. Smith as a reading teacher who has nothing to do with Mr. Jones, Susie has said nothing about her problems with homework or the classroom. And because Susie's parents think their daughter's difficulties are primarily due to her learning disabilities, they have not contacted anyone at school about their concerns; they are simply trying to help Susie keep up as best they can. As a result, Ms. Smith does not know that Susie's overall program is impossibly unfair. Unless someone—the classroom teacher, Susie, or Susie's parents—approaches her, Ms. Smith will probably remain ignorant of the problem until the failing grades on Susie's report card alert her.

Can coordination and communication among professionals really be this bad? Unfortunately, they can. At nearly every gathering of parents of students with learning disabilities, nightmares like Susie's are shared. There are tales of students who can't spell being humiliated by being required to participate in spelling bees, students who can't read being assigned college-level texts, and students who struggle to form letters being given zeros for sloppy or incomplete written work. Parents often report that they did not learn of the problems their children faced in school until months or even years after the fact. "When he was in high school, my son told me that his sixth-grade teacher made him sit in a kindergarten chair because his writing looked like kindergarten work," one mother remembers. "When I asked Sean why he never said anything about it then, he told me he was too ashamed—then added that he was doing so badly that year, he halfway figured he deserved the punishment."

To understand why problems like these occur, it is necessary to know something of the evolution of special education programming. First, we must recognize how new this field is. It was not until the mid-1970s that states were required by the federal government to educate children with disabilities. Before that, public schools could—and sometimes did—turn away students with disabilities, claiming they had neither the facilities nor the staff to cope with their special needs. In 1975 Congress passed Public Law 94-142, the Education for All Handicapped Children Act. (PL 94-142 has since been amended several times, and in 1990 it was renamed the Individuals with Disabilities Education Act, or IDEA.) This legislation, most recently revised in 2004, requires each state to provide a "free appropriate public education" to school-aged children with any of thirteen different handicapping conditions, including "specific learning disabilities."* The law further states that these students are to be provided with *individualized education programs* designed to meet their unique needs.

---

* For the federal definition of specific learning disabilities, see Chapter 5. The other disabilities recognized by IDEA 2004 are mental retardation, hearing impairments (including deafness), speech or language impairments, visual impairments (including blindness), emotional disturbance, orthopedic impairments, autism, traumatic brain injury, multiple disabilities developmental delays, deaf/blindness, and other health impairments (which includes ADHD).

Parents Share . . .

My daughter loves science, and she did exceptionally well in her junior high science classes in spite of her dyslexia. Yet at the end of eighth grade her teacher did not recommend her for the high school honors science class. When I asked why, the teacher said he had no doubt Kellie could handle the concepts, but felt Kellie's slow work rate would put her at an overwhelming disadvantage in the advanced class. I argued that Kellie's placement should be determined by her *abilities—not* her disabilities—and added that placing her below her intellectual level would undermine her motivation. I offered to meet with the honors science teacher and explain the adaptations Kellie would need in order to succeed—extra time on her tests and assignments, for example, and some adjustments to the reading list. A lot of teachers don't know much about learning disabilities, and people are afraid of what they don't understand. Once the honors teacher understood that working with Kellie wouldn't destroy his whole curriculum, he welcomed her in.

Federal law determines that special education can be provided in a variety of settings (including regular classrooms, special classrooms, special schools, the student's home, and hospitals or other institutions) but adds that an effort must be made to educate students in the *least restrictive environment*. To the maximum extent possible, children with disabilities are to be educated at their home schools with nondisabled peers. Placement in regular classrooms with appropriate supports and accommodations is considered preferable to placement in separate special education classes. According to the law, removal from the regular education environment is acceptable only "when the nature or severity of the disability of a child is such that education in regular classes with the use of supplementary aids and services cannot be achieved satisfactorily." Wherever they are placed, students are to have as much access as possible to the regular curriculum.

The law's emphasis on the least restrictive environment resulted in part from aggressive advocacy on the part of groups representing parents of children with disabilities. These parents were all too familiar with educators' tendencies to segregate special-needs students, placing them out of sight and out of mind of the typical school population. Parents felt that this practice unnecessarily stigmatized their children, robbed them of social support, and resulted in lowered expectations and a second-rate education. "Mainstreaming" children with special needs—that is, including them in regular education activities for all or part of the school day—was advanced as an important way of improving their opportunities.

Following this legislation, children with learning disabilities rapidly emerged as America's single largest special-needs group. (Nationally, students with learning disabilities now make up about 50 percent of the total special education population.) This generated a tremendous demand for teachers specializing in learning disabilities, and an explosion of university programs designed to prepare such teachers. Still, many schools found themselves identifying students with disabilities at a much faster rate than they could find specialists to work with them. Combined with the budget constraints chronically faced by many school districts, this shortage forced the development of programs that enabled available learning specialists to serve the greatest possible numbers of students. "Pull-out" programs (which placed students with disabilities in typical classrooms but removed them for small-group instruction with a special education teacher for an hour or two a day) made efficient use of the learning specialists' time and also fulfilled the least-restrictive-environment mandate. At the moment, most students with learning disabilities are educated in some variation of this model. (Coteaching and "push-in" programs—in which students with disabilities stay in regular classrooms full time, and special educators either coteach in the room or visit to work with students there—are being used with increasing frequency. This approach helps avoid the stigma of leaving class to get special help, improves communication between regular and special educators, and can lead to greater instructional flexibility in the classroom.)

But what about the regular classroom teachers? When IDEA was passed, very few of these teachers had any special education preparation. (Today most teacher education programs offer some information about learning disabilities, but it is often minimal.) Nevertheless, students with disabilities were placed in their classes on a regular basis. While some school systems made efforts to provide in-service training on learning disabilities to teachers, others simply assigned the stu-

Is Private School the Answer?

Parents who are frustrated with their public-school experience sometimes wonder if their children would fare better in private institutions. Are youngsters with disabilities likely to do better in private school? The answer is . . . maybe and maybe not.

Children who have mild information-processing problems may do better in private school if that school provides smaller classes, more individual attention, more elastic time constraints, and more flexibility in both curriculum and instructional style than the public school. If a student needs specialized instruction to master basic reading, math, or writing skills, however, these advantages alone will not produce improvement—the child must also have the assistance of a learning-disabilities specialist. Parents should also be aware that teachers in private and parochial schools are not necessarily any better informed about learning disabilities than teachers in public schools. It is still necessary to work with them closely to make sure that materials, assignments, and activities are consistently appropriate and meet the child's needs.

At the other end of the spectrum, students whose disabilities and/or attention problems are so severe that it is very difficult for them to function in a traditional classroom may benefit from attending a private school exclusively for children with learning disabilities. These schools are staffed primarily by learning specialists, and they offer a range of opportunities and services that is beyond the scope of most public institutions. A major disadvantage is that day schools of this type do not exist in most communities; many are boarding schools, where tuition can rival the cost of college. Students also have mixed feelings about "special" schools. Some are happy and relieved to discover there are other students like themselves (and teachers who can teach them), but others see placement in such schools as a mark of inadequacy and failure. Students who have positive attitudes are generally most successful in this setting.

Many parents straddle the public/private issue by supplementing a public-school education with private tutoring. This approach can work well if tutors are chosen with care, and if work is scheduled in a way that avoids overloading the student. It is also important to coordinate the activities of teachers and tutors in order to avoid unnecessary confusion (for example, if a student's teacher is working with one type of reading program and the tutor is using a system that is completely different, the child may end up becoming even more perplexed). Parent support groups are often a good source of information about tutors for students with different kinds of learning problems.

dents and expected teachers to cope as best they could—a practice critics refer to as "dump and hope" (that is, dump the children in the classroom without support and hope it will work out somehow). Often workshops on disabilities were offered to teachers, but they were optional. Understandably, many regular classroom teachers were uncertain about their responsibilities toward students with learning disabilities. Were they responsible for basic-skills instruction, or was the special education teacher? Were they expected to provide different materials or use different instructional methods for students with special needs? Were they supposed to modify the curriculum or grading practices for these children? Was giving "special treatment" to students with disabilities fair to typical learners in the class?

The confusion created by a lack of clear guidelines was compounded by the diverse yet highly specific needs of students with learning disabilities—as well as the fact that many students with information-processing problems did not appear to be handicapped at all. Since most children with learning disabilities spent more than half their time with teachers who were not quite sure what these students needed or who was supposed to provide it, it's no surprise that the quality of learning-disabilities programming varied tremendously from school to school, and even from classroom to classroom.

Parents Share . . .

My son is talented in art and loved drama. Those were two of the main things that kept him interested in school. One year I had to go toe-to-toe with the high school principal, who said Randy couldn't work on the school play because he was close to failing math that term. The principal came around when I pointed out Randy had started to fall when the math class switched from a geometry unit to an algebra unit. Randy does okay in geometry because it has a strong visual element, but he has problems with sequencing and memorization, so algebra is very hard for him. I suggested the teacher try to make algebra more visual and concrete—show Randy how to use math concepts to build models, for example. Sure enough, when she did that, Randy began to improve. Meanwhile, he designed a fantastic multilevel set for the play on his computer. Today he's a computer animator considering an offer from Disney.

A Word About Being Fair

"It's not fair to expect all the other kids to write out their book reports but allow Jane to give hers orally. She should do the same work as the others."

"Why should Johnny be allowed to use a calculator on tests when the other kids can't? It gives him an unfair advantage."

"If I take off points for everyone else's spelling errors, I should do the same for Sue. Otherwise, I'm not being fair."

Classroom teachers sometimes resist modifying assignments, materials, or grading practices to accommodate students with learning disabilities on the grounds that making these adjustments is not fair to other students in the class. Fairness, these teachers insist, means that everyone should be treated the same.

Yet these teachers would never demand that a student with a broken leg be deprived of his crutches and made to participate in gym. Nor would they suggest that hearing-impaired students attend class without their hearing aids, or that blind students make do with regular books instead of recorded texts or books in Braille. Perhaps it is necessary to give some additional thought to what *fairness* really means.

First, most of us would agree that being fair means you don't ask anybody to do the impossible. If you would not expect second-graders to do calculus problems or a child

Today it is well understood that teacher education and support are the keys to successfully including students with disabilities in typical classrooms. The National Education Association, for example, states that in order for inclusion to work, it must be accompanied by

- a full range of educational placements and services (so that students will not be placed inappropriately for lack of viable alternatives),
- professional development for staff,
- adequate time for teachers to plan and collaborate with one another,
- class sizes responsive to student needs, and
- appropriate staff and technical assistance.

with severe cerebral palsy to do broad jumps, you should not expect a child with fourth-grade reading skills to read tenth-grade books without help. Nor should you expect kids who are slow in processing information to perform satisfactorily on timed tests, or ask children with ADHD to sit at their desks for three hours without a break.

Second, being fair means you don't punish children for having disabilities. If the homework that takes most students forty minutes to do takes a student with learning disabilities three hours—leaving little time left over for recreation—*that* is not fair. Such situations make it much harder for the student with disabilities to learn and deprive that student of opportunities for normal social and emotional growth.

Third, being fair means you do not deprive children with disabilities of the means of doing what typical children can do on their own. If you do not object to giving a wheelchair to a student with a spinal cord injury, you should not object to providing the student who has trouble retaining math facts with a calculator, or allowing the student who has writing problems to demonstrate knowledge by dictating some assignments. These modifications equalize students' opportunities to participate in instruction and demonstrate their understanding; they do not give students with disabilities "advantages."

In short, treating students equally means sometimes you have to treat them differently. Fairness means giving children equal access to a quality education—not insisting that everybody must do everything exactly the same way.

We also now know that many of the strategies that have been developed to support students with learning disabilities are good for *all* children when implemented classroomwide. An encouraging new trend in education—called Universal Design for Learning—offers teachers a blueprint for "borrowing" methods and materials from special education to improve flexibility in schools that serve increasingly diverse student populations. (For more on Universal Design for Learning, see pages 185–87).

Many groups representing families of students with disabilities heartily support meeting the needs of students with learning disabilities within the regular classroom, and some are working actively with school districts to develop effective policies and improve local programs. Yet even where there is widespread support for inclusion, lack of adequate funding may still block appropriate staff development, new support services, and reductions in class size. As a result, general and special educators alike continue to struggle to do their jobs under difficult conditions in many classrooms, and the quality of programming available to children with learning disabilities remains extremely variable.

The collective wisdom of knowledgeable parents, therefore, is that *children with learning disabilities need advocates* to be sure that the education they receive is consistently appropriate and effective. Without active oversight, these students are too likely to end up overwhelmed and underassisted. Many parents state they stepped into the advocate role because there was no one else to perform it; in other words, they became education activists by default. "I knew nothing about education when I started out," one mother says. "I only knew that what my son was getting in school wasn't helping him. What I found was that there was almost no communication between the regular teachers and the special education staff at his school. I became sort of an unofficial go-between—explaining learning disabilities to the classroom teacher, and explaining the fifth-grade curriculum to the special ed teacher. I did the same in sixth grade, and again in seventh. On the way I learned a lot about education, and also about cutting through red tape and handling bureaucracies." Not only do parents like this secure better education for their children, but they are sometimes instrumental in creating new programs and services where none existed before. Parent-professional groups such as the Learning Disabilities Association of America (LDA) and Children and Adults with Attention-Deficit/Hyperactivity Disorder (CHADD) both provide information and support to families and work energetically for legislation that supports students with learning disabilities and protects their rights on local, state, and national levels. (For the addresses of these and other advocacy groups, see Appendix D.)

Exactly what does a parent need to do to provide students with adequate support and prevent problems? Experienced mothers and fathers advise that there are three basic areas where parental involvement and advocacy make a big difference.

PREPARING INDIVIDUALIZED
EDUCATION PROGRAMS

According to federal law, identification of a learning disability must be promptly followed by the preparation of an Individualized Education Program (IEP) for the student. An IEP document spells out annual goals, specifies all the services, supports, and accommodations to be made available, and identifies the type of classes to which the child will be assigned. The IEP is reviewed at least once a year (although the review can be waived if the parents and school district agree that major changes are unnecessary). Parental consent is required for first-time assignment of special education services and for changes in placement. Once a student has been assigned to special education, school districts can make some changes in the student's program without parental consent, but they may do so only after making a reasonable attempt to obtain parent input and approval. (School districts are allowed a certain amount of leeway to act on behalf of students whose parents choose not to participate in the IEP process.)

As we mentioned in Chapter 5, the IEP is in effect a contract: the school district is legally obliged to provide the assistance and services described in this document. The fact that specified services or equipment do not presently exist cannot be used as an excuse for failure to provide them (in other words, if a student's IEP states that he is to have access to a computer in the classroom and there are no computers there now, the school must get one). In addition, the IEP serves several other important functions:

- IEP meetings provide an opportunity for parents and educators to share their perceptions of the child's needs, resolve conflicts, discuss options, prioritize goals, and make decisions about the child's educational program. IEP meetings are held following the initial identification of a learning disability and usually once a year thereafter. Parents may also request a meeting to review or revise an IEP if a student is not making satisfactory progress, or if new concerns have arisen.

• The IEP serves as a management tool. It is used by school districts to ensure that children with disabilities receive educations and services that are in compliance with federal and state guidelines. Monitors from government agencies may review IEPs to make sure schools are fulfilling their obligations under the law.

• The IEP serves as a device for tracking and evaluating a student's progress from year to year. An IEP is not a "performance contract"—that is, schools and teachers cannot be held legally responsible if a student does not meet IEP objectives. Failure to make progress toward the goals specified on an IEP, however, strongly suggests that modifications need to be made in a student's program.

In the next chapter, we will discuss some of the most important questions that have to be resolved when preparing an IEP. Our purpose here is to emphasize the importance of participating fully in IEP meetings. Federal law requires public agencies to notify parents of the time and place of these meetings well in advance. If you are unable to attend a scheduled IEP meeting, it is reasonable to ask for the meeting to be rescheduled at a more convenient time. If it is impossible for you to

Parents Share . . .

I had to fight just to get my son *tested*. The school kept saying, "He's so bright, and he's not failing, so he can't have a learning disability." I *knew* he was bright—that's why I couldn't understand why some kinds of schoolwork were such a struggle for him. Finally I insisted on an evaluation. It showed he had both a learning disability and a gifted IQ. . . . So many people think "smart" and "LD" can't go together—even teachers, who you'd think would know better. Caleb was actually relieved to find out he had a learning disability. He'd been knocking himself out to get Cs—which was okay with the school, but not okay with Caleb. After his program was modified, he made the honor roll. He got one of those "My child is an honor student" bumper stickers—you should have seen the grin on his face when we put it on the car!

attend a child's IEP meeting in person, then the school district should make an effort to secure your participation through other means, such as conference telephone calls. The district is also required to provide interpreters if parents are hearing impaired or speak languages other than English. Despite these provisions to protect parents' rights, a surprisingly large number of parents never take part in preparing Individualized Education Programs. "I think many parents just don't realize what an important document the IEP is," one special educator says. "If it were my child, I'd take a day off from work—even a day without pay—to make sure her needs were being addressed properly."

MONITORING STUDENT PROGRESS

As Susie's story demonstrated, preparation of an appropriate IEP does not guarantee that a student's program will go smoothly. There are many things that can interfere with the implementation of an IEP, including unrealistic or badly stated goals, poor staff communication, large class size, scheduling problems, and shortages of space, materials, and support personnel. Student resistance can also be a problem, particularly among youngsters who experienced long periods of failure or frustration before their disabilities were identified. These young people often lack faith in themselves, and many have developed behaviors that contribute to their academic problems. Procrastination, misbehaving to get attention or avoid work, and manipulating others into reducing expectations or feeling sorry for them are just a sampling of the counterproductive coping strategies used by children with learning difficulties at school and at home.

Because so many of them have become discouraged, it is important for students with learning disabilities to start experiencing success as soon as possible. Once these students realize they are moving forward, their motivation and levels of commitment to academic tasks usually improve. To maintain their enthusiasm, these youngsters need to be able to see themselves making progress on a regular basis. Many are quite sensitive to setbacks; even short periods of frustration can be enough to cause these students to give up and revert to undesirable patterns of behavior.

Guidelines for Parent-Teacher Partnerships

Regular classroom teachers are not trained in special education, and they should not be expected to function as special education teachers. Teachers can be expected to respect students' basic human rights, however, and to make reasonable accommodations for a disability (for discussion of accommodations, see Chapter 8). The guidelines below outline what parents of children with learning disabilities should expect from any teacher (basic), what a good teacher will provide (better), and behavior that identifies the truly exceptional teacher (best).

BASIC	BETTER	BEST
1. Children will not be criticized, shamed, scolded, humiliated, or made to feel embarrassed or guilty about their learning disabilities. The teacher will not tell them they are lazy, stupid, stubborn, or worthless.	Students will be encouraged to work around their learning problems while facing them honestly. Teachers will be sensitive to the social and emotional issues associated with learning disabilities and protect special needs students from children who tease or try to make them feel inferior.	Teachers will help the class reach a better understanding of learning disabilities. Activities will be designed so that special-needs students can make real contributions.
2. Children will never be asked to do work they are totally incapable of doing.	Children will be asked to do as much of the regular classwork as possible. When necessary, they will be given smaller amounts of the regular work or alternate assignments.	The teacher will work with special education staff to see that class materials are consistently adapted to students' ability levels and learning styles, or that special materials are provided that teach the same concepts at levels students can handle.

For this reason, wise parents do not wait for report cards or IEP reviews to see how their children are doing in school. Instead, they monitor student progress much more closely—often on a weekly basis. When they see problems (either with academic progress or emotional well-being), these parents contact the school and seek intervention promptly. This proactive stance protects children from experiencing

BASIC	BETTER	BEST
3. In reading, writing, and math, children will be given instruction appropriate to their level of skill. (No child reading at a second-grade level will be asked to work independently from a fifth-grade reading book, for example.)	In addition to understanding students' weaknesses, teachers will nurture strengths. (For instance, a child with poor writing but good drawing skills might be asked to illustrate a story written by another student for the school literary magazine.)	Teachers will maximize opportunities to individualize instruction. Options like cross-age grouping, peer and volunteer tutors, and creative use of computers will be used to help reinforce learning.
4. Children will participate in subjects such as science, social studies, health, music, art, and physical education to the greatest extent possible. Either students' work will be adjusted so that they can do it alone, or assistance will be provided as needed.	Teachers will vary their presentation methods to accommodate students with disabilities (for example, overhead projectors will be used to assist children who need visual reinforcement; hands-on materials will be provided to assist concrete learners).	Children will be taught organization, good study skills, and appropriate educational strategies so they can succeed in these subjects.
5. Students will be tested fairly. Disabilities will not be permitted to interfere with demonstrating knowledge. (The knowledge of a student with handwriting problems, for example, would not be judged on the basis of handwritten essays.)	Teachers will be flexible about time limits imposed for tests and test settings (quiet rooms will be made available for distractible students, for example).	Teachers will use a variety of evaluation methods to accommodate different learning styles (students might be given a choice between writing a final paper and taking a short-answer test, for example).

continued

damaging lengthy periods of defeat, and often leads to important adjustments in student programs.

In order to monitor a student's progress effectively, it is essential to develop cooperative relationships with the child's teachers—and sometimes with school administrators as well. This is a prospect some parents find intimidating, since there is something about meeting a

BASIC	BETTER	BEST
6. Children will not be prevented from taking part in enrichment activities as punishment for poor performance in school work. Art, music, physical education, recess, or field trips will not be withheld on the grounds that work was not finished or that the student failed a particular assignment. (Of course, those activities might be withheld for bad behavior.)	Field trips, special projects, drama, art, music, and sports will be regarded as worthwhile elements of the student's program. Achievement in these areas will be recognized and valued.	Teachers will help children discover outlets for their talents and energy and actively encourage participation in extracurricular activities.
7. The child will not be allowed to disrupt the class. The teacher will not tolerate temper tantrums, lack of respect, rudeness, foul language, physical injury, or damage to property.	Behavior problems will be avoided by good classroom management. The teacher will encourage children to express anger and frustration in ways that do no harm to themselves, to others, or to property. Children will be recognized and rewarded for their successes so they will learn to find satisfaction in good behavior.	The teacher will plan activities that enable students to succeed in order to help them improve their self-concepts and build self-esteem.
8. The teacher will cooperate with parents and provide information about children's progress as needed.	The teacher will take the lead in seeing that the school and the home are working together in the best interest of the child. Teachers will suggest ways parents can help support the child academically and will remain flexible and open to suggestions from parents and other professionals.	The teacher will also attempt to coordinate instructional planning with psychologists, social workers, special education teachers, therapists, and others concerned with the child's welfare.

Adapted from Suzanne H. Stevens, *The Learning Disabled Child: Ways that Parents Can Help.* (Winston-Salem, NC: John F. Blair, 1980).

teacher (or, heaven help us, a principal) that makes almost everyone feel like a student again. If we were successful as students, this is usually not a big obstacle to communication. Parents who did not do well in school, however, may find themselves feeling frightened and powerless the moment they set foot on school property. Parents who felt they were treated unfairly in school (this group includes many parents who themselves have information-processing problems) may also feel hostile toward teachers and other education authorities. Such parents may have trouble dealing with teachers effectively because of a lack of assertiveness or a chip-on-the-shoulder attitude.

In Chapter 9 we will talk more about establishing relationships with your child's teachers and developing methods for monitoring student progress. It helps to begin, though, with a realistic idea of what you can expect from these important people in your child's life. The guidelines for parent-teacher partnerships on pages 178–80 will help you identify what you can expect from a regular classroom teacher. These guidelines can also be used to evaluate how effectively teachers work with students who are struggling with academic or behavioral issues.

PROVIDING APPROPRIATE SUPPORT AT HOME

The key word here is *appropriate*. Susie's devoted parents thought they were supporting their daughter by committing themselves, night after night, to helping her through her homework. The truth is, however, they might have been doing her more harm than good. Quite possibly, their assistance made Susie feel dependent on them and reinforced her certainty that she could not succeed on her own. By doggedly enforcing unrealistic academic demands (no fourth-grader should be doing three hours of homework a night!) these parents also endangered their personal relationship with their child. Rather than experiencing what Mom and Dad were doing as supportive, Susie likely perceived them as unsympathetic taskmasters!

Does this mean parents should not help students who have learning disabilities with their schoolwork? Of course not; these youngsters need help with assignments on a fairly regular basis. Parents

Parents Share . . .

My daughter's weakness is auditory processing—she needs extra time to understand what she hears. There was one third-grade teacher—if Jenny didn't respond to directions *right away*, this woman got right in her face and started yelling. This only confused Jenny even more. When she's bombarded with a lot of noise, she shuts down—like a soldier with shell shock. I learned it was very important to meet with teachers who were screamers early on. I would explain that Jenny needed extra time to process verbal instructions. I told them she did well with visual material, and suggested ways they could give her information that would help her succeed. Then I would talk about Jenny's response to loud voices, so that even if they didn't help her, at least they wouldn't shout at her. Fortunately, we didn't run into too many teachers like that—but wouldn't you know, Jenny's very first job supervisor was a screamer. Jenny did a good job handling that situation herself, though. She met with him and asked if he'd give her job assignments in writing.

do need to learn to distinguish, though, between the kinds of help that sabotage self-esteem and the types that build self-confidence, independence, and good study habits. For example, Susie would have been far better off if her parents met with her teachers about reducing her unreasonable homework load and structuring her assignments so that Susie could do more of the work on her own. Susie's parents could contribute to her success by helping her break down tasks and set realistic deadlines, by establishing a structured time and place for doing homework, and by offering praise or allowing rewarding activities (such as time on the family computer) when she finishes agreed-upon amounts of work. In addition, they might agree to read certain texts to Susie (the science and social studies materials that are beyond her reading level, for example), and get the teacher's consent for Susie to dictate some assignments into a voice recorder so that the amount of writing she has to complete does not become overwhelming. This kind of support lets Susie sidestep her disabilities while leaving her responsible for the actual work of learning and remembering information, interpreting concepts, and answering questions. Susie's life at home is likely to be a lot more peaceful, and when she succeeds, she will know she has done so on her own intellectual merits.

Even more important than providing academic assistance are the jobs of providing emotional support to children with information-processing weaknesses and making sure that these children feel they are valued and functioning members of a family. Many studies show that a sense of self-worth and belonging are more critical to a child's future success than academic skills. For this reason, the following types of activities may be just as valuable to your child as homework:

- taking a fair share of household responsibilities
- enjoying hobbies and recreational activities (such as sports, collecting, music, or arts and crafts)
- participating in group activities (such as scouts or 4-H Clubs)
- getting involved in community service projects (cleaning up the environment, helping the homeless, volunteering in political campaigns)
- taking part in religious observances and traditions
- enjoying travel and family outings

Try to avoid making participation in these activities or sharing in family fun conditional on success in school. All children need to believe that they belong and have value independent of their abilities to perform academically. This is especially important for students with learning disabilities, whose progress in school is so often slow or erratic. "Becoming overfocused on school performance is a trap that catches many parents of students with learning disabilities," says one special education teacher. "So many try to take on the job of trying to teach their kids what they have been unable to learn in school. What this can mean, though, is that the kids never get a break. What children usually need most when they get home is love, acceptance, and a reduction of stress. These are gifts parents are uniquely equipped to provide."

In the following two chapters we will discuss constructive things parents can do to support students academically. In Part IV we will talk more about emotional support, and we will also look at how different parenting styles affect children's progress in school. In the meantime, if your instincts are telling you that your student has struggled enough for one day, trust your gut and arrange something fun. In the end, your understanding and encouragement ("You're a hard worker, and I'm proud of you for sticking with that tough job! How about a popcorn break?") will do your child as much good as finishing those last three vocabulary words or math problems.

Once they become involved at school, many parents find themselves expanding their interests and activism beyond their children's immediate needs. Some volunteer in classrooms and become active in parent-teacher organizations, while others serve on administrative committees that oversee the educations of students with disabilities or plan new programs and services. When one mother found there were so few computers at her son's elementary school that he had problems getting access to one on a regular basis, she teamed up with another parent to write a series of grant applications that eventually provided the school with forty personal computers! Working with organizations like the Learning Disabilities Association of America, parents have also been instrumental in shaping state and national policies concerning the rights of students with disabilities and their families. In fact, without parent activists, it is unlikely that students with learning disabilities would have many of the protections and services to which they are now legally entitled.

There is still, however, a great deal of work to be done. In too many schools, a lack of awareness of the needs of students with disabilities, inadequate support for teachers, inflexible scheduling and curriculum requirements, shortages of appropriate equipment and materials, and the absence of a clear special education philosophy continue to impede quality programming. These issues need to be addressed on a school-by-school basis. The schools at which these issues are resolved successfully will almost certainly be those where parents have become actively involved, both in asking for change and in working to bring change about.

What Is Universal Design for Learning?

One of the most exciting trends in education today is growing recognition that many children who do *not* have disabilities benefit from the same kinds of curricula and teaching modifications that are traditionally used with special education populations. Teachers are being increasingly encouraged to apply these strategies classroomwide as a means of making instruction more accessible to students with a broad range of abilities and learning styles. This approach—called Universal Design for Learning (UDL)—can hugely improve educational opportunities in almost any classroom. When instruction is universally designed, the need for accommodations and modifications for students with disabilities is reduced. At the same time, the flexibility built into classroom activities supports other students who may be struggling and provides an environment in which typical and gifted students thrive.

Universal Design for Learning focuses on three major principles:

   1. Content to be learned should be presented in multiple ways and at multiple levels, so that all students will be able to understand it. For a unit on Greek mythology, for example, books at several different reading levels might be provided, a film based on Greek myths might be viewed, and the teacher might read some myths aloud to the class.
   2. Each student should be encouraged to engage with the material according to the way he or she learns best. Students might have the option of working individually or in groups to write and illustrate a myth of their own. Students working in groups would be offered multiple ways to contribute (for example, some students might dictate story ideas to a "scribe" who writes them down; others would plan and execute illustrations).
   3. Students should be provided with a variety of ways to demonstrate what they have learned. Instead of using a single test to evaluate all students, the teacher offers options: essays, multiple-choice tests, graphic and oral presentations, and a skit or play might all be acceptable ways of demonstrating knowledge of Greek myths, for example.

   Classroom teachers implementing UDL also make frequent use of such "special education" strategies as

* *Helping with task organization:* Students with learning disabilities benefit when teachers help them break down complex tasks (like science experiments or re-

continued

search projects) into a sequence of subtasks to be completed, but so do many others—and no student is harmed by this practice. All students gain when teachers show them how to organize information according to their strongest learning channels (make charts, lists, outlines, pictures; dictate questions and answers into a voice recorder . . .). Providing clear instructions and deadlines for completing stages of work helps all students organize their time.

- *Providing direct instruction:* Stating the main point of a lesson in advance, highlighting key subpoints, and summarizing the most important information to remember at the end of a lesson helps almost any student focus better on new material. Teaching the use of memory "tricks" (such as associating rhymes or pictures with new information) enables students who don't think of these strategies on their own to retain information better.

- *Using multimodal activities:* Many children do best when teachers encourage them to use their eyes, their ears, and their hands to learn. Since three-dimensional objects draw attention, use of concrete objects helps engage students in their lessons (as when children are encouraged to count poker chips when learning to add and subtract, or "hands-on" experiments are used to demonstrate science principles). Activity-based instruction (such as using algebra concepts to build a ramp) offers children who have difficulty with traditional paper-and-pencil exercises another path to success.

- *Adjusting for information-processing speed:* Very few students gain anything from timed assignments and tests. Offering options that take off the time pressure (take a multiple-choice test in one long or two short sessions, or write an open-book essay at home, for example) provides students who process information more slowly the opportunity to fully demonstrate what they know. Speaking slowly helps children who have auditory-processing weaknesses, but it will not bore the rapid learner. (Waiting three to five seconds after asking a question gives most children time to formulate a response.)

- *Matching tasks to students' strengths, needs, and cognitive styles:* No valid educational principle supports the idea that every child in a class must be given the same homework. In a class where UDL is being implemented, some students will read assigned books while others listen to them on CD or use talking e-book readers. (Book reports can be written or given orally, or even done through producing a mural or play.) Students will practice new skills at a rate that doesn't overload their cognitive capacity (some students can handle twenty-five vocabulary words in one night, but those who learn best with smaller chunks of information will be told to learn five each night). Students who work well independently will be encouraged to do so, but those who do not will be offered alternatives (students with attention deficits will be given work in small batches with appropriate rewards when each batch is completed; "study buddies" will be encouraged to review material together and quiz each other on new information).

- *Removing distractions:* Sometimes teaching materials in the classroom itself call children's attention away from what they are supposed to be learning. Reducing the amount of "stuff" hanging all over the room, separating students with bookshelves to cut down on noisy chatter, and covering pictures on a page to help students concentrate on text are just a few of the techniques that can help students focus their attention. Strategies that help students locate key information—such as color-coding the signs in math or different categories of information (red paper for the list of democracies, blue paper for the list of authoritarian regimes) can help all students focus better.

Does using UDL make a teacher's job harder? Not necessarily—but it does involve a significant "paradigm shift" from the way most teachers are used to doing business. Schools interested in implementing UDL need to provide teacher education and support to make it work. Many teachers who do invest in learning to implement UDL, however, say they are so impressed with the gains in student achievement and enthusiasm for education that they would never go back to traditional methods of instruction.

Parent advocates are often instrumental in introducing the concepts of Universal Design in Learning to their children's schools. Even if UDL is not being used schoolwide, you may be able to persuade your child's teachers to adopt elements of it (offering all students in the class a choice of alternative testing procedures, for example). At the very least, the principles of UDL give you a comeback to the teacher who insists that allowing your child to use a calculator (or any other accommodation) is unfair: "You may be right," you can say. "How about if we make calculators [or accommodations] available to everyone?"

8

Developing an Effective Educational Program

Once a learning disability has been identified, federal law requires that an Individualized Education Program (IEP) be developed within thirty days. The law also requires school districts to make an effort to include parents in the program-planning process.* Therefore, soon after eligibility for special education services has been determined, you will receive a written invitation to participate in an IEP meeting. The purpose of this meeting is to present professional views of your child's learning issues, inform you of available educational options, secure your ideas about what your child needs, and obtain your consent for special education services. At the IEP meeting the school district will be represented by a team that includes one or more representatives of the department of special education, at least one of your child's general education teachers, a school representative knowledgeable about children with disabilities and the school district's re-

* Federal regulations apply only to institutions receiving public funds. Private and parochial schools do not necessarily observe these procedures. Parents should be aware, however, that special-needs students enrolled in private and parochial schools are entitled to many free services from their public school districts, including speech therapy, physical and occupational therapies, and special education. For additional information, contact your school district's department of special education.

sources (often the director of special education or a principal); and an individual who can interpret the instructional implications of the evaluation results. You are entitled to bring anyone you would like to have present to support you or your child (friends, family members, or outside professionals).

Among the specific issues to be covered at an IEP meeting are the following:

- What are the child's present levels of achievement?

- How do the child's learning problems affect participation and progress in the general education curriculum?

- What special services does the student require? (Summaries of service must include statements of frequency and duration—for example, how many reading sessions a week, how many minutes per session.)

- Who will deliver these services, and where will they be provided?

- What specific goals for academic and behavioral performance should be established for the coming year?

- How will progress toward those goals be measured and reported?

- If the child will not participate with nondisabled peers in the regular classroom or extracurricular activities, why is alternate placement necessary?

- What special methods and materials will be used to teach the child? (This discussion should include information on why these particular materials have been chosen.)

- What (if any) special equipment or technical support will be provided?

- What kind of accommodations and/or modifications in the child's program will be allowed?

- How will the child participate in state and federally mandated testing? Which specific test accommodations will be necessary?

The outcome of the decisions made at the IEP meeting is summarized in writing in an IEP document. This document becomes the blueprint for your child's education for the following year. Once the IEP document is complete, federal law requires that the described program be implemented as soon as possible. The IEP must be reviewed and (if necessary) revised at least once a year.

Experienced parents note that it pays to go into IEP meetings prepared. "Don't count on the school district doing a thorough job of going over your rights or explaining how the special education system works," one mother cautions. "There usually isn't time. Our district schedules thirty to forty-five minutes for an IEP meeting—barely enough to discuss specific recommendations for the child." Unprepared parents also risk feeling outranked by professionals at IEP meetings; many say that, as beginners, they found themselves agreeing to recommendations without fully understanding the implications of their decisions. While programs can, of course, be changed if they prove ineffective or inappropriate, it is obviously better if a student can be put solidly on the road to success from the beginning.

What do you need to know to plan an effective educational program? The first step is to be clear on what types of help your child needs. Although IEPs must be highly individualized to meet the combinations of needs unique to each student, nearly all programs for children with learning disabilities must include four basic components in order to be successful. One of a parent's most important responsibilities is to make sure that the school district covers all four of these bases, described below.

THE PROGRAM MUST TEACH
AND REINFORCE BASIC SKILLS

Students with learning disabilities usually need both individualized instruction and a lot of extra practice in order to master basic skills (reading decoding, reading comprehension, written expression, math reasoning and/or performing arithmetic calculations). Specialized texts and teaching materials may also be required. The child's program should provide both teaching that is appropriate for the student's basic-skills level and adequate opportunities to practice new skills as they develop. Usually, this kind of instruction needs to be delivered one-to-one or in a small-group setting. Basic-skills instruction may require a substantial commitment of time in the early stages of a special education program. As students progress, time allocated for this work typically decreases.

Most students with learning disabilities benefit from a "back-to-basics" approach to skills development, especially for reading. Research indicates that nearly all these students need a thorough grounding in phonics (that is, learning to decode words by sounding them out) in order to read successfully. No matter what instructional methods and materials are being used, progress in basic skills needs to be closely monitored to make sure that the programs are consistently effective. If a student does not start showing improvement within three months of starting a new reading or other basic-skills curriculum, then the program should probably be reevaluated.

Basic-skills instruction must be governed by realistic expectations. Not all children with learning disabilities can reach average levels in reading, writing, and arithmetic, even with years of remedial help. For a student with severe language-processing disabilities, basic literacy (often defined as reading at a third- or fourth-grade level) might be the highest attainable goal. Many students with learning disabilities will never be good spellers, and higher mathematics will always remain a mystery for some. In cases such as these, it is very important to teach students *compensatory skills*—ways of getting around what remains of their disabilities—so they can go on to achieve their personal goals. "There is a big difference between being illiterate and being uneducated," a special education teacher explains. "Even a person who can't read or write at all can become educated if he knows other ways to get and give information. Part of the school system's job is to teach the student with disabilities exactly what those other ways are."

Note that students who are struggling with basic skills are at risk for being "tracked" into lower-achievement classes for *all* their academic subjects, a practice that contributes to underachievement and robs these students of self-esteem. For students with learning disabilities, selection of classes and activities should be guided by intellectual ability, not basic-skill level. A bright student with poor reading skills can succeed in advanced English and history classes given appropriate accommodations and supports. Parents may have to advocate for class placements that allow children to explore the full range of their abilities and talents.

THE PROGRAM MUST ENABLE THE STUDENT TO KEEP UP WITH CLASS CONTENT

Students with learning disabilities often have trouble keeping on top of subjects like health, science, and social studies, either because material is presented in a way that is inaccessible to them (for example, textbooks are beyond their reading capabilities, or lectures and demonstrations are too fast paced for them to follow) or because getting special help removes them from the classroom for substantial periods of time. To prevent this problem, it may be necessary to modify to some extent academic tasks for students with information-processing weaknesses. For example, if a student has trouble keeping up with assigned reading, material can be read to the child, a simpler book can be substituted, or—if text is not essential to understanding a subject—reading material can be reduced or eliminated. Students who have trouble writing can be provided with copies of lecture notes, allowed to take some tests orally, and permitted to dictate long reports. It is also possible (and a good idea) to restructure some assignments so that students can work from a position of strength. Instead of writing a report on a South American country, for instance, a student might be asked to build a relief map of South America for the class or to design a poster illustrating major exports.

The checklist on pages 194–97 describes some modifications and accommodations that are frequently used to help students compensate for learning disabilities. It is essential to employ as many of these as necessary to enable a child to keep up in class. It is also important to pay careful attention to scheduling so that valuable elements of a child's program do not conflict. If a student is to leave class for special help in reading, for example, every effort should be made to schedule that help during the class reading period rather than at a time that would compel the child to miss enrichment activities or instruction in other subject areas. When a child must miss instruction in a content area in order to get special education, it may be necessary to release the student from some academic obligations in order to avoid overburdening him. (For example, a fifth-grader who needs three hours of special basic-skills instruction a day might be exempted from health education and state history lessons, neither of which would be essential to success in sixth grade.) Whenever practical, basic-skills instruction and course work should be combined—as when a learning specialist uses a simplified version of the history text to teach reading, or a science lesson to reinforce math principles.

A well-designed special education program provides the support a child needs to participate as fully as possible in the general education curriculum. Beware, however, of the hazards of overaccommodation. "Don't let the school system get away with saying 'We've given Johnny all his books on tape, so we don't have to teach him to read,'" a special educator warns. "These supports are intended to help students keep up with class content—not to enable the school to avoid doing its job." Excessive accommodation can also rob students of the opportunities they need to practice what they have been taught: if you let Johnny dictate *all* his assignments, his writing skills will never improve. Overmodification of the academic program can furthermore leave a student ill equipped to pass tests that might have a major impact on his or her future (see High-Stakes Testing, page 198). "You don't want your child to be overwhelmed," a mother cautions, "but you *do* want him to be held accountable for the highest level of work he is capable of. Teachers tend to underestimate these kids. Accepting accommodations should not be accompanied by unnecessary lowering of expectations."

Modifications and Accommodations for Students with Learning Disabilities

Modifications and accommodations such as those listed below can be either formally specified on students' Individual Education Programs (IEPs) or worked out informally with teachers and school administrators. When they are specified on an IEP, all the child's teachers are legally required to comply with them. In most cases, accommodations and modifications specified on a high school IEP will continue to be honored by colleges and vocational programs, provided that the assessment on which they are based is fairly recent. Students with documented disabilities are also allowed some accommodations on college entrance exams (SATs and ACTs) and state and national competency tests. (For the SAT and ACTs, LD documentation within the past five years is required when requesting accommodations.)

Note that the term *modifications* usually refers to making changes (to texts, course content, teaching strategies, and testing methods, for example) that may alter and/or lower expectations for a particular child. *Accommodations* are supports that enable students to work around disabilities (slow reading or labored writing, for example) so they can meet the same standards as everyone else in the class.

In the Classroom

- Allow preferred seating (near the teacher, close to the blackboard).
- Allow extra time to answer questions and to complete written work.
- Provide copies of laboratory or lecture notes (notes can be provided by either the teacher or another student).
- Allow use of a device to record lectures.
- Allow use of a calculator.
- Provide access to a computer and/or allow use of a portable keyboard for writing.
- Allow alternative assignments (e.g., ask the student to prepare a video or submit an annotated bibliography instead of writing a report).

THE PROGRAM MUST HELP THE STUDENT LEARN APPROPRIATE EDUCATIONAL STRATEGIES

The most heroic efforts to keep a student on course with the curriculum won't count for much if they produce a young adult who cannot learn independently. That is what can happen, however, if

- Highlight texts and worksheets to help student focus on the most important material.
- Provide instructions both orally and in writing.
- Provide more or fewer visual aids (depending on the child's needs).
- Provide ready access to math tables, lists of formulas, maps, and so on (rather than requiring the student to memorize such material).
- Assign lab or study partners to help with particular tasks or subjects.
- Preview written material (discuss contents of assigned texts in advance); pre-teach key vocabulary words.
- Exempt student from selected requirements or activities (e.g., memorize periodic tables, oral math drills).
- Provide easier versions of reading material (e.g., a history text that contains fewer facts to memorize).
- Use "study buddies" to read difficult material to the child.

Testing
- Allow alternate settings (student may take tests in library, resource room, at home).
- Allow flexible scheduling (student may take tests after school or during study hall or resource period; tests may be completed in two or more sessions).
- Extend or waive time limits.
- Allow directions and test questions to be read to student and repeated if required.
- Rephrase test questions in simpler language as necessary.
- Allow the student to answer questions orally instead of in writing.
- Allow short-answer-only tests (true/false, multiple choice).
- Allow essay-only tests.

continued

youngsters with learning disabilities are not taught organizational and time-management skills, effective study habits, methods to improve memory, problem-solving and decision-making strategies, and self-advocacy skills. For most students, these skills are essential to academic survival; test and homework failures can have as much

- Allow use of a calculator or math-facts chart.
- If the student is unable to memorize, allow access to dates/facts/formulas on "cheat sheets."
- Allow tests to be taken on a computer (at school or at home).
- Allow the student to circle answers in a test booklet rather than use a computerized answer sheet.
- Reduce the number of test questions or problems (the student is tested on ten division problems or vocabulary words rather than twenty-five).
- Allow alternative evaluation methods (portfolio, oral or video presentations, plays, performances).

Homework

- Give students homework assignments in writing on a daily or weekly basis (as opposed to giving assignments orally or expecting them to be copied from board).
- Provide assistance with organization and planning of assigned work.
- Arrange for textbooks on tape, e-book reader, or MP3 player.
- Allow all or part of assigned texts to be read to student.
- Allow use of computers to scan and "read aloud" written material.
- Reduce the total amount of material to be read (teacher highlights key passages, for example).
- Provide texts rewritten in simpler language.
- Provide text alternatives (permit student to watch the movie version of *To Kill a Mockingbird* instead of reading it).
- Allow students to record assignments on CD rather than writing them.
- Arrange for students to dictate reports to a "scribe" (often a parent) or give reports orally.
- Reduce the number of questions to be answered and/or length of written

to do with forgotten deadlines, books that were left at school, and failure to ask for help as with basic-skills deficits or information-processing problems.

The Metacognitive Skills checklist in Chapter 6 (pages 148–49) lists areas in which children with disabilities are likely to need direct instruction. Help needs to be provided at a level that is appropriassignments (answer five comprehension questions instead of ten; write a three-page rather than a five-page report).

- Use a grading policy of no points off for spelling errors.
- Encourage assistance of a proofreader to locate and correct spelling/punctuation errors.
- Encourage use of computer with spell-checker.
- Allow use of *Cliff Notes* or prepared outlines for previewing, organizing, and reviewing text material.
- Provide the child a CD on which the teacher has recorded the text material (substituting easier language if necessary, deleting unnecessary details, highlighting the most important content [e.g., here is the overarching theme], or organizing the content [the three most important contributors to the war were . . .].

Overall Program Planning

- Consider extended time to complete the educational program (e.g., five years to complete high school) so the course load can be reduced to more manageable levels each year. Public school students are legally entitled to remain in school through age twenty-one. Students have successfully negotiated with colleges to spread four years of courses over five years without incurring additional tuition charges.
- Grant exemption from foreign language requirement. (If college graduation requires a foreign language proficiency, sign language often is an acceptable language alternative.)
- Encourage the student to take some courses in summer school in order to reduce the course load during the academic year.
- Allow computer technology courses to be substituted for higher-level math courses.
- Design independent study or work/study courses to meet some requirements.

ate to the student's age. For example, while youngsters can start to learn basic organizational skills (such as keeping books and school supplies in a special place, and having a regular time for doing chores or schoolwork) as young as five or six, not many are ready for work on memorization or problem-solving strategies before the fourth or fifth grade. (Keep children's memory capabilities in mind at home,

High-Stakes Testing

Before the passage of the No Child Left Behind Act of 2001 (NCLB), children with disabilities were often excused from state-mandated standardized tests. Tests of student achievement are used, in part, to judge how well *schools* are performing. Educators were concerned that including the scores of students with disabilities would "drag down" school achievement averages.

NCLB requires, however, that *all* students participate in tests of proficiency in reading/language arts and math (given annually in grades 3–8 and once during grades 10–12) and in science (given once during grades 3–5, once during grades 6–9, and once during grades 10–12). Although alternate assessments are available for students with multiple or severe disabilities (and those new to learning English as a second language) the great majority of students with LD take these tests alongside typical peers in regular classrooms, sometimes with accommodations (which must be permitted by law).

Including students with LD in these assessments has produced some meaningful gains. For the first time, both parents and schools have an objective means of measuring exactly how effectively students with learning disabilities are being taught. In many schools, this has resulted in a stepped-up effort to teach them. Since under NCLB students with disabilities are expected to meet the same proficiency standards as typical learners, it no longer benefits the school to isolate these students or offer them a "watered-down" version of the curriculum. Expectations for these students have been raised, and the students have responded: they are participating in the general education curriculum and passing standardized achievement tests in greater numbers every year.

Not all LD students are benefiting, however. Under NCLB, those who are significantly behind in reading or math must still take grade-level tests in these subjects, and the experience can be discouraging for them. If the state has attached *stakes* to standard-

too. Most first-graders will have to be reminded to do chores. Ten- and eleven-year-olds, however, can be taught strategies for reminding themselves, such as posting notes on a bulletin board or marking the chores on a calendar.) The importance of metacognitive skills increases dramatically when students enter secondary school. For this reason, the introduction of learning-strategies instruction should not be delayed beyond seventh grade if at all possible.

ized tests, consequences of failing them can be serious. For example, twenty-six states now have or plan to implement "exit exams," which must be passed in order to receive a high school diploma. Seventeen states now require students to pass standardized tests at some point in order to be promoted to the next grade. In some cases, these policies have been put in place by local education authorities even when the state does not require them. (NCLB itself attaches no penalties to failing required tests, but some state and local educational authorities use the same tests for promotion/graduation decisions and meeting NCLB requirements.)

Students with LD are disproportionately impacted by high-stakes testing. These children fail these tests at higher rates than typical learners, and are at increased risk for retention (even though retention usually has no benefit for these students) and failure to graduate (either because they drop out or are awarded alternate diplomas or certificates that are not recognized by most colleges and employers). It is therefore important for parents to make themselves aware of state and local testing and proficiency requirements. (NCLB requires tests of proficiency, but each state sets its own proficiency standards.) Among the questions to ask are these:

- What standardized tests will my child be expected to take? Which are state and locally mandated, and which are required by NCLB? Are alternative assessments allowed for students with learning disabilities?

- What are the consequences of failing these tests? Do scores impact promotion and/or graduation? Note that under NCLB, public schools must provide additional support to students who fail required tests; if your child does poorly, it is reasonable to ask what additional instruction or other programming will be offered to help him improve.

continued

Self-advocacy is among the most important skills a student with learning disabilities can master, yet teaching this skill is often overlooked. Both parents and teachers sometimes get so used to "managing" a student's program that they forget that a time comes when it is proper to step aside and let the student take over. Children need to be helped to understand their own learning strengths and weaknesses, taught when and how to ask for assistance, and encouraged

- Are students being taught the same information they are to be tested on? Do both regular and special education teachers understand the state's standards for both skills and content? Most classroom teachers do (at least for their own grade levels), but recent surveys suggest that many special education teachers do not. What is the school district doing to improve special educators' abilities to help students meet proficiency standards?

- What accommodations can be used during these tests? NCLB mandates that accommodations must be allowed for children with disabilities on required tests. The accommodations allowed for testing, however, won't necessarily be the same as those permitted in the classroom. Ask your special education department for a list of accommodations that are approved by your state for standardized testing, and make sure the ones your child will need are listed on her IEP. It is wise to practice with a given accommodation (giving dictation or

to communicate and negotiate with teachers on their own behalf. Youngsters must also learn appropriate uses of self-advocacy: seeking a reasonable accommodation like extra time to finish a test is fine, but using a disability as an excuse to avoid taking an exam altogether is not.

Self-determination, knowing what one wants—and figuring out how to get it—is another important life skill. Both at home and at school, students with learning disabilities need encouragement and guidance to identify important issues in their lives, set goals, recognize problems or obstacles, and devise solutions or work-arounds. Practicing these skills becomes especially important as students approach the transition from school to the world of work or higher education. Students who are adept at these processes have the greatest potential to become independent young adults.

Note that it is appropriate for secondary-school students (and mature younger children) to attend IEP meetings and participate in setting educational goals. Teens especially tend to become more cooperative and enthusiastic about their programs if they are involved in the planning process.

listening to a reader, for example) so that the child is comfortable with its use well before the test. (Note that accommodations cannot avoid the objective being measured. When the ability to read itself is being assessed, for example, the material cannot be read to the student.)

- How can we connect IEP goals to proficiency standards? Some school districts now use *Standards-Based IEPs*, in which a child's levels of achievement are described in relation to requirements for the student's enrolled grade, and goals are written specifically to address how a student's skills and content knowledge can be brought closer to grade-level standards. Whether or not your school uses this system, IEP committees should demonstrate awareness of state proficiency expectations for each grade level and be prepared to address how to close any gaps between that standard and your child's present level of performance.

THE PROGRAM MUST HELP THE STUDENT ADDRESS PROBLEM BEHAVIORS

Students with learning disabilities often need help learning how to modify behaviors that interfere with functioning in a classroom. Most common among these are difficulties with focusing attention, staying on task, controlling impulsive behavior, and managing anger. Some shy students need help learning to become more assertive about asking for help and/or participating in class activities. Learning appropriate social skills, an important (but often overlooked) element of school survival, can pay off in improved peer acceptance of students with learning disabilities.

Teachers use many methods of behavior management, but the most successful tend to employ *positive reinforcement*. This involves making an effort to "catch the child being good" and rewarding desirable behavior, as opposed to giving children attention mostly when they act up or step out of line. Methods centered on punishment rarely succeed in effecting long-term behavior changes; sarcasm, ridicule, and humiliation are bad for all children and should never be used as methods of "motivation." To be most effective, sys-

Discipline for Students with Disabilities

Schools have a responsibility to provide a safe environment, and to take action when students violate established codes of conduct. If disruptive or disorderly conduct is substantially caused by a student's disability or an improperly implemented IEP, however, the school must follow federally mandated guidelines when considering suspension or expulsion in order to avoid penalizing the student unfairly.

Suspension: Students with disabilities who violate rules may be suspended for up to ten days. If the student's behavior requires a suspension longer than that (or if the student is receiving repeated suspensions), the law requires a special IEP meeting to

- assess the problem behavior and identify reasons for it;
- develop a Behavior Intervention Plan that includes strategies, program modifications, and supports that will help improve the student's behavior; and
- establish a short-term Interim Alternative Education Setting in which the student will continue to receive both regular and special education instruction while problem behaviors are being addressed. Students must be provided with the means of making satisfactory progress toward IEP goals even though they are not in their regular classes.

Expulsion: A student cannot be expelled for behavior that is found to be related to a specific disability. Schools may move a student to an alternative setting for up to forty-five school days, however, when conduct violations involve any of the following:

- weapons: applies if students bring weapons to school or school functions beyond the school grounds
- drugs: applies to possession, use, or sale of illegal drugs while at school or at a school activity
- serious bodily injury: applies if a student inflicts serious harm to another person either on school premises or at a school function

Note that federal guidelines do not apply when problematic behavior is not related to a student's disability. For example, an impulsive student with ADHD who damages property in a rage over being chosen last for the relay team would probably be covered under the law. If a student with language-processing delays behaves the same way, the behavior likely would be considered unrelated to his disability, and he would be disciplined like any other student.

tems of behavior modification need to be practiced by all the child's teachers—and also reinforced at home. Parent-teacher cooperation is often the key to real improvement. (If parents and teachers both agree to recognize and praise efforts to improve handwriting, for example, children will probably improve faster than when either parents or teachers target the issue on their own.) Note that the IEP process requires the team to plan for positive behavioral interventions to address any behavior that impedes a child's learning. In the case of seriously disruptive or violent behavior, schools must follow federally mandated guidelines when meting out discipline to students with disabilities, if the disability contributes substantially to rule violations (see box).

For children who suffer from attention-deficit/hyperactivity disorder (ADHD), medication (most commonly with stimulants like Ritalin) can also play a role in behavior management. The decision to use medication must be made cautiously, however. Some experts feel that Ritalin has been vastly overprescribed and is too often given to normal, high-energy youngsters by physicians who know little about ADHD. It must also be noted that stimulant medications can have side effects that need to be weighed against potential benefits. In the box on pages 204–7 the pros and cons of medication for ADHD are discussed so that you can make an informed choice on this issue. Keep in mind, though, that medication should be viewed as only one element in a multilevel program of support. The best medication can do is improve focus and help children become better prepared to learn; skilled instructors still need to be on board to do the teaching.

In IEP meetings, parents may have to advocate for measures that address a student's individual needs in each of the four key areas described above. "Special education committees often suffer from tunnel vision," one mother comments. "They focus on academic goals, sometimes to the exclusion of everything else. Behavior modification might be suggested if a child is really out of control—but for a child who is quiet and doesn't speak up enough? Not likely." Social-skills training and help with learning strategies and self-determination may also not be provided unless parents specifically ask for

Medication for Attention Deficits and Hyperactivity

For more than fifty years, stimulant medications such as methylphenidate (Ritalin), dextroamphetamine (Dexedrine), and pemoline (Cylert) have been used to "normalize" the behavior of children who exhibit symptoms of attention-deficit/hyperactivity disorder (ADHD, described in Chapter 2). More recently introduced stimulants include Adderall and Concerta. These medications are believed to stimulate children's underaroused central nervous systems by increasing the amount or efficiency of neurotransmitters that regulate attention, concentration, organization, and planning. Studies indicate that as many as 80 percent of students with ADHD respond to stimulants positively.

Research indicates that use of stimulants to improve availability for learning can lead to short-term gains in academic achievement. Several studies have found improvement in test scores and accuracy, quantity and speed of completing daily assignments, short-term memory, problem-solving, and handwriting after students with ADHD started taking stimulants. Improved motor coordination and social relations, increase in appropriate behaviors and emotional control, and reduction of disruptive behavior (breaking rules, leaving one's place, talking out of turn) are also commonly reported. While medication alone is very effective, many studies find that when behavior modification and special education intervention accompany medication, learning, behavior, and self-esteem can improve even more and medication dosage may be reduced. Research shows that students who receive multiple interventions are the most likely to make long-term gains in their behavior and educational achievement.

The most common side effects associated with use of stimulant medications are reduction of appetite, weight loss, and difficulty falling asleep. These problems sometimes disappear after children become accustomed to the medication; if they persist, a change in dosage or type of drug may bring improvement. (Some doctors recom-

them. Even when addressing academic concerns, committees can overfocus. "My son's reading problems always got attention at IEP meetings," another mother remembers, "but I usually had to remind the committee that he needed some help with his writing, too."

Since a student's program must be described in terms of written goals and objectives on the IEP document, it will help if you arrive at the IEP meeting prepared to state in the clearest terms possible what mend medicating students during school hours only, so that stimulants won't interfere with dinner and bedtime. Others say use of Ritalin at bedtime may help children calm down for sleep.) Research also indicates a mild slowing of the growth of children taking stimulants. The growth of children taking low to moderate doses of Ritalin usually rebounds after the first year. The growth of those taking Dexedrine or higher doses of Ritalin may be slow as long as they remain on medication, but studies indicate these students also return to normal growth patterns when drug therapy stops. Some experts advise "drug holidays" during vacation periods to allow children's growth to catch up. Others note that because not all education takes place during school hours, it may be best to leave children on medication so they can take full advantage of all their learning opportunities.

Less common effects of stimulants include headaches, dizziness, stomachaches, lethargy, irritability, talkativeness, nausea, euphoria, depression, nightmares, dry mouth, constipation, anxiety, hallucinations, nervous tics, and tremors. If a child seems depressed, or the child's personality appears dulled, the dosage may need to be lowered or a change of medication considered. Parents should be aware that Cylert has been occasionally associated with liver problems. Some research indicates that stimulants can bring on symptoms of Tourette's syndrome or make tics worse, so treatment with stimulants should be avoided by children who are anxious, tense, or at risk for tic disorders.

Students who are interested in competitive sports, careers in the military, or jobs requiring drug testing need to understand that stimulant medications will register as a controlled substance on urine tests. When such tests are required it is important to alert coaches and employers that the student takes stimulants as a legitimately prescribed medication.

continued

you want for your child. The final goals and objectives should have the following characteristics:

> *Realistic:* Objectives must take into account the student's present levels of achievement, and they should describe gains that can be made within one year. "Tim will score within the average range for math computation" is not a realistic objective if Tim is

If adjusting dosage does not eliminate adverse side effects or does not improve attention and concentration, parents may want to discuss alternatives to stimulants with their physicians. Clonodine (a medication normally used to treat hypertension) has helped some people who have both ADHD and Tourette's syndrome. Antidepressant drugs such as imipramine have also been found to help some youngsters who cannot tolerate or do not respond to stimulants. Strattera, another nonstimulant, has been found helpful to many with ADHD, but this medication has been associated with an increase in liver problems and suicidal thoughts in some children. Since the research on the safety and effectiveness of nonstimulants is sparse, these medications generally are considered only when stimulants have proved unhelpful.

Concerns about use of stimulants leading to addiction are not supported by research to date. While some stimulants (notably amphetamines) can become addictive if abused by adolescents or adults, low therapeutic doses appear to be safe for children. Children do not build up a tolerance for these medications or become dependent on them, nor do they become more likely to abuse other drugs later on. In contrast, there are studies suggesting that *untreated* children with ADHD may be at increased risk for alcohol and drug abuse as teens. Authorities relate the substance abuse to the high rate of academic failure and low self-esteem often found in this population.

Successful drug therapy depends on finding the right medication, as well as the lowest effective dosage for each child. Since optimum dosage cannot be predicted from a child's weight, children need to be tested on a range of doses to determine the one that best enhances attention and engagement at school. Since children often respond favorably to one stimulant but not another, it may also be necessary to try two or three different drugs before finding one that works. (Note that youngsters may remain energetic and somewhat impulsive even after starting medication; the goal is only to improve their attention, not to drug them into a zombie-like state.) Since drug responses are

a sixth-grader starting out with second-grade math skills. "Tim will complete three-column addition and subtraction problems with 90 percent accuracy and learn to use a calculator for problems involving multiplication and division" is more realistic.

Specific: "Darnell will improve his self-esteem" describes a worthy goal, but how will Darnell's program accomplish it? "Darnell will be given leadership responsibility as a crossing guard" highly individual, frequent monitoring and adjustments of dosage may be needed at the beginning of treatment. This process involves collecting ratings of attention, hyperactivity, impulsivity, and academic and social functioning from parents and teachers. Periodic dosage adjustments may also be required as children get older. In addition, parents must be alert to potential drug interactions (the antihistamines in some cold and allergy medications, for example, can neutralize the effects of stimulants). Note that stimulants come in short-acting (wears off in five hours) and longer-acting (wears off in eight to twelve hours) dosages. The longer-acting agents are becoming more popular, as they avoid the attention ups and downs of short-acting agents and also relieve school personnel of the responsibility for distributing and monitoring student medications.

It is important to be aware that medication is a long-term treatment. The National Institute of Mental Health (NIMH) estimates that 80 percent of individuals who need medication for ADHD as children will continue to need it as teenagers; 50 percent will benefit from taking stimulant medication as adults. (Note that stimulants are not approved for use by children under the age of six.)

Experts at NIMH urge parents to "remember that many things, including anxiety, depression, allergies, seizures, or problems with the home or school environment can make children seem overactive, impulsive or inattentive." In addition to finding a physician knowledgeable about treating ADHD (this might be a neurologist, a psychiatrist, or a pediatrician), it is important to conduct a comprehensive educational evaluation so that all factors contributing to a student's behavior and achievement problems can be understood. About a third of students with ADHD have additional learning disabilities that require special education intervention. Psychotherapy, social-skills training, and vocational counseling may be needed to address social, emotional, and employment issues. Sometimes dealing with these concerns effectively makes use of medication unnecessary.

and "Darnell will use his advanced art skills to make posters for school activities" are specific objectives targeting self-esteem.

Measurable: "Nicole will improve her vocational skills" is too vague an objective to be useful for guiding instruction. "Nicole will complete the career-explorations program, target an area of interest, and participate in a short internship" is a statement describing expectations that can be measured.

All the modifications, accommodations, and exemptions to which the child is entitled should also be included in the IEP document. (Remember that accommodations recorded on an IEP are binding on all of a child's teachers unless otherwise specified. "May take tests orally" means a high school student can take oral exams in any class or subject.) If the student is to be provided with access to any type of assistive technology, such as a computer, a calculator, or a voice recorder, this, too, must be included in the IEP. When an assistive device is listed in the IEP, it is the school district's responsibility to purchase the equipment. Use of the equipment may be restricted to school property, however—students will not necessarily be allowed to bring it home. (For a fuller discussion of assistive technology, see Chapter 9.)

If the student needs services in addition to those offered by regular and special education teachers, the IEP document must specify those as well. For example, a child might receive direct or indirect help from the following school specialists:

Reading or math specialists provide remedial instruction to nondisabled low achievers and also help organize and evaluate the reading and math curricula at the school. While the law requires students with learning disabilities to receive basic-skills instruction from special education teachers, reading and math specialists are sometimes called in to help pinpoint problems and advise special educators on materials and methods.

Speech-language pathologists are trained to work with students who have articulation, voice, fluency (stuttering), or language-development disorders. They often help screen entering students for developmental delays.

School psychologists participate in teams that evaluate students for learning disabilities. They also counsel students about a wide variety of nonacademic problems and advise teachers on behavior management and instructional techniques.

Physical and occupational therapists can assist students who have persistent coordination difficulties in addition to providing services for students with physical disabilities.

Audiologists can determine if sound-processing problems or hearing deficits are contributing to learning disabilities. These findings can be used to modify instructional approaches (e.g., teachers need to face students, rather than the board, when speaking) or student seating arrangements. The audiologist may also recommend hearing aids or other assistive devices.

Social workers and guidance counselors are available to help families resolve issues that may be having an impact on a student's learning. They are often instrumental in helping families connect with support services or resources in the community (such as health care or adult-literacy training).

Vocational educators assist with career exploration and help students learn specific employment skills. They can sometimes place students in job-training positions in the community.

If the child is to receive direct services, the duration of each service must be specified on the IEP in addition to specific objectives (it might be determined, for example, that the child will receive speech therapy for three half-hour sessions each week, and that the goal is to increase intelligibility from 60 percent to 85 percent). Once services have been specified on an IEP, the school district is expected to initiate them as soon as possible. (Short delays are permissible if needed to make arrangements for transportation, personnel, or new equipment.)

If assistance from several different specialists is recommended (a speech pathologist, an occupational therapist, and a psychologist, for example), ask who is going to be responsible for coordinating these services and monitoring the student's overall program. Too often, it turns out that nobody is. When this is the case, services can start conflicting with instruction, with recreation, and with each other, and children can become more and more confused because of all the "help" they are getting! To achieve a well-integrated program, somebody has to be watching out for the interests of the whole child—and parents frequently inherit this role.

Be aware, then, that providing too many services can be as troublesome as providing too few. When children have multiple problems or disabilities, prioritizing goals and tackling a few problems at a time is usually better than trying to take on everything at once. If a student has become very depressed about school, for example, get the academic program adjusted, involve the child in satisfying and rewarding activities, and look into counseling first; speech and occupational therapy can wait until the youngster has regained some self-confidence and enthusiasm for education.

An issue of urgent concern for most parents at IEP meetings is "In what kind of class should my child be educated?" School districts are required to provide a range of educational options for students with special needs. The most common—organized from least to most restrictive—are described below (the actual choices in your own district may be greater or more limited than those presented here):

- The child is placed in a regular classroom full-time. The classroom teacher individualizes the environment and modifies the curriculum for the student with the help of an LD specialist (the "teacher-consultant" model).

- The child is placed in a regular classroom full-time. A learning specialist visits the classroom on a regular basis to help special-needs students (the "push-in" model). Sometimes the learning specialist will also work with some nondisabled students (such as the advanced readers) in order to avoid "spotlighting" or stigmatizing children who need special education.

- The child is placed full-time in a class in which there are special education and general education coteachers. Usually there will be a number of special-needs children in such a class, and several different kinds of disabilities may be represented (for example, the class may include children with mild retardation and/or children with emotional problems as well as typical learners and children with learning disabilities).

- The child is placed in a regular classroom, but leaves to get help from a special educator in a learning center or resource room for one to three periods a day. (This—the "pull-out" model—is currently the most common arrangement for students with learning disabilities.) Instruction in the resource room is delivered one-to-one or in small groups.

- The child is placed in a self-contained special education class (a smaller class with more teaching support; all the students have special needs), but is included in regular classes for subjects in which the child's disability will not have a major impact (for example, health, art, music, and gym).

- The child is placed in a special education class full-time. Ideally this class will be located at the student's home school, but it might be necessary to transport the child to another facility. This could be a regular school where there is more in the way of staff, space, equipment, or services for students with disabilities, or a school where all students have special needs. (*Note:* School districts can contract with private schools or individuals to provide pupil services rather than provide them directly. A district *must* seek private placement or support if it cannot provide appropriate services for a special education student in a timely fashion. In these cases, the school district pays tuition and related charges. There is no cost to the family.)

- The child is placed in a residential school. This option is likely to be exercised only if the child has needs so unusual or severe that they cannot possibly be met locally, or has behavior problems serious enough to have involved the criminal justice system.

- The child is schooled at home or in an institution such as a hospital. This option is available for children who have serious illnesses, have been suspended for disciplinary infractions, or have other issues that keep them out of school for extended periods. Teachers visit the home or facility daily to provide individualized instruction. Some parents also choose to teach their own children at home (see box on pages 212–13).

Is Homeschooling the Answer?

"Michael was born two months prematurely and has several disabilities," explains his mother, Mary. "He has very poor fine motor coordination, which affects his writing and his ability to take care of himself; all through elementary school, he needed help with things like tying his shoes and getting his coat buttoned. He also has problems with spatial awareness, some problems with reading comprehension, and attention deficits—it's very hard for him to stick to things." In his nine years of school, Michael has been assigned to several different types of special education programs. Self-contained classes provided the structure and supervision he needs, but they did not always challenge Michael to work up to his full intellectual potential. "His progress in those classes was so slow I ended up hiring tutors after school to teach him to read and write properly," Mary says. Regular classes, however, did not provide Michael with enough individual attention and guidance to keep him on track. "When we tried putting Michael in regular classes, he just fell apart," Mary remembers. "His behavior went all to pieces—like I suddenly had a devil child on my hands."

For junior high, Michael was placed in an inclusive program cotaught by regular and special education teachers. He did reasonably well in this environment, and a similar program was recommended for ninth grade. Unfortunately, the program was not available in Michael's home high school; he would have to be bussed across the city. "I don't think the school and the neighborhood where it's located are safe," Mary explains, "especially for a kid like Michael, who has been protected and isn't that 'streetwise.' I also didn't want to cut Michael off from his neighborhood friends—I think having a social support system is very important." Since nothing the school district could offer looked right for Michael, Mary decided to homeschool him for ninth grade.

Mary and Michael are part of a growing trend in the United States. In the last decade the number of students being educated at home has more than tripled: nearly 3 percent of school-age children (1.5 million students) are now educated at home. It is a choice that has gained increasing acceptance by the educational "establishment." Some school districts have explicit policies of cooperation with homeschoolers, providing books, library privileges, testing, and other support services to parents who wish to educate their own children. Increasingly schools permit children who are homeschooled to participate in sports, extracurricular, and other enrichment activities. In addition, homeschoolers can now turn to a network of local, state, and national organizations for help and information about resources, research, and legal news. While many states don't regulate homeschooling, at least twenty-one states provide online education support specifically for homeschooling families.

Parents who homeschool cite many advantages to their way of life, including their ability to ensure high academic standards, physical safety, moral education, and an education tailored to children's individual talents, needs, and interests. Most admit, however, there is a downside to homeschooling. Social isolation is one difficulty that is widely acknowledged. Some parents note that access to educational materials and resources can also be a problem, and others say they could use help with choosing educational activities and with testing. Parents who have support from their school systems, churches, families, and/or communities have fewer complaints than those trying to "go it alone." In one survey, 92 percent of homeschooling parents indicated that such support was integral to the process. A current trend is for homeschoolers to band together in cooperatives so that the children are educated in groups, with different parents taking responsibility for different parts of the curriculum. Some cooperatives also hire teachers for specialized courses (such as chemistry, physics, calculus, or foreign languages), put on shows, go on field trips, develop competitive sports teams, and even build lending libraries. Many of these parents are doing an excellent job: recent research finds that homeschooled children score higher than the national average on standardized achievement tests.

Parents interested in making the serious investment of time and energy that homeschooling requires should begin by contacting their superintendent of schools for information about state and local policies. All states permit homeschooling and some place no restrictions on homeschoolers. Others hold parents more accountable by overseeing and regulating homeschooling: obligatory standardized testing, specific parental qualification for teaching, and home visits by certified personnel may be required. Keep in mind that federal law guarantees access to special education services for children with disabilities who are educated at home (as well as for those educated in private and parochial schools). Available services include testing for disabilities; speech, physical, and occupational therapy; and individualized help with arithmetic, reading, and writing.

For now, homeschooling is working for Michael and Mary. Mary says two things have helped make the program successful: Mary's aunt (a teacher) set up math and reading programs on a computer for Michael ("I don't have the academic background to teach reading or high school math," Mary admits), and Michael regularly participates in sports at a local recreation center ("That's where he gets exercise and connects with his friends," his mother explains). Mary is undecided, though, about whether she will continue homeschooling next year. "Michael is almost sixteen, and we have to start thinking about how he's going to support himself," she says. "I expect to continue to help Michael with academic skills, but we're also looking over our options for vocational education."

Over the course of a student's education more than one of these options may be utilized. For example, starting out, a third-grade nonreader with a history of behavior problems might need the structure and low student-teacher ratio of a self-contained special education class. When his behavior stabilizes, he can be included in classes that do not require too much in the way of reading. When his reading skills reach "survival" level, he can be educated in a regular classroom with some accommodations and receive continued reading instruction in the resource room. If he learns appropriate self-advocacy and compensatory strategies, this student may well reach a point where he can function successfully in regular classrooms with minimal outside help.

Education experts and parents agree that the type of class in which a child is placed is ultimately less important than what happens *in* that class. "Attaching too much importance to the type of program a child attends can distract parents from looking at issues that could have a far greater impact on the child's success," says the director of a university learning clinic. "The fact is that the 'place' in which services are offered is not a critical factor. What really count are things like the skill and attitudes of the teacher and the atmosphere in the classroom. Is the learning environment pleasant and peaceful or is it noisy and distracting? Do students respect one another or are they disruptive and at odds? Is the teacher organized or disorganized? Rigid or flexible? Are the teacher's instructional style and the student's learning style compatible? All of these considerations are more important than whether a class is labeled regular or special education." Experienced parents echo this view emphatically. "The bottom line is that you have to locate the best teachers," a father of two children with learning disabilities summarizes. "Nine times out of ten, it's the teacher that makes or breaks the program."

Remember that IDEA requires that your child be placed in the "least restrictive environment," as close as possible to the regular educational setting. Before you give final approval to *any* placement, it is a good idea to visit the school, talk with the teacher(s) who would be working with your child, and observe those teachers at work in their classrooms. Although this involves a commitment of time and effort, it is by far the best way to determine whether or not a proposed placement is likely to meet your child's needs. In Chapter 6, we discuss qualities that distinguish excellent teaching. Among these, the ten characteristics of an effective class environment that are of particular benefit to children with learning disabilities are

A manageable class size. Research finds a consistent relationship between class size and academic achievement. Not only are teachers more likely to individualize instruction in smaller classes, but they also tend to have more positive attitudes about students when student-teacher ratios are low. This translates into both greater student participation and higher student self-esteem. When class size exceeds twenty-five students, the quality of education usually declines sharply.

Limited distractions. Excessive background noise and/or clutter can compromise the learning potential of an entire class. Studies show that all students—not just those with learning disabilities—do best in relatively quiet environments with limited visual distractions. Some teachers try to limit distractions further for youngsters with learning disabilities by placing them in isolated corners of the classroom, but this practice is counterproductive (it usually results in less supervision and encouragement from the teacher). Research indicates that students with disabilities do best when seated near the teacher in the front of the classroom.

A teacher who provides effective guidance. Beware of teachers who give the class an assignment and retreat to their desks to grade papers. The best teachers for kids with learning disabilities (and for typical learners as well) are those who spend a high percentage of their time directly involved with students. When students are working independently, good teachers are found moving around the classroom monitoring individual progress, helping students stay on task, checking for understanding, and offering encouragement. Effective teachers also model and reinforce respect for others and good social manners in the classroom.

A noncompetitive atmosphere. Many teachers use "contests" like science fairs, math competitions, and spelling bees to encourage youngsters to study. The classroom's top academic performers may also be given rewards such as stickers, gold stars, or special privileges. This type of motivational technique is likely to *discourage* kids with learning problems. They feel they cannot possibly compete, and in addition may feel shamed and betrayed because their limitations have been publicly exposed. In general, children with learning disabilities do best in classrooms in which students work cooperatively toward shared goals. A team approach to assignments can make a student a valuable player in spite of disabilities (for example, a student who does not read well but has strengths in math might prepare the statistics for a group science report). Look also for a teacher who values personal progress over high grades; the child who moves from a D to a C in spelling ought to get the same recognition and approval as the child who moves from a B to an A.

An orderly approach to learning. Nearly all students with learning disabilities need structure. They do their best work in classes that have consistent routines, clear rules and procedures, and predictable schedules. A disorganized teacher will make it very hard for these students to do their best, as will a schedule that requires many changes of class and the need to absorb several sets of rules and requirements (the transition to secondary school is often difficult for this reason). Inefficiency in the classroom not only compromises students' abilities to perform, it also cheats them of valuable instructional time. One study of elementary school classes found that *one third* of students' time was spent waiting for teacher directions, getting and putting away materials, and lining up and moving to new activities. Time spent on task and academic achievement are clearly related, so look for a teacher who keeps noninstructional business to a minimum.

A focus on basic skills. "Enrichment activities" like field trips, music, art, and drama are valuable components of the curriculum and often offer students with learning disabilities opportunities to stand out. In some schools, however, there is so much enrichment going on that basic-skills instruction has been compromised. One mother found that her son's sixth-grade curriculum had been organized around a theme of discovering other cultures. "Every month they focused on a different ethnic group," she remembers. "They really got into it—watched movies, cooked ethnic foods, dressed in costumes. I thought it was great until I realized that my son hadn't brought home one written paper all year. Later I found out there wasn't much reading going on, either." Students with learning disabilities need continuous instruction and reinforcement of their basic skills. Worthwhile goals like learning about other cultures should be tied to skill-building activities such as reading stories connected to the culture, using a computer to find more information about it, writing related reports, and/or corresponding with pen pals.

Instructional flexibility. As we have said more than once, rigidity in the classroom is toxic to students with learning disabilities. These students are limited in the ways they can understand, remember, and/or communicate information; if they are not matched with teaching styles and curriculum materials that target their strengths, they make poor progress. In addition, because these youngsters process information more slowly than typical learners, many need extra time to understand material and complete tasks successfully. When uncompromising time limits are imposed on instruction and testing, students with learning disabilities find it hard to succeed. One way of evaluating flexibility is to ask teachers about basic-skills curricula. Does the teacher stick with one reading and math program or (far better) select materials from several different programs according to student needs? Look also for classes that group students by skill level (groups might include students of different ages) and change groupings for different subjects (a student who is a poor reader but has great math skills should be in the top math group, and can participate in a heterogeneous group for social studies). Instructional groupings should not be cast in concrete; students should be able to move easily from one group to another as skills improve. Creative approaches like assigning peer tutors, study partners, or volunteer "mentors" to students who need extra help can also improve the options of students with learning disabilities.

Clear expectations for achievement. There are many studies that show that children rise to the occasion when teachers expect them to do well. Unfortunately, high expectations are not always extended to the student with learning disabilities. Regular classroom teachers sometimes assume that special education students will do poorly; as a result, some invest less effort in these students, apply lower expectations, and even avoid assigning them homework. (Kids don't want to hear it, but doing homework *is* clearly related to academic success.) "Don't allow the teacher to accept anything less than your child's best efforts," one parent advises. "If you feel your child can do better than the work that's coming home, make an appointment to talk to the teacher about raising stan-

Curriculum-Based Measurement

Teachers monitor classroom learning daily in myriad ways. They give quizzes and tests, hold discussions, ask questions, grade homework, note the quality of performances and projects, or simply ask children to record and hand in three things they learned before leaving the classroom. These methods use authentic classroom material to evaluate whether a child is learning the content that is being taught. They also help teachers note the kinds of errors that require reteaching. These evaluation measures do not, however, inform teachers about whether their methods and materials are helping a particular child make satisfactory progress in basic skills.

To help teachers judge the rate of basic-skill growth of particular students in comparison to their peers, a system of curriculum-based measurement (CBM) has become popular in recent years. CBM offers teachers a quick and easy method of keeping tabs on an individual student's progress, using everyday class materials.

If your school's teaching team is unfamiliar with CBM, most recent books on assessment describe how it is done. Below are brief examples of how CBM can be used to evaluate progress in particular subjects. These exercises can be repeated every three to four weeks. If progress is not rapid enough, then a change in teaching materials or strategies is called for.

Reading: The number of words your child reads aloud correctly in one minute is compared to that of classmates reading the same passage (children are given the cor-

dards." Students with learning disabilities benefit most when goals for achievement are clear, attainable within a reasonable time period, and tied to specific learning practices. "You can do better in Spanish" is not as motivating as, "If you practice with the flash cards for fifteen minutes a day, you will probably do much better on the Spanish quiz next week."

Effective monitoring of student performance. "My son brought home great math grades all year, so I was expecting real improvement on the year-end standardized achievement tests," remembers the mother of a fourth-grader with learning disabilities. "But those tests showed he was still two years behind; he'd made very little progress. I was disappointed and angry. What happened?" What happened is that this student earned good grades on the second-grade math work he had been given, but had not been challenged sufficiently to close rect word if they hesitate or stumble for three seconds). Since reading comprehension is closely tied to reading rate, this simple test predicts reading comprehension levels accurately for most children.

Math: The class is given three minutes to work a series of problems representative of what has been taught that year, or of what children their age are expected to know. The number of correct digits in the answers provided by your child is compared with the number in the answers supplied by other students. The percentage of correct digits will rise as comprehension of concepts and ability to compute improve.

Spelling: Twenty spelling words are dictated to the class; students have seven seconds to write each word before the next one is dictated. The number of correct two-letter sequences is counted, as well as correct first and last letters. As in the other areas, repeating this test can tell the teacher whether your child's spelling skills are developing, and whether development is slower or faster than other children in the class.

Writing: A "story starter" is provided; children are then asked to write for three minutes. The length of the passage (total number of words) your child has written is compared with that of classmates. Usually, length of passage and writing quality (sophistication of thoughts expressed) improve together. Teachers also can analyze story elements (themes, sequence, development, supporting ideas, cohesion) and mechanics (spelling, handwriting, grammar, punctuation, and capitalization).

the gap between his math performance and that of his typical peers. The As on his report card were therefore somewhat deceptive. Does this mean the student should have been given Ds and Fs? Of course not; students with learning disabilities should be graded fairly on the highest level of work they are capable of doing. Comparisons with achievement of typical students, though, should not be left until the end of the year. If this student's math achievement had been analyzed earlier, he might have been placed in a more difficult math program and moved ahead faster. *Curriculum-based Measurement* (described on these pages) is one effective way of monitoring student progress on an ongoing basis. Whatever monitoring methods are used, it is important for teachers to keep parents informed about both performance on current lessons *and* progress toward annual goals (as listed on the IEP).

Ample feedback. Research shows that all students benefit from frequent and timely feedback. Tests and papers that are returned promptly, weekly or monthly progress reports, and charts or graphs that illustrate progress toward stated goals have all been shown to have a positive effect on learning. Students with learning disabilities often need extra feedback and encouragement. Because these youngsters so frequently advance by fits and starts (two steps forward, then one back again), many have trouble understanding they are actually making progress. "These kids are very easily discouraged," adds a special education teacher. "You have to keep *proving* to them that they're getting somewhere. They need cheerleaders to keep them on task, to keep them from giving up." Cheerleaders must remember, however, that students with disabilities can be very sensitive about feedback that isn't fair or honest. As Jeff's story illustrates, these youngsters

Jeff

A self-employed computer software designer, Jeff struggled with dyslexia throughout his school and college years.

My mother remembers me coming home from school and saying, "I am so much smarter than those guys. Why are they so dumb and they can read and I can't?" I always had a little of that constructive arrogance, you know. I never really thought I was stupid, and I think that's fortunate for me. But I remember being overwhelmed, and just downright obstinate about the way I wanted to do things. . . . One thing I was very sensitive about throughout my elementary education was, you know, just evaluate me on what I *do;* don't say, "Well, you misspelled nine out of ten words, but you did a great job on this one word so we'll give you 100 with two smiley faces at the top." I mean, don't lie to me in terms of my performance. I was always really aware of how I was doing, and I was also aware of how everybody else in the class was doing. I was quite on top of that.

I remember in fifth grade we had to do a report. The subject I chose was "Arms and Armor in the Middle Ages." My dad took me to the Metropolitan Museum in New York City and I pawed over every single piece of armor in their collection. We bought tons of books and my father read all these books to me. Then I basically created my own book. I cut up all the books Dad bought me—I cut pictures out and I cut words out and I created this report. I didn't really type anything or write anything but I took all the things I wanted want applause for actual achievement; they need teachers who recognize, value, and validate small steps forward and real work that has been done differently.

Recommendations for how to get a student placed in a preferred setting vary. "I hear some schools are responsive to parent requests for a particular class, but ours wasn't," says a mother who admits to "shameless manipulation" to get her son placed with the school's best teachers. "I found out *teachers* could recommend a particular class for a student, so each year I enlisted the help of my son's teachers in selecting the best class for the next year. The teachers were usually happy to cooperate because I went out of my way to be helpful to them—I could always be counted on to sew costumes for the class play, or bake four dozen brownies for the bake sale." Other parents have found that *suggesting* a teacher for a child (and backing the

to say out of all the different books and I pasted them together. It was a great report, and it was obvious that for me to accomplish this had taken enormous effort—I mean, I can't begin to tell you, hours and hours. So I handed in this report like it was nothing, like everybody hands in their report, and that's how I wanted it treated. I mean I just wanted to know if I really worked hard and did my best, how would I do? In this particular school the grades were E for excellent, then B,C,D and F. I don't know why they didn't use A, but they didn't. Everybody in the class who got an E on their reports got an E for excellent, except me. The teacher gave me an E for *effort*. I was so irate about this particular event; I mean—irate is an understatement. My parents had this medication to give me when I got out of control and after school that day I had everybody piling on top of me to get one of these pills down my throat. But I was behaving this way because of these tremendous *injustices*. It was just the most incredibly offensive thing to me at the time. I would have been happy with a B or a C, but instead I got an E (an A anywhere else) for *effort*.

After that I decided I was not going to let this thing and these people run my life. So I began to run everybody else's life. I was very, very intrusive on other people, to the point where my sixth-grade teacher—one day early in the fall he left the classroom without saying a word. I found out later he went to my parents' home and he broke into tears and said, "I can't have this kid in my classroom. He has to go."

Interview by Jennifer Kagan.

suggestion up with logical reasons for such a placement) sometimes works where a straightforward request would not. "Our elementary school had a policy against parent requests for individual teachers," one mother remembers, "but if I said 'Ms. Smith is so calm and patient, I think Rashaan would do really well with her, don't you?' the principal usually went along." Many parents swear by the "squeaky wheel" or "broken record" approach: "I just kept politely asking for what I wanted until they gave it to me," a mother explains, "I think it got so the principal got a headache as soon as she saw me coming." "I always got a better reception when I showed up at school dressed like a professional," another mother adds. "My advice? Don't go to school meetings in blue jeans."

More than one mother has observed that requests made by fathers—or by mothers and fathers jointly—sometimes carry more weight than those made by mothers alone. "It's sexist and it's disgusting but it's reality," one says. "When a man walks into the conference, people sit up and pay attention. Use it to your advantage if you can." With or without Dad in tow, many mothers say knowing their legal rights and understanding the available educational options helped them be assertive in the program-planning process when they needed to be. "When they send you this dull-looking publication about your rights as a special education parent, *read* it," one urges. "That's how I learned what it was possible to ask for. Asking for what you want is important. Frankly, I think I got more out of our school district most years than they were planning to provide."

As we discussed in Chapter 7, the school district cannot initiate special education services or change your child's placement without your permission. If you feel the program offered to your child is inappropriate or inadequate, you also have the right to request professional mediation or challenge the school district's decisions at a due-process hearing before an independent hearing officer (that is, an official not employed by the school district). These proceedings cannot resolve all disputes—you cannot ask for a hearing because you don't like your child's teacher, for example—but the law does protect your right to be heard in the following cases:

- You feel your child has been incorrectly identified. (*Example:* You think the child has learning disabilities; the evaluation team says the child has mild mental retardation.)

- You feel your child needs more services than are being offered. (*Example:* You feel the child needs speech therapy; the district says the speech problems are not severe enough to interfere with academic performance.)

- You feel the school or class placement recommended for the child is inappropriate. (*Example:* You feel your child's problems with ADHD justify placement in a small class with structure and close supervision; the district recommends inclusion in a regular class with behavior modification.)

- You feel the program described in the IEP is not being implemented effectively. (*Example:* The IEP calls for the student to learn computer keyboard skills; due to a lack of equipment, only one period a week of computer time is being provided, and little progress has been made.)

- You feel your child's rights have been violated. (*Example:* Although an IEP was completed three months ago, services have not started.)

Keep in mind that formal mediation and due-process hearings should be resorted to only after reasonable attempts at negotiation have failed. Since hearings are time-consuming and expensive for you and the school district—a case must be prepared and legal representation is usually involved—it is in everyone's interest to avoid one if you can. Aim for compromises that get most of what you want: if the district won't provide your child with a personal computer, for instance, will they guarantee there will be a computer he can use as needed in his classroom? Suggest making changes on a temporary or "trial" basis, such as allowing some accommodations for three months and seeing if skills and behavior have improved at the end of that period.

Don't allow shortsightedness, shallow mindedness, or cost consciousness on the part of the school district, however, to result in half measures that seriously compromise your child's right to the "free, appropriate public education" guaranteed by law. If you feel your child must have a higher level or quality of support in order to achieve, fight for it. "I started out assuming the school district would know and do what was best for my son," says the mother of a boy with multiple learning disabilities, "but I soon found out differently. It seems like half the time the district doesn't know what Ryan needs, and the other half they're arguing that they can't afford to provide it. Parents of kids with disabilities have to be prepared to go to bat for them. Planning a child's education is far too important a matter to leave to educators."

Since time at IEP meetings is limited, it pays to prepare as much as possible in advance. The following IEP meeting planner will help you get organized.

Preparing for Your IEP Meeting

Before the Meeting

- Review your rights. Before your first IEP meeting, the school district is required to provide you with a *Procedural Safeguards Notice* outlining the rights of parents and students receiving special education under federal law. (This information is also available on the websites of several learning disabilities organizations: see Appendix D.) Take the time to read this information carefully; it is unlikely that the IEP committee will explain your rights to you.

- Gather information about state and local policies. For a first-time meeting to discuss an evaluation, make sure you understand the criteria your state uses to identify students with learning disabilities. You also want information on district or state assessments that will affect your child (see High-Stakes Testing, page 198), alternative evaluation options, and allowable test accommodations. Ask for a copy of the forms your school district uses for IEP documents; they will help you understand what specific information has to be included. All of this information should be available from your school district's department of special education.

- Gather and review records of your child's current level of performance. These might include past IEPs (if applicable), report cards, state- or districtwide test scores, and examples of your child's work. The last can be particularly helpful: test scores identify reading and math problems, but work samples do a better job of highlighting many other issues (such as strengths in drawing or struggles with writing).

- Request an advance copy of your child's evaluation reports. Reading this material before the IEP meeting will help you understand how the evaluation team "sees" your child and the interventions they think are most important. If you need more explanation, schedule a private meeting with the most relevant evaluation team member to review the results prior to the IEP meeting. If you have a different perspective on any of these results, be prepared to share your insights with the evaluators.

continued

- Organize your thoughts about your child's talents, interests, and needs. Prepare a written outline or notes summarizing your view of how your child is doing at school, how you see your child's strengths and weaknesses; what kinds of teaching materials and strategies work best/worst for your child; and what types of assistance (including technology assistance) you think would help your child improve. Do not limit your concerns to academic issues: many students with learning disabilities need help learning appropriate behavior, social skills, organizational skills, and self-determination and self-advocacy skills. The IEP committee should address these needs as well.

- Decide who will attend the IEP meeting. You are entitled to bring anyone to the IEP meeting who can contribute to the process, including family members, outside experts, and the child him/herself. It is a courtesy to inform the IEP committee in advance who will attend. Federal law requires the IEP committee to include at least one of your child's classroom teachers, a qualified special education teacher, an individual who can interpret evaluation results (if first-time identification is to be discussed), and a representative of the school district who is knowledgeable about the general education curriculum, school district resources, and specially designed instruction. Team members may be excused in certain circumstances, but *only with parents' permission*. If your school district proposes excusing a member of the committee (your child's classroom teacher, for example), and you believe that person should participate, notify the school district in writing in advance that you prefer that this member of your child's IEP team *not* be excused.

- Request a copy of the IEP draft. It is illegal to prepare an IEP document in advance of a meeting, but many districts save time by preparing rough drafts of IEPs covering issues such as evaluation, placement, services, goals and objectives, progress reporting, and accommodations. If your district does this, reviewing the draft before the meeting will give you an opportunity to see how the IEP committee is thinking. Remember that this document is only a draft: in the course of the meeting it may undergo many changes.

At the Meeting

- Arrive on time and dress for success. While there is no official "dress code" for IEP meetings, many parents observe that you get more respect if you look like you are dressed for business or a job interview.

- Ask for introductions. Take a moment to learn the names and positions of anyone on the IEP team who you do not recognize (if your child is to receive special education services, you will likely be meeting them again). If you have brought anyone with you, introduce them to the team.

- Remain calm. Although discussions at IEP meetings sometimes tackle emotionally loaded issues, raised voices, accusations, and name-calling never help. It is in your child's best interests for you to avoid taking an adversarial position. Keep in mind that everyone wants the child to succeed. Try to stay positive and cooperative. Polite negotiation usually works better than demands.

- Take notes. A great deal of detailed information is presented at IEP meetings; without notes, it's unlikely you will remember it all. If you would prefer to stay focused on the discussion, bring a designated note taker with you, or ask to record the meeting.

- Don't let the meeting overfocus on your child's weaknesses. You may have to remind the team that your child has strengths that you want to encourage, or that can be used to help solve problems ("My son gets along very well with others and benefits from a teamwork approach." "Although my daughter needs help with reading, she loves math, and I'd like to make sure she gets a lot of encouragement in that area").

- Make sure all the bases are covered. If time runs out before all your views have been heard, all your concerns have been addressed, and/or all the components of the IEP have been developed satisfactorily (including specific services to be provided, individualized goals and objectives, guidelines for monitoring and reporting progress, determination of assessment participation, and allowable accommodations and technology support), ask for a time

continued

extension or another meeting. If it is inconvenient for you to meet in person, the district should offer options such as videoconferencing and conference telephone calls.

- Finalize the IEP document. Or, if you have concerns about it, don't. Special education services cannot begin until a parent consents (often indicated by signing the IEP document). It is reasonable to ask if you can bring the final document home to review and share it with other family members, to delay consent until you have had a chance to visit classrooms proposed for your child, or to postpone approval until you get a second opinion or gather information from outside professionals. When parents and IEP teams cannot agree on major components of an IEP, mediation is the next step. (Your rights to mediation and due-process hearings are described in your *Procedural Safeguards Notice*.) Note that once given, consent to an IEP can be withdrawn at any time. Parents may also request meetings to review and change an IEP whenever they develop concerns that a child's program is not working or new issues arise.

After the Meeting

- Visit classes that have been proposed for your child, meet the teachers, and try to observe for at least an hour. Use the guidelines in Chapter 6, What Should I Expect from My Child's Teacher?, pages 157–60 to help assess whether your child will function well in these settings.

- Explain to your child what changes to expect. If your child did not attend the IEP meeting (attendance is not recommended for children younger than middle school), explain why his or her school program has been altered, in encouraging terms ("We know you have been having a hard time with reading, and the school has some expert teachers who are going to help you"). Going over specific changes in the schedule and visiting new teachers can help reduce student anxiety.

- Monitor progress closely. While the school district is obliged to report student progress several times a year, many parents work with their children's teachers to check on basic-skills progress more frequently—often on a weekly basis. Once an IEP has been implemented, your child's skills should start to improve within three months. Substantial lack of progress toward IEP goals after six months calls for review and revision of the IEP.

9

The ABCs of
Success in School

It is no secret that children with learning disabilities must work harder than others in order to get ahead in school. These youngsters often have to be more motivated, more dedicated, and spend more time involved with academic tasks than their classmates just to stay afloat. "It used to make me crazy when teachers criticized my writing and told me to try harder," a high school student with visual-perception and fine-motor disabilities remembers. "In third grade it took me almost an hour to finish a simple worksheet. I sweated out two or three of those every night, while my sisters got to watch TV. How many eight-year-olds did my teachers know who tried harder than that?"

Children can't be expected to maintain this level of discipline and motivation for long unless their efforts meet with some degree of success. It's not hard to understand why. Just imagine yourself trying to learn a new skill on the job and getting absolutely nowhere. How long would you have to fail before you give up and quit? A month? Two? Maybe you're stubborn and you're making a little progress, so you hang in longer. But could you keep it up for thirteen *years* (the period we want children to remain motivated in order to graduate from high school)? Not many of us could. If we don't succeed at our work, we figure pretty quickly that we're in the wrong business. That's just what happens to our kids: if they try and don't succeed in school, they decide they're unfit for the business of education.

Unfortunately, failure to believe in your own capacity to learn is the most serious kind of learning disability there is. Students who do not believe they are able to achieve rarely put forth the effort necessary to do so, making continued poor performance inevitable. Experience proves, however, that if you can show children with learning problems that they *can* achieve in school, their levels of interest and motivation improve dramatically. While positive reinforcement and rewards can help get kids moving forward, success is the only incentive that works in the long run. Just as unrewarded effort can set up a failure cycle ("I'm no good at reading, I'm no good at school, there's no point even trying . . ."), achievement sets up a success cycle: it creates self-confidence and positive expectations, which in turn support more success.

The fundamental task facing adults who care about kids with learning disabilities, then, is to stack the deck so that these children can experience success on a regular basis. Without that experience, you cannot expect a child to sustain the energy and attitudes necessary to overcome information-processing problems. Happily, a little success can go a long way. Children need not be successful in everything they undertake in order to keep trying, nor must they be at the top of the class in order to feel successful. All children need *some* areas of accomplishment, however, to which they can point with pride, saying, "I did that! I worked hard and I made that happen!" From these empowering experiences comes faith that effort can influence events, that obstacles can be overcome, and that goals and dreams can be realized.

In this chapter we will discuss seven important ways parents can help children improve their levels of accomplishment in school. As you review them, keep a few general guidelines in mind:

Sometimes it's best to work behind the scenes. You will note that not all of these suggestions involve providing direct assistance to the child. Whenever possible, the goal is to structure circumstances so that children can succeed on their own by drawing on their strengths and abilities. The best kinds of help are those that encourage children to take responsibility for themselves and their work.

Learn to Recognize Little Victories

Peanuts is reprinted by permission of United Feature Syndicate, Inc.

Forget the old saying "If at first you don't succeed, try, try, again." Perseverance may be a virtue, but a major source of frustration for children with learning disabilities is that they are often urged to "try harder" using unsuitable methods or materials. When reasonable goals are not being met, a change of approach may be far more effective than more effort.

Be sensitive about how you define success. If your idea of achievement is straight As and an admission letter from Harvard, it's time to adjust your thinking. Youngsters who have become discouraged about school need their "success cycles" kicked off and maintained with short-term, readily attainable goals. As the cartoon above affirms, little victories can mean a lot. Learn to recognize them (and to help your child recognize them as well).

With those principles in view, let's look at some strategies that can support success.

GET ORGANIZED

Most children with learning disabilities have some difficulty organizing objects and information; many also have trouble with concepts involving space and time. As a result, these children's problems with basic skills are often compounded by a host of difficulties with educational procedures. "These are the kids who forget to copy the as-

David

Parents can be very creative about making it possible for children to succeed, as David's story shows:

Fifth grade was a low point for David, an eleven-year-old with mild language-processing disabilities. Although he had received special help in reading for two years, David still read slowly and had trouble keeping up with assigned work. His written work usually came back to him covered in red ink. Arithmetic was nearly as bad; David was struggling with math reasoning, and during much of math period he felt totally lost.

"About the only subject David did well in was art, and he only had that once a week," David's mother remembers. "David was making academic progress, and the resource teacher assured us he would be fine once he got on top of his basic skills, but meanwhile his self-esteem was taking a beating. He felt incompetent at everything."

David's family enjoyed visiting art galleries, and on one of those outings David saw an exhibition of watercolor landscapes. He fell in love with the delicate paintings and told his mother, "I want to learn to do that!"

"I was so glad to see David motivated about *anything* that I became determined to find someone to teach him," his mother says. "But I had no luck—the art teacher at school said watercolor painting was too difficult and 'sophisticated' for kids David's age, and people who ran children's art programs in the community said pretty much the same thing. Then I saw an ad for an evening introductory watercolor course to be given at a local senior citizen center. I contacted the instructor, explained our situation, and asked if she would consider including an eleven-year-old in the class. She said if David didn't mind being in a class of retirees, she'd be willing to give it a try.

"What a blessing that class turned out to be!" David's mother continues. "Not only did David learn the fundamentals of watercolor painting—something no one else in his class could do—but he became the darling of his 'classmates.' It was like he suddenly inherited a dozen extra grandparents who thought everything he did was wonderful. He just bloomed. When his teacher put some of his pictures on display at school, it was like the icing on the cake."

David's success with watercolors also helped keep him motivated about practicing basic skills. "He no longer felt like a total loser," his mother says. "That boost to his self-confidence affected everything he did."

signment from the board," a special education teacher says, "or they copy it, but they copy it wrong. Or they copy it right, but they forget to bring the book home. Or they bring the book home and do the assignment, but leave it on the kitchen table when they go to school. Kids with learning disabilities often lose points to this kind of thing even when they're on top of their lessons."

As students get older and demands on organizational ability increase (because of more classes, more teachers, and more complex assignments), youngsters with learning disabilities often find themselves at a growing disadvantage. Transitions to new schools can be especially difficult, and many students remember junior high school as a low point in their academic careers. "It took me forever to learn my way around the new building," one student remembers. "I couldn't remember the combination to my locker. I had seven teachers, and they all had different rules. I got in trouble for being late to class, for not having the right kind of notebook, for having no sneakers on gym day. I felt sure the other kids were all laughing at me for being so out of it."

Because organization is not a gift that comes to them naturally, children with learning disabilities benefit from external structure. Four general areas where assistance is particularly helpful are described below.

Providing an Organized Work Space

Students with learning disabilities often have trouble settling down to work, and frequent interruptions to look for paper, pencils, calculators, or other tools and supplies don't help their concentration any. A well-lit, uncluttered work space with adequate supplies of most-used materials close at hand will help students make the most of homework time. In planning this space, keep in mind that many children with learning disabilities are easily distracted by movement or background noise. Remember also, however, that these children often need some help and supervision with their assignments. "Don't make their work area so isolated that you can't comfortably get to it several times a night," one mother warns.

Elementary-aged children often prefer to be close to where the family "action" is when they are working on school projects. The kitchen or dining room can be fine places for homework sessions as long as noise in the general vicinity can be controlled. (Big earphones may cancel just enough background noise to help children concentrate. Some children find that music helps them focus, so a radio or CD playing softly may be okay.) Children also need a permanent place for books and supplies. "We set a kitchen cabinet aside for the school stuff," one mother says. "How often do you need the good china, anyway?"

Managing Time

No work space for a student with learning disabilities is complete without a calendar with large spaces for recording school events, activities, and assignments (some families like to include family events and chores also). In the early stages of getting organized, maintaining this calendar is probably going to have to be the parents' job (if the student can't remember where he's supposed to be and what he's supposed to do, you don't really expect him to remember to write it down, do you?). "The point is to get the child in the habit of *looking* at the calendar," an experienced parent explains. "Check it with her every night, so she can see what's happening tomorrow and what she has to bring to school. Look ahead to see if there's anything later in the week that needs advance preparation. Don't assume your child will know how long an assignment or a project will take—kids with learning disabilities are notoriously bad at estimating time." Later, students can record assignments and events on the calendar themselves. Children are usually more responsible about doing this after they have become used to working with a calendar and are convinced of its value.

Children with learning disabilities also thrive on routine. Most benefit from predictable schedules for meals, recreation, homework, and bedtime. "These kids often have trouble with transitions," a teacher explains. "It can be hard for them to let go of one activity and get into another. Consistent routines make transitions easier. After a while, the kids know that they can play after school but must do homework after dinner, and they don't fight it."

In addition to helping students manage time at home, parents should alert teachers and other staff that children with learning disabilities may need help getting on top of schedules at school. "When your child is going to start a new schedule, walk him through it or get another student to walk him through it a few times when the building is quiet and empty," one family suggests. "Think the whole schedule through, so you can say, 'On your way from science to social studies you go right by your locker, so that would be a good time to pick up books for the afternoon.' Get that stuff worked out in advance so the child doesn't have to try to figure it out when the halls are packed with students, bells are going off, and announcements are coming over the loud speaker." Walk-throughs are especially important whenever a child starts a new school. Many students with learning disabilities have trouble with mental maps; several trial runs and extra attention to landmarks ("See, the steps you want are the ones *after* the bathroom") may be needed to help them become comfortable in an unfamiliar building.

Note that some students respond better to visual prompts than to verbal ones. Photos of the dog and a trash can posted on the refrigerator can remind a student that walking the dog and taking out the trash are his chores for the evening (the photos can be turned over when the job is done). A bulletin board with computer-generated images illustrating the after-school schedule (soccer practice, dinner, math homework, social studies report, TV; clock hands can be attached to symbols for each activity) may help a student organize her time better than a plain calendar.

Structuring Tasks

Many children with learning disabilities have difficulties with sequencing—that is, putting pieces of information into a logical or meaningful order. As a result, these children often have trouble breaking down complex tasks into simpler components, and figuring out which of those subtasks to tackle first. This applies equally to schoolwork and chores at home. "You can't just tell kids with sequencing problems to set the table or wash the dishes," a mother says. "With most jobs, you have to break it down and walk them through it many times before they get it right." While it can take time and patience to teach household tasks to children with learning disabilities (many an irritated parent concludes, "It would be faster to do it myself!"), experts advise that the effort is worth it in the long run. Taking responsibility for a share of the family's work can help build independence and create a sense of belonging and importance. Both are important to a child's self-esteem.

Students need help structuring school assignments, too. When asked to plan a science fair project, create a collage, or prepare a report on Uruguay, children may declare, "I can't do it!" because the project seems overwhelming in its entirety—not because it is actually beyond their abilities. When you help them break down the task into steps or phases, it often looks much easier. To organize a science fair project, for example, you might explain to the child: "First we'll go online and look for some ideas. Then you'll choose a project that can be completed in four weeks. Next you make a list of the materials we need so we can go shopping. Then we will make a schedule for doing the experiment and set up a notebook for recording results."

Remember that *the point of restructuring tasks is to create a set of simpler tasks, each of which students can handle mostly on their own*. If students have trouble following steps even after a job has been broken down, an alternate strategy may be what is needed. A youngster who cannot yet handle a science project independently, for example, might need a modified assignment (a simple experiment with directions provided, perhaps) or to work with a partner or a team. "Flexibility is the key to success in the classroom and at home," a special education teacher says. "If the child has fine-motor problems, teaching him to set the table or wash dishes may be a lost cause. That kid can handle a vacuum cleaner, though. You have to choose the tasks that allow kids to make their best contributions."

Keeping Track of Schoolwork

It is a fact of life that kids with learning disabilities lose things. But when they start losing school things, it can translate into unnecessarily lowered grades (not to mention frustrated parents, annoyed teachers, and students with reduced self-esteem). It is therefore important to work out a system for keeping track of materials that go to and from school. Parents say the following items are among the most important to keep tabs on:

Assignments. Does the child actually know what he is expected to do? Youngsters with learning disabilities sometimes do not because they could not interpret what was on the blackboard, missed the quick announcement made as the bell rang, copied the assignment wrong, or trusted themselves to remember it instead of writing it down (short-term memory is not always trustworthy for these students). To make sure that all assignments are understood, it may be necessary to ask teachers to give students their assignments in writing, or to pair students with a "study buddy" who reliably writes down test dates and homework assignments.

Books. "I left the book in school" is a familiar refrain for students with learning disabilities (second only to "I left the homework at home"). If this is a problem for your child, ask the school for a second set of textbooks to keep at home. "Saves a whole lot of aggravation," one parent says.

Homework. "Whenever a teacher said my son had missed turning in homework assignments, he was always so surprised," one mother remembers. "He'd insist, 'I did that work!' Then we'd clear out his backpack or his locker, and there the assignments would be, along with old spelling tests, gym socks, and candy wrappers." To avoid this familiar scenario, try providing the child with a heavyweight folder with pockets for each school subject (some have handy information like multiplication tables and standard weights and measures printed right inside). Label one side of the folder "Things to Hand In," and the other side "Things to Bring Home." Make sure completed homework assignments—and also items like notes to the teacher and signed permission slips—are in the correct folders before the student leaves for school each day, and teach children to check their folders for papers to hand in as soon as they arrive in class (it helps to have teachers' cooperation for this). Check the "Bring Home" side of the folder daily for assignments, graded work, and school announcements. "If you punch the folders and insert them in a three-ring notebook, they'll be harder to lose," a special education teacher advises. "If that makes the notebook too bulky, try making two notebooks, one for the morning classes and one for the afternoon. I saw one parent color-coordinate folders and textbook covers—red for reading, blue for math, and so on." If children have chronic problems keeping track of papers, it is also a good idea to encourage them to check with teachers once a week to make sure all required work has been handed in. That way they can catch up on what's missing before the load of unfinished business becomes overwhelming.

Experienced parents add that it is also a good idea to clean out lockers and backpacks every week or two. As one mother put it, "This greatly improves your chances of getting the note about the class trip before they actually go."

Not surprisingly, parents who have the most trouble helping their children get organized are those who are disorganized themselves. For them, however, efforts to provide appropriate support for their children can produce unexpected benefits. "Stabilizing our routines and writing everything down on a calendar helped me become more efficient and organized about my own work," one parent says. "I don't procrastinate as much as I used to, and I feel more on top of things."

HELP CHILDREN FIND THEIR PREFERRED LEARNING STYLES

Everyone has a preferred learning style, including the authors of this book. Lisa, for example, learns best from books and visual materials; she doesn't get much from lectures unless she takes reams of notes. She looks for the "big picture" (details bore her), can juggle a lot of information in her head, and deals well with abstract concepts. She is also an introvert who prefers to work independently. In contrast, Corinne learns best by listening and talking; she likes lectures and discussions but finds reading slow going. She's superb at organizing information and keeping track of details. She is outgoing and thrives on interaction with other people.

Obviously, our learning styles are distinct and very different (between us, we figure we have a whole brain). The only thing that distinguishes us from an individual with a learning disability is that we have a little more flexibility—Corinne does plow through mounds of printed material, and Lisa can cope with details and work with others when she has to. Youngsters with learning disabilities must stick with their preferred learning styles, however, because other means of handling information are inefficient or blocked. Yet many do not know what their preferred learning styles are; they understand only that they don't respond to the methods promoted at school.

To help children understand their preferred learning styles, you need to consider three separate areas:

Which Senses Make the Most Sense?

Some individuals learn best with their eyes; they are most likely to retain information presented in the form of visual materials (such as pictures, maps, charts, and diagrams) or demonstrations. Auditory learners, on the other hand, rely more on their ears. Educational techniques that work for them include discussions, lectures, and reading aloud. There are also children who find that touching and manipulating objects helps them focus; hands-on experience is often their best teacher.

While any student will do better when educated according to his or her strongest sensory channel, research suggests that a *multisensory approach* to education may be even better for many. A first-grader who has a hard time recognizing letters, for example, may be able to learn them by saying them out loud while tracing them in sand or cutting them out of colored paper. A high school student who retains little of what she reads may benefit from creating "graphic organizers" such as colored outlines, charts, lists, and drawings relating to the work and/ or forming a study group to discuss material in the text. Many good teachers use multisensory techniques in class (especially in the lower grades), and special educators sometimes use special multisensory curricula to teach reading and math. Even when teachers prove single-minded, however, students can learn to vary their own approaches to academic tasks, adding different sensory dimensions.

Abstract Versus Concrete Thinking

Albert Einstein once said that fantasy and imagination meant more to him than his ability to handle facts. This famous physicist was the quintessential abstract, or conceptual, thinker. He was comfortable in a world of theories and ideas and did not need to see or touch things in order to understand them. (Einstein, by the way, did not learn to read until he was nine. He also failed the language requirement for admission to technical school.) Abstract thinkers can usually visualize and manipulate information easily in their heads. Many like to take their time considering different aspects of a problem; they may resent being rushed or pressed for answers while they are thinking things through.

Concrete thinkers, in contrast, are most comfortable with applied or practical knowledge. They prefer to deal with real objects and situations. They learn by exploring the physical world, and are likely to be bored by abstract theories and ideas. The inventor Thomas Edison was a gifted concrete thinker, who even as a child had a driving need to figure out how things worked. (Edison proved so unsuited to traditional methods of education that his mother withdrew him from public school after only three months and taught him at home.) Today, of course, Edison is known for his technical brilliance and ingenuity.

Nearly all small children think concretely; the ability to deal with abstractions develops over time. Traditional methods of education reflect this normal pattern of development. There are usually lots of multisensory, hands-on activities in primary school, but students are expected to do more and more "in their heads" as they get older. In high school, students who become accomplished abstract thinkers can expect to do well in most academic subjects. Students who remain primarily concrete thinkers, however, may find that the only classes taught *their* way are shop, home economics, and gym. These students are educationally disadvantaged. No matter how bright they are, their learning style limits their opportunities in a conventional educational environment.

Research suggests that many students with learning disabilities are concrete thinkers. It is necessary to find ways of rooting these youngsters' educations in reality. Teaching methods that work for them include interactive demonstrations; hands-on experiments; field trips; providing case studies, illustrations, and examples; and placing skills and information in a practical context (for example, you use fractions and measuring skills when you follow a recipe or build a house). When teachers fail to provide a bridge between abstract concepts and the real world, parents can sometimes build one. Everyday activities like meal planning, cooking, and shopping offer many good opportunities for helping concrete (or "experiential") learners learn and remember information.

Concrete thinkers also benefit from structured tasks and precise instructions. Care may have to be taken to help them understand the purpose of their lessons and assignments. "Never assume these children understand the point of work they are doing," a special educator warns. "Often they are clueless—which easily undermines their motivation. It's necessary to explain objectives carefully and draw these kids' attention to key facts and concepts as you go along. Don't expect them to make inferences or draw conclusions on their own; if it's important, spell it out for them."

Frequent reference to a lesson's goals or main ideas helps the abstract thinker, too. Some of these youngsters overanalyze problems

Never Assume

A special education teacher offers these words of wisdom to parents.

In the twenty-five years I have taught children with learning disabilities, I have learned to always expect the unexpected and never, NEVER assume a student has prior knowledge of a subject, no matter how old, how intelligent, or how "streetwise" s/he is. . . . I remember the high school student who was learning how to plan and prepare a meal in life-skills class. After the class selected burgers and fries as their main course, they had to construct a grocery list—rolls, ground hamburger, potatoes . . .

"Potatoes?" one young man inquired. "What do you need potatoes for?"

"The fries!" came the response.

"No kidding!" said the student. "Fries are made out of potatoes?"

Source: Mary Ann Coppola, 1996.

and become bogged down in side issues. A child who feels the need to understand *everything* in a textbook is a good candidate for early academic burnout! (One student who tried to memorize all three thousand terms in her science textbook started to perform much better after being taught to concentrate only on terms mentioned by the teacher in class.) Explicit explanation of what is most important helps students like this make more efficient use of their time and intellectual energy.

Sequential Versus Global Processing

Many school teachers are *sequential processors*. They take a logical approach to learning, sorting information into linear sequences and presenting it in a methodical, step-by-step manner. They like to keep things systematic and orderly. They are good at outlining, categorizing, and analyzing. They pay attention to details. Not surprisingly, these teachers reward students who process and present information the same way.

Not everyone, however, thinks in a linear or logical fashion. Some individuals are *global processors*. These people don't learn step-by-step; they learn by making mental leaps. They grasp information intuitively (as a result they may have trouble explaining to others how they know what they know). Because they do not sort or categorize data in a conventional manner, they may perceive links between different kinds of information that are not obvious to others. Global processors hunger for insight; they tend to be impatient with details (which they consider unimportant). Often they are perceived as jumping the gun, or jumping to conclusions. Still, their conclusions are right often enough—and even when they are wrong, these students' views are often creative and interesting.

Like concrete thinkers, global processors can be at a disadvantage in school because their preferred learning style is out of sync with the dominant teaching style. When these children don't understand something, logically minded teachers usually backtrack, slow down, and become even more systematic: for example, they'll reorganize a task into six steps instead of three. This further frustrates the global processor, who only wants to know where all this explanation is *going*. To reach these students, it is important to summarize the main points of a lesson *before* it is taught. As one special education teacher puts it: "You give them the answers and work back toward the questions. Once they have the 'big picture,' these students usually become more willing to attend to details and follow procedures."

This teacher adds, "You don't meet many students with learning disabilities who are sequential thinkers." The students she works with most often have styles that are abstract/global ("They get accused of being ditzy airheads," she says) or concrete/global ("They look like restless troublemakers; their motto is "Ready, fire, aim!"). "It is important to teach these kids appropriately—and also to assure them that theirs is a legitimate learning style," the teacher concludes. "I always remind them that life's agenda is a lot more flexible than the curriculum at school. Once they graduate, they'll have more freedom to do things their own way."

Three additional factors that affect learning style are described below:

Attention span. Some youngsters must put so much effort into focusing attention that they tire after a relatively short time. If they keep trying to work beyond this point, their skills deteriorate rapidly. Attention problems are most obvious when children are attempting to master new skills, or are required to do work they find boring. (Motivation boosts attention, so attention levels may be good for creative ventures or for projects the child really wants to do.) For students with attention difficulties, work needs to be broken up so that it can be completed in short sessions. A list of twenty spelling words might be too much to take on at a sitting, for example, so limit spelling practice to five words a day. For difficult work, ten or fifteen minutes of concentration may be the most a child can handle without a break. Length of time on task can often be increased as the work becomes more familiar. Attention-grabbing strategies—like letting children practice "writing" letters and numbers with shaving cream, or using colored highlighters to identify new or important information in texts—can also increase time spent on academic tasks.

Sociability. Some people like working alone, while others prefer interacting with other people. Successful "loners" tend to be internally motivated, self-disciplined, and goal oriented. If this does not describe your child, look for cooperative learning opportunities: team projects, discussion groups, and study partners. Socially oriented learners may have difficulty maintaining their motivation without frequent input, feedback, and encouragement from others.

Information-processing speed. Some folks grasp information quickly; their minds can absorb large "chunks" of information at a time. They seem able to keep several lines of thinking going at once, which makes it possible for them to perform mental tasks like comparing, contrasting, and analyzing very rapidly. Many equally intelligent individuals, however, process information more slowly. These people often handle information best in small chunks, and they prefer to focus on one thing at a time. It is important to avoid throwing too much information at these students too fast because "data overload" produces confusion and undermines memory. These children also need additional time to respond to requests and to answer questions. The best way to support these students is to reduce or eliminate extraneous material and just . . . slow . . . down. Remember that many students with learning disabilities read and write over 30 percent slower than their classmates. Sometimes simple changes in strategy—like copying homework assignments from the board at the beginning of class, rather than rushing at the end—can do wonders for the student whose work has been chronically late or incomplete.

How much information is too much? Research finds that around seven pieces of information is what typical learners can handle at any given time before becoming overloaded. Reducing that number—or clustering information into a handful of categories that "package" the information to be remembered—will help most students with learning disabilities succeed.

In addition to paying attention to their children's learning styles, parents need to understand their own. If you are a visually oriented, concrete, sequential thinker, for example, your natural way of explaining things might be all wrong for your abstract, global, auditory child.

"Whenever my son had trouble memorizing something in elementary school, my first thought was *flash cards*," one mother says. "I would never have made it through school without flash cards. But RJ learns best through his ears and his hands. Verbal rehearsal worked better for him—he learned his times tables by reciting them over and over while bouncing a basketball."

KEEP ON TOP OF THE CURRICULUM

Many parents are unaware of the fact that a great many different programs exist for teaching reading, writing, math, science, and social studies. Publishers of these programs (which include student texts, teachers' guides, and sometimes workbooks, films, computer software, and other learning aids) aggressively compete with one another for the dollars of America's school systems. Every school district has some kind of committee responsible for periodically reviewing newly developed curriculum materials and comparing them to materials in use. New materials may be chosen because they better address student needs—or because they have been heavily promoted by publishers and/or reflect some currently popular trend in education.

As we have said earlier, there is no one program or type of program that is best for all children. Good teachers know this, and many use materials from several different teaching programs (as well as designing curriculum materials of their own) in an effort to reach the greatest possible numbers of students. Inexperienced or less talented teachers, in contrast, often attempt to teach classes "by the book" regardless of students' individual needs. If the curriculum materials supplied are unsuitable for some students, it is usually the students—not the publishers or the teachers—who are blamed for resulting problems.

Because students with learning disabilities are less adaptable than typical learners in the ways they assimilate information, the programs used in their classrooms can either speed or wreck their academic progress. It is therefore important for parents to investigate materials and methods and evaluate how well they are likely to meet children's needs. Two good ways to do this are to preview textbooks and workbooks, and to ask to see the "scope and sequence charts" supplied to teachers by publishers of different curricula. These charts describe what skills and content will be covered in the course of a semester or the year (the *scope* of the curriculum), as well as the order (or *sequence*) in which skills and information will be taught.

When you preview the curriculum, you can anticipate—and prevent—many kinds of trouble. It should be clear from the start, for example, whether text materials are appropriate for the child's reading level. Materials are appropriate if the child can read 95 percent of the words automatically (that is, without stumbling or stopping to sound them out). If they are too difficult, discuss modifications—such as using a detailed outline or a simpler text—with the teacher, or arrange for the text to be read to the child aloud. If you are familiar with your child's learning strengths and weaknesses, you will be able to spot other problem areas also (for example, the math class will be doing a unit on word problems, and the history materials call for memorization of names and dates) and work out methods of helping the youngster through them in advance (students may need to be assigned fewer homework problems each night when math material is difficult; open-book essays might be substituted for short-answer tests in history). If the skills of the special education teacher will be needed to help the student cover some material, you can draw both teachers' attention to this so they can plan to coordinate their efforts.

It is particularly important to explore how basic skills are being taught at your child's school. Some methods of teaching reading, writing, and arithmetic are notoriously problematic for students with learning disabilities. A few to look out for are discussed below.

"Whole-Language" Reading Programs

These are not as popular as they used to be, but they are still in use. Whole-language curricula stress recognition of entire words and textual meaning. There is little or no formal instruction in phonics; it is assumed that students will associate letters with sounds "naturally" as they go along. Fans of this system say it promotes comprehension of complex language and appreciation for literature (students are introduced to good literature at an early age) and is less boring than other methods of teaching reading. Reading lessons are often taught in conjunction with whole-language writing curricula, which encourage youngsters to express themselves freely on paper without worrying about spelling, punctuation, or other conventions.

Unfortunately, students who have visual-perception problems are very poor at whole-word recognition, and children with language-processing disabilities are unlikely to connect sound sequences with written words naturally. Whole-language programs do not provide these students with alternative strategies for deciphering words they do not recognize. Children with both types of disabilities need explicit instruction in phonics (decoding words by sounding them out) in order to read successfully. Some children need special exercises to help them recognize the positions of individual sounds in words before phonics can be attempted. Students with severe disabilities may need a multisensory approach to phonics that combines seeing, hearing, saying, and sometimes touching (cutting letters out or tracing them, for example). This type of instruction is usually available only through specialized reading programs. Note that building reading skill requires substantial investment of time: the most successful strategies provide thirty minutes or more of reading instruction every day. Since the reading rate of children with LD is often much slower than typical readers, working specifically on *fluency* (recognizing words faster and faster) is critically important. The faster and more effortlessly children can recognize words, the more attention and time they can give to understanding the material and trying to remember it.

The point of reading, ultimately, is comprehension. Vocabulary enrichment and improving students' wealth of background knowledge both help make new material more meaningful and memorable for children. Youngsters with LD also need to be taught explicit strategies to use when comprehension breaks down (such as rereading, stopping to rephrase or mentally picture what has just been read, and scanning ahead for clarification). Higher-level comprehension skills (which become important in secondary school) include evaluating, comparing, and synthesizing information from different sources, applying what has been learned to new situations, and developing awareness of character, theme, and plot development. It is an important part of a teacher's job to help your child learn to *think* in these increasingly sophisticated ways, in addition to building vocabulary and improving reading fluency.

Writing Programs That Overemphasize Mechanics

Ask students with learning disabilities how do you become a good writer, one researcher found, and you get answers such as "practice and hope and hold your pencil right." For many of these students, writing means heroic struggles with penmanship, spelling, and grammar. These issues may be so consuming that the children give little thought to content or style. Studies find that students with learning disabilities seldom plan what they write; many believe a successful paper simply means not too many spelling and punctuation errors.

For these youngsters (as well as for most typical learners), drilling mechanics is far less important than teaching them how to communicate effectively. Programs that emphasize planning, review, and revision of written work (often called writing-process curricula) are best; they focus students' attention on what they want to say and how to say it clearly. (Note that emphasizing content does *not* mean that teaching spelling and grammar can be overlooked. This sometimes happens when teachers urge children to be creative about expressing themselves but do not help them review and revise results.) Hallmarks of a good writing-process curriculum include *prewriting activities* in which students select topics, "brainstorm" ideas and vocabulary for addressing the topic selected, and organize the ideas logically (using tools like concept maps to connect a main topic to different subtopics); *conferences* in which students read early drafts to the teacher or to another student and receive feedback; a *revision phase* in which compositions are reworked for style, clarity, and effectiveness; and a final *editing phase* in which spelling, grammar, punctuation, and so forth are corrected. These programs often conclude by producing publications of student efforts.

At each step along the way, explicit instruction is necessary. For example, to develop an essay topic, students must be taught to ask questions like "Did I introduce the problem?" "Did I suggest several ways to solve the problem?" "Did I include reference to the five Ws [*who, what, where, when, why*]?" "Have I used topic and concluding sentences to help guide the reader?" "Do sentences and paragraphs transition logically from one to another?" Checking spelling, grammar, and punctuation comes at the end of this process.

Note that children who have trouble with handwriting (including some students with visual-perception disabilities, as well as those with fine-motor problems) may find it impossible to focus on what they want to say in writing until they are relieved of the burden of trying to form legible letters. The act of writing is so slow and arduous that they produce far less than they intended.* Allowing these youngsters to dictate to a "scribe" or teaching them to use a voice recorder as a prewriting tool sometimes improves the content of their written efforts dramatically. Most students also find that word processors (which make revising and correcting easy) greatly reduce the difficulties involved in writing. For youngsters with disabilities, typing is a survival skill that should not be left until high school; try to get computer keyboard skills built into the student's educational program by fifth or sixth grade. (Many schools now teach basic computer skills to all students routinely, but it may be necessary for you to arrange an early introduction to word processing through special education.) If a student's fine-motor skills are not equal to typing, there are voice-activated computer programs that take dictation. (Students can then "hunt and peck" to edit their work.)

Arithmetic by Rote

The traditional "drill-and-kill" approach to arithmetic is not very good for any student. Studies indicate that rote memorization of facts and formulas in preparation for tests does not equip children to handle math reasoning or higher-order problem-solving. Students with learn-

---

* Questions sometimes arise about whether a child who has struggled to perfect printing should be "transitioned" to cursive writing (usually around third grade). Some experts feel students should stick with printing, as it requires less complex movements and avoids the confusion of trying to learn two systems. Others argue that cursive writing is faster and more rhythmic, makes spacing easier (since letters are connected), and makes reversals less likely. As with other aspects of programming for the child with LD, an individualized approach is needed: the decision should be made according to what works best for each child.

ing disabilities may not even learn to handle basic computation using this system. A great many of these students have trouble with tasks involving rote memorization (the methods others use to memorize do not work for them). Nevertheless, the pressure to memorize math facts can become intense in elementary school. When the mother of a third-grader who had not learned his multiplication tables suggested that he be given a calculator so he could get on with the math curriculum, for example, the teacher replied, "In third grade, memorizing multiplication facts *is* the math curriculum." (This parent got permission for the calculator from the school district's special education committee, and also asked that her son's class be supplied with concrete materials—such as pennies, poker chips, or Popsicle sticks— that could be used to demonstrate basic math concepts.)

Another problem that can interfere with math education is that some students with learning disabilities have trouble with abstract ideas. Young children may not even understand that numbers on paper represent real things. Until the relationship between numbers and objects is made clear, these students will see little point in paper-and-pencil addition and subtraction exercises. Hands-on activities that involve counting real objects (such as blocks or Cuisenaire rods) are often essential to understanding basic number concepts and relationships. (Children should also be encouraged to use their fingers to "count up" as long as they need to; research has found that finger counting helps children learn math facts faster.) An explicit, tangible approach may also be necessary to help these youngsters learn about money, measurement, fractions, graphs, and time. Throughout their math educations, students with learning disabilities need instruction that emphasizes understanding concepts and reasoning (steps in problem-solving). These are the things that ultimately define math competence. What is the use of memorizing substraction tables, after all, if the child can't judge whether he has enough money left to make a purchase, or has received the right amount of change?

Problem-based curricula have become popular in recent years, and these are helpful to all students. Activities involve students working together in groups to solve real problems, such as how fast a go-cart will get to the finish line depending on such variables as the angle of descent, the angle of release, and the angle of the curve in the road. Students use computers or build models to calculate answers. All this is fun and motivating, but children with learning disabilities usually need explicit teacher guidance during the problem-solving process: asking probing questions, providing prerequisite knowledge, demonstrating and giving guided practice and feedback, and having students reason through their problem-solving aloud are all helpful.

Elementary school teachers are sometimes poor at explaining math concepts because they don't understand math very well themselves. Many freely admit they teach math by rote because they learned it that way and know no other means of handling math information. "If your child has one of these teachers, look for help from special education personnel or get a good math tutor so the child can build a solid conceptual foundation," one parent suggests. "You may find—as we did—that the student actually does better in math in secondary school where teachers are better at explaining the how-and-why of it all and memorization is less of an issue."

Sometimes, the most practical way of keeping on top of any curriculum is simply to read a chapter or two ahead in a student's textbooks. Parents say this practice helps them spot problems and plan supplementary or enrichment activities that give students a head start. "When I saw my son had an introduction to fractions coming up, I made a point of getting him involved in some cooking activities," one mother remembers. "He did all the measuring, which helped him understand concepts like one-half and one-third." Another mother increased her daughter's interest in an upcoming unit on Roman history (and effectively previewed the subject) by visiting a museum to see ancient Roman sculptures and artifacts. At the end of this book, Appendix B reviews the academic gains in reading, writing, math, and thinking skills that are typically expected at different grade levels. You can use this information to help determine whether your child is being challenged at the appropriate rate and level.

An important final word on curriculum: Do *not* assume your child's special education teacher is familiar with the programs being used in general education classrooms. Not many special education teachers

Is Your Child's School Failing?

In 2001, the No Child Left Behind Act (The Elementary and Secondary Education Act of 2001) was passed by Congress to ensure that all children have a fair and equal opportunity to obtain a high-quality education and to reach a minimum level of proficiency on challenging state academic-achievement standards. Among the requirements of NCLB are these:

- States will define academic content for each grade in reading/language arts, mathematics and science.
- States will establish challenging standards for proficiency in each of these subjects.
- Schools will hire highly qualified teachers (certified or with demonstrated competency in every content area they teach) in every classroom; these teachers will provide instruction that has been scientifically validated.
- The educational needs of all children will be met.
- States will assess how well public schools are teaching these subjects to all students and make this information available to the public. States must report the performance of public school students broken down by subgroups—including gender, race/ethnicity, poverty level, English language learners, *and disability status*—once each year.

NCLB requires states to bring 95 percent of students up to proficiency standards in reading and math by 2014. (Students with the most significant disabilities and those who are new English speakers are permitted to take alternative assessments using different standards.) Each year, the state determines whether or not each school has made adequate yearly progress (AYP) toward that goal.

While NCLB has been criticized for several reasons, this law does hold schools accountable for how well *all* students—including students with disabilities—learn. As a result, expectations for children with disabilities have been raised, and their access to the general education curriculum has been improved. NCLB also provides parents with information that was hard (if not impossible) to get before; parents must now receive annual "report cards" measuring the effectiveness of all the public schools in their districts. When a school fails to meet AYP requirements, families have important rights, including these:

- *The right to change schools.* If a school fails to meet AYP standards for two years in a row, parents may choose to enroll their child in a different school that is meeting AYP standards. The school district is required to pay for transportation to the new school.

- *The right to Supplemental Educational Services (SES).* If a school fails to meet AYP standards for three years or more, children there are entitled to additional instruction to bring them up to speed. Supplementary services include free tutoring, after-school programs, and summer school. States must develop a list of approved providers of these services. (SES providers may include agencies and individuals outside the school district.)

When considering a change of schools, parents of students with learning disabilities need to ask some key questions:

How are students with learning disabilities performing? Look at the performance of the special education subgroup at the schools you are considering. Are most students with disabilities meeting grade-level expectations and passing competency tests? (For more information on tests, see High-Stakes Testing, page 198.)

How are students with special education needs taught? Research finds that the more isolated students with special needs are, the less access they have to the general curriculum. Students with special needs should be fully integrated into the school environment, including extracurricular activities.

How qualified are the teachers? Do all teachers and learning specialists meet new standards established by NCLB? Are special education teachers certified in both special education and the subjects they teach? Have general education teachers received professional development in the area of working with students with learning disabilities?

Are specialized staff available? If your child needs the services of an aide, a speech therapist, a psychologist, or another professional, does the staff at the new school include these people? Can the school implement everything in the student's existing IEP?

Is the student comfortable with a change of schools? If the child is uneasy with being bussed or miserable about being separated from friends, a change of school may be unwise—unhappy students are not usually successful students. Students remaining in underperforming schools will likely need additional help to meet state achievement standards, however, either in the form of Supplementary Educational Services or private instruction.

Adapted with permission from *No Child Left Behind: Making the Most of Options for IDEA-Eligible Students* by Candace Cortielle © 2010, National Center for Learning Disabilities.

have the time to keep track of how all subjects are taught in each of their students' classes. If you become concerned about the methods or materials used by a particular general education teacher, alert the special education teacher promptly and ask for help with intervention.

Since the passage of the No Child Left Behind Act (NCLB), parents have some new ways of evaluating how well mathematics and language arts are taught in their district's public schools (see box, *Is Your Child's School Failing?*). This federal law has substantially raised the bar on expectations for the nation's elementary schools. Under NCLB, the majority of students with disabilities are expected to meet the same achievement standards as typical learners. Parents need to make sure students with LD are receiving enough exposure to the general education curricula to meet these standards.

PAY ATTENTION TO BASIC SKILLS

Research indicates that significant delays in reading, writing, and arithmetic increase students' risk for academic failure and dropping out of school. This is why children who are making slow academic progress are sometimes encouraged to repeat kindergarten or first grade. Educators want to make sure children get the best possible basic-skills foundation before they move on to more complex subject matter.

Basic-skills acquisition, then, is obviously a matter of concern to any parent. What many parents do not realize, however, is that schools offer children a relatively small window of opportunity for learning these skills. In a typical grade school, basic skills are pretty much what the curriculum is about from kindergarten through third grade (everything else generally falls in the category of "enrichment"). In the fourth through sixth grades, however, increasing amounts of additional subject matter (science, health, social studies, and so forth) are introduced, and explicit instruction in reading is phased out. Math begins to focus on complex operations (such as working with decimals and fractions, long division, and word problems) for which knowledge of basic arithmetic is necessary. Writing instruction shifts to matters of composition, and competence with basic grammar and usage (punctuation, capitalization, and so on) is increasingly expected rather than taught. What this means is that children who have failed to master the fundamentals of reading, writing, and arithmetic by the fourth grade have substantially missed the educational boat. At age nine or ten, Johnny may be ready to learn basic skills, only to find that his teachers aren't teaching that anymore.

While continuing basic-skills instruction is usually available through remedial and special education programs, these programs do not always provide the intensity of instruction students need, or the time and opportunities they require to practice new skills. If they do not, the gap between Johnny's skills and those of his classmates will start to grow. As a result, Johnny will become less and less prepared to handle his academic subjects as the years go on, and find it harder and harder to maintain interest in school. This scenario is the sad experience of too many students with learning disabilities. To avoid this kind of educational tragedy, there are several things parents can do:

Monitor Progress Frequently

Most schools give achievement tests once a year to establish how students are doing in basic skills. The progress of students with learning disabilities, however, needs to be checked more often. Failure to move forward in reading, writing, or arithmetic is a red flag signaling that intervention is needed, and children should not have to languish for a year—or even half a year—before appropriate help is provided. Understanding where your child's basic skills stand with respect to other students will also help you determine what kinds of support will be necessary to help him or her keep up in class. A sixth-grader who is a year behind in reading may only need a little extra time to handle class texts, for example, while a student who is three years behind will probably need to be paired with someone who can read texts aloud or be provided with materials written at a lower reading level.

It is therefore important to discuss ongoing monitoring systems with your child's teachers. Curriculum-based Measurement (explained in Chapter 8) offers teachers a simple way of checking on skills development using ordinary class materials. Weekly progress reports like the one illustrated on page 258 can help parents and teachers keep

What About Retention?

Retention is frequently recommended for kindergartners and first-graders who have not made satisfactory progress in prereading, writing, and counting skills. Repeating a year may also be advised (or required) for students who have not passed basic-skills competency tests at various educational "checkpoints" such as third, fifth, and/or eighth grades. Does retention actually help children?

Research suggests retention is valuable in very limited circumstances. Repeating kindergarten or first grade can give children who were not ready to start school or who are "late bloomers" the time they need to catch up in their academic-readiness skills. Retention is therefore a viable option for students who have started school very young, and for youngsters who have mild developmental delays. Children who have been deprived of *opportunities* to learn (due to illness, frequent moves, or emotional stress, for example) can also benefit from retention—given the opportunity to learn what they hadn't been exposed to, they thrive. Research shows that the best candidates for retention are youngsters who are of average intelligence, show normal social and emotional adjustment, and who have no serious academic deficits. In all cases, retention is likely to succeed only if children's parents are thoroughly supportive of the idea and children themselves do not oppose it. It is important for children to understand the difference between failure and needing extra time to grow. When youngsters think they are repeating because they have failed or are stupid, sinking self-esteem is likely to wipe out any benefit an extra year of education might provide. One alternative to retention for such children are transition classes between kindergarten and first grade where children's learning skills are given time to mature.

Studies show that youngsters with more severe academic deficits and students of below-average intelligence benefit less from retention. Although they may make some gains during a repeated year, their progress typically remains slow and so the gap between their skills and those of average learners grows. Evidence suggests these stu-

in touch about both academic skills and classroom behavior (an issue that is important to teachers). You can also keep tabs on your child's progress using the basic-skills charts supplied in our Appendix B. Be especially watchful for lags in areas that are building blocks for higher education. (Spelling problems are less worrisome than trouble-sequencing ideas in written compositions, for example.)

dents' failure to make progress is due to their need for a different type or intensity of instruction, not a need for more time. Rather than make them repeat what did not work for them before, it is better to refer these students for remedial programs or special education intervention at the earliest possible point.

Research indicates that after sixth grade the effects of retention are almost entirely negative. Repeating a year in junior high school is associated with increased rates of failure, truancy, and behavior problems. Students who have been retained in later years, retained against their will, or retained more than once are also at significantly higher risk for dropping out of school before graduation. As students grow older, potential for academic gain appears to be sharply undercut by the decline in social status associated with repeating a year of school. Other means of assistance (tutoring, remedial and summer programs, special education) are therefore better choices for secondary students with achievement problems.

It should never be assumed that repeating a year of school will solve all a child's academic problems, especially in the early elementary school years. Children repeating kindergarten, first, or second grades should also be exposed to an expanded range of teaching methods and materials to see if they benefit from new approaches. If children have not shown satisfactory progress two or three months into a repeated year despite intensified efforts to reach them, special education intervention should be sought without delay. Note that special education services can be provided to young children without formally identifying a specific disability. Changes to federal law enacted in 1997 made it possible to offer this support to *any* child aged three through nine who is experiencing persistent physical, cognitive, communication, social, or emotional difficulties. Through age nine, the child is referred to as "developmentally delayed," regardless of the nature of the disability, and special education services are provided.

If your child is not making progress in basic skills, ask for a conference with his general and special education teachers to discuss intervention. Sometimes a simple adjustment to the child's program (providing more practice with a new skill, for example) will bring improvement. At other times more substantial changes (such as intensifying time in remedial instruction or placement in a smaller or more

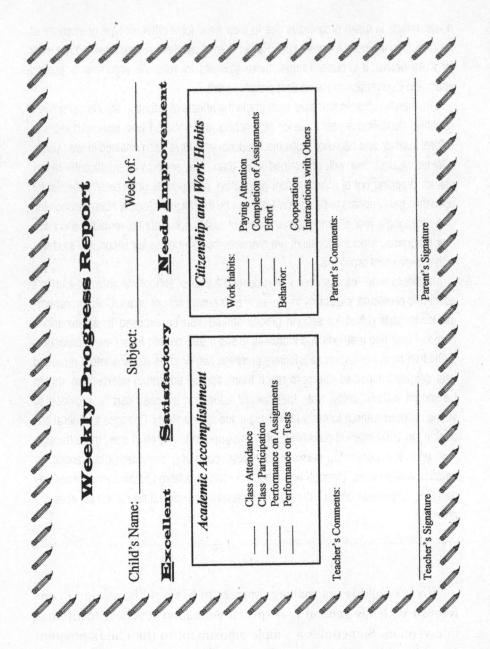

Weekly Progress Report

Child's Name: _____   Subject: _____   Week of: _____

Excellent   **S**atisfactory   **N**eeds **I**mprovement

Academic Accomplishment

	Class Attendance
	Class Participation
	Performance on Assignments
	Performance on Tests

Citizenship and Work Habits

Work habits:
	Paying Attention
	Completion of Assignments
	Effort

Behavior:
	Cooperation
	Interactions with Others

Teacher's Comments:

Parent's Comments:

Teacher's Signature

Parent's Signature

structured class) might be called for. The point is to address the issue promptly so that your child does not become unnecessarily discouraged or frustrated.

Communicate with Teachers About How Your Child Learns

While special education departments often collect a great deal of data about how a child with disabilities learns, only some of this information may trickle down to the child's regular classroom teachers. As a result, you cannot assume these teachers know what teaching methods and materials are most likely to work with your child unless you tell them. Information that is most useful to teachers includes

- how the child's disability might affect performance in different subject areas (for example, the child has trouble with word problems in math; spells phonetically; tires and loses focus during long periods of reading);
- areas of particular strength or interest (the child is talented in music; loves computers; gets along well with others);
- teaching or management methods that have proved successful (the child needs the main points of a lesson to be summarized in advance; does best when seated in front row; responds to particular positive behavior interventions);
- accommodations or special grading policies that have been approved (the student may take tests in resource room, use a calculator to retrieve math facts, receive assistance with note taking).

Many parents schedule a parent-teacher conference to discuss these concerns—or provide this information in writing—at the beginning of each school year while children are in elementary school. This practice not only reduces the chances that your child will be taught inappropriately, but it can also help dispel the negative attitudes some classroom teachers have about students who have learning disabilities. A father explains: "Teachers have egos, too, and few enjoy working with students who don't succeed. Anything you can do to help a teacher work with your child more successfully will pay off in increased acceptance and approval."

Reinforce Basic Skills at Home

Many students with learning problems see basic skills primarily as a series of academic hurdles they have to leap—not as pathways to knowledge or tools that can help them in real-life situations. Because they fail to see the relevance of these skills, their level of commitment to learning them remains low. When children are encouraged to apply their skills in daily life, however, both motivation and performance often benefit. Not only does experience make learning more relevant, it may actually improve the child's capacity to handle new information. A growing body of research suggests that growth in different areas of the brain can be stimulated by mental exercise. Some authorities believe, for example, that living in a language-rich environment promotes neural connections in parts of the brain that are concerned with language.

Parents are in a far better position than teachers to help children place basic skills in a practical context. Some of the most valuable things parents can do include the following:

Talk with children. Although it's obvious, many never think of it: a child's first experience with language is through speech, and those who don't learn to handle language competently at that level rarely become skilled at reading and writing. Talking with children can also help them learn to express ideas and put them in logical order.

Read to children . . . and help them find appropriate reading materials of their own. Reading to children builds vocabulary, encourages interest in books, and stimulates thinking—and children love the "quality time" that reading with a parent provides. In addition to reading to children, show them that reading is a tool they can use to entertain themselves or get useful information (try asking children to help you look up information—anything from how to cook a turkey to who scored the most touchdowns in a single season—on the internet). Subscribing to publications that focus on areas of interest to young people is another good way to keep them reading (even a basketball-crazed teen might make time for a magazine like *Sports Illustrated*). For more suggestions on reading with children, see pages 262–65.

Play games. Word games like Scrabble and Boggle can help build vocabulary skills, while Battleship and chess encourage youngsters to plan and develop logical strategies. Almost any kind of game is better for intellectual development than TV.

Let children manage money. An allowance can be a valuable math-teaching tool, if you are clear about when cash will be handed over and what it is expected to cover. In Chapter 11 we will discuss guidelines for helping children with learning disabilities to handle money wisely.

Encourage correspondence. Exchanging letters with pen pals, writing to public officials or the newspaper about issues of importance, even writing fan letters to celebrities helps students learn to put ideas on paper. A father mentions that email and instant messaging may have rescued the art of letter writing from the scrap heap of history (kids love it because they don't have to wait a long time for replies).

Show children how you use your own basic skills. Bringing children to work can give them insight into how academic skills are used on the job. Involving young people in cooking, shopping, and other activities can also show them how you use basic skills in daily life (get them to help you figure out gas mileage for the car or adapt a recipe for four to serve six).

Do remember that progress in basic skills for youngsters with learning disabilities is not always smooth. Many develop skills in bursts of learning activity separated by relatively stagnant periods. When this is the case it is important not to let either yourself or the child become discouraged. Think of these plateaus as opportunities to consolidate skills by applying them in new ways. It is also vital not

Guidelines for Reading with Your Child

One of the best ways to become more proficient at reading is practice, practice, and more practice. Children are unlikely to be motivated to persist with reading, however, if it is all work, all the time. There are a number of things parents can do to help children get the most out of the reading process:

Read to your child, **and listen to your child read to you.** Most children find the process of being read to by a parent a pleasurable bonding experience. Children also like to show off new skills to their loved ones, and the positive feedback they receive helps keep them motivated. Don't limit your reading activities to academic subjects—students will have more positive attitudes about reading if you also read entertaining stories (such as the Harry Potter or Little House on the Prairie books) together.

Monitor reading material for difficulty. Processing text requires effort, and students lose their motivation rapidly when reading material is too difficult. Research finds that students are unlikely to persist if they cannot read 95 percent of a text fluently (that is, without stopping to sound out a word). If your child is stumbling over five (or more) words in every hundred, the text is too hard. Look for an easier book, or—if the text is required for school—consider alternative ways of covering the material (such as asking the teacher to provide a simplified text or making a voice recording of it).

Note that the motivation of struggling readers is sometimes undermined by the fact that the material they are given is not age appropriate: a seventh-grader who is three years behind in reading will be bored and embarrassed by most fourth-grade texts, for example. To address this problem, look for high-interest, low-readability materials that use simplified language to discuss topics of interest to older students and adults. These books look more like "grown-up" books; they are smaller and have smaller print than books designed for younger children, and the illustrations depict older children or adults. There are publishers who specialize in high-interest, low-readability reading materials. Your local librarian, bookstore, or

to let poor performance in reading, writing, or arithmetic interfere with a child's intellectual development in other areas. Children who do not read well, for example, can be exposed to literature by other means (try listening to an actor read Mary Shelley's *Frankenstein* on CD during a long night car ride), and they can excel in almost special education department should be able to help you find "hi-lo" publications. Reviews are also available online. Besides classic novels rewritten in easier-to-read vocabulary and simpler sentences, you will find hi-lo sports and news magazines, newspapers, reading series (such as the world's greatest heroes or natural disasters), and much more. Reading these materials is enjoyable, and children are delighted with how "aware" they are becoming.

Correct reading errors the right way. Many parents fear that interrupting a child to correct him will distract him, cause the child to over-rely on the parent for help, undermine comprehension, or injure the child's self-esteem. Research finds, however, that students who receive prompt feedback on oral reading errors both reduce their errors and improve their comprehension.

When your child stumbles over a word, stop and suggest "try it another way." If the child is still unsuccessful, encourage her to sound out the word by asking, "What does this syllable or letter sound like?" (Skip this step for children who have very poor decoding skills.) If the child continues to falter for more than three seconds, supply the word and move on. Students given this kind of feedback tend to recall words two to three days later that they hadn't recognized on their own initially.

You can prepare your child to read a passage by previewing the hardest words. Or since vocabulary tends to repeat itself from page to page, your child might prefer you to read a chapter, followed by your child reading a chapter. You can also switch page by page. Some children enjoy "modeling" your reading by listening to you read a page, then rereading it aloud to you; because the child has been made familiar with the vocabulary and message, she will be delighted with how much faster she can now read the passage.

Help your child focus. Reading a child's school texts aloud verbatim may not be the best way to present the material. Some students with LD find that their ability to focus breaks down rapidly during long periods of reading, and many need help isolating

continued

any subject provided they learn alternative methods for gathering information. Remember that our brains keep developing into early adulthood and beyond. Possibly the greatest tragedy in education is that every year many children stop learning because adults give up and stop teaching them.

the most important points in their lessons. Studies find that most students do best when essential concepts are taught deeply, and less important material briefly summarized (or skipped altogether). Instead of starting right in on a new social studies chapter, for example,

- *Consult the teacher* to find out which is the most important material to emphasize and what can be briefly summarized or skipped.
- *Preview the text,* pointing out how chapter introductions, subheadings, topic sentences, and illustrations can be used to do this. ("This chapter is about building the Erie Canal. Here are pictures of some of the people we will learn about. People made fun of the canal and called it 'Clinton's Ditch.' Let's find out why. . . .")
- *Draw the child's attention to the most important material as you go along.* Try numbering important points ("So, three ways the Erie Canal improved life in New York were . . ."). Material that is not essential to understanding the main topic can be briefly paraphrased or passed over.
- *Insert questions or reminders that encourage your child to stop and think.* These reminders should occur at least once per page. ("Where did the canal start and where did it end? How did people travel on the canal? Do you think the canal was a good idea? Why?"). Try encouraging your child to read a page silently, then ask her to answer three questions about the material (both fact questions and idea questions).

Improve comprehension. Many children with LD—including some who read fluently—have trouble remembering what they read because they have not fully understood it. Most of the strategies described in this box help improve comprehension (students must reach a certain level of fluency before they can apply their brainpower to issues of comprehension, for example, so providing materials appropriate for students' reading levels is important.) Two other means of improving comprehension are these:

- *Broaden your child's horizons:* Research has found that ability to understand and remember new information is influenced by cultural background, vocabu-

TAKE ADVANTAGE OF TECHNOLOGY

As one student put it, "If you have to have a handicap, this is the era to be handicapped in." He was referring to the array of technological supports that have become available in recent years to students with learning disabilities and other handicaps. Chief among these are personal lary, and the prior knowledge a child brings to the process of reading and listening. Basically, the more a child already knows, the easier he will find it to learn. Children who have parents who read with them and encourage them to try new activities (anything from a museum visit to foreign travel) therefore have a distinct advantage in school and in life. In addition to reading books that relate to your child's interests, try a few that introduce new subjects you think your child might enjoy. (Make sure to explain vocabulary words that are unfamiliar.) Doing internet research together on topics of interest is another wonderful way to increase your child's knowledge and motivation to learn.

- *Talk about what you read:* Studies have found that when students discuss questions related to a new text *before* reading, comprehension improves. (Questions motivate children to find out the answers.) Discussing text *after* reading helps reinforce important concepts and information. (Simply stopping after every paragraph or page to restate the main idea can work marvels.) Breaking up long periods of reading with questions and discussion can also help keep children engaged. The next time you read a story aloud, try stopping and asking the child to predict what happens next—or tell you how the story should end—to pull the child into the storytelling process. Then read on and compare endings or developments.

Emphasize reading in your daily activities. Engage your child in "real life" reading activities such as helping you find information on the internet (search for movie times or shopping bargains, for example), looking for specific signs on the road (or particular labels in the supermarket), and helping you follow written directions (as in trying a new recipe or putting together a bicycle or bookshelf for the child's room). Whenever you can relate information gained through reading to positive outcomes ("Great—winter coats are on sale downtown—let's go!") your child's attitudes about reading will be reinforced.

computers, which now include a variety of useful programs even in the most basic packages (see What Can a Computer Do for My Child? on pages 266–69). Some of the most helpful devices, however, are less costly and complicated. Below is a list of some familiar electronic aids that can help children with learning disabilities cope. (In Appendix C an expert on adaptive technology discusses this subject in greater detail.)

What Can a Computer Do for My Child?

The father of an eleven-year-old with severe language-processing disabilities sits down at his keyboard to show us some of the ways his family has been able to use a home computer for educational support. "My daughter was interested in reading *Little Women*," he explains. "That's a great book for her age, but she would have a lot of trouble reading it herself. So we got on the internet *(click, click)* and found *Little Women* in a university library. Then *(click)* we downloaded the book into our computer's memory—we can do that because it's not copyrighted material. Now I call the text up on our screen *(click)* . . . here's Chapter 1. Okay, now we choose a voice *(click)* and the computer starts reading the text aloud." The computer does indeed start reading Louisa May Alcott's classic in a pleasant baritone, highlighting each word on the screen as it goes along. "If you like a female voice better, we can do that," our guide says, clicking away on his mouse. The computer now sounds like a woman. "You want it slower? We can do that, too *(click, click, click)*. See? We're all set, and we didn't even have to go to the bookstore or the library."

Welcome to the brave new world of computers. The technology demonstrated above was included in a fairly standard home-computer package. The cost of such packages in this highly competitive industry has been dropping steadily, putting computers in range of more and more American family budgets. Before you buy, however, it is important to understand the educational applications of computers and determine which (if any) would be useful to your child.

Computers' usefulness in education falls into three basic categories: *drill and practice, instruction,* and *tools.* All three can have value for youngsters with learning disabilities, but applications must be carefully chosen with individual students' specific needs in mind.

Drill and practice. Youngsters with learning disabilities often need extra drill and practice to master new skills. Gamelike computer programs can make drills in math or vocabulary skills more fun, thereby increasing the time students are willing to spend on these tasks. On the downside, students may find the graphics in some programs too confusing, distracting, or overstimulating to be helpful. Rapidly paced programs are inappropriate for some students' information-processing speeds and reaction times. In addition, use of the keyboard and joysticks requires a fairly high level of manual dexterity.

Instruction. You can find tutorial programs that teach a huge range of subjects at a variety of levels. Because the child controls the speed at which information is introduced (lessons can be stopped and repeated at any time), these programs can help students with learning disabilities master new material at their own pace. Some programs use sophisticated graphics and sound effects to introduce new skills and concepts in creative ways. Students particularly like simulation programs, which take a "you are there" approach to subject matter (the computer simulates a road test to help a student learn driving skills, for example, or enables the student to decide moves in an important historical battle). The best of these programs teach more than content: they also help students learn such important problem-solving skills and strategies as forming and testing hypotheses, planning ahead, evaluating risks, analyzing clues, interpreting directions, and using maps. Not all programs, however, are well designed and educationally sound—many offer more flash than substance. Overreliance on computer instruction is also a problem at some schools. If your child is using a computer in the classroom, make sure this instruction is being used to reinforce what a teacher has taught, not as a substitute for professional teaching assistance.

Tools. Computers can be used as tools for communicating; for finding, organizing, and storing information; and for solving many kinds of problems. Given the right kinds of software, for example, you could use a computer to access library materials and research a report, organize and file your notes, write the report, and illustrate it with charts, graphs, and pictures (sophisticated graphics programs even make animation possible). At many colleges, your report can be submitted to professors electronically instead of on paper. When you are finished doing that, you can email a few friends, pay your bills online, and play a game of chess or solitaire, all without leaving your keyboard. As we have already seen, computers can be used to assist students who have learning disabilities with reading in many ways. Voice-activated writing programs have made it possible for computers to take dictation (originally developed for busy executives, these programs were rapidly adapted for special education use). The wizards of the world of microchips seem to be coming up with additional applications every day.

Of all these tools, by far the most useful to students is word processing—in fact, some parents say it is worth buying a computer for word-processing capability alone. Good word-processing programs offer a host of advantages to youngsters with learning disabilities. By making manipulation of text easy, they facilitate brainstorming and organizing ideas, creating outlines, writing rough drafts, and making improvements and corrections. Modern programs come equipped with spell-checkers and a built-in thesaurus (which can help students expand their vocabularies). Most programs even advise students on issues of grammar and style (for example, the computer might indicate that sentences are too long

continued

or that certain words have been overused). All these features reduce the agony involved in getting ideas down on paper, and can therefore improve motivation and the overall quality of student work. (Of course, a teacher is still necessary to help students learn the basic principles of organization and good writing.)

If you are convinced a computer can help your child, it is important to research this investment carefully. Prices and the types of equipment included in different packages vary, and not every system will meet your needs. Some important questions to ask when looking for a home computer are listed below:

- *Will the system do everything I want it to do?* Try to think through in advance all the ways different family members will use the computer. If you are interested in computers that can read aloud, for example, you need a machine equipped with a particular type of sound card. To scan your child's books and worksheets, you must also have optical character recognition (OCR) software. (Always listen to computers "talk" before you buy; voice quality varies considerably.) Students interested in creating computer graphics usually want high-resolution monitors and top-quality printers. Families interested in email and other online services will need access to telephone or cable lines by means of a modem. Computer salespeople can demonstrate different options and help you separate the necessities from the frills.

    Decide also whether you want a desktop computer or a laptop. Laptops save space and offer the advantage of portability. Desktops can be equipped with better monitors and are usually less expensive.

- *Is the memory provided adequate? Expandable?* Memory capacity affects speed at which word-processing and high-tech graphics programs run, as well as how much material can be stored. Buying an expandable system will make it possible for you to update your machine to handle new programs and applications.

- *What equipment is included in the system?* Does the package include a monitor? Speakers? A printer, a modem, a mouse? Can a scanner, copier, and/or fax machine be added? Find out what the cost of upgrading or adding components would be, and shop around for the best prices. The high-volume, low-overhead companies that advertise in computer magazines sometimes offer good deals. (The lowest-cost equipment may be found online.)

- *What software is included?* To make packages more attractive or competitive, dealers sometimes "throw in" programs with the machines. If they are programs you actually want, you can save hundreds of dollars. Word-processing programs usually have to be bought separately and must be investigated carefully—some are much easier to use than others. To learn more about word-processing and other software, check computer magazines for reviews of software created for the home market (many reviews are available online). Computer-savvy teachers and parents are among the best sources of software reviews and recommendations. Learning-disabilities organizations support groups (such as www.ldonline.org) are also a great resource for learning about special education applications. If your child is using a word-processing program at school, using the same one at home will cut down on confusion and "glitches" when transferring material from one machine to another.

- *Who will I call when things go wrong?* Sooner or later, something will. If you have a friend or relative who is computer-wise, great. If you don't, forget about internet or mail-order sales. Buy your system from a reputable local dealer that has an accessible and well-informed staff.

Note that when use of a computer has been determined to be essential to a child's educational development, school systems must provide a computer and appropriate software for the child's use at school. Students who have severe or multiple handicaps are the most likely to qualify for this type of assistance (a child whose learning disabilities are compounded by severe speech problems, for example, might need a computer in order to communicate). Access to computers at school can also be negotiated for specific situations (for example, a student with learning disabilities might be permitted to take notes on a computer in the classroom, or take tests in the school computer lab). If students intend to carry work on computer disks to and from school, it is important to make sure your home computer is compatible with the system used at school.

Be aware, however, that checking out systems at school may lead you into the heart of a computer controversy. Apple (the manufacturer of Macintosh systems) has very successfully marketed its products to schools for many years. IBM personal computers (PCs) and their compatible cousins, however, have developed an increasingly firm grip on the home market. As a result there are some good educational programs that run only on Apple systems and some popular word-processing and data-management programs that run only on IBM-type machines. If you're new to the computer game, veterans suggest you choose the *programs* that best meet your needs first, then look for value in a machine that runs the software you have selected. (See Appendix C for further discussion of specific technology that could be helpful to your child.)

Calculators

Research has consistently shown that use of calculators in elementary school increases skill acquisition, improves attitudes toward math, and frees youngsters to reason more intelligently about mathematical concepts. As a result, many experts now urge that *all* children learn to use calculators in math class (although teachers have resisted this recommendation). For children with learning disabilities, use of calculators is even more important. Ready access to addition, subtraction, and multiplication facts via calculator enables these students to keep up with the curriculum and allows them to focus their mental energy on problem-solving strategies. Seeing correct numbers pop up over and over again also helps these youngsters learn their basic math facts (when calculating on their own, these students often produce many errors). To use calculators to the greatest advantage, students should be taught to employ them to solve each step of a complex problem—not to jump straight to the final conclusion. (For example, students would use the calculator only to retrieve division, multiplication, and subtraction facts while actually doing the process of long division by hand.) Oversized calculators are available for children with weak fine-motor skills, and "talking calculators" help children who need auditory feedback (the student can wear headphones when the calculator is used in class).

Students with documented disabilities can be permitted to use calculators on tests, including many standardized achievement tests (make sure this modification is recorded on the student's IEP). On some tests—including the SAT mathematics section and the level 1 and 2 SAT subject tests in mathematics—*all* students are now encouraged to use scientific or graphing calculators. Students taking these exams should learn to use scientific and/or graphing calculators in their advanced math courses.

Note that some students find a math-facts chart easier than using a calculator for retrieving basic math information. "Cheat sheets" can also be used to give students access to formulas, theorems, or equations that they are unable to memorize. As with calculators, proper use of these materials frees students to develop a better understanding of math concepts.

Watches

Many inexpensive digital watches have calculators built in ("When you strap the calculator to their wrist, it makes it that much harder for them to lose it," one mother comments). Some store telephone numbers and have calendars with alarms that beep reminders at preset times (useful for students who have difficulty keeping track of appointments). These watches are not always easy to program, however, and their tiny buttons may be hard for young children and students with fine-motor problems to use. Some youngsters also find it hard to tell time on digital watches—for example, students who have trouble making sense out of number sequences will probably do better with an old-fashioned big hand and little hand. (Teachers add that watches with second hands are best for helping young children understand how the passage of time is measured.) The consensus seems to be that programmable watches work best for older kids and teens.

Wristwatches are also great for helping kids distinguish right from left; remembering that the watch is worn on the left (or right) wrist is a trick many keep using into adulthood. "But don't invest a lot of money in a watch until you are sure your child can be responsible about keeping track of it," cautions the mother of a boy who managed to lose four wristwatches in one year. "Even then, I recommend going for a watch that's shock resistant and waterproof. That way they can wear it to gym, swimming, in the shower. The less they take the watch off, the less chance of misplacing it."

Digital Recorders

Voice recorders can be valuable tools for students with many types of learning problems. For example, youngsters can record lectures in addition to taking notes. They can use recorders to complete assignments (a student who has difficulty writing might answer some homework questions orally and submit a recording to the teacher instead of a paper). Recorders can also be used as a prewriting tool. Students who feel paralyzed at the thought of writing a paper sometimes find it easier to begin by dictating their thoughts into a machine; the recording is then played back, and the ideas are written down.

Students who learn best through their ears can also use recorders as a study aid. Young people who have trouble understanding what they read, for example, may improve their comprehension if they read text material aloud into a recorder, then play the recording back and listen to it. Recorders can also be used to help students review class material and prepare for tests. Dictate (or have the student dictate) a question into the machine, then count slowly to five before recording the answer. When the recording is complete, the student listens to each question, pushes the Stop button and writes or recites the answer, then restarts the machine to see if the answer is correct.

For students who have reading disabilities, textbook chapters and other printed materials can be recorded—something some parents do for children on a regular basis. It should be understood, however, that simply transferring written material to a recording may not be enough to help these children learn. Most children with learning disabilities also need help organizing information and determining which material is most important. Experts recommend use of the following guidelines when preparing voice recordings for children:

- Read at a comfortable rate and in a natural tone of voice.

- Provide a short advance organizer or "preview" of what is to come ("This chapter concerns the first European explorers to reach South America. The explorers we will learn about are . . .").

- Do not record chapters verbatim. Instead, read key sections and summarize or paraphrase sections of lesser importance.

- Insert questions and reminders that will encourage the listener to stop and think about what has been read ("Why were the kings and queens of Europe interested in South America? What was their view of the people who already lived there?").

- Summarize the most important material ("The main point of this chapter is . . ." "The three most important consequences of European exploration were . . .").

Parents of students who are poor readers may also want to look into professionally recorded materials. Organizations that record materials for the blind (such as Recording for the Blind and Dyslexic in Princeton, New Jersey; the American Printing House for the Blind in Louisville, Kentucky; and the National Library Service for the Blind and Physically Handicapped at the Library of Congress in Washington, D.C.) can provide recorded textbooks as well as recordings of popular nonfiction books, novels, and magazines. (If the book is not already recorded, there may be an eight-month waiting period—so plan ahead.) Commercial publishers also produce books on CDs and MP3s, many read expertly by professional actors (the Harry Potter books recorded by Jim Dale are a real pleasure). Appropriately equipped computers and the latest generation of e-book readers can also read text aloud—including books, magazines, newspapers, and text from the internet.

E-Books

In the near future, the use of e-books (texts designed to be read on computers or e-book readers), is likely to grow not only in homes but also in the nation's schools. In "paperless classrooms," students need only carry a notebook computer into which their texts and workbooks have been downloaded. Students can use the same computer to complete assignments, referencing both their assigned texts and information on the internet. Sound like science fiction? A few schools are already experimenting with this system.

Meanwhile, there are several ways that students can benefit from e-book readers. Some readers can alter the size and color of text, making words easier to read. There are also machines equipped with voices that can read any text downloaded into them—including text from the internet—aloud. (Though still somewhat robotic, these machine voices are becoming increasingly sophisticated and pleasant to listen to.) Before buying an e-book reader, however, make sure you can access the texts you want with it (you may find, for example, that while you can easily download current best sellers, few textbooks are available). Ask also if the e-reader can access newspapers and other periodicals and the internet; these have the greatest potential for assisting students in school.

Cell Phones and PDAs (Personal Digital Assistants)

Even the simplest cell phones allow students to store and organize information such as phone numbers, addresses, appointments, and events such as due dates for assignments and friends' birthdays. The camera function can be used to create memory joggers (a photo of the cat, for example, can be used as a reminder to feed it). The latest generation of "smart" phones puts the entire internet in a student's pocket, and may also include features such as global-positioning devices and minikeyboards for sending or storing text.

Beware, however, of PDAs' and cell phones' considerable potential for creating distractions (a reason many schools do not allow students to carry them). During homework time, it may be best to put these aside—though time to text friends or play games might be allowed as a reward for finishing an assignment.

Electronic Spellers

These clever gizmos were originally developed for crossword-puzzle fans, but they rapidly found a larger market. When a student types a word into the handheld device, a list of correctly spelled words resembling what has been typed appears on a small screen. The machines also recognize fragments of words (if a student types in the first three or four letters, for example, the machine will start scrolling possible word choices). Most youngsters will tell you this beats thumbing through a dictionary hands down. Electronic spellers can be helpful for students who spell phonetically (the spelling of youngsters with auditory-processing weaknesses may be too irregular for the machines to recognize). Students must also be able to recognize the word they want when they see it. Electronic spellers work best for younger children—once students plug into computers, word-processing programs take over the correction of spelling errors.

Electronic Notebooks and Laptops

Designed for busy people on the go, these miniaturized data managers range from pocket-sized communications devices to minicomputers that can do anything their larger relatives can. Laptop computers run on rechargeable batteries; they can be taken to class, to a friend's house, or away on holidays. The newest notebook computers offer all the features of a laptop in a package smaller than some textbooks. Portable computers make wonderful tools for high school students with many types of learning disabilities, and they are essential for students in college. As with most electronic gadgets, prices are dropping steadily, and laptops are becoming a more familiar sight in public school classrooms.

Note that none of these devices—personal computers included— can take the place of good teaching. There is no substitute for human warmth and skill, for example, when it comes to planning lessons, selecting appropriate learning materials, and offering encouragement. At its best, however, technology *can* reduce the penalties for having a disability and help students adapt tasks to fit their strongest learning styles. As a college student puts it, "As long as I can get to a computer, I can wipe out eighty percent of my learning disability. My written work looks terrific. My life would be perfect if only the thing could help me meet girls and find the things I've lost in my room."

AVOID HOMEWORK TRAPS

Let's be clear about one thing up front—no parent should have to spend all evening, every evening, helping a child do homework. Mom and Dad need some time for themselves, for each other, and for their other children. Yet parents of kids with learning disabilities often find themselves parked at the kitchen table night after night, helping frustrated, teary-eyed youngsters through piles of reading-comprehension checks, vocabulary lists, math problems. . . . Then there are those special evenings before big projects like book reports and term papers are due (often made even more memorable by the fact that the student has procrastinated and left everything until the last minute). "I remember a night when my husband and I were both up until three in the morning helping our son finish a paper on the Civil War," one mother says wryly. "At any given point in the evening two out of three of us were hysterical."

How do parents get entangled in this sort of mess? That's easy to explain: parents love their children and they don't want the kids to fail. But overinvolvement in homework rapidly becomes counterproductive. First, when you regularly sit down and do homework with your child, you start to blur the issue of whose responsibility the work is. Some youngsters become expert at exploiting confusion in this area. Many a parent, for example, has heard a child whine, "I'm going to *flunk* this test, Mommy, because you're not *helping* me!" "That really gets the guilt machine going," a mother says. "Before you know it I'm convinced my daughter's grades really *do* depend on me!" The truth, of course, is that satisfactory completion of schoolwork is the student's obligation, not the parent's. The presence of a learning disability does not alter this basic fact. (This mother eventually learned to respond to her daughter's manipulation by saying, "The spelling test is not a problem for me, sweetheart; I've already passed fifth grade.")

A second problem is that students who receive a great deal of "help" may become increasingly convinced they cannot swim on their own academically. As their self-esteem plummets these youngsters become increasingly dependent on adults (who often respond generously to their obvious neediness, thus reinforcing an unhealthy pattern). Young people who become hooked on excessive academic nurturing can become truly panicky at the thought of tackling anything on their own. They are at high risk for failure in college or on the job—if in fact they find the courage to attempt higher education or apply for employment.

A third problem is that parents don't always make good teachers—and even when they do, children would usually rather have them act like parents, instead. The bottom line is most mothers and fathers are too emotionally involved with their children to teach them effectively. Parents often take setbacks personally. They become frustrated and disappointed (and show it) when they try to explain something and children don't get it. Sometimes their fears for their children's futures lead them to increase academic pressure, urging youngsters to shape up, try harder, put in more time . . . (parents who are high achievers themselves are most likely to exhibit this kind of response; fathers are observed to be somewhat less patient with children's forgetfulness and short attention spans than are mothers). Of course it's all for the children's own good (parents say), but children rarely see it that way. What they want most from their parents is emotional support and help structuring an environment in which they can function successfully. If they get chronic tension and discontent over school issues instead, they may react by developing a distaste for learning, by withdrawing from parents emotionally, and/or by rebelling against parental authority.

What, then, is a concerned and caring parent to do? Experts (including experienced parents) offer the following guidelines for helping youngsters with homework:

Make Sure the Homework Is Doable

If it is taking a child all night to struggle through one or two assignments, the solution is not necessarily to provide more help. It might be more appropriate to discuss the problem with the student's teacher(s) and see what can be done to modify assignments and/or cut down on the total workload. "Teachers may not even *know* that it takes a child twenty minutes or more to work a certain kind of math problem, or that the combined assigned reading from several classes has become overwhelming," a parent says. "There is a limit to the amount of work any child can do in a night."

How much time is a reasonable amount to spend on homework? A special education teacher suggests that an hour a day is the most children in first through third grades can handle. Students in the third through sixth grades should be able to manage sixty to ninety minutes a day (a bit more, perhaps, when they are working on a special project). Students in the seventh through ninth grades can be expected to work on homework for two to three hours a night, and motivated tenth to twelfth graders can apply themselves for three to four hours (the level of effort typically invested by ambitious college-bound students).

Means of modifying assignments for students who are overburdened with homework include reducing the number of problems to be solved or questions to be answered (for example, do ten selected problems from each math unit instead of all twenty-five); reducing reading to the essentials and/or providing other means of keeping up with text (such as asking teachers to highlight the most important areas or pairing youngsters with a "reading buddy"); providing alternative strategies (dictating or illustrating a story instead of writing one); and eliminating some types of work entirely (for instance, exempt the student from answering questions at the end of social studies chapters so more time can be invested in math). Your child's special education teacher can help you negotiate these adjustments with regular classroom teachers. *Remember that the purpose of homework is to practice or reinforce what has been learned in class.* Homework should not be assigned to introduce new important information or to cover content that students have missed. (Research suggests that 75 percent or more of homework should involve practice and reinforcement of skills or concepts that the student already knows. As long as 25 percent or less of homework presents a challenge, students will stick with the task and thinking will be stimulated.)

Set Aside a Regular Time for Homework

Having a predictable homework time accomplishes several things. First, most children with disabilities find security in routine (these youngsters don't much like surprises, and many find changes of schedule unsettling). Second, a daily homework-time period communicates to children that homework is considered important and is not optional. Third, this practice gives parents some control over the amount of time they are going to turn over to providing academic assistance. "My kids knew I'd be available between seven and nine," a mother explains. "After that they could keep working, but I was on my own time." Experienced parents add that it is a good idea to involve children in decisions about when homework time will be. This avoids creating the impression that parents are being unreasonable or arbitrary about imposing rules and restrictions.

Be Specific About What Kinds of Help You Will Provide

Many kids will let you do as much of their work as you're willing to do, and some are adept at sucking parents into providing much more assistance than parents had planned. It is usually best, however, if parents establish some clear boundaries about what they will and will not do; this helps young people understand and face their own responsibilities. The best types of assistance are those that leave the "thinking" part of schoolwork to students. Appropriate roles for parents include the following:

Help getting organized. This includes checking calendars and assignment notebooks, making lists of things to do, going over directions, and making sure assignments are understood. Students may also need help prioritizing tasks and breaking down complex assignments (like writing a research paper) into steps or stages. In general, it is best to encourage children to do the most difficult work first—when their energy levels are highest—or sandwich the difficult task between two easy ones. Complete each assignment before moving on to the next (as opposed to jumping from assignment to assignment, as kids sometimes do when they are frustrated).

Help managing time and staying on task. Youngsters with learning disabilities often have difficulty estimating how long tasks will take, so they may need help planning their study times. (Typically, the time needed to complete assignments or prepare for a test is underestimated, so work tends to pile up at the end of the day, the week, or the semester.) For children with limited attention spans, homework may need to be scheduled in short sessions, with minibreaks and rewarding activities in between. Frequent feedback may also be needed to help children stay on course—but don't let the child trap you into continuous involvement. Some children find soft music or "white noise" (like the hum of a fan or an air conditioner) helps them concentrate; you might see how they like commercially available tapes of nature sounds (waves, wind in the trees, rain falling . . .). Some youngsters also find that rhythmic or repetitive movement helps them focus their attention. If their pencil or toe tapping drives you nuts, see if chewing gum or squeezing a soft ball provides the same benefits. Sitting on a large exercise ball instead of a chair may also help "twitchy" types concentrate.

Reading aloud. The job of reading assigned material aloud to the student or into a voice recorder often falls to parents—and many enjoy it. Do make sure, however, that students do as much of their own reading as they can; they cannot learn this skill without practice. If you do not enjoy this kind of activity or lack time to do it consistently, there are other ways to meet the child's needs: ask teachers to match the student with a peer reading partner, or hire a high school student to read to the child, for example. You may also find that a family member (such as a grandparent), a church member, or members of local community-service organizations would be willing to take on the job of recording text material.

Serving as a secretary or scribe. Students who have trouble getting words on paper sometimes have an easier time explaining what they know if they are allowed to dictate to someone. As with reading, it is important to encourage students to write out as much of their own work as they can (students can often manage short assignments on their own, but they may need help with long written projects such as reports). When serving in this capacity, it is important to record students' words faithfully—it can be very tempting to make "improvements" as you go along. Note that a common problem for students with weak handwriting skills is lining up the numbers in math problems correctly; this sometimes leads to needless confusion and errors. Some parents address this problem by writing out homework problems for students in large numerals. Also try writing out math problems on lined paper turned sideways to create vertical columns, or on graph paper.

Reviewing and proofreading written work. Students with learning disabilities are notoriously bad about checking their own work. Sometimes this is due to their disabilities (students with visual-perception problems, for example, may be unable to identify their own errors), and sometimes it is because when a difficult or boring assignment is done, students never want to see it again! By helping students check over their work, however, parents both provide some "quality control" and communicate to children that they are expected to meet high standards. Just make sure that these standards are attainable and that students are not unnecessarily penalized for making improvements. You might offer to type a corrected composition, for example, rather than asking a child to copy it over. (For many students with disabilities, copying is a task that involves generating a whole new set of mistakes.)

Students with learning disabilities also need to have information that they couldn't understand from books or lectures reviewed and/ or interpreted for them from time to time, but parents are not always the best people to do this. "Working with my son took the patience of a saint," a mother confesses, "and half the time I didn't understand his homework either. Usually I contacted his teachers when he had trouble understanding something." This sensible policy also helps teachers figure out which materials and methods work best for children and which give them trouble. If teachers are unable to give children the individual attention they need at school, finding a competent tutor may be preferable to tying up all the time you and your child have together with schoolwork or leaving yourself no free time. Even when students have learning disabilities, schoolwork should not be allowed to consume all a family's energy.

Look into Study Buddies

Peer study partners (these partnerships are usually brokered by teachers) can assist youngsters with learning disabilities in several ways. Partners can help children record assignments in a notebook or on a calendar, help copy material from the blackboard into notebooks correctly, share class and/or lab notes, and quiz or drill in preparation for tests. In addition to providing direct assistance, peer study partners serve as positive role models in the classroom. Students who are good choices for partnerships are those who are well organized, have good social skills, and have a firm grasp on class subject matter. It is also best if the partner volunteers for this duty (there is usually no shortage of volunteer helpers in classes where teachers recognize and praise cooperative effort). Partners who are required to work with a student who has learning problems may be too resentful to offer much in the way of patience and understanding. Children with learning disabilities can also benefit from working with older student "mentors." A fifth- or sixth-grader, for example, might provide valuable one-on-one instruction for a fourth-grader who is struggling with long division. (Educators know this kind of relationship is usually good for the older students as well; teaching helps them consolidate and expand their own knowledge.)

With teachers' permission, youngsters can also team up to tackle tasks such as research reports; this practice helps keep students who have trouble working independently in the game, and it also helps reduce big projects to manageable proportions. Take care, however, that students do not coast through group projects on the coattails of energetic achievers. In the best cooperative ventures, each participant has well-defined responsibilities.

Note that homework hassles are frequently related to emotional issues. Homework makes a convenient battlefield, for example, for a student intent on challenging parental authority. If this appears to be the case, parents need to back away from the power struggle—pounding away at the issue will only make matters worse. "*Refuse* to fight over homework," a teacher advises. "If your child is avoiding it, talk to teachers about your concerns and let them work on the kid for a while. Continue to express support and willingness to help if asked. Once the pressure is off, most students realize that doing well in school is in their own best interests." If conflict over homework is part of a larger pattern of rebellion that includes defiance of authorities at school—or if a student has become withdrawn and apathetic about nonacademic activities, as well as schoolwork—the situation is more serious. These circumstances signal an emotional crisis and call for prompt intervention from a mental-health professional.

Sarah

Sarah is a twenty-one-year-old college senior who has an auditory-processing disability. She began studying the flute in fourth grade.

It's funny: I have a very hard time remembering things people say to me, but remembering music is no problem. I've always loved it. Some years music was the only thing that kept me going to school. For example, when I was in middle school I did very poorly academically. I don't mean in just math or English; I was doing horribly in *everything*. I was unhappy and unmotivated—except in band and chorus. I made an effort for my music teachers, and they gave me a lot of encouragement. When I was in eighth grade, the high school band director came and auditioned all the kids who wanted to play in the band the next year. It seemed like besides me, there were about a hundred other kids who wanted to play the flute, and we all had to play solos. The director chose me for the second seat in the high school band! That success lifted my self-esteem tremendously. I was a lot less afraid of high school, knowing I had such a good place in band waiting for me. . . .

In high school, music turned my life completely around. I eventually became involved in the Pep Band, the Marching Band, and the Concert Orchestra; I participated in three different choral groups and sang and acted in musical theater performances. I won awards for musical achievement—when our concert band was invited to play at the Epcot Center at Disney World, I even got to play the featured solo. The amazing thing, though, was the way success in music carried over to my other studies. At some point it clicked that I was successful in music *because I worked at it*—and that working hard could make a difference in my other classes. I started to apply myself, and my grades went up. When I graduated, my first-choice college awarded me an academic scholarship.

Music did wonderful things for me socially also. I would guess that eighty-five percent of the people I feel close to and keep in touch with today are friends I met through musical theater or band. Looking back, it's easy to see that without music my high school career would have been nothing. Music gave me friends and teachers who supported and believed in me. It taught me the value of effort and self-discipline and gave me self-confidence. I think I would be a very different person now if my family and my school hadn't supported my love of music the way they did.

Reprinted by permission of Sarah DeWan Litchfield, speech/language pathologist, Amherst, VA.

GIVE YOURSELVES A BREAK

Conscientious parents who have stuck with us to this point may be feeling fairly panic-stricken by now. "Good Lord!" some will be thinking. "How am I going to check up on my child's basic skills, build her a study corner, record her textbooks, find her a mentor, preview the curriculum, hold down a job, and take care of my other children, too?" Relax. You're not going to do all those things today, or probably even this year—and your child can still grow into a splendid human being if you don't ever do all of them. What we have provided in this chapter are suggestions for things parents can do to help children academically *as opportunities arise*. We wouldn't advise anyone to rush out and try them all immediately.

Instead we want to warn parents here of the hazards of becoming overly focused on academic performance. In today's achievement-oriented culture, this is a problem many families face. While any child can suffer from too much scholastic pressure, there are some special risks for students who have learning disabilities.

The greatest danger of academic "tunnel vision" is that children will be required to spend so much time and effort struggling with what they do badly that they have no energy left over to do what they do well. Many children with learning disabilities find that their spheres of success—the areas of activity or endeavor that are most satisfying to them and give them the most confidence in themselves—lie outside the academic arena. These children may be unusually creative and able at expressing themselves through art, music, or drama, for example. Some are exceptionally sensitive to the feelings of others and demonstrate strong leadership skills or commitment to their communities. They may be skilled craftspersons, clever with machines, talented athletes, enterprising entrepreneurs . . . the list of what these youngsters *can* do goes on and on. But if adults overfocus on what children *cannot* do (reading, writing, or arithmetic), these children may be deprived of the opportunities they need to explore these other areas of achievement. Even when opportunities are provided, children whose lives have been dominated by disability may lack the courage and self-confidence to risk trying something new.

Another by-product of academic overkill is that children end up leading unbalanced lives. All children need exercise (children with ADHD need it more than most), time to be with friends, and time to "veg out" and rest. Children who are never allowed to forget that they are doing poorly in school, however, may be shortchanged in any or all of these areas. Should we really be surprised when such children display explosive tempers or rebel against authority's heavy hand? Note that pressure to excel in school does not come only from parents. Teachers and guidance counselors also issue dire warnings about finding a job or getting into college—and ambitious youngsters who are competitive by nature sometimes do a great job of pressuring themselves. Parents may have to help children like this learn how to relax, lighten up, and enjoy life.

A third consideration is that overemphasizing school achievement can start to warp relationships between adults and children. When school concerns dominate the time parents and children have together, children may come to see their parents as demanding taskmasters instead of sources of warmth, acceptance, and support. It is therefore important to distinguish between encouragement to achieve ("I know you can do it") and behavior that sounds encouraging but carries a heavy subtext ("I know you can do it, and if you don't do it soon we're going to be really fed up and disappointed"). In Part IV of this book we will discuss in greater detail how parental behavior influences motivation and learning. The point to keep in mind here is that if you made a list of what children with learning disabilities need most from their families, help with schoolwork wouldn't even make the top ten. Do *not* allow your concern about school performance prevent you from playing with your child, talking with your child, enjoying outings, and sharing activities that have no academic value whatever. Those are the times that make meaningful memories—not the hours you spend helping the child look up vocabulary words.

Realistically, what all this means is that parents of children with learning disabilities must often make choices. Allow the child to go to the movies or insist that she finish her history homework? Hire a piano teacher or a math tutor? Can the teen handle chemistry given three hours of soccer practice every day? If not, should the chemistry or the soccer be given up? Sometimes the choices are very tough: should a student who is falling significantly behind, for example, be signed up for summer school or abandon the college-preparatory curriculum? Although parents sometimes feel unprepared to make these decisions, they are usually the best qualified to do so, because choices like these have to be made with the whole child in mind. Teachers and school officials can usually be counted upon to push for academic achievement; it's Mom and Dad who know how much music means to the child, how much soccer has done for the student's self-confidence and self-esteem, how much the youngster needs relief from academic stress. At the bottom line, academic potential should never be nurtured at the expense of a child's emotional security and well-being. What children need most is parents who will make humane decisions on their behalf—and teach them to establish healthy priorities and make sensible decisions for themselves as they get older.

The director of a parent-professional support group in New York (herself the mother of a successful college student with learning disabilities) adds that young people aren't the only ones to feel the pressure in our competitive society. Parents can also be tripped up by unreasonably high expectations of themselves. "Perfectionism is an awful trap," she says. "Expecting ourselves to be perfect parents is hard on us and hard on the kids, too, because perfect parents are supposed to produce perfect children. Sometimes I think the best thing we can do for our kids is relax and accept ourselves. My kids have seen me screw up a million times—and I'm glad, because that's what tells them they don't have to hate themselves if they try something and don't succeed."

What else has this authority learned from working with hundreds of parents over the years? "Hold on to your sense of humor!" she says. "The mothers who I see making it are the ones who know how to laugh. Certainly, that's been my own experience. My daughter's junior high school years were a nightmare—not only was she failing several courses and hanging out with a dangerous crowd, but her father walked out on us and I ended up in the hospital facing major surgery! We're much stronger as individuals and as a family for having survived all that, but part of the reason we did survive was that even at the worst times, we could laugh a little."

Part IV

A QUALITY LIFE

10

Social and Emotional Growth

Although parents understandably fret about school performance, research finds that "book learning" often has less to do with achievement in life than do personal attributes like optimism, ambition, adaptability, willingness to work hard, and persistence in the face of difficulty. These qualities make the difference between average and outstanding performers, and often characterize exceptionally resilient individuals who rise above disabilities and oppressive circumstances again and again.

Social competence also has an impact on how comfortably an individual functions in the real world. Not only does the ability to form and maintain relationships improve quality of life, it is a basic building block of self-esteem. Among teens, for example, connecting with a peer group is an essential part of establishing an identity. It is so important to have friends at this age that child-guidance experts view adolescent "outsiders" as extra-high risks for emotional disturbance. Significantly, teens and adults with learning disabilities consistently cite social life as an area with which they most want assistance. In surveys, this concern is often ranked as more important than finding educational opportunities or employment.

This is not to suggest that schoolwork is unimportant; educational achievement does affect students' career choices and prospects for higher learning. There is no doubt, however, that social and emotional development are equally important to a student's success and sense of well-being. There is also no doubt that the most powerful influence on a young person's social and emotional growth is the family. Many of children's feelings about themselves and other people are formed long before they start school. As they grow, the attitudes and expectations of parents and other family members continue to have an enormous effect on how they interact with others, approach difficult tasks, and view their own abilities. For an example of the impact that family can have on achievement, we need look no further than the current generation of Asian immigrants to the United States. In part because of strong family support systems that emphasize the value of hard work and education, many children who endured tremendous hardships to reach this country, lived much of their lives in poverty, and started school speaking no English at all are now leading their classes at high school and college campuses across the nation.

It is important for parents to recognize the crucial role they play in helping children develop aptitudes for living and learning. It is also important for parents of children with learning disabilities to understand that information-processing problems can affect social and emotional growth. Learning disabilities often have as great an impact on life at home and in the community as they do on performance in school. One expert suggests these handicaps should really be called living disabilities because their effects are so pervasive. Yet parents do not always connect "problem" behaviors such as bad table manners, difficulty completing chores, chronic inability to be on time, or a tendency to go bananas at Grandma's house with the neurological irregularities that cause trouble with reading or writing. As a result, some children with learning disabilities get punished for laziness, carelessness, and disobedience at home as much as they do at school. Accusations and repeated family clashes, of course, help erode these youngsters' self-esteem and add to their burdens of anger and anxiety.

Even when the link between learning disabilities and personal problems is clear and families are eager to offer support, parents may feel uncertain about how to help youngsters cope with life's challenges. Finding appropriate assistance with reading, writing, and arithmetic can seem simple compared to figuring out how to help a child who has trouble with language learn how to make conversation, or to teaching a teen with no sense of direction how to drive a car. Some parents find themselves keeping children with learning disabilities close to home in an effort to protect them from failure, hurt, or rejection. These good intentions can backfire, however, as oversheltered children tend to remain immature and often lack confidence in their own abilities to survive independently.

Also challenging for parents is managing the impact a learning disability has on family dynamics. How to deal with a spouse, for example, regarding differences over spending savings on tutoring or on private school tuition? With siblings who are resentful that the child with learning disabilities does fewer chores while grabbing *all* of Mom's free time for help with homework? Or with the grandparent who insists that what the child needs is "a little less spoiling and a lot more discipline"? When and how to apply discipline can become a divisive family issue that may find mother and father on opposing sides (about the only thing the family may agree on is that no known form of discipline seems to work). As one mother put it, "Learning disabilities are really a family affair. The stress and the emotional fallout have a ripple effect. One way or another, the problem touches everyone."

Obviously a discussion of learning disabilities cannot end with a discussion of the child's needs at school. In this section we will therefore look at some of the nonacademic factors that contribute to a quality life. In this chapter we will discuss stages of development and talk about how learning disabilities can influence social and emotional growth. In Chapter 11 we will discuss some strategies for helping young people maintain their self-esteem, develop a sense of responsibility, and form healthy relationships, both in- and outside of the family. In Chapter 12 we will look at skills that are necessary for independent living, and talk about helping young adults make the transition from school and home to the world of work or higher education. Along the way, we think you will discover that many of the problems that afflict children with learning disabilities and their families are avoidable. While living with these youngsters may never be stress free, a little understanding can go a long way toward finding solutions that preserve everyone's sanity and dignity.

LEARNING DISABILITIES AND CHILD DEVELOPMENT

On their way to maturity, all children go through a series of fairly predictable stages, each with its own set of needs and characteristic behaviors. Children with learning disabilities, however, do not always move through these stages at the same rate as their typical peers. Just as cognitive, verbal, and motor skills are often delayed among these youngsters, lags in emotional development and social skills can occur.

Chad

When Greta remarried, she was delighted how well her eight-year-old son, Chad, related to his stepfather. Greta had married Chad's father young; he was a high school dropout and a "rebel" who deserted her soon after Chad was born. Mike was a totally different kind of man: responsible and kind. The family lived on a farm, and Chad followed Mike everywhere, begging to be allowed to help with chores.

Over the next two years, however, Mike and Chad's relationship changed. "I tell Chad what I need help with but he doesn't follow through," Mike complained. "I can't trust him." Privately, Greta thought Mike's perfectionism was contributing to the problem. "Take it a little easier on him," she suggested. "He's just a kid, and he already has enough people on his case at school." Chad's grades could have been a lot better, and his fourth-grade teacher was always nagging him. "Take it easy!" Mike replied. "I'm giving him the simplest jobs as it is. He's just goofing off!"

Greta felt hurt that Mike was so rough on Chad, but Mike was hurting, too. "Lately Chad avoids me," he confided to Greta later. "I try to make time for him and show him how to do things, but it seems like he wants nothing to do with me." When Greta urged Chad to spend more time with his dad, however, Chad only replied, "He's not my dad," and retreated to his room with a video game.

At the end of the school year Chad's teacher said he had made so little progress that he ought to be tested for a learning disability. He was evaluated over the summer,

As a result, the thinking and behavior of children with learning disabilities may sometimes seem babyish or resemble that of younger children (causing exasperated parents to exclaim, "Why can't you act your age?").

In addition, many children with learning disabilities seem to enter the world with intense personalities that challenge parents to the max (it has been observed that children with learning disabilities are just like other kids—only more so). These children may be *extra*energetic, *extra*sensitive to their surroundings, *extra*moody, or *extra*insistent on doing things their own way. As a result, their behavior at any given stage of development may seem magnified. While virtually all kids go through a "no" stage at around age two and a half, for example, an intense child's "no" may seem resistant to all forms of persuasion or be accompanied by hour-long tantrums.

and found to have language-processing problems that interfered with both reading and understanding verbal directions. With help, his performance in school improved in fifth grade, but relations at home became even more strained. Mike became increasingly irritated with the boy's "carelessness and irresponsibility," while Chad's mother felt obliged to defend him. They argued about what Chad should be expected to do on the farm, and how to punish him if he failed to do it. When Mike lost his temper and told Chad he could sleep in the barn if his chores weren't finished by suppertime, Greta responded by packing a bag and taking Chad to her sister's apartment.

Neither Mike nor Greta realized that Chad's learning disability accounted for much of his problem with chores. He could not remember the lists of jobs Mike told him about, nor follow all the instructions for how to do them. (If *shown* how to do something Chad usually got it right, but Mike's teaching style leaned toward long, detailed explanations.) Aware that he was disappointing his much-admired stepfather, Chad dealt with his growing sense of inadequacy by withdrawing and masked his feelings with a hostile attitude. Because it was assumed that a learning disability was exclusively an *educational* problem, everybody in the family was miserable. Fortunately, this family's crisis led them to get counseling, which helped them identify these issues. The lesson remains: it can be perilous to address learning disabilities at school but ignore them at home.

It is important to understand that children cannot be hurried through basic stages of development. A great deal of stress can be created when cognitive or social expectations are far beyond children's levels of developmental readiness. Just as important, it is necessary to understand that some elements of personality are difficult to modify. Although the environment has a huge influence on personality, scientists now believe that some aspects of our temperaments are genetically programmed. The traits listed on pages 296–97 are those most likely to be inherited and to persist in some form throughout life. While environment can influence these traits to some extent, they will always underlie a person's personality in obvious as well as not-so-obvious ways. (In other words, a very shy child can learn good social skills and even to have fun at parties, but that child is unlikely to grow into a gregarious extrovert who looks forward to mixing in big crowds.) Parents who are not respectful of temperamental differences sometimes end up labeling a child whose approach to life is different from their own as "wrong" or bad—an attitude that can strain parent-child relationships. We will talk more about temperament in Chapter 11. For the time being, remember that a great deal of conflict and aggravation can be avoided by learning to work *with* a child's basic temperament instead of struggling against it.

Maturation is also affected by personal circumstances. A. H. Maslow, a psychologist who studied motivation, observed that as they grow, human beings attempt to get their needs met in a particular order; his hierarchy of human needs is presented on page 295. Maslow believed that all of an individual's needs must be met at one level before he or she can succeed on the next. (Maslow also observed that if several needs are present at once, people will devote their energies to meeting the needs that are most basic first.) In other words, while everyone needs affection and acceptance, children who lack shelter, safety, or family stability often have a harder time attaining emotional support than children who are securely provided for. Similarly, if teens are unable to find acceptance in a peer group, their ability to develop self-respect and set goals for themselves may be compromised. Maslow's hierarchy reminds us that concerns such as safety, stability, and acceptance are not merely "early childhood issues" or "adolescent

Maslow's Hierarchy

Psychologist A. H. Maslow ranked human desires according to importance. Individuals who are unable to satisfy basic needs (at the bottom of the pyramid) have a hard time attaining "higher-order" goals. Maslow's principles are sometimes used to explain why economically disadvantaged children are often less self-confident and successful than more privileged youngsters.

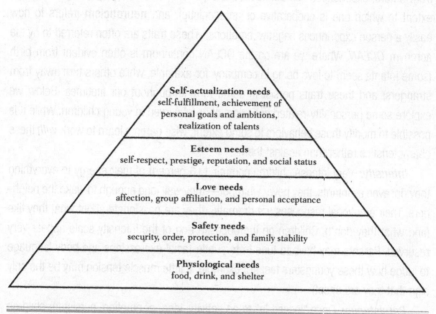

Self-actualization needs
self-fulfillment, achievement of
personal goals and ambitions,
realization of talents

Esteem needs
self-respect, prestige, reputation, and social status

Love needs
affection, group affiliation, and personal acceptance

Safety needs
security, order, protection, and family stability

Physiological needs
food, drink, and shelter

issues." These needs remain important throughout our lives. Whenever circumstances or disabilities interfere with getting basic needs met, social and emotional progress can be delayed.

With these general ideas in mind, let's look at how children behave at different stages of their development.

THE PRESCHOOL CHILD

A remarkable amount of social and emotional development takes place during the first three years of life. It is during this critical period, for example, that children discover whether or not it is safe to explore their environments and trust other people. The quality of a child's relationships at this stage can have a significant impact on his or her

Genes and Personality

Researchers have found that there are five aspects of human temperament that are substantially influenced by heredity: **openness** (ability to appreciate new experiences and ideas); **conscientiousness** (ability to discipline oneself, plan one's behavior, apply oneself to meeting goals); **extraversion** (the extent to which one seeks stimulation from others, experiences self-confidence and positive emotions); **agreeableness** (the extent to which one is cooperative or antagonistic); and **neuroticism** (refers to how easily a person experiences negative emotions). These traits are often referred to by the acronym *OCEAN*. Where we are on the OCEAN continuum is often evident from birth (some infants seem to love being in company, for example, while others turn away from strangers) and these traits persist in some form throughout our lifetimes. Below we explore some personality-related behaviors often observed in young children. While it is possible to modify these behaviors to some extent, wise parents learn to work *with* these characteristics rather than against them.

Intensity: Very intense children commit 110 percent of their energy to everything they do: even as infants, they never whimper—they wail loud enough to wake the neighbors. Their emotional responses are dramatic; they are passionate about what they like (and what they don't). Children on the opposite end of the intensity scale appear very reserved. Parents may have to tune in to subtle facial expressions and body language to judge how these youngsters feel (for example, a little muscle tension may be the only sign that they are upset).

Persistence: Once "locked in" to an activity, idea, or emotion, persistent children pursue it to the limit—and even then they have trouble giving it up. These kids will not take "no" for an answer and are not afraid to assert themselves. Less-persistent children are more easily redirected; they are also more easily "turned off" when things don't go their way and may need extra encouragement to follow through on difficult tasks.

Sensitivity to environment: Some youngsters are very sensitive to noises, smells, light, and textures. They are easily overwhelmed in busy, noisy, or crowded situations, and can be very picky about the comfort of their clothing. These children can also be extraordinarily sensitive to others' moods (they may know how you're feeling before you do). Less sensitive youngsters will wear anything and sleep through fireworks, but plan to tell them when you're getting angry or stressed out—they may not notice the storm clouds gathering.

Adaptability: Slow-to-adapt children don't like change. They are distressed by variations in their schedules and often have difficulty with transitions (both shifts from one activity to another and changes of environment). They really hate surprises (*don't* expect these kids to be happy about getting a cherry Popsicle when they were expecting grape). These children have a greater need for routine than more flexible youngsters, who change activities and settings with relative ease.

Distractibility: "Distractible" children are in fact ultraperceptive; they are very attentive to details in their environments and often see things others miss (who else would notice that the little stain on the ceiling is shaped like the state of Texas?). They may be so interested in their surroundings, however, that they have trouble following through on tasks. Less distractible youngsters are usually better at focusing their attention (but they may be so intent on homework that they completely miss the sunset glowing outside the window).

Regularity: Very regular children become hungry and sleepy at predictable intervals; even as infants, it is easy to settle them into schedules. Other children seem wired to a different kind of clock: you never know when they're going to sleep or want food. Irregular children can resist all attempts to establish routines; their parents' most frequent complaint is that they will *not* sleep through the night. (The mother of an irregular teenager says, "Take heart; eventually they learn to amuse themselves at two a.m. and they don't wake you up anymore.")

Activity level: Even when they sleep, very active children aren't still; they crawl all over the beds, tangling their covers or dumping them on the floor. They are typically curious and "into everything"; they shift rapidly from one activity to another and don't stop until they drop from fatigue. When required to sit (as at dinner or at church) they fiddle, tap, and squirm. Less-energetic children are more likely to sit quietly absorbed with a book or game. Since they are by nature less exploratory, however, parents may have to make an effort to expose these youngsters to new activities and areas of interest.

Mood: Some children are upbeat and optimistic by nature; they look for each cloud's silver lining and usually express satisfaction with their lot in life. For others, however, life is a more serious matter. These "Eeyores" tend to focus on the flaws and drawbacks in every situation and may try parents' patience with their criticisms. There is an upside to a "down" personality, however. These children are naturally analytical (definitely the companion you want with you when you test drive a used car) and can be excellent at troubleshooting all kinds of problems.

emotional outlook. In general, children who have secure, stable relationships with their adult caretakers are most likely to be attentive, motivated, and responsive to challenges. Even at age three or four these fortunate youngsters appear to have optimistic expectations and a certain amount of self-confidence. Children who have not had consistent nurturing from adults, on the other hand, are more likely to be passive, easily discouraged, withdrawn, and/or fearful of new situations. Research indicates that these early attitudes can be very persistent, enduring into the school years and even into adulthood.

The ability to play cooperatively with others typically develops at around age three (before that, children tend to play *near* each other rather than *with* each other). From this age on, peer relationships (as well as relationships with adults) present the growing child with opportunities to learn and practice social and language skills. Since children who are open, enthusiastic, and outgoing are attractive to other children, they often garner more social opportunities than those who are shy or passive. By the time they start school, these socially advantaged youngsters have a significant head start over children whose social and language skills are less developed. Children who are good communicators, comfortable with both peers and adults, and confident of their own abilities usually make good students, sometimes outdistancing peers of higher intelligence academically.

Preschoolers who have learning disabilities benefit no less than others from loving support from their parents and appropriate opportunities to interact with peers. Children who have these advantages are typically more resilient and able to compensate for their disabilities than those who are socially isolated or whose family systems are disengaged, rigid, or chaotic. Youngsters who have immature or unevenly developing nervous systems, however, can be challenging to raise and they sometimes present their parents with special problems. As infants, for example, these children are sometimes irritable and hard to comfort. They may defy all efforts to settle them into a schedule for eating and sleeping and react to attempts to play with or cuddle them by screaming or turning away. These behaviors usually leave parents feeling helpless, incompetent, and rejected. As a result, parents do not always "bond" with these infants as successfully as they do with

Eden

Eden is a seven-year-old girl of average intelligence from a middle-income family. Every child in her family has inherited a language-processing disability that results in serious reading delays. Eden's family is supportive, understanding of her disability, and hopeful about her future. Her parents have formed a cooperative relationship with Eden's teachers at school, and Eden is making steady progress. In her family picture, Eden shows her father presenting flowers to her pregnant mother, while Eden plays ball with her older sister. Her self-portrait (top left) shows a happy little girl. When she was given incomplete sentences to finish, Eden's answers reflected satisfaction with her family and high self-esteem: "Boys think I am . . . pretty"; "My father never . . . shouts"; "I know I can . . . read"; "My family is . . . important to me"; "People are always . . . nice"; "Other children . . . play with me."

their other children. Indeed, Mom and Dad may not be able to help resenting the baby who keeps them up night after night and refuses to respond to their loving efforts to relieve the child's discomforts.

Children with learning disabilities can continue to be challenging as toddlers. Difficulty processing verbal or visual information makes it harder for them to follow directions, remember rules, or play games; delays in learning to talk, dress, or feed themselves may also disappoint and frustrate parents. Children who are hyperactive often seem completely out of control as preschoolers. Many cannot seem to avoid mayhem when taken out: parents watch helplessly as supermarket displays tumble; the company picnic becomes a shambles as the child climbs all over the table, upsetting everyone's food; Grandmother's furniture and carpets sustain new damage with every visit. Even when parents go out alone, they may spend their time worrying about what kinds of catastrophe are befalling the babysitter at home.

Parents of hyperactive children often come to feel increasingly isolated from friends and extended family members—all of whom may be generous with advice on child management without fully understanding the realities of the situation. If parents disagree about how a child should be "handled" or blame each other for the child's behavior, the stress can undermine a marriage and family stability as well as parent-child relationships.

Sadly, in circumstances such as these parents and children sometimes become increasingly estranged. Research finds that parents of children with learning disabilities often feel more negatively about these youngsters than about their other children and behave toward them in a harsher or more remote manner. Sometimes parental affection is transferred to a more successful or less troublesome sibling, effectively rendering the child with disabilities "odd man out" in the family group. As the drawings on pages 299 and 301 illustrate, parents' feelings about their children directly influence how children feel about themselves. Kids who become labeled "family screwups" or "family troublemakers" usually end up with poor self-concepts and low opinions of their own abilities.

Some preschoolers with learning disabilities are also at a disadvantage when it comes to establishing peer relationships. Toddlers who are maturing slowly, for example, may remain in the possessive "mine" stage longer than usual, making them unpopular with peers who are learning to take turns, cooperate, and share. Youngsters who are impulsive human whirlwinds are usually no more welcome at nursery school or the playground than they are at the family dinner table. Preschoolers who have trouble processing verbal or visual information can have a hard time understanding the rules of even

Rebecca

Rebecca is the same age as Eden and has the same type of learning disability. Her mother and father are both physicians, and her older brother is a straight-A student. Rebecca's parents are unable to accept her disability. They are angry about her poor academic performance and have demanded that the school do something to "fix" their disappointing daughter. Their dissatisfaction and lack of respect for Rebecca's teachers has spilled over to Rebecca, who is ambivalent about investing energy in her school-work. In Rebecca's family picture, the cats are more animated than the people. Rebecca's parents and brother are together, but Rebecca is segregated, looking in from a doorway. Her self-portrait in the corner is angrily scribbled out. In response to questions about her drawing, Rebecca stated: "I'm pretty stupid"; "I'm sad because my mom and dad yell and scream"; "My brother's mean to me"; and "My mom and dad wish for me to get away for real and in the picture."

the simplest games, and they may be impatient with activities that other children enjoy. A child with auditory-processing problems, for example, is likely to be restless and disruptive during "story time" and may be frustrated to the point of tears by games like Simon Says. As games and play activities selected by others become more complex and language based, children with learning disabilities sometimes get left behind. By the time they start school, many are doubly disadvantaged: not only do they have problems with academic tasks, but they have not yet learned to interact with other children successfully. Even when youngsters come from very supportive families, the combination of poor school readiness and unsuccessful peer relationships can test their emotional defenses to the limit. Unless appropriate social opportunities are provided along with academic help, the result can be plummeting self-confidence.

THE ELEMENTARY SCHOOL STUDENT

During the elementary school years, friendships play an increasingly important role in children's sense of success and well-being. At school, matters of who sits next to whom at lunch, who gets invited to which birthday parties, and who gets selected as a best friend often get at least as much attention as reading, writing, and arithmetic. Social relationships in elementary school are increasingly governed by unwritten rules, and conformity to these rules is expected if one wants to "belong." Rigid codes may be developed for behavior, language (use of slang), and dress. This is an age when fads sweep the school with predictable regularity. A particular haircut or shoe style initially identifies peer leaders and others "in the know"; by the time everyone else catches on, a new trend is embraced or invented.

Throughout these years, same-sex friends are typically preferred. Research finds that younger and older children have somewhat different expectations of friendship—as do girls and boys. Six- to eight-year-olds, for example, say a friend is someone to play and share with, while nine- to eleven-year-olds increasingly value friends' abilities to help out and be loyal and dependable. As they approach middle school, an important element in girls' friendships is trying to *look* like one another. Boys, on the other hand, look for friends who enjoy similar pastimes—guys to "hang out" with.

Elementary-age children become very astute at "reading" the requirements and values of the different groups they interact with. A fifth-grader, for example, not only can recognize that peers and adults have different attitudes about clothes, entertainment, and grades but is also capable of distinguishing attitude variations among several different peer groups (what's "in" at one's own school, for example, may be different from what's "in" at a cousin's school or at summer camp). Desire to conform to a chosen group's standards typically becomes stronger as students get older. By the end of fourth grade most children are choosing their clothing and amusements with the opinions of other children—not their parents—uppermost in their minds. The lust to possess what "all the other kids" have can seem quite maniacal at this point. Some weary parents report almost daily requests for popular collectibles, the latest style in a particular brand of sneakers or jeans, the newest thing in electronics, and/or other items pertaining to some currently "in" activity. Even what goes into the lunch bag may be accepted or rejected on the basis of peer tastes and preferences!

Clearly, children who look "different," who are not skilled at popular sports and games, or whose behavior is erratic or unpredictable are at a disadvantage in the elementary school environment. Many youngsters with learning disabilities fall into these categories. Children who are immature or who have visual-perception deficits, for example, are often *socially imperceptive;* they do not pick up on "cues" in their environments as easily as others do. Not only do these youngsters fail to appreciate the finer points of fifth-grade fashion, they may be totally unaware that appearance influences popularity. These children also have difficulties recognizing the effect that their behavior has on others. A child with visual-perception disabilities who is describing the plot of a television show in tiresome detail, for example, may miss facial expressions and body language indicating that her audience is becoming bored or that others would like a chance to speak. Caught up in her own excitement, she rattles on and on, then wonders why no one wants to sit next to her on the bus. Frequent failure to observe social conventions can lead to a child becoming labeled unfriendly, "lame," or weird. Among youngsters with learning disabilities, however, the problem is more often ignorance of what the prevailing social conventions are, or difficulty applying social skills correctly. Children who understand the value of sharing, for example, may stumble by passing gum around during reading period rather than when on the school bus. Or they may find themselves on the periphery of the playground because they don't realize that children negotiate who will play with whom well before recess.

Some children understand social rules but nevertheless have a hard time following them. Youngsters with language weaknesses who are poorly organized, for example, may endanger friendships by their inability to remember names and phone numbers, frequent tardiness (thereby holding up group activities), or failure to return borrowed items ("I have your hat? Uh, what does it look like?"). Children who are impulsive (a common characteristic of attention-deficit/hyperactivity disorder) exasperate others by speaking and acting without thinking about the consequences. They blurt out embarrassing observations, try to insert themselves into activities that are already underway, and reach for what they want without regard for whom it belongs to or whose turn it may be to use it. (These children may later realize they have caused offense, but honest regret does not prevent them from blundering and barging in again and again.) Young people can also alienate peers with their rigidity and need to do everything one way (theirs), or their emotional immaturity (they may be so intolerant of losing, for example, that they will cheat or overturn the checkerboard rather than allow someone else to win). Predictably, youngsters such as these are avoided and sometimes ostracized; eventually many come to expect rejection. Frustration over their inability to connect positively with peers can have a corrosive effect on these children's self-esteem. Hostile attitudes ("I'll reject you before you have a chance to reject me") are sometimes adopted to mask feelings of personal inadequacy.

Youngsters who have difficulties processing language also encounter a variety of social problems. These children not only have trouble following and participating in conversations (a problem that typically gets worse in group situations) but also may appear to lack humor because they fail to appreciate wordplay or recognize the point of jokes. They make embarrassing social gaffes because they choose the wrong words or misunderstand explanations and instructions. (The child who fails to grasp that the rules of Musical Chairs call for sitting down *after* the music has stopped, for example, may feel like the laughingstock of the birthday party whether she is or not.) Learning the rules of games can be such a problem that children avoid games altogether—which of course deprives them of valuable social opportunities. ("Klutzy" kids with poor muscle coordination and children with severe perceptual disabilities can also find themselves shut out of sports and games.) Often youngsters with language disabilities cope by adopting the role of passive followers in a crowd. They find they can achieve a certain amount of acceptance by hanging watchfully around the fringes of activities, copying others' behavior. The price of this acceptance, however, may be a feeling that it is not all right to be oneself or to strive for positions of leadership.

Because of their sensitivity to issues of social status, elementary-aged children may display increasing reluctance to participate in special education interventions as they get older. To escape the stigma of a special education "label," middle school students may try to refuse to participate in these programs altogether, and many young people attempt to hide their disabilities from classmates. In surveys, students voice a variety of concerns about "going public," from risking the ridicule of poorly informed peers to jeopardizing chances for success with the opposite sex. Concerns of this kind do need to be taken seriously. The way teachers are managing classes may be contributing to the problem, and a more sensitive approach at school may improve the students' comfort levels. It is equally important, however, to probe children's own understanding and attitudes. Do they think they need special education because they are stupid, bad, genetically defective, or otherwise "messed up"? This is often the case when students lack information about learning disabilities. Students who have a thorough understanding of their own strengths and weaknesses are more likely to express confidence in themselves and in their abilities to overcome negative stereotypes. Research reveals that the secondary and college students who are most successful are those who have accepted their disabilities, know how to compensate for them, and have learned to identify situations in which they can prosper. Helping children understand their own learning patterns and empowering children to deal with them is therefore a better strategy than cooperating with efforts to hide or deny handicaps.

Note that both children and adults with learning disabilities are often observed to be somewhat egocentric. Their preoccupation with themselves and their own concerns is often interpreted as an irritating lack of sensitivity or failure to appreciate the needs and concerns of others. It is important to remember, however, that people who are literal or concrete thinkers do not easily generalize or transfer information from one set of circumstances to another. Just as children sometimes have difficulty seeing that basic number principles can be applied to word problems in math, they can have trouble placing themselves in other people's shoes. It may therefore be necessary to *explain* to them what others are thinking and feeling—even when you'd think it would be obvious. For example, a fourth-grader might be capable of being very considerate and compassionate once you tell him "Cindy is feeling very sad now because her grandmother died." Fail to provide that information, however, and he may try to tell Cindy his latest joke the moment she returns from the funeral! This is one area where understanding the child's thinking process can significantly improve family relations. If those who are close to the child get in the habit of spelling out how they feel and what kind of behavior is expected, everyone may be amazed at how sensitive and helpful the child has suddenly become.

THE ADOLESCENT

During adolescence, typical youngsters experience a "cognitive leap" that makes it easier for them to understand and reason about the world around them. It is during this time, for example, that most young people become capable of distinguishing between objective and subjective realities. They start to recognize that what you see is not always what you get, that what you are told is not always true, and that different people sometimes see things different ways. As a result, teens usually spend a great deal of time comparing their own thoughts, feelings, and experiences with those of others. This process eventually leads to the formation of independent views and opinions.

Parents—who are all too aware that their values and judgments are being scrutinized and questioned—often feel that their adolescent children are pulling away from them. Typical teens, however, want not so much to terminate as to renegotiate their relationships with their families, placing these relationships on a more grown-up basis. Often teens seem more eager to claim adult privileges than adult responsibilities (which they do not yet fully understand). What the adolescent most longs for, however, is respect for his or her emerging individual identity.

The road to an adult identity can be rocky, however. Along the way, teens must resolve some major developmental issues. On the adolescent agenda are such tasks as

- learning to accept one's changing body,
- becoming comfortable with one's sexuality and learning to express it in a safe and responsible manner,
- learning to become less emotionally dependent on parents through the development of closer relationships with peers of both sexes,
- selecting an educational and career path and preparing for economic independence, and
- developing an ethical code or set of values by which to live.

This is a tall order, and these goals are seldom achieved without a certain amount of *angst* and conflict. Typically, teens are excessively self-conscious and self-centered, wary of adults (whom they judge harshly, having only recently discovered that we can be fallible, hypocritical, or otherwise imperfect), and committed to the concept of their own "specialness." Most adolescents—including those who sincerely love and respect their parents—also develop a passion for privacy and a desire to keep the worlds of family and friends separate. Affiliation with a peer group becomes a matter of urgent importance at this stage. Friends provide the often-insecure teen with social status, a

Martin

Martin is a forty-four-year-old commercial baker. His attention-deficit/hyperactivity disorder (ADHD) was identified last year. Experts estimate that up to 50 percent of individuals with unaddressed ADHD abuse alcohol and/or other drugs at some point in their lives.

I had a lot of problems in school from the beginning—I flunked first grade. Later on I had trouble focusing on what I was reading and I could not take notes. . . . I did real well on some quizzes and short-answer tests, but essays and writing papers, that was something else. No way was I going to college. . . . By the time I graduated from high school I thought I'd never amount to anything.

I was an angry kid, too—I had a real bad temper and I got into a lot of fights. I always felt like other kids were laughing at me. Later on, when I tried to get close to girls, I'd try to get intimate too fast so of course I got rejected a lot. But I didn't understand what I was contributing to the problem. I just thought everybody hated me and that helped feed this terrific anger I felt all the time.

When I was a senior in high school I discovered alcohol and drugs and I felt like my troubles were over. I liked booze and I *loved* marijuana—it calmed me right down. Before you knew it I was partying all the time. The only problem was, alcohol made me completely crazy. I was always getting into trouble. I couldn't work steady—I kept getting mad at my bosses and quitting. I drifted from job to job, working on assembly lines, driving forklifts, doing maintenance—whatever I could get. At night I'd go to bars and get into fights . . . Or I'd buy everybody drinks, like I was trying to buy friends.

One good thing did happen in those years: I met my wife. She was a nurse at this nursing home where I worked as a security guard. Claire has been a real miracle in my life. She's always believed in me, even though I put her through a lot. She used to say, "Marty, there's something going on with you that we don't understand yet." She sensed that there was something behind all this restlessness and anger. But back then we'd never even heard of ADHD—so of course it never occurred to us that I could have it.

Meanwhile, drugs and alcohol started taking over my life. I was smoking pot all day—I smoked on the job when I could. At night I'd drink and pick fights with Claire so I'd have an excuse to storm out of the house and run around the bars. At one point things were so out of control I thought I was losing my mind. I went to a psychiatrist, who said I was paranoid schizophrenic. He put me on antipsychotic drugs, which made everything even worse (especially when I mixed them with pot and booze). I ended up locked in a psych ward for three days. The docs told my wife, "We'll look after him; go get yourself another life." She didn't buy it, thank God—she signed me out of there and we went looking for another counselor. This therapist said, "Marty, you better get yourself to Alcoholics Anonymous, and if you don't, there's not much point in coming back here."

I stopped drinking with AA in 1984, but it took me almost three years longer to give up the marijuana. It's hard to explain how much I loved that stuff; it just relaxed me and made me feel all right about things. But in the end pot twisted me and started making me even *more* hyper and nervous—yet I couldn't quit. I checked into a treatment center to get help for my drug addiction in 1987, and with the support of AA I haven't used a drink or a drug since.

After that my life got better in a lot of ways. I was able to work steady and got a job in a commercial bakery. My mom taught me how to make bread when I was a kid and my dream has always been to have a bakeshop of my own. But I was still disorganized—the house was always a mess and I had a lot of trouble remembering where I was supposed to be and being on time for things. I also had a hard time managing money. Then my wife's aunt read a book about ADHD and said, "Marty, this sounds like you." I read the book and it was like they were telling my story! I found a psychiatrist who specializes in ADHD. She recommended medication.

At first I was afraid—I was worried that I would become addicted to the medication like I had been addicted to alcohol and marijuana. But the doctor said she would monitor me carefully, so I decided to give it a try. It took a while to find a medication that worked without side effects, but what a difference the right medicine makes! It's like giving my brain a tune-up. I can organize myself. I write appointments down and get to places on time. I pick up after myself and put things away. I can sit still. I can listen. I can read! And so far I have no desire to abuse the medication at all—I take it exactly as directed.

Best of all, I have started my own business. It's part-time now—I bake Italian bread at home and deliver it to restaurants—but my customer list is growing. We're saving our money so that one day my dream of having my own shop will come true. Claire and I just celebrated our 23rd anniversary, and it feels like everything is finally coming together. Claire says she loves coming home to the smell of bread baking. She says that when I'm baking, I smile all the time.

place to "belong" outside the family, and a transitional support system that helps the child face those all-important questions: "Who am I and where am I going?" Studies suggest that teens who do not develop peer-group attachments have difficulty resolving these questions satisfactorily. Such young people may remain either inappropriately dependent on their parents' support and authority or end up separating from their families prematurely, without a reliable "inner compass" to guide them. Strong peer relationships, therefore, play a crucial role in enabling teens to grow into responsible, self-respecting adults.

Of course, the yearning to "belong" has its downside, too. Because their need to find acceptance among peers is so compelling, adolescents are exceedingly vulnerable to social pressure. To achieve popularity, even basically level-headed youngsters may sometimes engage in behavior that is foolish, harmful, or illegal. By far the most common reason teens cite for using alcohol and drugs, for example, is a desire to "fit in with the crowd"; even young people who understand and fear the consequences of drug and alcohol abuse (car accidents, arrest, addiction . . .) may fear being ridiculed or rejected by friends much more. Desire to achieve the status of having a boyfriend or girlfriend—as well as longing to experience the romance and passions glorified in movies and on television—stimulates widespread sexual experimentation among teens. Recent studies indicate that nearly half of adolescents (girls as well as boys) become sexually active during their high school years. Sadly, nearly 40 percent of sexually active teens report that they do not protect themselves against pregnancy and sexually transmitted disease. As a result, three in ten girls become pregnant before the age of twenty; 80 percent of these teens are unmarried and their pregnancies unintended. Half of sexually active youth contract a sexually transmitted disease by age twenty-five: the human papillomavirus, trichomoniasis, and chlamydia—a virus that often produces no symptoms but can damage the reproductive system and increase the chances of contracting AIDS—now infect teens in epidemic numbers. Even more tragic, teenagers have become this country's fastest growing risk group for AIDS, with half of all new HIV infections occurring in this age category.

Teens who have stable family support systems are most likely to negotiate the hazards of adolescence successfully. It is therefore critically important for parents to strive to appreciate teens' fears and concerns, to keep lines of communication open, and to uphold their own value systems by both word and deed. Adolescent children do continue to rely on their parents for guidance, security, and affection, even when their behavior suggests otherwise. Children also rely on their parents for information. Accurate facts about sex (including the risks of sexually transmitted disease, pregnancy, and sexual abuse) and about drug and alcohol use need to be provided in a tactful, nonjudgmental manner. To avoid this responsibility is, in essence, to leave a child's education in these matters to other children and the media. Recommended reading for parents who want to learn more about adolescent issues and how to address them is *Your Child's Emotional Health: Adolescence* by Jack Maguire, prepared by the Philadelphia Child Guidance Center (available in paperback from Macmillan). This easy-to-read guide includes suggestions for discussing sensitive issues with teens and also lists warning signs of dangerous adolescent crises that require intervention, including substance abuse, sexual abuse, eating disorders, and depression. (Making an effort to learn about child development at any stage is a good investment in your family's mental health. You may be relieved to discover how much "strange" behavior is normal!)

For the child with learning disabilities, the risks of adolescence can be significantly magnified. Slow-to-mature teens, for example, may find themselves in hazardous situations that they lack the cognitive awareness, emotional maturity, or basic good judgment to handle. An immature girl, for example, may fail to understand that boys could interpret friendly touching as a sexual come-on. A boy who has not yet reached the stage of mature moral reasoning may be unable to think through an older friend's invitation to go joyriding in a "borrowed" car (how annoying and unfair to cut the evening short by being arrested!). Youngsters who are particularly naive or socially imperceptive may even become the butts of cruel humor or abuse. One mother recalled her sixteen-year-old daughter dressing carefully for a "date," only to be driven to a parking lot and told how to perform oral sex. "Fortunately she had enough self-confidence to say no," Mom reports, "but she was humiliated and heartbroken because she thought this boy really liked her." Too often it's the kid with LD who is put up to a robbery or other dangerous prank by "the gang." Anxious to be accepted and included, he goes along, only to find himself the only one who is caught. (Once arrested, he does not understand his rights, so he helpfully incriminates himself and ends up paying a high price for the malicious joke of his "friends.")

Sometimes teens with learning disabilities become relatively eager participants in their own undoing. Those who have not yet established successful peer relationships, for example, may now be driven to extreme behaviors to find a place among other adolescents. A ticket to acceptance in the drug culture or party crowd is relatively easy to obtain (as one young man put it, "A friend with weed is a friend indeed"). Habitual use of alcohol and other drugs can also blunt the pain of loneliness and provide escape from other uncomfortable realities. The search for love can lead to sexual promiscuity among teens who have low self-esteem; some girls in this group actually hope for pregnancy, believing that a baby will provide focus for an aimless existence and fulfill their longings for someone to love and belong to. There are also teens who seek thrills and excitement as a means of escaping unpleasant or humdrum lives; they are attracted to risky behaviors (such as fast driving, gambling, and shoplifting) and seem to go out of their way to generate crises in their personal relationships. Experts speculate that risky or otherwise highly stimulating activities are particularly rewarding to some individuals with ADHD because they help focus attention in a way ordinary experiences cannot. Unfortunately, individuals who do not learn to channel their needs for excitement productively often find themselves at odds with the law. Young men with ADHD and other learning problems are significantly overrepresented in the juvenile justice system and adult prison population—a fact increasingly recognized by authorities who hope to improve methods of crime prevention and rehabilitation.

As with typical teens, young people with learning disabilities rise to the challenges of adolescence best when they have informed, supportive parents who model responsible behavior. Parents whose beliefs, values, and personal habits are under frequent attack from adolescents do not always find it easy to be supportive, however! (It can be even more difficult to remain understanding when the children are also blowing off family obligations and doing poorly in school.) In addition, many fathers and mothers feel threatened by the repeated assaults teens launch on their authority. In an effort to regain control, some parents become rigid and didactic and "lay down the law"—a strategy that usually succeeds only in escalating the levels of conflict. Teens who are both in conflict with their families and unable to find support among their peers are very high risks for emotional disturbance. This helps explain why research finds higher-than-normal rates of depression, anxiety, and antisocial or hostile conduct among adolescents with learning disabilities, as well as higher rates of failure to complete school. Alienated adolescents who are doing poorly in school are among the most likely to drop out. Too many teens with learning disabilities (including some who never got identified) fit that sad profile.

Even teenagers who have good family support and avoid these emotional extremes may develop counterproductive defense strategies to mask the shame of not fitting in. For example, a child who is "out of it" at school may respond by

- becoming angry and aggressive ("Move out butt-face! This is my seat!");
- cutting up or becoming the class clown ("Of *course* I'm not burping intentionally, Mrs. B. . . .");
- claiming that school is too dumb or boring to bother with ("Algebra is so stupid, like who's ever going to need it?");
- shifting blame or adopting the role of victim ("Nobody ever gives me a chance . . . they don't know how to teach . . . this family sucks . . . It's not *my* fault!");
- becoming manipulative ("Do it for me just this once! I really need your help, pleeeeeeeeeeeease!"); and/or
- creating distractions ("Look, Ma! I dyed my hair blue!").

Creative and resourceful youngsters may also use verbal intellectualism or performance in areas of relative strength to distract attention from a disability ("I'm an artist! I don't need to read; I need to *express* myself.") These self-protective postures do help youngsters cope with the pain of failure or rejection, but they can become self-defeating in the end. Children are not likely to give up these be-haviors, however, unless they are provided with alternate tools and strategies that address their real needs (this is why nagging, bribes, and threats are so rarely effective). Remember that teenagers can-not take responsibility without learning the skills (communication skills, reasoning skills, organizational skills . . .) that are the foun-dations of responsible behavior. Just as they often need special help with reading or math, teens with learning disabilities may need to have social and emotional growth opportunities tailored to their special needs.

THE YOUNG ADULT

Leaving home and entering the larger worlds of college or career can be difficult and stressful for any young person, and we should not be surprised that it is sometimes even harder for the young adult with learning disabilities to make this transition successfully. Continuing problems with academic skills, organization, taking responsibility, and establishing a personal support network can all undermine the individual's attempts to achieve economic and emotional indepen-dence. Poor self-image often exacerbates the problem. Studies find that young adults with learning disabilities often have lower expecta-tions for their futures than do their typical peers. They are less likely than others to complete college, and likely to live at home longer with their parents. Many go to work directly out of high school; they are often engaged in part-time and low-wage work, and have frequent job changes. Individuals with severe language disabilities, attention defi-cits, and/or hyperactivity are generally found to be the highest risks for low educational achievement and underemployment.

Yet many young people with learning disabilities do function suc-cessfully in demanding jobs and in institutions of higher learning. Studies of these productive young adults find a number of factors that relate to sustained good performance. Among the most impor-tant are these:

Self-awareness. The students with learning disabilities most likely to succeed in college are those who recognize their strengths and understand and accept their weaknesses. Based on this understanding, they set realistic goals, seek appropriate accommodations, and identify situations in which they are likely to perform well. Realistic understanding of disabilities is also linked to successful employment. Adults who have this insight choose appropriate careers and are resourceful about modifying tasks or developing other compensating strategies on the job.

A strong work ethic. Successful adults with learning disabilities usually frankly admit, "I had to work harder than everyone else to get where I am today." These high achievers are characteristically ambitious, goal directed, determined, and creative about overcoming obstacles. They accept the necessity of putting more time and effort into completing some tasks than other people. They may not like having disabilities, but they have put resentment and self-pity largely behind them.

A positive personality. The personal characteristics of optimism, adaptability, curiosity, and tenacity are strongly associated with both academic achievement and success on the job. Research finds that self-confidence (defined as belief in one's own ability to bring about change) also has a tremendous impact on performance. Individuals who have a strong work ethic and a "can do" attitude have been known to become successful in spite of severe disabilities and limited educations. While some aspects of personality are inborn, self-confidence and attitudes about work are most often learned from parents and other role models.

An effective support network. The support and guidance of family and/or significant others (teachers, counselors, girlfriends/boyfriends, job mentors) is frequently cited by young adults with learning disabilities as essential to their success. Families are very influential in helping young people develop

Jeff

Self-confidence (defined as belief in one's ability to influence events), persistence, and willingness to work hard are important contributors to success among young people with learning disabilities. Here, Jeff (a dyslexic adult whom you met in Chapter 8) describes how he went about getting into college:

In my last couple years of high school, the whole idea of college seemed incredibly out of reach. Everybody sort of had the attitude that "Well, you're a bright guy, but, you know college is just not in the works for you." But that never sat right with me. Maybe it was because my father is the Dean of a university, but I don't think that's the only reason. I just had ideas about what I wanted to do in life and they were going to require that somehow or other I get a handle on using my mind. But I had no study skills, and even after five years of high school I could not write. I had no clue as to where a period went or what commas were for. I had sort of got reading understood, but writing was overwhelming. . . . So my senior year wound down and out of the blue I decided to call the new headmaster of a boarding school for students with learning disabilities where I had gone for seventh and eighth grade. I introduced myself and told him I had been a student at the school, and I didn't have a good plan for next year. And he said, "Well, come on down and we'll talk about it." So I hopped on a bus and spent the weekend at this school and we threw around some ideas. And the plan we came up with was that I would work at the school as a janitor, and they would give me a small salary plus room and board and tutoring from the faculty so I could take courses at the local community college.

In my first semester at the college I took two courses. It was an incredible experience, because I really started to feel that "Hey, I can do academic things." I never had that academic confidence in high school. I don't think my school had a very good idea of where they were going academically, let alone where they were going with someone who had disabilities. There was no plan, and when they saw I wasn't making progress they just let me do whatever I wanted. So high school was pretty much a lost situation. But my two years at the community college were great. They changed the way I perceived myself as a thinker. I took basic writing—like a precollege writing course—and I really enjoyed it.

We talked about structure—things like an introduction, and argument paragraphs and a conclusion. I found out once I had a *system* for writing I could do it. Another good thing I learned was to have someone proofread so I got credit for what I was saying and didn't get an inordinate number of points deducted for misspelling every other word (this was precomputer for me, so I had to type everything out, which was a remarkably cumbersome process). I started getting As and B+s and learned that I could think, and that made me more confident. I liked working at the boarding school, too. The next year they gave me a position as a dorm master; I lived with thirty kids. They were all learning disabled one way or another and some had been so protected by their environments—well, they all had low self-esteem but some were completely incapable of handling basic tasks, like how to make a bed or get your shoes on the right feet or take a shower. So that was challenging, but I felt good because I could identify with these kids and the incredible satisfaction they got from learning to do things on their own. . . .

Then one of the teachers at the community college who had worked with me a lot suggested, "You know, you ought to apply to some four-year colleges." We wrote away and got some applications to some great schools. A lot of them seemed pretty over-whelming but I sent several in and went to one interview, which was actually very useful. I mean, a lot of students going through high school have everyone grooming them for college, but I had no clue. So this interviewer gave me a lot of tips about the application process, which was great. Still, I did not get into this very selective small college I wanted. When I got the rejection letter, I called the Dean of Admissions and I just said, "I'd like to drive there tomorrow and review my application with you." And to my total surprise he said, "Sure, what time will you be here?" So I met with him, and explained really simply that I had worked harder to have the opportunity to just sit down with him than any other student he would be accepting this year, and that no matter how carefully he screens all those applications somebody is going to drop out. So what did he have to lose? The worst thing that could happen was I would be one of those . . .

Anyway, halfway through the summer I got a letter from the college. And they accepted me.

Interview by Jennifer Kagan.

visions for their futures, set reasonable goals, and make specific plans for achieving objectives. Both family and friends provide advice and emotional support when young adults encounter obstacles or become discouraged. The availability of this kind of support often separates individuals who "bounce back" from setbacks or defeat from those who give up.

A positive school experience. Research finds that satisfaction with one's high school experience is related to high expectations for the future and enthusiasm for higher education. Students who have achieved a certain measure of success in secondary school are most likely to see themselves as competent and in control of their own destinies. Academic achievement, extracurricular activities, and social interactions all contribute to high school satisfaction (a student who has the lead in the class play, a position in student government, and many friends, for example, may feel successful in spite of spotty grades). However, as Jeff's story shows, individuals who are flexible, upbeat, and willing to work hard can transcend even disastrous school situations.

Even a glance at this list makes it obvious that young people with disabilities who grow up in families that model positive values, support children's individuality and autonomy, and advocate for children appropriately have a tremendous edge on success. Research indicates that these youngsters often manage to succeed even where the destructive forces of poverty, discrimination, poor health, and limited educational opportunities are at work. Sometimes individuals who lack family support are able to find mentors and role models elsewhere (young people with upbeat personal characteristics are particularly good at attracting people who want to help them). Individuals who do not feel loved and accepted and who lack effective advocates and advisors, however, often continue to struggle uphill in many aspects of their adult lives.

Sadly, young adults with learning disabilities sometimes have as much trouble with personal relationships as they do with higher education and employment. Some feel so inferior and fear rejection so much that they become socially isolated and withdrawn. Others plunge into one relationship after another, but their immaturity, insecurity, and emotional instability defeat partner after partner, and the love and acceptance they long for remains ever elusive. The most common complaint expressed by this group is loneliness; even those who are successfully employed often say they need help learning to meet people and make friends. Finding appropriate recreational activities and helping individuals with learning disabilities learn social and "courtship" skills is therefore an important part of helping them make a successful adjustment to adult life.

Clearly, experiencing success at home and in the community are as important to a child's future as experiencing success at school. Fortunately, parents do not require college degrees or teaching certificates to provide what children need most from them. As we shall see in the next chapter, common sense and parents' own nurturing instincts are the best qualifications for helping children reach a healthy, happy maturity. Remember that children with learning disabilities are *children* first. They need what all children need: love, understanding, acceptance, responsibility, and discipline. The point is to not let the child's disabilities interfere with a family's ability to effectively provide those things.

11

Strategies for Promoting Personal Success

While quality of schooling may determine how skilled a child becomes at reading, writing, and mathematics, it is families who provide children with the self-confidence, determination, and resourcefulness they need to put their skills to effective use. Children's homes are also the laboratories in which they learn (or fail to learn) such important survival skills as how to set goals and make plans, how to evaluate choices and make decisions, and how to solve problems and resolve conflicts. Competence in these areas can ultimately have a greater impact on a young person's success in life than the ability to read or write.

Parents are therefore a child's most influential teachers. While this is the good news (parents can help youngsters overcome the negative effects of poor schooling), some parents may wonder if it isn't the bad news, too. Many mothers and fathers find the responsibilities of parenthood sobering (if not flat-out overwhelming) and worry that they are not equal to the job. This insecurity is not hard to understand. After all, nobody taught us in school how to raise children. Most of us don't even have a wise aunt or grandfather in the neighborhood to help us over the humps (an advantage often enjoyed by earlier generations). We therefore go through much of our parenting careers as on-the-job trainees—a role that can present some serious challenges to our own self-confidence. There is nothing like spending a night with a baby who will not stop crying to make one feel like a complete incompetent (although taking a teen who has just pierced her nose and shaved her head to your mother-in-law's for Thanksgiving dinner comes close). No matter how many parenting books we read, children have a way of presenting us with situations that make us feel as if we have no idea what we're doing.

Mothers and fathers of children who don't grow up "by the book" often feel even more uncertain of their parenting abilities. We note that the neighbor's little boy does better somersaults than our son does, and we start to wonder where we went wrong. When a youngster's deficits prove to be more severe—for example, the child is still struggling to decipher the alphabet in second grade, or is not "college material" according to the guidance counselor—parents often assume they are responsible and suffer enormous guilt. In an achievement-oriented culture where many parents wear their children's accomplishments like merit badges ("Johnny got elected captain of the baseball team!" "Great! Susie got a scholarship to Princeton!"), parents of children with learning disabilities sometimes feel like second-class citizens. The well-intended (and frequently conflicting) suggestions these parents receive from others often serve only to fuel the fires of doubt and confusion.

Before we discuss ways to help children maintain their self-esteem, therefore, we would like to offer a reminder for parents who may be struggling to hold on to their own. Learning disabilities are physiological problems that can occur in any kind of family. They are not reflections of your lifestyle, your intelligence, your skill as a parent, or your worth as a human being. There is therefore no reason to let anyone trap you into feeling ashamed of yourself or your child. As for those who offer unsolicited advice or try to engage you in games of parental one-upsmanship, try to forgive them their arrogance and their ignorance. If you continue your search for creative solutions and don't get defensive, you and your family may discover opportunities for personal growth that average achievers never dreamed of. As one mother put it, "My sister's children get good grades in school, and sometimes I'm jealous that so much comes easily to them. But I know her children don't know half of what my son knows about courage, and I think my sister is sometimes jealous of the close relationship Chris and I share."

Refreshed by this reality check, let's look at what parents can do to help children with learning disabilities grow up feeling like winners.

BELIEVE IN YOUR CHILD

Parents' attitudes about children's capabilities have a powerful effect on how children regard themselves. Youngsters who see themselves as essentially able and responsible usually have parents who see them the same way. Research finds, however, that children with learning disabilities sometimes have parents who view them as bumbling, helpless, fragile, or otherwise incompetent. Many of these children approach life, not surprisingly, as if it were a war that they had already lost.

It is not hard to fathom how parents come by these damaging attitudes. By the time their problems are identified, many children with learning disabilities have established a losing streak both at school and at home. These are the kids who can't seem to do anything right: in addition to bringing home disappointing grades, they spill orange juice all over themselves at breakfast, forget to feed the hamster for days on end, and lose three backpacks in a month. After the family has been made late for the hundredth time because the "problem child" can't find his jacket (or his glasses, or his shoes), even patient parents may erupt with messages to the effect of, "You dimwit! Why must you screw up *everything*?"

When the child's learning disability is identified, parents may regret these earlier accusations, but they do not necessarily adjust their basic perception of the child. Some accept the learning disability as an excuse for continued poor performance and irresponsibility. Earlier expectations for achievement may be lowered and the amount of work the child is expected to do at home and at school, reduced. Children absorb the view that they are hapless, helpless, and hopeless all too readily. Surrounded by low expectations, young people quickly settle into a pattern of low achievement, and may even stop trying to do things they can do well.

Parents who are fearful about children's ability to cope in a world that can be insensitive to people with special needs sometimes kill their children's self-confidence with kindness. Overly protective mothers, for example, sometimes run so much interference for their offspring that the children never get an opportunity to advocate or care for themselves. In the saddest of these cases, Mom may start to build her identity around being the child's champion. She may so "need to be needed," for example, that she actively resists others' efforts to help the child become more self-sufficient—this resistance often takes the form of repeatedly rejecting or finding fault with professionals on the grounds they don't understand what the child really needs. In this pathological twist on the scenario of the genuinely supportive parent (who usually welcomes professional assistance), youngsters tend to develop low opinions of their own abilities and become progressively more dependent. All too often, children like these grow into adults who are passive, friendless, and virtually unemployable.

Obviously, it is important to avoid being overwhelmed by children's problems and to stay positively focused on their *abilities*. Some suggestions for helping you keep your outlook optimistic follow.

Develop a Positive Vocabulary

What words do you use when you describe your child? When dealing with a youngster with learning disabilities, words such as *difficult, stubborn, wild, obnoxious,* and *impossible* are sometimes among those selected. Negative labels like these can hurt children even if they are never spoken aloud. Words influence perception, and when we use words like these we render ourselves incapable of seeing our children in their best light. Educator Mary Sheedy Kurcinka—herself the parent of a boy "who could scream for forty-five minutes because his toast had been cut in triangles when he was expecting rectangles"—notes that changing the words we use can help us think of our children more positively. She suggests we begin by thinking of our "difficult" children as "spirited," then go on to select new words for as many spirited traits as we can. Some alternatives suggested in Kurcinka's book, *Raising Your Spirited Child,* follow:

Instead of saying the child . . .	*Try saying the child . . .*
is wild	is energetic
is demanding	holds high standards
is stubborn	is assertive
is anxious	is cautious
is picky	is selective
is explosive	is dramatic
is loud	is enthusiastic
is argumentative	is opinionated
is distractible	is perceptive

The more negative labels you can replace with neutral or positive ones, the easier it will be for you to appreciate your child's spirit and individuality.

While you are working on your vocabulary, take a good look at the words your children are using also. Siblings can be vicious to one another when they are angry, and children with learning disabilities sometimes get into the habit of using derogatory words to describe themselves. Parents need to take the lead in teaching children that name-calling and put-downs are an unacceptable way to express feelings. When children put themselves down, it is important to confront and correct them gently, offering positive views to replace negative ones ("I know you are disappointed about your grade on the spelling test, but you are not stupid. Spelling is very hard for you. I'm proud of the effort you put into studying. You're a hard worker!").

Search for the Strengths

The very word *disability* focuses attention on what the child cannot do. It can be easy to forget that children with learning problems are for the most part interesting, unique individuals with many virtues. Their energy and enthusiasm are charming (if somewhat exhausting).

They may excel in art, music, and other creative endeavors. Some who have difficulty with reading and writing become verbal virtuosos who can talk their way into—or out of—anything. (These "natural salespeople" excel in politics and sometimes become successful entrepreneurs.) The compassion some children with learning disabilities develop for people who are "different" or who struggle with hardship is remarkable; these young people are often attracted to volunteer service and the helping professions, where their sensitivity is an asset. Because of their slightly skewed way of looking at the world, many young people with learning disabilities also have a delightful, offbeat sense of humor.

Speaking to a Massachusetts chapter of Children and Adults with Attention-Deficit/Hyperactivity Disorder (CHADD, a national support group), Dr. Edward Hallowell, coauthor of *Driven to Distraction: Recognizing and Coping with Attention Deficit Disorder from Childhood Through Adulthood*, explained there are also hidden benefits to this kind of problem:

> *ADD people are highly imaginative and intuitive. They have a "feel" for things, a way of seeing right to the heart of matters while others have to reason their way along methodically. . . . This is the man or woman who makes million-dollar deals in catnip and pulls them off the next day. This is the child who, having been reprimanded for blurting something out, is then praised for having blurted out something brilliant. . . . It is important for others to be sensitive to this "sixth sense" many ADD people have and to nurture it. If the environment insists on rational, linear thinking and "good" behavior from these kids all the time they may never develop their intuitive style to the point where they can use it profitably.**

A mother suggests: "Try sitting down and making a list of ten things about your child that you *like*. I do that when I'm feeling

---

* Thanks to Carson Graves and the Concord Special Education Advisory Council in Massachusetts for posting Dr. Hallowell's comments on the internet.

discouraged, and it helps me keep things in perspective." In addition to keeping her own thinking positive, this parent has found a good way to give her child a head start on self-esteem. What parents value in their children, the youngsters usually come to value in themselves. By thinking about why she likes her son, this mother gives him a fresh and frequently updated list of reasons to see himself as a great guy.

Learn to Put Failure in Perspective

Inventor Thomas Edison made about a thousand lightbulbs that *didn't* work before he made one that did. When asked how it felt to fail that often, Edison is reported to have replied: "I didn't fail one thousand times; the lightbulb was an invention with one thousand steps." Like most scientists, Edison knew that discovering what doesn't work can help you figure out what does. Progress is often a matter of trial and error, and people who are afraid of making mistakes limit their opportunities for advancement.

Unfortunately, children are often taught in school to fear failure and to take it personally. In many classes, learning is not presented as a matter of interest or exploration, but as a tournament in which students must prove their worthiness. To the victors go the spoils: the esteem of teachers and other students, college acceptances, prizes, and scholarships. Failure restricts youngsters' options and reduces their status. Rarely are students encouraged to analyze failures and learn from them.

If children are to learn that failure can be educational, they are probably going to have to learn it at home. In order to help them, parents must examine their own attitudes about making mistakes. How do you react when a youngster botches a chore or an assignment? Do you berate the child ("What's wrong with you, Johnny? We've told you a hundred times the trash goes out on Friday, and here you've forgotten again!"), or do you take a neutral position, helping the child backtrack and discover what went wrong ("You seem to be having trouble remembering this chore. Let's talk about how we can get around that problem.")? Children who frequently get the first kind of treatment will eventually learn to see themselves as incompetent losers. The second approach eliminates the emotional penalty for failure and encourages youngsters to see themselves as creative problem-solvers.

Emphasize Education

"My parents never talked about 'If you go to college,'" says a sophomore psychology major. "It was always, '*When* you go to college.' They said that even when my grades were bad. When we found out I had a learning disability, the position became, 'We'll have to look carefully for the *right* college.' Not going to college was never considered."

This young woman's parents helped her keep her sights set high—a fact that almost certainly helped seal her success. Research indicates that parental attitudes about education have a tremendous impact on students' expectations. One study determined that the most significant predictor of adult occupational status was parents' attitudes about school. (Occupational status and income are closely linked to the number of years of school completed. Parents who encourage children to finish high school and to go on to complete postsecondary education programs therefore help boost kids into better jobs.)

While college-educated parents are among the most likely to encourage their offspring to pursue higher education, many teachers, doctors, and lawyers recall parents who worked long hours at blue-collar jobs so that their children could get advanced degrees. "My mother could barely speak English, but she checked all my homework every single night," a social worker remembers. "I'm not sure how much of it she understood, but I sure got the idea that homework was important." Students like this always have an advantage over those whose parents are indifferent to school performance. It is the respect, interest, and enthusiasm parents convey for education—not the parents' level of educational achievement—that make the point.

For students with learning disabilities, high expectations must be coupled with careful planning based on a solid understanding of youngsters' strengths and special needs. As we shall see in the next section, self-esteem plummets when children are presented with expectations they cannot hope to meet. Parents must also recognize the difference between having high hopes and attempting to impose their will on children. The third-generation businessman who insists that his son carry on in the family tradition (even though the boy dreams of a career in the arts) is both interfering with his child's growth and endangering their relationship. Young people usually apply their greatest efforts toward goals they set themselves. The wise parent therefore combines enthusiasm for education with a certain amount of open-mindedness as to what the ultimate objective of that education ought to be. (For more on postsecondary, college, and career planning, see Chapter 12, where we discuss preparing for life after high school in greater detail.)

ESTABLISH REALISTIC EXPECTATIONS

No parent would intentionally ask a child to do the impossible. We know, for example, that babies can't ride bicycles and first-graders can't read advanced physics texts. When children's personalities, stages of development, and/or learning capabilities are poorly understood, however, parents may unwittingly establish expectations that are almost as unreasonable as these examples. Children with learning disabilities are especially vulnerable to this kind of misplaced confidence. Since they look "normal" and are able in many areas, it's easy to forget these kids can't do everything like other children their ages.

Unrealistic expectations set up children for failure—and when children fail, they can suffer tremendous guilt for letting Mom and Dad down. (Since children assume that adults know what they are doing, they almost always blame themselves in these situations.) If they let their parents down a lot, young people often come to see themselves as intrinsically inept and unworthy. To protect children's self-esteem, it is therefore essential for adults to keep what they ask in line with what youngsters are capable of delivering. The bottom line is that kids don't *know* enough to say, "Sorry, Mom and Dad, I don't have the cognitive ability to manage that request at this stage of my development." They trust us to be aware enough to make that judgment for them.

There are three areas in which it is especially important for parents to know their children well enough to align their expectations with the children's capabilities: temperament, moral development, and learning style.

Temperament

Some aspects of temperament have a genetic component and are therefore more resistant to change than other personality traits (for a description of these traits, see pages 296–97). Parents who do not understand this may overestimate a child's ability to adjust to different circumstances and environments. Mom and Dad may look forward to showing off their talented five-year-old at a family reunion, for example, only to be disappointed when Johnny whimpers and turns away from people he doesn't recognize. As Johnny becomes increasingly overwhelmed and irritable, they may find themselves urging him not to be such a tiresome crybaby. When they are forced to take their quickly disintegrating son home early, we hear Mom muttering, "You've ruined the day for all of us when we were so looking forward to this!" In addition to being tested beyond his limits by overexposure to new faces, Johnny now knows his inability to cope has made his mother unhappy—an emotional double whammy.

If this naturally reticent child has been born into a family of outgoing socializers, variations on this scenario may be repeated many times over the years. Eventually Johnny may well become convinced that his reluctance to mix with strangers means there is something seriously wrong with him. Even though he may have largely outgrown his fear of new situations by the time he enters junior high school, if he accepts his family's labels (Johnny is a loner, Johnny is antisocial), he may not even try to make friends. Such a child ends up paying a heavy price for his parents' failure to recognize and respect his basic personality.

Researchers have found that when a child's temperament is very different from a parent's, the level of stress and conflict in the household often increases. In the story on page 330, the result is tragic. How different Norman's life might have been if his father had been

Norman

Stella Chess, a psychologist who did groundbreaking work on the persistence of temperament over time, once described an unfortunate patient, Norman. Chess followed Norman from the age of four because of his persistent "behavior problems." As a preschooler, Norman was active and highly distractible. Although his behavior was well within the normal range, Norman's parents were concerned that his difficulty sticking to tasks showed a lack of character and self-discipline. Norman's father—a successful professional—was particularly critical and expressed his low opinion of his son's abilities openly in front of the child.

When he started school, Norman's short attention span often interfered with finishing his work. When Norman failed to rise to the top of the class, his father became increasingly hypercritical of the boy's performance, which he continued to attribute to a lack of backbone and willpower. Norman wanted to please his father and tried hard to apply himself to his schoolwork, but the stress of trying to maintain behavior so incompatible with his basic temperament took a toll. Over time, Norman's problems began to compound: he started to wet his bed, had trouble sleeping, bit his nails to the quick, and developed facial tics.

Norman's mother eventually came to understand his needs, but no amount of discussion could convince Norman's father that his son's temperament was normal; he continued to insist that Norman was irresponsible and doomed to failure. Counseling was arranged for Norman during his high school years, but by then Norman seemed to see himself as beyond help; he made little effort to cooperate with the counseling process. When Chess saw Norman at age seventeen, he was a college dropout with vague ideas about "finding himself" but no real plan. Chess noted that Norman was also extraordinarily self-derogatory—he told her he was lazy, could not follow through on anything, and deserved his father's low opinion. Sadly, the father's misguided predictions about his son's future appeared to have become a self-fulfilling prophecy.

Adapted from A. Thomas and S. Chess, *Temperament and Development* (NY: Bruner/Mazel, 1977).

able to accept the differences between his son and himself, instead of rejecting the boy and branding him a failure!

Parents who are sensitive to their children's temperamental needs can both establish realistic expectations and help manage their environments so that the youngsters are not unduly pressured. Johnny's parents, for example, might warn relatives that he will need time to warm up to them at the family reunion (children like this sometimes need to be defended from overeager huggers). They might also decide not to subject him to an entire day of festivities—or find a comfortable place on the sidelines until Johnny is ready to approach the crowd. In this way, they would set up their son for success rather than failure and frustration.

Awareness of temperamental characteristics also helps parents appreciate their children as unique human beings, especially if they are able to recognize positive aspects of temperamental traits. (The flipside of Johnny's "shyness," for example, may be that he forms considered judgments about people and chooses his companions wisely—character assets most parents would value.) To help children make the most of their temperaments, it is also important to understand that personalities do not always match traditional cultural roles. If shyness is seen as acceptable for girls but a mark of cowardice in boys, for example, half the shy people in the world will be condemned (and feel guilty) unnecessarily.

Moral Development

Children's ability to judge what is right and what is wrong develops in stages. Mothers and fathers who do not understand moral development sometimes find themselves trying to enforce rules that are beyond children's comprehension and/or punishing youngsters who don't understand what they have done wrong. Misinterpretation of youngsters' motives can also convince parents that children are sinful or wicked when their behavior is actually normal and innocent.

Let's take a brief look at how a child's morality develops. Experts agree that children under the age of two have no real sense of right or wrong; their controlling principle is pretty much, "If it feels good, do it." At this stage of their development, children are not capable of understanding "rules." Punishing toddlers for behavior deemed unacceptable (such as touching their genitals or breaking fragile knickknacks) is therefore pointless and cruel. A more appropriate strategy is to distract the child from behavior you don't like, or to eliminate temptations. (If offering a toy doesn't keep the baby from playing with the buttons on the TV, move the baby—or the TV—to another room.)

As they grow older, children learn that some behaviors are acceptable and others are not. Children younger than seven or eight, however, don't have the reasoning ability to understand *why* a particular behavior is right or wrong; their moral code is borrowed whole from parents and other authorities. This tends to result in a black-and-white view of the world and a rigid interpretation of rules—for example, a five-year-old will tell you that lying is *always* wrong; suggesting that it might be okay to tell a "white lie" to avoid hurting someone's feelings will only confuse her. It is necessary to explain rules and expectations clearly to these youngsters; without adult input, they have no idea how to behave. (Children who have not received consistent adult guidance can be expected to behave inconsistently.) Appropriate discipline for this age group is often more a matter of education than punishment. Lecturing early elementary-aged youngsters is ineffectual, but they do understand concrete consequences closely tied to events. ("These markers belong to the store. You are not allowed to take things from the store unless you pay for them. We are going to take the markers back right now.")

Around the time they enter third grade, children begin to use their own judgment instead of relying entirely on adult guidance. Whereas for younger children "being good" is primarily a matter of pleasing adults, youngsters eight and older also consider rules and standards established by their peers. This divided loyalty sometimes presents them with ethical dilemmas ("Mom says I should invite Emily to my birthday party because she lives next door, but my friends at school think Emily is a pain"). Discussing problems like these gives parents opportunities to share values. Although children younger than twelve deal poorly with abstract concepts and prefer simple solutions, they are capable of understanding that the "right" choice can depend on circumstances. Children this age often need help thinking through different aspects of a problem, but should be encouraged to make their own decisions whenever possible. Parents who arbitrarily impose their own judgments ("You have to invite

Emily, or there's no party!") rob children of opportunities to practice thinking and acting maturely.

Elementary-age youngsters do test the rules. Since most do not yet reason logically, concrete rewards and consequences remain the best means of modifying their behavior. When it is necessary to discipline these children, an explanation of the punishment is appropriate (even if they do not fully understand your judgment, children need to know you have a reason for what you are doing and are not acting on a whim). You can spare them lengthy analyses and philosophical observations, however—short and to the point works best. At any stage of development, it is important to distinguish between criticizing a child's *behavior* and criticizing the *child*. Criticizing behavior ("Hitting is not all right. Hitting hurts people!") establishes boundaries, but criticizing or shaming the child ("You bad boy! Why are you so mean?") is a form of character assassination that can leave lasting scars.

By the time they reach junior high school, most children understand that rules arise out of mutual consent and involve a certain amount of give-and-take. They no longer think exclusively in terms of good guys and bad guys, and they understand that real justice takes mitigating factors into account. (This insight sometimes gives them an incentive to try excuses; these are the kids who plead, "Really, Mrs. Jones, I wrote the book report, but my dog ate it!") As a result, teenage children want to *negotiate* rules and consequences. Parents need to not become inflexible in response to these challenges; experts find that a certain amount of debate and negotiation is characteristic of healthy family systems in which generations respect one another. During the teenage years children also start to develop a "social conscience." As they mature intellectually, teens begin to appreciate abstract ideas like altruism, brotherhood, and patriotism, and these concepts reinforce their desire to become good citizens.

Parents must note, however, that adolescents' moral judgment is not yet fully developed. Young teens' respect for the law, for example, is still based partly on fear of being found out and punished; they may be tempted to break rules if the risk of being caught is small. It is not until late adolescence that children fully understand that laws preserve society, and that compliance is necessary

Matthew

Understanding a young person's level of moral reasoning can be the key to effective intervention:

Thirteen-year-old Matthew had an explosive temper. When things didn't go his way, he often took out his feelings on furniture—he overturned desks and chairs and once threw a wastebasket through a window. Unfortunately, Matthew was often unhappy in eighth grade. His difficulty maintaining attention and his problems with written language had been recognized late; this year was Matthew's first experience with special education. He resented being separated from his friends for reading, and some classmates teased him about having to go to a reading class with "retards and dummies." His attitude toward his resource teacher and the other students in his reading group was hostile at best. On his bad days, Matthew's behavior was so aggressive and disruptive that the teacher had no choice but to send him to the principal's office.

The middle school principal made many efforts to reason with Matthew. She pointed out that his behavior interfered with other students' right to learn and also set back his own education. None of these talks had much impact. Matthew's mother also tried to reach him; she was a religious woman and made it clear that his destructive outbursts violated the teachings of their faith as well as the rules of the school. Matthew loved his mother and wanted to please her, but her words didn't help him deal with the anger that kept building up inside his small, wiry body. Giving Matthew detention didn't work either—in fact, being forced to stay after school and miss playing ball with his friends made him even *more* angry. On his way to a recent detention, Matthew

to maintain the social order. (Youths who feel victimized by the established social order will not be highly motivated by this consideration.) Wise parents therefore continue to provide teenage children with structure and help them think their actions through. Since slipups tend to generate their own consequences at this age (shoplifting can get you arrested; unsafe sex can result in illness or unwanted pregnancy), threats of punishment may be superfluous. When parents act like advisers instead of police officers, adolescents often find it easier to see that responsible behavior is in their own best interests.

deliberately swept three students' books off their desks and "accidentally" overturned the teacher's coffee.

In a last-ditch effort to avoid suspension, Matthew was referred to a guidance counselor. The counselor recognized that generalized appeals to Matthew's instincts for good citizenship were not going to modify his behavior. Matthew was immature in several respects (his favorite television programs were cartoons, for example); this suggested the need for a more concrete approach to managing his anger. The counselor offered a deal: if Matthew would come to the counselor's office to talk when he got angry instead of disrupting class, a red star would be placed on the cover of his folder. When Matthew had five stars, the counselor would take him out for a pizza at lunchtime. When he got ten, Matthew would get two tickets to a movie of his choice.

The system worked. By the time he got his movie tickets, Matthew had built a trusting relationship with the counselor and begun to learn how to talk out his anger instead of attacking property. Once he settled down in class, his resource teacher was able to help him understand his learning disabilities. Matthew became less hostile when he understood that you could have a learning disability and still be smart. He started to apply himself, and his academic skills improved. The key to these positive outcomes was the counselor's understanding of Matthew's level of moral development. Although most thirteen-year-olds are beginning to develop a "social conscience," Matthew's development was somewhat delayed. His thinking was more like that of a fifth- or sixth-grader, and children that age are motivated by tangible rewards. The counselor's point system was therefore successful where attempts to reason "maturely" with Matthew had failed.

To be effective, efforts to discipline children must be based on their stages of moral readiness, not their ages. Children who are slow to mature (including many children with learning disabilities) are sometimes punished unfairly because parents misjudge their ability to understand rules and evaluate consequences. As Matthew's story illustrates, treating children as if they had the social judgment and moral reasoning ability of a child two or three years younger is sometimes the key to bringing successful solutions within a young person's reach.

Learning Style

In Chapter 9, we discussed how learning preferences affect students' performance in school. Since parents also have a great deal to teach, insight into how children learn is just as important at home. Yet, as one mother puts it, "It's amazingly easy to forget about learning disabilities when you're trying to get the kid to clean up his room. Even though I know my son doesn't deal well with verbal directions, I still tell him to do things sometimes and get angry when he forgets."

Too often, parents don't consider at all how a child's learning style might affect behavior at home. When this is the case, expectations for the child are likely to be unrealistic; family friction usually follows when the child fails to perform. To avoid this unhappy situation, parents may want to keep a few basic guidelines in mind when trying to teach tasks to children with learning disabilities:

It takes them longer to learn. The task that your typical five-year-old learned after one explanation may take your eight-year-old with learning disabilities longer to master. Some can attend to tasks for only short periods at a time, which slows their rate of learning. In addition, most of these children need to practice a new skill many times before they are comfortable with it. Parents who expect quick results from children with learning disabilities are often disappointed. If you plan to invest two or three weeks in teaching your youngster to set the table, on the other hand, you can probably count on results you and your child will both be proud of.

You have to show them as well as tell them. Many children with learning disabilities have difficulty following verbal directions. Some process language poorly. Others have difficulty visualizing information; no matter how many times you explain a sequence of events, they have trouble "picturing" it. Nearly all children with learning disabilities do best when new skills are demonstrated as well as explained. In the box on page 337, a noted special educator suggests a teaching sequence that is usually very successful.

You need to break big jobs into little ones. No child welcomes an order to "clean up your room," but most can handle it without a

Teaching New Tasks to Students with Learning Disabilities

Parents! Ask yourselves, "How many things do I do for my child every day . . . tasks that I complete out of habit . . . tasks that are within the child's range of ability?" Do you still iron for your fourteen-year-old? Do you continue to ban the sixteen-year-old from the power tools?

If so, consider this simple sequential approach to teaching the child with learning disabilities. This four-step method can be applied to nearly any common task. We will use teaching Jimmy to make his bed as an example.

STEP 1: Do it for him.
Make the bed while Jimmy observes you. Carefully point out the stages of the task while you complete each step. Encourage him to ask questions. Continue to do this daily until he is ready for Step 2.

STEP 2: Do it with him.
Slowly integrate Jimmy into the process. Have him assist you with various stages of the task. Praise and encourage his increasing involvement. Continue this step daily until he is ready for Step 3.

STEP 3: Watch him do it.
For a few days, watch Jimmy make his bed. Provide encouragement and gently point out any mistakes he may make. (This will prevent bad habits from forming.)

STEP 4: Have him do it.
Now that the task has been mastered, require Jimmy to make his bed every day. Make this part of his routine. Often parents will make a great effort to teach children a skill and then not allow them to *use* that skill. Do not fall back into the old unproductive habit of making Jimmy's bed for him!

Source: Richard D. LaVoie, M.A., M.Ed., executive producer, How Difficult Can This Be? The F.A.T. City Workshop.

---

great deal of supervision. To a child who has trouble with sequencing or visualizing what an orderly room looks like, however, a task like this presents many bewildering choices. Pick up the toys or put away the clothes? Deal with the trash or make the bed? Without help, the youngsters cannot devise efficient strategies, so the job drags on and on. To help youngsters complete a complex job like this, break it down into a series of simpler tasks (put dirty clothes in hamper, collect and throw out trash, put toys and books on shelves, and so on). Older children can be given a list to follow; younger ones (and children with short attention spans) may need to check results with you after each subtask has been completed.

You must teach memory strategies. A frequently heard complaint from parents of children with learning disabilities is that the kids are forgetful; they forget the time, their chores, and where clothes and possessions were left or last seen. (On this page, we have a note

Note to the Tooth Fairy

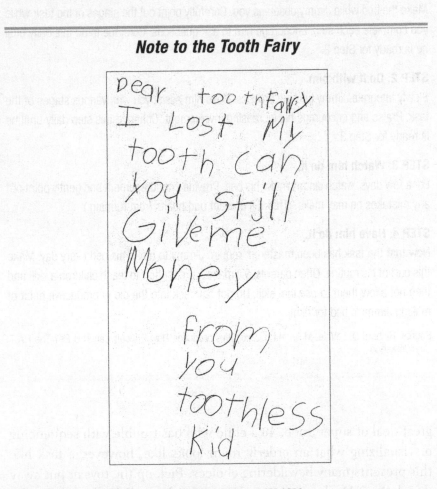

from a child who hopes the Tooth Fairy can overlook the fact she's misplaced her lost tooth!) Carelessness is not the issue here; most children with learning disabilities have difficulty entering some kinds of information into their memory banks. It is therefore important to teach memory-boosting strategies, such as writing commitments on a calendar, posting daily lists of things to do on a bulletin board, putting away possessions promptly, and/or wearing a watch with an alarm that warns of upcoming appointments. Even when using these techniques, however, the child with learning disabilities is likely to remain the least organized member of the family. Sanity sometimes lies in accepting our "free spirits" the way they are—and developing family strategies to compensate for their disorganization, such as allowing ample time to get ready for events.

Reward direction, not perfection. Children with learning disabilities are often frustrated by their own inability to achieve perfect results. Help them see that progress—not perfection—is the point. When children do a job partly right, praise what was done well before showing them what was overlooked. Children who understand that they are getting somewhere are far less likely to get fed up and quit.

GIVE THE CHILD RESPONSIBILITY

Research indicates that giving children responsibility is highly important to their overall development. Many studies have found that children who do helpful work in their homes and neighborhoods gain both skills and self-esteem. For example, a long-term study that followed a group of individuals with learning problems on the island of Kauai, Hawaii, found that those who were given useful work (usually in middle childhood and adolescence) were most likely to grow into caring, competent adults. The young people's work typically involved helping out parents at home and assisting neighbors or needy members of the larger community.

Learning to take responsibility for oneself is another key to successful independent living. Unfortunately, research finds that adults do not always encourage youngsters with learning disabilities to think or do things for themselves. As a result, many of these young people feel unable to influence events and drift passively from day to day rather than making plans or decisions that might improve their lives.

Parents sometimes sabotage their children's initiative with the best of intentions. Presented with a disorganized child who is struggling with simple tasks, it's natural to offer help. As children with learning disabilities grow, help with eating, dressing, and getting to the top of the jungle gym flows naturally into help with homework, help with housework, help with money, and so on. Before we know it, helping has become a habit that neither we nor our children are very motivated to break. The children enjoy the attention (and are not averse to having us do their work for them); we want to protect them from failure—and besides, it's really easier to do their laundry than to teach them to do it themselves.

A habit of helping, however, can eventually become a destructive cycle. The more parents do, the less children accomplish; the less they accomplish, the more persuaded parents become that the children are basically helpless and incompetent. This often leads to the parents becoming even more protective and "helpful" (although efforts to shore up the child sometimes start to be tinged with resentment). Escalating parental involvement continues to prevent children from analyzing or solving their own problems. By the time the kids reach adolescence, a pattern of "bawl them out and bail them out" may have become established (parents bawl out children for their failures, then jump in to fix the situation). The teens resent Mom and Dad's interference and lack of trust in them—but they have never learned to take care of themselves, and by this time have real doubts about their ability to do so. Nobody sees the future as promising.

Although children with learning disabilities need energetic advocates, it is important to avoid doing for young people what they *can* do for themselves. A number of proactive steps parents can take to help children become more responsible and independent are outlined below.

Give Children Regular Chores

As we pointed out in the last section, it can be harder to teach household tasks to children who have learning disabilities. Enabling these children to contribute to the work of the household, however, pays off in several ways. First, children enjoy a boost in self-esteem when they feel they are helping their families. These youngsters feel more capable and more valuable to their loved ones than do kids who are always on the receiving end of assistance. Second, children who pitch in at home learn skills that are essential for independent living. Since youngsters with learning disabilities usually need more practice than others to master new skills, it is wise to start teaching both boys and girls about cooking, cleaning, shopping, and other aspects of household management as early as possible. Third, when children with learning disabilities do a fair share of the family work and are expected to meet the same obligations as their brothers and sisters (for example setting the table, writing thank-you notes, and taking a turn walking the dog), sibling relations improve. A common complaint of siblings is that children with learning disabilities get less work and more help doing it—a perception that is often accurate.

It is sensible, of course, to assign chores with a child's strengths and special needs in mind—you would probably not want a child with fine-motor problems dusting your collection of antique porcelain figurines, but weeding the garden should be no problem for her. You may also have to modify tasks from time to time in the interest of fairness (the mother of a thirteen-year-old with weak handwriting skills allowed him to type forty thank-you notes on a computer following his bar mitzvah, for example). At other times, however, you will have to accept that children with disabilities must work a little harder. It is going to take a poorly coordinated teen longer to sort, wash, and fold his clothes than it would his sister, for example, but that doesn't mean you should do it for him. He's going to have to know how to do laundry when he's living on his own, and will feel more self-confident for his ability to do it.

Let Children Handle Money

Money management is a particularly common stumbling block for young adults with learning disabilities. Poor math skills, lack of experience with planning, and impulsive temperaments can all lead to overdrawn notices from the bank. This essential life skill is seldom taught successfully in school. The bottom line is that the best way to learn to manage money is to manage it; young people who handle their finances responsibly usually learn to do so at home.

Like other children, a child with learning disabilities benefits from receiving a weekly allowance. (Experts advise that to be an effective learning tool, the allowance should not be tied to chores or academic performance; it should be an income the child can count on.) They may need more help than their brothers and sisters, however, in learning to spend it. It may not occur to these youngsters to compare prices, for example: the addition and subtraction involved in comparison shopping may be too much for them. (Try shopping together with a calculator in hand until children can use the calculator themselves.) Impulse shoppers—the ones who didn't know they needed a purple-spangled pixie wand until they saw it—need encouragement to look around and explore what different things their money will buy. You might point out, for example, that the cost of the pixie wand is about the same as that for a poster, a package of barrettes, or a box of modeling clay. This gives the child practice considering her options and making decisions.

Involve children in spending your money, too. One family asked their children to propose how $2,500 might be spent on a family vacation; the suggestions—accompanied by price estimates for food, lodging, and entertainment, as required—ranged from a theater weekend in the city to two weeks of wilderness backpacking. While parents are sometimes reluctant to talk to children about income and household expenses, doing so can help youngsters develop realistic expectations and understand the point of establishing a budget. Financial candor, however, should not be taken to the point of frightening children or burdening them with adult concerns. Letting kids know the amount of the monthly car payment is fine, but telling them you're having trouble making it because Dad is late with the child support again creates unnecessary anxiety and adds nothing to the children's education.

As children acquire experience handling cash, trust them with larger amounts. A quarterly clothing allowance can be educational for secondary school students (one mother says that her daughter learned all about discount stores within days of being put on a clothing budget). Since most students this age have some impulse control and can delay gratification, this is also a good time to start encouraging saving. Most students become motivated to save only after identifying a desirable item that is within reasonable reach. Since some youngsters cannot delay gratification very long, you may want to start off discussing purchases that could be made after saving for only a few weeks. Some parents like to add incentives at this point—for example, a fourteen-year-old was told that if he could save $200 toward a mountain bike, Dad would match it.

Consider providing a high school student with a checking account and debit card (it's better not to allow students to use credit cards until they prove able to plan a budget and stick to it). Students with long-term savings goals need to explore various financial instruments (savings bonds, certificates of deposit, mutual funds, and other types of investments) for helping their money grow. It's a good idea to have these tools in place *before* a child starts working; paychecks that get cashed rather than deposited in the bank have a way of evaporating quickly, leaving little of value behind. Some parents expect working teens to pay some of their own expenses, such as gasoline, auto insurance, and telephone bills. If you do, think about establishing separate accounts in children's names so they can become familiar with paying monthly bills (and, if necessary, with the loss of service that comes with failure to pay them). Beware of overbudgeting, however—if kids don't have some "play money" left after bills are paid and savings goals are met, they rapidly lose interest in working.

Most youngsters with learning disabilities will need to be taught how to keep financial records, and they will have to be walked through the process of balancing their accounts several times before they can manage this task on their own. Monthly bookkeeping sessions can be a good time to review goals and spending habits. ("Did you plan to spend eighty dollars on pizza last month?") Youngsters who receive this kind of guidance become educated consumers and gain confidence in their abilities to make financial decisions.

It doesn't guarantee they'll never bounce a check, but it makes it much more likely that they will be able to live within their means down the road.

Help Children Get Around on Their Own

Nearly every parent remembers the gut-wrenching anxiety that accompanies taking the training wheels off the bicycle, putting a teen behind the wheel of the family car, or seeing a child off on her first solo trip on the subway or the bus. For parents of children with learning disabilities it's worse. In addition to the fears all parents face when letting go, we think about how easily the children are distracted, how rotten their sense of direction is, how confused they are by noise, and so on. Sometimes we scare ourselves so much with these considerations that we decide not to let the children go after all.

There is no question that teaching young people with learning disabilities to get around on their own can be a challenge. General immaturity and specific skill deficits (such as poor coordination, short attention span, difficulty judging speed and distance, and/or problems reading signs) often delay the age at which they can learn to ride a bike, drive an automobile, or use public transportation safely. Achieving this kind of independence is so important to growth and self-esteem, however, that parents should make every effort to help these children learn the basics of transportation as soon as they are ready.

As with any other skill, teaching a youngster with disabilities to ride a bike or interpret a bus schedule or a city subway map takes time and patience. Parents should be prepared, for example, to take several trial runs on the bus to likely destinations, answering questions and pointing out landmarks (gradually, have the child start pointing out landmarks to *you*). Learning to ride a bike may take hours of supervised practice. (Older children struggling to learn this skill may fear ridicule and want to practice out of public view—or at least out of the neighborhood—until they can stay upright.)

Deciding to trust a teen with the car is a more complicated issue, because driving requires both skill and good judgment. Skill issues for young people with learning disabilities include trouble reading signs, right-left confusion, difficulty coordinating hand and foot movements, and problems with estimating speed and distance. Situations that call for integrating several of these skills quickly (such as looking left and then right upon approaching an intersection, or checking street signs and judging the speed of oncoming traffic before making a left turn) can be particularly challenging. Young people with attention-deficit/ hyperactivity disorder (ADHD) present some additional concerns. These teens often have trouble keeping their minds on the road; they are easily distracted by the music on the radio, the airplane overhead, the blonde on the sidewalk, and so forth. When impulse control is poor, these adolescents may also be tempted to drive too fast and too aggressively—tailgating, weaving in and out of traffic, and cutting off other drivers—placing themselves and others at risk for accidents. When problems such as these are severe, it is best to delay teaching teens to drive (be prepared for vigorous objections from your sixteen-year-old). Coordination and judgment may improve when the nervous system matures (although some individuals with severe learning disabilities never become good drivers). It is important to make sure that teens and young adults who do not drive know how to make efficient use of available forms of public and private transportation so they do not feel "trapped" at home.

Young people with mild to moderate disabilities can usually learn to drive successfully, given appropriate instruction and support. In the box on page 346, parents share some helpful tips for putting these teens behind the wheel.

Before youngsters are allowed to travel alone by any means, of course, you must make sure they know how to conduct themselves safely among strangers. Some young people with learning disabilities are very trusting and affectionate—a charming trait at home but potentially dangerous for a child out on his or her own. Anticipate and discuss situations and approaches that should make children wary, and explain exactly what they should do if they become uneasy. If you have doubts about a youngster's maturity, you may want to encourage a more limited kind of freedom (such as allowing the child to visit

Tips for Teaching Teens to Drive

- Invest in professional driving instruction. Individual instruction may be a better bet than the group instruction that is available through many high schools. Make sure the driving instructor understands the nature of the child's disabilities and how best to approach them.

- Forbid use of the radio/CD player until driving basics have been mastered. (If youngsters are very distractible, keep the car radio off permanently.)

- Tape labeled arrows indicating left and right on the dashboard.

- Spend extra time studying the section in the driver's manual on road signs (many can be identified by shape and/or color and do not have to be read).

- Drive with your child through the neighborhood and along most-used routes (to school, to friends' houses, to the mall, and so on), pointing out landmarks, road signs, and areas where extra attention is needed (such as awkward intersections or a stop sign partly hidden by trees).

- If children have to drive someplace new (as to a job interview or to pick up a new friend), study the route on a map and/or make a few "trial runs" so they can familiarize themselves with the roads and drive with confidence later.

- Consider buying a GPS (Global Positioning System) if your car is not already equipped with one.

- Do *not* assume children understand the meanings of the dials and indicators on the dashboard, auto maintenance ("Check the oil? I thought the car ran on gas"), how to read a road map, or what to do in the event of an emergency or an accident. Take the time to review each of these things before your teen hits the road.

Remember that passing a driving test does not make a child a good driver. Parents need to clarify their *own* rules and standards for safe driving, and ride with children until they are certain these rules are understood and regularly observed. A mother adds, "Having friends in the car can be a major distraction for teenage drivers. We didn't allow our children to carry passengers until they had several months driving experience and we were sure they knew how to stay alert and drive defensively."

selected stores in the shopping mall alone while you wait in the snack area). These intermediate steps toward independence help build self-confidence while protecting children's safety.

Encourage Decision-Making

Many youngsters with learning disabilities don't realize that decision-making involves a number of steps, such as establishing priorities, identifying and examining options, researching and ruling out alternatives, and testing several solutions to see what works best. Children who lack awareness of this process usually make choices on impulse or by guessing. When these strategies produce poor results, children often conclude that they are unlucky, incompetent, or both. Eventually many give up trying to influence events and adopt a passive approach to life.

To avoid this situation, it is important to teach decision-making strategies to children. Unfortunately, many schools actively *discourage* decision-making (in authoritarian classrooms, for example, it is passive compliance that is valued and rewarded). Students with learning disabilities are sometimes perceived as even less competent to make choices than their peers. Often these young people are not even encouraged to participate in discussions (such as IEP reviews) that have a direct bearing on their futures.

To help children learn decision-making skills, it is important to encourage them to make their own choices, starting with small ones and working up. Too often, when children ask us what we think they should do, we make the fatal mistake of telling them (sometimes we tell them even before they ask us). Instead, try helping children think through their alternatives. Expressing confidence in the child's initiative is vital ("The sweater and the jacket both look great! The jacket is warmer; have you checked the weather report?"). For big decisions, children need to be encouraged to do things such as brainstorm possibilities, write down priorities, research alternatives, and make lists of pros and cons. ("Let's make a list of the things you most want in a college and rank them according to importance. Okay, now we can

Julie

The summer before she entered high school, Julie announced that she was no longer in need of special education. She said reading was not a big problem for her anymore—and her reading skills had indeed improved considerably in the five years she had received special education help. Julie was still poorly organized, however, and lacked study skills. This compromised her written work; Julie's compositions and reports were not well researched and showed little evidence of logical thought. It had therefore been recommended that she continue to receive help in the resource room for one period a day in ninth grade.

Julie became more and more adamant about her decision to abandon the resource room as the opening day of school came closer. Her parents thought they knew what was going on. Over the past two years, Julie had become increasingly sensitive about being "different" in any way. It had been hard for her to make friends at the junior high school, and she blamed her special education label for this (although her parents thought Julie's shyness probably contributed more to her social isolation than the fact that she needed help with basic skills). It was obvious that Julie wanted to start at the central high school with a clean slate. By shedding the special education label, she hoped to put herself on an equal footing with her peers.

Still, Julie's parents were frustrated by her obstinacy. They pointed out all the ways special education had helped her in the past: not only had she received instruction in reading and writing, but also the resource teacher had helped negotiate extra time for

compare that list with these books and decide which campuses to visit.") The more children are walked through this process when they are growing up, the greater their chances are of making effective decisions when they are on their own.

The hardest part of teaching children about decisions is that sometimes you have to let them take the consequences of bad ones. As Julie's story reminds us, experience is sometimes the only teacher a youngster is willing to respect. Although the temptation to rescue children from mistakes is great, it can be wiser (if the situation is not dangerous) to let young people play their choices out. An important aspect of taking responsibility is accountability; children who are protests and assignments when needed. Did she want to give that up? These reasoned arguments only made Julie angry. "You don't think I can do it on my own!" she accused her parents through tears. "You don't have faith in me!" Bewildered and uncertain as to what course to take, Julie's parents called her junior high school resource teacher and explained the situation. "I think you should let her try it her way for a year," the teacher suggested. "Tell her to give it her best shot, and in June you'll reevaluate the situation."

"That ninth-grade year was rough," Julie's mother remembers. "Julie was swamped with homework every night. Her midterm grades were awful; she failed history and English. There was a week she had three research papers due when she did nothing but cry. She had no *time* for a social life. All she did was work, work, work." At the end of the year, Julie had Bs in math and Spanish, a D in English, and an F in history. "She knew it was the essays and research papers that had hurt her in English and history," Julie's mother said. "She hadn't done badly on short-answer tests."

Julie took history again in summer school and passed with a C (all the tests were multiple choice). She offered no objections to a resource period in tenth grade, and used it to work on her research and written-composition skills. "The hardest thing I ever had to do was watch Julie bottom out in her freshman year," her mother recalls, "but letting her try it her way was the right thing to do. She learned what kind of help she needs, and I learned something, too. I learned I've got a spunky kid who doesn't give up easily. Her determination and willingness to work hard earned our respect. In tenth grade those things really paid off; with minimal help, she finished the year with As and Bs."

tected from the consequences of their choices seldom learn to be accountable for their actions.

IMPROVE SOCIAL SKILLS AND OPPORTUNITIES

Research indicates that winning social acceptance can be even more important to children's self-esteem than achieving good grades in school. The ability to make friends and hold up one's end of a relationship is also one of the keys to making a successful adjustment to adult life. Among the most important things parents can do for children with learning disabilities, therefore, is to help them learn and practice social skills. Parents can also support children's development by learning to identify the environments in which youngsters are most likely to succeed, and structuring social opportunities accordingly.

What do we mean when we talk about social skills? Much is a matter of simple good manners: being on time, playing fair, respecting others' rights and property, and considering others' feelings. Conforming to group standards in these respects provides an important foundation for social interactions. Studies of school-aged children, however, find that other factors influence personal popularity as well. Among them:

Appearance. Children who are perceived as unkempt or unfashionable are more likely to be excluded than children who are neat and clean and dressed like their peers. It is therefore a good idea to teach good grooming habits, and to help youngsters keep their wardrobes up to date. Since children with learning disabilities are often slow to pick up on fads and fashion trends, you may have to sharpen your own awareness of what's "in" at school. (Other children, such as siblings and neighborhood pals, make good consultants in this regard.)

Attitudes. Youngsters who are "fun," enterprising, optimistic, and enthusiastic are generally perceived as more attractive than those who act gloomy or helpless. While you cannot change a child's basic temperament (some kids are naturally more "up" than others), encouraging your child to maintain a positive outlook on life will improve his or her social outlook, too. Note that school-aged children are drawn to others who make them feel good about themselves, and children who express interest in others are viewed as more friendly than those who are self-absorbed. Encouraging your youngster to notice and comment positively on what other children are doing ("You did a good job on the science project," or "I liked your sculpture in art") can help boost acceptance.

Ability to express thoughts and emotions. Studies find that children choose friends based in part on companions' ability

21 Questions That Help Children Set Goals

Asking youngsters the following questions can help them assume greater responsibility for their futures:

- What would you like to do, have, or accomplish?
- What do you wish would happen?
- What would you like to be able to do better?
- What do you wish you had more time for? More money for?
- What more would you like to get out of life?
- What are your ambitions?
- What angered you recently?
- What makes you tense or anxious?
- What do you complain about?
- What misunderstandings need to be straightened out?
- What changes for the worse or better do you sense?
- Who would you like to get to know better?
- What would you like to get others to do?
- With whom would you like to get along better?
- What changes will you have to make?
- What takes too long?
- What is too complicated?
- What blocks or "bottlenecks" exist in your life?
- In what ways are you inefficient?
- What wears you out?
- What would you like to organize better?

Once a goal has been identified (e.g., "I wish I had a bike"), children may need help examining alternatives and forming realistic plans ("Let's find out how much bikes cost and figure out how long you would have to save your allowance. Let's talk about how you could earn some extra money to save faster"). Don't take on too much! Most youngsters do best if they focus on one goal at a time.

Adapted from J. Canfield and H. C. Wells, *100 Ways to Enhance Self-Concept in the Classroom*, 2nd ed. (Boston: Allyn & Bacon, 1994).

to express caring and admiration, be helpful when needed, and be counted on to work out disagreements. Children who lack the ability to put their needs and feelings into words are more likely to have trouble with these skills, and may even make themselves unwelcome by barging in or acting out when things don't go their way. It is therefore important to encourage youngsters to use language to ask for what they want, resolve conflicts, and express feelings. Learning to express anger appropriately can be a particular challenge. Asking kids to take "time out" to cool off and providing a safe means of releasing anger physically (such as a punching bag or a big soft ball to kick) are often helpful—some children need to do this before they can talk. Educator Mary Sheedy Kurcinka advises that a wordless "Tarzan yell" (complete with beating one's chest) can discharge a lot of tension without causing specific offense. Once youngsters have calmed down, help them find words for what they are feeling. A playful approach ("How mad are you? Mad enough to bust a brick? Mad enough to bite a bear?") sometimes helps kids put things in perspective. Be careful not to belittle children's emotions, though. Children whose feelings are not taken seriously learn to repress their emotions—a habit that can lead to depression.

As children approach adolescence, planning and decision-making skills become an important part of the social tool kit (there is no point suggesting a group of kids get together, after all, if you can't decide where to go or what to do). Teenagers also need to learn to be appropriately assertive and to handle stress. The box on page 353 lists fifty social skills that have been identified as important during adolescence. In addition to facilitating social relationships, these skills support responsible behavior in school and in the workplace, so they remain important throughout adulthood.

Because young people with learning disabilities cannot be counted upon to learn correct social behavior by observation alone, a direct approach to teaching social skills and repeated reinforcement may be needed to help them learn to act appropriately. Role-playing and

Social Skills

Group I. *Beginning Social Skills*

1. Listening
2. Starting a conversation
3. Having a conversation
4. Asking a question
5. Saying thank you
6. Introducing yourself
7. Introducing other people
8. Giving a compliment

Group II. *Advanced Social Skills*

9. Asking for help
10. Joining in
11. Giving instructions
12. Following instructions
13. Apologizing
14. Convincing others

Group III. *Skills for Dealing with Feelings*

15. Knowing your feelings
16. Expressing your feelings
17. Understanding the feelings of others
18. Dealing with someone else's anger
19. Expressing affection
20. Dealing with fear
21. Rewarding yourself

Group IV. *Skill Alternatives to Aggression*

22. Asking permission
23. Sharing something
24. Helping others

25. Negotiation
26. Using self-control
27. Standing up for your rights
28. Responding to teasing
29. Avoiding trouble with others
30. Keeping out of fights

Group V. *Skills for Dealing with Stress*

31. Making a complaint
32. Answering a complaint
33. Sportsmanship after the game
34. Dealing with embarrassment
35. Dealing with being left out
36. Standing up for a friend
37. Responding to persuasion
38. Responding to failure
39. Dealing with contradictory messages
40. Dealing with an accusation
41. Getting ready for a difficult conversation
42. Dealing with group pressure

Group VI. *Planning Skills*

43. Deciding on something to do
44. Deciding what caused a problem
45. Setting a goal
46. Deciding on your abilities
47. Gathering information
48. Arranging problems by importance
49. Making a decision
50. Concentrating on a task

Source: A. Goldstein, *The PREPARE Curriculum: Teaching Prosocial Competencies* (revised ed.). Champaign, Ill.: Research Press, © 1999. Reprinted by permission.

rehearsal ("Let's imagine we're at Grandma's and she's offered you that juice you hate. I'm Grandma. What do you say?") and what-if games ("What if you were over at your best friend's house and he offered you alcohol? How might you respond?") are both useful ways to help youngsters practice responding to different kinds of social situations. Even relatively rigid personal styles can be modified with patience. (If your daughter tends to ramble endlessly before coming to the point, for example, ask her to give you the conclusion of the story before launching into all the details; eventually she will do this with her friends, too.) Noticing and rewarding good behavior play a vital role in cementing new skills into place ("What a great job you did staying quiet through the whole church service! You must be ready to cut loose—how about a trip to the park?").

To do a really effective job of social education, it is necessary to make an effort to understand the peer value system at school—if you don't, you won't know what social situations to prepare your child *for*. One mother was shocked to learn, for example, that some youngsters were sexually active in junior high (she'd assumed that she had until high school to deal with sex education). Another discovered that athletes were the social aristocrats of the local high school (the school had a tennis team, so she encouraged her well-coordinated eleven-year-old to take lessons). Among the best sources for this kind of information are kids a few years older than your own; a respectful relationship with a neighborhood teenager can be well worth cultivating if you want to know what really happens at school.

Peers can also help youngsters with disabilities learn social skills. Some high schools match youngsters who have learning and other types of disabilities with volunteer "coaches" who introduce them to a variety of activities, eat lunch with them, answer questions, and serve as models for appropriate social behavior. Programs like this offer the advantage of providing teens with guidance when and where they need it most. If your school does not have such a program, ask your school principal about approaching student organizations that promote service and leadership (such as the student government or the National Honor Society) about starting a peer-mentoring project.

What else can parents do to promote social development? Three important strategies that can help children grow in the right direction are described below.

Turn Off the TV Set

Many American children spend more time watching television than doing any other activity except sleeping. Three or four hours of television viewing a day is not unusual, and some children regularly watch much more. Experts object to excessive TV watching on a variety of grounds. One is that television introduces children to questionable content and values. It is estimated, for example, that by the time they graduate from elementary school, American children will have witnessed more than 8,000 murders and more than 100,000 other violent acts (including rape and armed assault) on television. This has been connected to a rise in both anxiety and aggression among young people, as well as to increased indifference to human suffering. Much of the punching and kicking parents try to prevent or punish can be traced to what children see on the small screen (where impulsive or violent behavior is sometimes represented as a way to solve problems by the *good* guys). While there is more diversity on television than there used to be, racial and gender stereotyping are still common. There is so much sex on TV that teenagers now report that the greatest pressure to become sexually active comes from television—not from their peers. Studies find that children who watch a great deal of television are also more likely to smoke and drink alcohol.

Wait, it gets worse. Television has been connected to weaknesses in verbal fluency, reading ability, and creative thinking. Low school achievement has been associated with watching TV as few as ten hours a week. A study of a small Canadian town before and after TV reception became available found that reading fluency and community participation both went down after television was introduced to the community. Verbal and physical aggression went up. Add to all this the fact that the average child is bombarded with more than forty thousand commercials a year (many for junk food and other questionable products) and the argument for switching off the set becomes pretty powerful.

Does "educational TV" have value? Studies have found that quality children's programs—such as PBS's *Sesame Street, Cyberchase, Electric Company,* and *Word Girl,* or Nickelodeon's *Dora the Explorer* and *Go, Diego Go!*—do help young children make gains in vocabulary and early-reading and school-readiness skills. Benefits (more book reading and better English grades, for example) have been found to persist well beyond grade school. Unfortunately, truly educational programming beyond the preschool years is sparse.

Even if all programming were acceptable, television would still interfere with development because it robs children of social opportunities. The most compelling reason to unplug the TV may be a brief list of what children are *not* doing while they are glued to the tube: they are not learning to play cooperatively, learning to make decisions or solve problems, having conversations and developing language skills, reading, or getting exercise. So while the children are sure to object, the evidence suggests that restricting television is in their best interests. As we will see shortly, other kinds of activities have much more to offer them.

Promote Social Awareness

Youngsters with learning disabilities are often less aware of social issues than others their age. Research finds that current events and hot topics like drug abuse, racism, sexual harassment, environmental issues, homelessness, poverty, and religious intolerance are not often discussed in class; when they are, students with learning disabilities are more likely to be absent (getting special education help) or unable to participate because information is not presented in a form they can use. As a result, these young people are frequently either ignorant of these issues or have opinions that have been heavily influenced by the entertainment media.

This general lack of awareness contributes to the impression that kids with learning disabilities are "out of it," and it can also lead to behavior that is viewed as inconsiderate, irresponsible, or just plain offensive (efforts to act like TV tough guys, for example, are rarely appreciated by teachers). To prevent this situation, parents may have to make an extra effort to help children become more aware of the world around them. Some suggestions follow:

Keep children abreast of current events. Discussing what is going on across the country and around the world helps students develop their awareness of such important issues as civil rights, religious freedom, economic inequality, and environmental safety. It can also help children appreciate cultures other than their own. To help kids tune in, watch TV news with them and ask their opinions on the issues. Subscribe to newspapers and news magazines (which are preferred by some students because they are illustrated), and invite youngsters' comments on events of local, national, and global importance. (Remember that high-interest, low-readability news magazines are available for children; check with your school librarian.) Even if children do not read the news themselves, discussing it with you will increase their awareness; it will help develop their thinking and language skills as well.

Involve children in community service. There is no better way to learn about the important issues facing our own community than becoming a volunteer. Not only does volunteer work help youngsters find a focus outside themselves, but also being helpful to others can provide a big boost to self-esteem. In addition, young people who volunteer regularly often acquire skills that help them later on the job (learning to be on time, to operate computers and other office equipment, and to deal with the public in person and on the telephone are likely benefits). In most communities there are many service opportunities, ranging from helping out in museums to staffing soup kitchens and assisting with environmental education and political action campaigns. For ideas, check your local list of United Way agencies. Many of these nonprofit organizations welcome reliable volunteer workers.

Relate issues to personal conduct. Concrete thinkers will not automatically apply general observations about issues like sexism, racism, and religious tolerance to personal behavior. (A youngster who knows that racism is wrong, for example, may still thoughtlessly repeat racial slurs he has heard used on television or at school.) It is therefore necessary to make the connection explicit. When talking about environmental concerns, for example, emphasize how the child can personally address the issues (such as by assisting in recycling efforts or conserving water). Be equally explicit about behavior the child should avoid (such as littering). This promotes social awareness at a personal level.

As youngsters approach adolescence, it is particularly important to connect social responsibility and sexual behavior. While courtship rituals can be tough to figure out for any teen, socially imperceptive adolescents have an even harder time understanding how to behave properly around the opposite sex. A list of sexual survival skills is presented in the box on page 359. These issues need to be discussed with youngsters before they leave junior high school (earlier may be even better; preteen children are often more open to discussing sexual matters with parents than teenagers are). To be effective, it is important to go beyond talking about what to avoid ("Make sure that boy respects you and keeps his hands to himself!"); you must also talk about how to avoid it ("Let's imagine he wants to get physical before you're ready; what are some ways to say no? What if he's not listening?"). This kind of preparation can both reduce the risk of embarrassing blunders and help ensure teens' sexual safety.

Encourage Outside Interests

Getting involved with hobbies, extracurricular activities, sports, and/ or community-based programs like scouts or 4-H clubs can increase a child's opportunities for social contact. Shared interests also provide a basis for friendly interaction (two baseball fans or coin collectors usually have no trouble finding something to talk about, for example, even if their conversational skills are limited). Improving opportuni-

Sexual Survival Skills

Learning to behave in a sexually responsible manner is an important part of growing up. Parents need to make sure their adolescent children know how to do the following:

- turn down unwanted sexual advances in a manner that suits the child's personality and the situation at hand (this skill is equally important for girls *and* boys)

- display romantic interest in someone in a respectful, nonintimidating manner

- recognize and respect someone else's rejection of romantic or sexual advances (understanding that the phrase "Let's be friends" is usually a turndown, for example)

- convey relationship expectations to a partner openly and honestly (rather than behaving in a way that is offensive or misleading)

- elicit the relationship expectations of a partner in direct conversation (instead of guessing them and/or being misled)

- negotiate dating activities that are mutually agreeable as well as reasonably safe and responsible (for example, that don't involve a high risk of being stranded somewhere or winding up in unwanted company)

- establish terms of intimacy with a partner that are physically safe, responsible, and respectful of both parties (if not abstention from sex, then the practice of safe sex)

Adapted from Philadelphia Child Guidance Center with J. Maguire, *Your Child's Emotional Health: Adolescence.* (New York: Macmillan, 1995).

ties for quality interaction is important because research suggests that the better children come to know one another, the more they get to like one another, regardless of differences in their academic-achievement levels. Participating in sports and recreational programs can also help develop children's skills and boost their self-confidence. On pages 360–61 a college student with learning disabilities describes the many benefits that came from running with his high school track team (an activity he needed more than a little "encouragement" to join).

Ben

Ben is an anthropology major and an officer of the photography and outing clubs at Bates College. His hobbies include fly-fishing, drawing, ballroom dancing, mountain biking, and guitar (an instrument he says helps him make friends wherever he goes).

When I started high school, my father insisted that I go out for a team sport. It was part of his scheme to get me involved in my new school. I remember feeling very disgruntled about being forced to occupy my time according to my father's plans. I was tall, gangly, not in terribly good shape, and certainly not interested in organized physical activity. I saw myself being hit by balls, crushed by three-hundred-pound freaks with no necks, and being told to grin and bear it when I was in pain. My interests strayed more toward the arts spectrum, where my coordination could be put to use in a manner that did not involve damaging my limbs. But for me it was a sport I must choose, or risk the wrath of my father standing tall and dark above me.

I consulted my gym teacher. She introduced me to her nephew Joe, a senior who had run on the cross-country team since middle school. Joe introduced me to his coach, who told me to show up for practice the next day with shorts and running shoes. Thus my career as a runner began.

When I showed up for practice, the coach sent me out on a five-mile run. I woke up the next morning hardly able to walk. When I hobbled into school, the muscles in my legs felt like they were being flayed by red-hot pokers. Other members of the team noticed and sympathized with my condition. Older team members encouraged me to keep running and told me it would get better.

As I continued to attend practices, I discovered that I was not so different from these other runners. Yes, there were some stereotypical "jocks" on the team, but there were also artists, drama enthusiasts, and mathematicians participating for various reasons. Some of us ran for fun, some ran for fitness, and some ran for scholarships. We all hurt at the top of the hill, and when the race was done.

Often experienced members of the team would help new members. They offered encouragement when exhaustion set in and passed on bits of advice about warming up, reducing fatigue, getting rid of cramps. I liked the fact that even if you weren't a "star," you were accepted and respected as a member of the team. I remember one runner who was obese. Every year he ran to lose weight. He wasn't any good—in fact, he usually came in last—but he always finished. And every time he crossed the finish line, his teammates would clap and cheer.

As I began to get in shape, my times started coming down. I became more interested in how I was running; I enjoyed setting personal records and breaking them. I wasn't running because my father said I had to anymore—I was running because I liked it. I developed a friendly rivalry with another freshman as we competed for the same spot on the team roster. I found myself wanting to win. I made sure I got plenty of sleep before race day and ate spaghetti for dinner so I would have plenty of energy.

At the end of my first semester, I made varsity. My mother had promised me that if I earned a varsity letter, she would get me a jacket like some of the older members of the team wore. We went to the mall, picked out the jacket, and had it monogrammed. At home, Mom sewed on the bright orange letter. The next day I felt great wearing that jacket to school, like I'd made the big league! Looking back, I guess I must have looked pretty funny, a skinny freshman "art geek" in a size-too-big varsity jacket. But I felt proud of earning it, and that jacket still keeps me warm on autumn days.

I know now my father was right to have me go out for a team. In addition to becoming a source of confidence and personal pride, the team offered a great way of getting to know people. My high school is the most culturally diverse in our city. Its population includes African-Americans, Latinos, Native Americans, Middle Easterners, and Asians. Unfortunately, the school is fairly socially fragmented, and people of different races and nationalities do not always mix. People from nearly all these groups run, however, and on the track team there were fewer cliques. Because of my participation in a sport, I developed a much wider base of friends.

From joining the team I also learned to be more open-minded about trying new things (and maybe to listen to my dad). I discovered that if I want to be part of something, I can't just wait to be invited in. I didn't intend to join a club or activity when I started high school, but after I started running I realized how much I could learn from extracurricular endeavors. I went on to become involved in many other school activities. I joined the ski club. I helped build sets for the drama club and eventually worked up the courage to audition for parts in the school plays. I became a photographer—and ultimately photo editor—for the yearbook. Each of these activities involved a different kind of teamwork, and each gave me opportunities to make new friends. These experiences added so much to my enjoyment and growth in my high school years that I really hate to think of what they would have been like for me if my father had not insisted that I become a member of a team.

Studies show that recreational pursuits can also ease the transition to adulthood. For example, the landmark study in Kauai, Hawaii, cited earlier, found that most of the individuals with learning disabilities who coped well in adulthood took pleasure in interests and hobbies that relieved stress when other things in their lives fell apart. Most of these people had participated in cooperative recreational programs (such as cheerleading, 4-H clubs, and YMCA programs) as teenagers.

Obviously, there is a great deal to be gained from these endeavors beyond physical fitness and fun. To involve youngsters with learning disabilities in these activities successfully, however, it is helpful to observe a few guidelines:

Take the time to prepare the child for the activity, and the activity for the child. Many children with learning disabilities are somewhat fearful of new situations and anxious about their ability to succeed. Some children also have difficulties learning new procedures and rules. Before starting a new activity, give your child as much of a "preview" of what is going to happen as you can. (Before the first Girl Scout meeting, for example, arrange to meet the troop leader, visit the site where meetings take place, and read some Girl Scout literature together.) It is also a good idea to tell group leaders about a child's learning disability so they can help the child do her best and avoid placing her in embarrassing positions. (Mentioning to the coach that a child has trouble hearing directions against background noise, for example, could make the difference between an ice-hockey player's success and failure.)

Choose activities on the basis of interest, not age. Having friends is important to self-esteem, but there is no rule that says all of your friends have to be the same age you are. Because children with learning disabilities can be slow to mature, they are sometimes most comfortable with people somewhat younger—or older—than themselves. A twelve-year-old who is too impulsive and distractible to play baseball with other seventh-graders, for example, might have a great time gardening with a group of adults or working on a model railroad with a ten-year-old neighbor. A youngster who builds a rock collection with his grandfather both benefits from the special attention and develops a body of knowledge with which he can impress his peers. By encouraging cross-age activities, you can often improve a child's social opportunities considerably.

Avoid cutthroat competition. Cooperative activities that emphasize enjoyment, individual growth, participation, and making a contribution to a shared endeavor tend to be the best confidence boosters for children with learning disabilities. Many youngsters prefer individual or recreational sports such as swimming, tennis, golf, skating, or skiing to more competitive team athletics. If your child does want to play a team sport (in many communities these are high-status activities, especially for boys), make sure the coach is interested in building up the individual player as well as the team.

When it comes to making friends, parents can help a lot simply by engineering proximity—bringing children with similar interests together (as through arranging family outings and sleepovers, or involving children in organized activities based on their talents or enthusiasms). Keep in mind that it's quality—not quantity—that counts. Many children with learning disabilities are most comfortable sharing an activity with one or two special people; larger groups may overtax their receptive- or expressive-language capabilities or provide too many distractions. A youngster who has a couple of regular buddies is probably doing fine, and he or she may need no more. Hobbies and group activities still provide wonderful opportunities for exercise and intellectual stimulation, of course, so whatever your children's interests, look for opportunities that will help them follow through.

BE CONSISTENT ABOUT RULES AND LIMITS

All children need the security of a system of rules and limits. The way rules are established and enforced, however, can have a significant impact on both family relationships and a child's self-image. Let's take a look at three types of child-rearing practice that are particularly common:

Strict parents. These parents communicate high standards to their children and tolerate little in the way of deviation. Energy is typically focused on correcting negative behaviors. Standards are enforced by power measures (threats or punishment), unaccompanied by explanation or discussion. Children are given few or no choices. Obedience is seen as a virtue and valued for its own sake.

Authoritative parents. These mothers and fathers also have firm standards for obedience, school performance, and responsible behavior at home. They explain the reasons for their rules, however, and are willing to listen to children's points of view. Parents recognize and reward good behavior as well as punish wrongdoing. Children are given a limited range of choices. Independence and initiative are traits that are valued.

Permissive parents. These parents are very accepting of their children's behavior and impulses. They are often warm and affectionate, but do not insist on standards or limits; rules are rarely enforced. Freedom is valued. Children are given many choices but little support or guidance in making them.

Research indicates that it is the authoritative parents who are most likely to inspire trust and respect, and to have offspring who are responsible, self-reliant, cooperative, confident, and creative. Strict parents are more likely to inspire fear and resentment; their children are often withdrawn, distrustful, and discontent. Children of very permissive parents tend to be the least self-controlled and self-reliant of the lot. Lack of structure and effective role models frequently leaves them irresponsible, disorganized, and drifting.

Studies of children with learning disabilities find that their problems can be made worse by parenting styles that are either overly strict or overly permissive. Overprotective parenting, for example, has been associated with hyperactivity and delays in child development. Parents who are inflexible about their standards frequently set youngsters with developmental differences up for failure; loss of self-confidence and motivation usually follows. In contrast, authoritative parents give children with learning disabilities four of the things they need most: a strong model, belief in their abilities to reason through problems with adult guidance, structure, and encouragement. Following are some experts' suggestions for those who would like to make their parenting styles more productive.

Keep Rules to a Minimum

Too many rules create a repressive family atmosphere. Parents end up acting like parole officers—ever vigilant for wrongdoing—and their kids become either fearful or sneaky (depending on their ages and personalities). Either way, the children feel devalued. Don't issue mandates when friendly give-and-take will do, or for chores that enforce themselves (you really don't have to tell children to do their laundry, for example; they'll do it when they run out of clean clothes). Lay down the law only for important matters, such as insisting that your children keep you informed about where they are and/or call to tell you when they are going to be late. Rules like these let children know parents value and care about them.

Remember also that the point of rules is to regulate behavior—not thoughts or feelings. Attempts to dictate matters of personal taste or opinion are usually unwise. Telling children what they must wear or whom they may have as friends, for example, invites unnecessary conflict and risks your relationship with your child. So even if you hate your son's ponytail, try to live with it. (An experienced guidance counselor refers to this as "choosing the battles you're going to lose." "If you give the kids room to rebel with safe items like fashion and hair," he explains, "you'll be in a much better position to enforce standards on bigger items, like drugs.")

Seek to Educate and Negotiate Rather Than Dictate

Educating children about standards and negotiating mutually acceptable solutions to problems can be a much more effective means of improving their behavior than punishment. Consider the case of a five-year-old who snatches a toy from her baby brother and knocks him over. We could yell at Susie or punish her for her aggressive behavior, but instead let's ask her what went wrong. Ah! It appears the doll Susie snatched was her own, and she didn't like baby brother chewing on its head. If we hear Susie out, we may realize she was rougher than she meant to be and is frightened that she may have hurt the baby badly. Clearly, there is little to be gained from sending the little girl to her room; what she needs is a strategy for dealing with this kind of situation in the future ("Now that the baby can crawl, it's best not to leave your toys on the floor. Maybe we need a special shelf for your things. If you are feeling angry with the baby, come tell me and I will help you solve the problem").

As they get older, it becomes increasingly important to involve children in establishing standards and rules. Attempts to control them with arbitrary commands ("You'll do it because I said so!") both convey a lack of faith in the child's judgment and make rebellion his or her only option for expressing individuality. Even when their views seem outlandish it is essential to hear youngsters out. Listening communicates respect and interest in them as people. Children who feel respected and understood are most likely to trust their parents' opinions. You may therefore find that young people become much more open and flexible once they have had their say.

Learn to recognize the point at which negotiation starts to deteriorate into a power struggle, however. When discussions degenerate into accusations and character bashing, nobody can win. If you or your child is "losing it," declaring a time-out can be a sanity saver. Sometimes a quiet meal, a warm bath, or a night's sleep can do wonders to restore one's perspective and ability to appreciate a child's better qualities. Remember, too, that the final responsibility for making and enforcing rules does rest with adults (*don't* let kids talk you into the idea that family issues should be decided "democratically"). If reasonable attempts at discussion and negotiation have failed to produce a workable compromise, it is appropriate to tell your children, "Thank you for your input; here is my decision," and put an end to further discussion.

Apply Logical Consequences

Sooner or later, all kids test the rules. Ignoring these violations is not in the best interests of the child; authoritative parents respond promptly when rules are broken. Following a brief discussion in which the rule is reviewed and children are given a reasonable opportunity to explain their behavior, discipline is carried out.

Whenever possible, consequences for wrongdoing should be logically connected to the misbehavior. If a child is chronically careless about where he leaves his bicycle, for example, it is logical to take the bike away for a period of time; this punishment is likely to be more effective than a lecture or a spanking. (Hitting children rarely accomplishes anything other than humiliating them and stimulating a desire for revenge.) Try to explain punishments in a way that is respectful to the child. "I see you are not old enough to be responsible for a bicycle yet, so we will put it away until next month" does not call the child's character into question. In contrast, "How can you be so careless! Your father paid good money for that bike, but obviously you don't appreciate it!" implies that the child is a bad person who is undeserving of his parents' generosity.

When undesirable behavior produces its own unpleasant consequences, the best strategy is sometimes simply not to interfere. If a child forgets to return library books, for example, a whopping fine from the library may be all that is needed to encourage her to change her ways. If the consequences children face are not really dangerous, resist the impulse to rescue them from these helpful learning experiences. Note also that enacting logical consequences can be a much more effective motivator than nagging. If children are having trouble remembering to put dirty clothes in the hamper, for example, don't browbeat them about it. Don't wash anything that isn't in the hamper, either; they'll get the point.

Generally speaking, the best time to determine penalties for breaking rules is before wrongdoing takes place. When you establish an expectation (that Johnny's stuff will be removed from the kitchen on Saturday, for example) also establish the penalty for failure to comply (no social engagements will be allowed until the job is done). This helps prevent misunderstandings, and it also spares you from trying to think of a fair punishment when you are angry—a time when life imprisonment at hard labor may seem reasonable. If you discuss consequences in a calm moment, children can sometimes be surprisingly helpful. "When I asked my seventeen-year-old son what the penalty for being late to dinner should be, he said, 'Well, Ma, I guess I should cook my own dinner,'" a mother remembers. "Sounded reasonable to me. From then on the rule was that if he hadn't come home or called by five thirty, I didn't cook for him."

Remember that whatever consequences are established, you are the one who is going to have to enforce them. Don't set up consequences that are harder on you than they are on the child! Forbidding a teenager to use the car for a month may seem like an effective penalty, for example—until you realize that you are now stuck with driving your daughter wherever she needs to go. Similarly, if assigning extra chores puts you in the position of nagging children to do them and/or standing guard to see that they are done right, the punishment may be more grief than it's worth. Since rules are pointless unless they are enforced consistently, the best consequences are simple and easy to execute. (Grounding a teenager on Saturday night for breaking curfew may be as effective as grounding her for a month, and you will only have to listen to her complain for one day instead of thirty.)

Use Positive Reinforcement

One of the most powerful tools for changing children's behavior is to "catch them being good" and reward them for doing right. Positive feedback also boosts self-esteem because it helps children see themselves as capable and responsible (frequent punishment tends to underscore the idea that children are irresponsible or inherently bad). Taking a youngster out for dinner to celebrate a good report card or posting an improved spelling paper proudly on the refrigerator is usually a more effective motivator than is nagging about homework. Similarly, telling a teenager "You look sharp today!" is often worth more than a week's worth of "Don't tell me you're leaving the house dressed like *that!*"

Offered the wrong way, however, rewards can actually undermine children's motivation. Children who are given indiscriminate positive feedback, for example, sometimes become "praise junkies"—the point of performance becomes getting attention and recognition; personal satisfaction in achievement declines and performance falls off as soon as praise is withdrawn. Children may also find themselves so impatient to receive a promised reward that they have trouble focusing on the task at hand. A child who is told he will be given popcorn after he finishes his math homework, for example, may rush through the assignment and do a worse job than if no incentive is offered! Youngsters who perceive rewards as an attempt to coerce their compliance (and therefore limit their choices) are also likely to find their motivation slipping. Praise that is vague and unrelated to specific behavior (such as "You were a good girl today") can leave a child feeling uneasy and insecure (what exactly did she do that was "good," and what if she forgets to do it tomorrow?).

To make positive reinforcement effective, experts advise following these guidelines:

Use rewards only when they are needed. Offering rewards when they are not needed shifts a child's motivation away from the satisfaction of doing well and toward working for "payback." *Do* let success be its own reward whenever possible, and *don't* offer rewards if a child's level of motivation or satisfaction in an accomplishment is already high. By all means acknowledge children's achievements ("I'm so proud of how well you've done in math!"), but be aware that offering additional incentives ("Here's twenty dollars for getting an A") may only confuse the issue.

Tie praise and rewards to specific behavior. Children need to know *exactly* what they have done right if you want them to do it again. "I noticed you took a time-out when you started to get angry—that was smart!" will therefore have a more powerful effect on behavior than the more general "It's nice to see you and Steve are getting along better these days." Whenever possible, link rewards to the particular type of effort being made. If a child is working hard in art, for example, rewarding her with art books or a generous supply of paints and brushes is the most meaningful way of expressing your approval.

Use the least powerful incentive that is effective. Research shows that a little encouragement can go a long way. A study of high school students, for example, found that praise worked best when offered sparingly (5 to 10 percent of the time); if it was used more often, the kids stopped hearing it. (Young children usually need more frequent reinforcement than do teens.) Excessive rewards can also undermine inner motivation and set up an understanding that the only reason to achieve is to get bigger and better prizes. (If the effort to pass math in a given year is aimed at getting a new bike, for example, what's the point of continuing to work hard in math next year?) A hug and a sincere "Well done!" is often all a youngster needs. (For some alternative ways to say "Well done," check the box on page 371.)

Respond promptly. Praise and rewards do a good job of reinforcing desirable behavior only if they are provided close to the time the behavior occurs. If you have promised your son a banana split if he improves his citizenship grade, don't put the trip to the ice-cream parlor off until next week—go the day he proudly brings home his report card.

Reward effort and initiative as well as achievement. Working hard and being persistent are as praiseworthy as outstanding performance. For the child with learning disabilities, effort may be especially worth celebrating; these youngsters often need extra encouragement to "hang in there" and see difficult or frustrating tasks through. When a child with at-

50 Ways to Say "Well Done!"

Your hard work is paying off.	You've learned a lot.
You made my day.	You remembered!
How clever of you!	I really like that.
You're on the right track.	Good try.
You're good at that.	Wow!
Much better!	Look at you go.
I knew you could do it.	You're a hard worker.
A big improvement!	Congratulations!
Now you have it.	Nice job.
Beautiful!	Good thinking.
Good Idea.	You did it yourself!
You haven't missed a thing.	A new record!
Good start.	You're almost there.
That's what I like to see!	That's it!
A first-class job.	Couldn't have done it better myself.
The best yet.	You're right on target.
Good for you!	Yes!
I'm proud of you.	You got it.
Way to go!	Outstanding!
Very original.	Good move.
Super!	You've outdone yourself.
Coming along nicely.	A lot of effort went into that.
You're really on top of it.	Creative!
I'm impressed!	You're really applying yourself.
You must have been practicing.	Let's celebrate!

tention deficits has put in a solid thirty minutes on a task, he deserves praise even if the task isn't finished. Remember that it's *behavior* you want to reinforce; rewards can never guarantee results.

A special educator adds, "Showing a sincere interest in what a child is doing is often even more effective than praise." The most valuable reward a parent can bestow, after all, is *time*. Asking a child to play you the new song she has learned on the violin or show you his stamp album clearly states, "I'm proud of who you are and what you have done."

TUNE IN TO FAMILY DYNAMICS

The mother of a fourteen-year-old boy with attention-deficit and language-processing disabilities relates:

> *I don't think the stress of coping with a child who has a learning disability would cause a couple to split up, but it sure will open up any cracks in the relationship that are already there. My husband and I have fought about a lot of things having to do with both education and discipline. For instance, my husband says I spoil Justin and help him too much with things. But I think my husband is too critical—he hasn't put in the time with Justin that I have and I don't think he has a realistic idea of what Justin can do. We fought over giving Justin piano lessons. My husband said Justin would only quit (which he did), but I thought he deserved the same chance to learn to play as his sisters. The most difficult time in our marriage was when we were trying to decide if we should move into the city. We had our dream house in the country, and we loved the space and being able to have animals. But the school district was in the dark ages where services for learning disabilities were concerned—we had to fight for every single thing Justin needed, and it seemed like all his teachers hated him. They have a lot more experience with his kind of learning problems in the city schools, but that would mean a smaller house, higher taxes, a tiny yard. . . . Even if it was best for Justin, would a move be fair to the girls? We argued about it for a year. In the end we did move, but even now we don't always agree that it was the right thing to do.*

This story highlights some stresses that are very common in families of children with learning disabilities: ambivalence about how much to expect of the child at home, frustration over the difficulty of securing adequate help at school, and guilt about the impact of the disability on nondisabled children.

Although she may not realize it, this mother is also describing a pattern of family interaction that is common: the "problem child" has formed an alliance with one parent against the other. It is often (but not always) Mom who becomes the child's protector, while Dad gets to be the bad guy (the one whose job it is to enforce limits and find fault with household policies and educational plans). Sometimes the family becomes increasingly locked into these roles as time goes by. If Mom feels she is the only one who really understands the child, for example, she may invest more and more of her time and energy in meeting the child's needs. When this happens, Dad—who feels as though no one is listening to his point of view—often responds by becoming even more demanding and critical.

Nondisabled children in families like these sometimes adopt roles, too, including these that are seen frequently:

The superkids. These children get good grades, star in sports or other extracurricular activities, and generally strive to do everything right—almost as if they are trying to compensate for their siblings' problems and failures.

The troublemakers. These children keep parents involved with them by having one problem after another. If attention is diverted to other children, these may respond by producing a crisis of some kind.

The mediators. These kids are exquisitely sensitive to other people's feelings and invest a lot of energy in trying to patch up arguments and smooth out problems so that stressed family members will feel better.

The clowns. They keep us laughing with their antics or distract us from our worries by being generally winning and adorable.

Each of these roles represents a bid for a place of importance in the family. To some extent, these youngsters are all trying to compete with the child with disabilities, whose family role is being dysfunctional.

Although roles such as these are seldom entirely comfortable, over time a family can become so habituated to them that change poses a significant threat to the family system and the identities of the individuals within it. If one member of the family tries to change—Dad attempts to become more supportive of Mom, for example—other family members may display considerable resistance or even initiate counterbalancing tactics. (If Dad becomes more supportive, Mom doesn't get to be the child's lone "savior" anymore; if she is unwilling to give up that role, she may go out of her way to provoke disagreements and arguments. Likewise, a child who fears losing Mom's undivided attention may attempt to regain it by becoming even more "disabled" and helpless.) These reactions are instinctive attempts to protect what is familiar; often, the family members who are following these scripts have little conscious awareness of what they are doing. The problem with patterns of this kind is that they allow little room for individual growth. Family members trapped in roles are also unlikely to work together to solve problems—indeed, if the family has become organized around a problem, members may fight to keep it in place.

Awareness is the first step toward addressing this and other damaging patterns that occur in families with "problem" children. Before we discuss prevention, let's look at a few other familiar family traps:

Scapegoating the child with disabilities. This occurs when a family focuses on a child's dysfunction as a means of avoiding other painful issues. Virtually everything that goes wrong in the family is laid at the "difficult" child's door. For example, the fact that all children in a family are doing poorly in school might be blamed on the presence of an "out of control" hyperactive teenager; the facts that Dad is abusive and Mom drinks too much remain safely buried. (If these secrets are discovered, the alcoholism and anger may be blamed on the teen, too.) This pattern confers a spectacular amount of guilt upon children with disabilities, who often come to believe they really are responsible for all of the family's problems.

Giving in to denial. In this scenario, one or more family members refuse to accept that a disability exists, then pressure the rest of the family into playing along. The person leading the parade is most often a parent ("There's nothing wrong with my son! Those teachers just don't know how to deal with a boy who has real spunk!") or a grandparent ("Please don't tell anyone about this evaluation; I don't want people to think she's retarded. I'm sure it's wrong, anyway—it's obvious that Carly is perfectly normal!"). If the individual in denial holds a powerful position in the family, help for the child may be blocked or delayed. Alternatively, the learning disability may be acknowledged in some family settings but not in others ("Don't tell Auntie Ellen . . ."). Denial is frequently rooted in guilt and fear ("Everyone will think it's my fault . . . I can't bear to give my mother-in-law one more thing to hold against me"). Concerns about social status may also play a role. Cooperating with denial, however, protects adult egos at children's expense. It often convinces young people that having learning disabilities is bad or shameful.

Slighting sibling interests. The primary complaint of brothers and sisters of children with learning disabilities is that Mom and Dad expect more of the siblings while giving them less time and attention. Even when parents bend over backward to be fair, unavoidable inequities can breed resentment and strain sibling relationships, as Eli describes (see box on pages 376–77). Siblings of youngsters with learning disabilities can also experience a lot of ambivalence. For example, a girl may feel protective of a brother with disabilities but also feel embarrassed about his behavior when friends come to call, and she may fear peer rejection on his account. A boy might become a superachiever, then feel guilty about succeeding where the sibling with disabilities cannot. Younger children may fear "catching" a learning disability, or try to copy "disabled" behavior in an effort to win attention (the latter problem can be unwittingly enabled by teachers, who

Eli

Being the younger child is not easy—especially in a family of two boys. My memories are filled with competition and jealousy. In some ways, my older brother's learning disability made our relationship even more complicated and difficult.

I admit, when I was first told that my brother had a learning disability I was thrilled. He's two years older than I am and had been ahead of me in almost everything. Now *I* was going to be better at a few things! When I was angry with my brother (which was pretty often) I sometimes felt like taunting him with his handicap: "I'm smarter than you are in school! You have brain damage and I don't!" I never said it; I knew it would be a low blow. I thought it, though, and I think he knew I did.

But at times I had trouble believing in this disability. I couldn't see anything in my brother that was "different." At my elementary school there were a lot of students with disabilities, and he didn't look or act like any of them. He didn't have distorted features or make odd noises or need a wheelchair or walk with a tilt. He looked about as normal as a big brother can get.

I watched for signs of his handicap. It was taking him a long time to learn his times tables, but I knew lots of kids who were bad at math. Nobody was making excuses for them! I began to wonder if having a learning disability wasn't more of an advantage than a disadvantage. My brother got to use a calculator for math tests (blatant cheating, it seemed to me) and was given extra time for some assignments and exams. He didn't even have to take a language in high school. Hey, I had some trouble with social studies and Spanish, but nobody was giving me any breaks! At one point in high school, my brother and I landed in the same math class (I was a year ahead in math, and he was a year behind). I worked

sometimes expect less of siblings of youngsters known to have learning problems). When learning disabilities are severe, nondisabled children may worry about becoming responsible for siblings after parents die. All these stresses can take their toll; studies have found up to 25 percent of siblings of children with disabilities experience significant emotional problems. If siblings have no safe means of resolving their rivalries, jealousies can erupt into vicious open family warfare. The risk for emotional distress is greatest when parents are hard and got 90s while he got 70s. My parents seemed equally pleased with those grades (because the learning disability made math especially hard for him, they were happy my brother had passed). They expected each of us to do our best and maybe that was the fairest way to look at it, but it sure didn't feel right to me at the time.

When my brother got extra time to take his college SATs, I thought, "These learning disabilities sure are handy!" It seemed like I was going to have to do twice the work to get into college that he did. One day when I was swamped with homework, I remember telling my mom I wished I had a learning disability so I could get all kinds of help and forgiveness if I screwed up. (Nobody was happy with *me* when I brought home a C on a test!) She told me to be grateful that I could succeed in every class if I worked hard— small comfort to a kid who thought he had too much to do.

Today I can think of my brother's learning disability with a little more compassion. It couldn't have been easy for him, sharing a class with a cocky younger brother. Looking back, he handled that situation with an amazing amount of dignity. I understand also that I do have more options than he does. When I look at my college catalogue, for example, my choices are unlimited, and there are no roadblocks between me and my choice of a career. My brother has a lot of talents, so I know he will succeed, but I wonder if he'll have to explain learning disabilities to his employers. That's going to be a lot harder than explaining to teachers at school. I know from experience how difficult it is to make people believe in something they can't see. No matter how much my mother told me about learning disabilities, the extra help and attention my brother got always seemed unfair. I was never one hundred percent sure he wasn't just fooling everybody and coasting.

so intensely focused on a child with disabilities that siblings' concerns are ignored or devalued ("How can you complain about being late to a silly soccer game when your brother has slammed his finger in the car door again!").

What can be done to avoid these snares? The key is often effective family communication. An effort may have to be made, however, to break counterproductive habits. Four strategies that can help get families headed in the right direction are discussed below.

Avoid the Blame Game

When we are feeling frustrated or angry about a problem, we often start looking around for someone to blame. After all, if we can figure out whose fault the problem is, we can demand that they fix it! In the families of children with learning disabilities, you often see blame being sprayed all over the place. Dad blames the school and the incompetent teachers who have mismanaged his child's education. Mom blames Dad's genes ("Just look at his side of the family!"). Big sister blames her brother for complicating her life and her parents for neglecting her needs. The child with learning disabilities blames everybody for misjudging him, and himself for making his family miserable.

This kind of behavior, of course, can be very hurtful. But an even bigger drawback of the blame game is that it inhibits action. Since the problem is always the *other* guy's fault, no one takes responsibility for solving it. Describing this state as "the paralysis of analysis," one mother recalls:

> *When he was in eighth grade, my son brought home a note that said he was failing science because he had handed in less than half of his homework assignments. I was horrified! Science was his favorite subject—how could this have happened? Maybe it was my fault; that year we were encouraging Jay to take more responsibility for himself and I'd supervised his homework less than usual. Or maybe the science teacher was disorganized and had forgotten to check that Jay had his assignments written down. Surely the resource teacher should have been on top of the situation and not let things get this far! Or maybe the issue was simply that Jay had started spending a lot of time on the phone talking to girls. . . . After several days of fretting I realized that analyzing the problem was getting us no closer to a solution. Jay needed to make up his missing homework and learn to keep better track of his assignments—everything else was a distraction.*

When a family has gotten into the blaming habit, it can take considerable effort to reroute energy along more constructive lines. It's useful to begin by recognizing that when a family has a problem, everyone has a stake in solving it regardless of the problem's origin. Instead of asking who *should* resolve a difficulty, try asking who *can* contribute something that might help. This helps family members refocus their attention and encourages them to work together cooperatively.

Don't Make Learning Disabilities a Secret

"My mother said I shouldn't tell the neighbors about needing help in reading," recalls a dyslexic adult. "It was like I had this awful secret. We didn't tell my grandparents or my cousins, either. I felt like if anyone found out about me getting special education help, it would bring shame on my entire family. Even now I'm not really comfortable talking about it."

No child should suffer shame or guilt for having a learning disability, but when parents attempt to hide these conditions from friends or family members, youngsters almost always do feel ashamed. Most children assume that what can't be talked about is either painful, dishonorable, or both. The best policy, therefore, is to talk about learning disabilities openly and honestly, emphasizing positive aspects of the situation. A matter-of-fact acknowledgment ("Johnny has a learning disability and has been getting some extra help in reading. We're so proud of how hard he's been working!") tells both the listener and Johnny that his good qualities are admired and that his learning disability is no big deal.

When you adopt this open approach, you may have to learn to deal with the occasional insensitive individual ("A learning disability? How awful! My neighbor's son has one of those; he dropped out of school and he's in jail now"). A mother advises, "Try not to get defensive when you run into one of these clods. I usually say, 'Ah! I see you don't know very much about learning disabilities,' and smile. If they really want to know more, they can ask me. If not, we change the subject. Either way, we've communicated that we're not ashamed and we've gotten out of my son's personal business."

Sometimes parents will be honest about a child's learning disability with everybody except the child. Behind this policy is usually fear that telling children the whole truth about their disabilities will be hugely harmful to their egos. In fact, keeping youngsters in the dark can do far more damage. Children who lack knowledge about their learning disabilities often assume they are stupid (why else would they be having such trouble in school?). Without accurate information, these young people also cannot devise efficient compensatory strategies, which effectively intensifies their handicaps. Don't be afraid to tell children about learning disabilities; the news that they are different hardly ever comes as a surprise to them, and learning *why* they are different often comes as a relief ("You mean I'm not retarded?" is a fairly common response). The kids will take their cues from you about how bad the news really is. If you talk to them through tears, sighing "My poor, poor baby" at odd intervals, they will probably be worried. If your approach is accepting and optimistic ("It's good we know about this; now we can find better ways of teaching you"), they will very likely share your positive attitude.

Remember that there is a difference between talking frankly about learning disabilities and *harping* on them. Educators sometimes meet parents who are so worried about their children's school problems that they talk about learning disabilities obsessively, ignoring the children's many charms and virtues. These unbalanced monologues can frighten children or leave them feeling humiliated or guilty for causing so much concern. If you are frightened and worried yourself, it is best to talk to professionals without your child present. Put off talking to the child until you have learned enough about his or her learning profile to talk knowledgeably about strengths as well as weaknesses.

Give Siblings an Even Break

Children with learning disabilities often need more time, more attention, more help, and more encouragement than their siblings. If tutors, private school, or special equipment such as computers are needed, the child with disabilities may also require a larger share of the family's financial resources. This situation is to some extent unavoidable, and it is therefore necessary for all the children in the family to accept it. The question is, will they accept it with equanimity—or with jealousy and resentment?

Siblings will almost certainly react with resentment if they are given no reason for differences in treatment. It is therefore important to explain learning disabilities to all children in a family. Avoid making the child with learning disabilities an object of pity, however; "Poor Mary isn't as good as you are at reading" invites Mary's siblings to look down on her—an attitude you can't expect Mary to tolerate serenely. (Comparing kids almost always promotes jealousy and rivalry.) "Mary has a learning disability that makes it hard for her to understand words in print" puts a more neutral spin on the discussion.

As children get older, they normally ask plenty of questions about perceived inequities ("Why do you write out Danny's math problems for him? How come you type Danny's papers and not mine?"). These occasions make good teaching opportunities. Providing straightforward answers to questions ("Because of his learning disability, Danny has trouble with small print. . . . It is hard for Danny to control a pencil; next year he will learn to type for himself") works better than becoming defensive ("You know I love you both! Didn't I bake brownies for you last week?"). Try to avoid scorekeeping—it invites kids to keep tally sheets and become manipulative. Children who constantly whine "It's not fair!" usually do so because there's a payoff in it for them somewhere. If you stop rewarding this behavior ("All right, I'll buy you one, too!"), the whining stops eventually.

Siblings are also less likely to be resentful if parents help them to understand that being fair does not necessarily mean treating all children the same. A more mature view is that being fair means everyone gets what he or she most *needs*, and that it is unusual for different people to need exactly the same things. For example, Dan's sister, Sue, needs recognition and encouragement for her achievements in track, so Mom and Dad make an effort to attend every meet and help organize the athletic-awards dinner at the school. Dan's brother, John, has a passion for music, so he is the one being given piano lessons. Dan needs help doing better in school, so the family invests in a computer primarily for his use. Although the time and money being spent on the children may not be exactly equal, these parents are being fair.

Siblings who feel that Mom and Dad are tuned in to what's most important to them are least likely to complain about what other children
in the family get—but this means that parents must learn to recognize
and honor their children's priorities. Perhaps your eleventh-grader's
agony over whether to wear a short or a long dress to the junior prom
seems insignificant compared with the fact that her brother is flunking
out of school; if this decision is very important to *her*, however, it deserves your respectful attention. If you devote the weekend to helping
her find that perfect dress, she probably won't care if you spend the
next month trying to straighten out your son's academic problems.

As we mentioned earlier, siblings' perceptions that children with
disabilities "get off easy" when it comes to housework is a frequent
cause of resentment, so an effort does need to be made to involve
children equally in chores. Parents sometimes wonder if this policy is
entirely fair to the child with disabilities. Is it reasonable to ask these
kids to wash dishes and take out the trash even though it takes them
longer to do their homework? Sure it is. The fact is, individuals with
learning disabilities often have to work harder to meet all their obligations, and those who are successful eventually accept this. When you
exempt children from responsibilities in an attempt to "equalize" their
loads, you set up unrealistic expectations for the future. (The child's
employers are *not* going to say, "Hey, take the afternoon off, buddy, I
know you have a lot of laundry to do.") Of course, if children are really
swamped you can always do them a favor ("I'll walk the dog for you,
honey, so you can keep up that good work"), but be equally sensitive
when your nondisabled child has a term paper due. (Sometimes kids
devise their own ways of adjusting workloads. One mother recently
overheard her son offer to do his sister's laundry if she'd correct his
spelling and type his book report.)

A final caution: if parents give siblings too much responsibility for
the care of children with disabilities, considerable resentment can
develop. Older girls in a family are most likely to be drafted as caregivers, but boys may also be enlisted or urged to "take your brother along"
when they go out. "My mother had no concept of how embarrassing it
was to have this hyperactive kid around when I was with my friends,"
a college student recalls. "A couple of times she made me take him

along to the movies; he went back and forth to the popcorn stand ten times, disturbing the whole row. After that, when my friends went to the movies, I just said I couldn't go." While it is reasonable to ask older siblings to help with child care, it is important to limit the number of hours that care is expected, and to give older children some choices about how they provide this help (the teenager quoted above said he wouldn't have minded taking his brother to the park once or twice a week; he just didn't want the child bothering his friends). If the amount of child care you need starts to limit siblings' abilities to pursue their own interests or significantly interferes with their social relationships, consider hiring a babysitter. This is sometimes the best investment you can make in good family relations.

Note that some parents of youngsters with learning disabilities establish unrealistically high expectations for achievement for their nondisabled children. Since they do not have handicaps, these siblings are expected to perform perfectly and fulfill all the hopes and dreams that the child with disabilities cannot. While this pressure may not create sibling hostility, it can seriously undermine the self-esteem of the nondisabled children. Remember that each child in the family deserves a chance to explore his or her own interests and make a fair share of mistakes and wrong turns. Children should never be pressed to achieve in order to make up for the perceived failures of a sibling, repair a family's social status, or bolster parents' own sagging sense of self-worth.

Learn How to Listen

Parents are often much better at talking to kids than they are at hearing what they have to say. Similarly, when husbands and wives discuss problems, each is sometimes so bent on getting points across that no real effort is made to listen to the other's views. The problem is that people who don't feel heard rarely feel understood or respected. Those who don't feel heard over an extended period of time have a limited number of options: they can quit trying to communicate and withdraw (often silently nursing a growing list of grudges and resentments); they can become more aggressive about pushing their opinions; or they can flee this frustrating situation. Counselors sometimes see all three responses at work in troubled families (a father and son launch escalating attacks on each other nightly, Mom escapes to the bedroom, and the boy's brother runs off to party with friends). Once these habits are entrenched, it becomes very hard for the family to address problems, so difficulties tend to compound (the brother starts abusing drugs; Mom becomes clinically depressed). Eventually, professional help may be needed in order to restore the family's health and stability.

When families do seek help, listening skills are often among the first things family members are encouraged to learn. Learning to listen can help prevent problems, too. Three suggestions for parents who want to help keep family members in close and respectful contact follow:

Take time to debrief. In previous generations, families didn't need to make time to talk; they gathered around the table for a meal at least once a day, and as often as not everyone spent the evening at home. Today, it is not unusual to find family members heading off in several different directions at night; dinner may be eaten in shifts in front of the TV. The result is less conversation and less information being shared. The smaller trials and triumphs of everyday living may not be communicated at all. Only relatively urgent matters may cause family members to seek one another's attention, giving conversation a frenzied quality.

If you can't reliably remember the names of your children's friends . . . if you don't know who their most and least favorite teachers are or what musical groups they like . . . if most of your conversations seem to fall into the "Mom, I've gotta have poster board and a report cover for tomorrow" category, you need more time to debrief. Successful debriefing involves four steps, described in the box on page 385. For children with learning disabilities, regular debriefing is especially important. These sessions provide youngsters with opportunities to practice their language skills in a safe, supportive environment (essential for the development of linguistic confidence) and give them a forum for problem-solving.

Debriefing

Debriefing is a method of keeping up with what is going on in your children's lives without making them feel as if they are victims of an inquisition. The objectives are to learn more about your children's experiences, to help them explore feelings, to identify problems, and to set goals. Successful debriefing consists of four steps:

1. ***Provide an opportunity for relaxed togetherness*** (a walk after dinner, a leisurely Sunday breakfast, or something similar). You need to find a time when you won't be interrupted or feel pressed about getting other things done.

2. ***Ask specific questions*** ("What's your favorite class this year?" works better than the more general "So how are things going at school?"). Avoid questions that imply criticism or judgment; this is not the time to ask if the child's math grades are improving. To make the most of your time, keep questions focused on one area—don't try to cover school, dating, and career goals in one lunch.

3. ***Keep the child talking by being a good listener.*** Sometimes a nod and a sympathetic "Mm-hmm" are all that is needed to keep the ball rolling. At other times you may need to offer supportive feedback ("I bet that made you mad"; "Sounds like this really excites you"; "How did you feel when she said that?").

4. ***Acknowledge what you have heard.*** This involves reflecting children's thoughts and feelings back to them in your own words ("Sounds like what Raicine said to Naomi made you wonder if Raicine is really your friend"). At this stage, letting children know you have listened and understood them is much more important than analyzing their problems or offering advice. Indicate that you are willing to help solve problems, but don't push. This tactful approach conveys respect for the child's own problem-solving abilities, and makes it more likely the child will want to talk things over with you again.

Polish your listening skills. Listening involves more than being quiet so your partner or child can have a say. A good listener also makes an effort to understand the speaker's feelings and opinions and lets the speaker know that he or she has been understood. This is easy enough to do when you're in agreement with views being expressed; in the middle of an argument, however, it can be much harder. A listening exercise that can be used in times of conflict is described on page 387. Try it and see if the level of cooperation among family members improves.

Listen to the feelings, too. Children who can talk about how they feel are usually more resilient than those who keep their emotions stuffed inside. They are also less likely to resort to inappropriate behaviors as a means of expressing themselves (a child who can tell his sister how angry he is, for example, is less likely to strike out physically). Many children grow up, however, with the idea that some emotions are bad and should not be expressed. Anger and fear are among the feelings most likely to be judged unacceptable. Parents who react to emotional outbursts with phrases like "Stop making a scene!" or "Stop being such a baby!" are usually the architects of the belief that getting mad or being scared is wrong.

To avoid this pitfall, encourage young people to talk through their emotions. When your son comes home and denounces his math teacher with a string of unprintable adjectives, for example, try to tune in to the feelings as well as to the inappropriate behavior. Saying, "I don't like that language, but I can hear that you're really mad—what happened?" gives him room to keep talking. Telling him, "I won't tolerate cursing! Go to your room immediately!" may make him feel that anger and swearing are both wrong. Similarly, saying, "Don't be silly! There's nothing to be afraid of!" to the child who is anxious about going to a sleepover party invites her to shut down her emotions (not only will this kind of "encouragement" fail to reassure her, it labels her feelings as wrong). Asking her to sit down and talk about what's worrying her helps your daughter confront her fears—the first step toward overcoming them.

When children talk about problems, they don't necessarily want adults to "fix" them. What youngsters often need most is a sympathetic listener who will allow them to vent. Once intense feelings have been discharged, children's perspectives often improve to the point that they can once again manage life's challenges on their own. "I remember a day my son came home mad as a hornet," a mother remembers. "He exploded as soon as he got inside the door—his English teacher was unfair, the lunch aide was a jerk, he hated the girl who sat behind him in social studies; it went on and on. . . . After about twenty minutes he wound down. Finally he said, 'Thanks, Mom; I appreciate talking things like this over with you,' and went outside with his basketball. Through the whole episode I hadn't said one word!" Even so, this parent was communicating with her child very well. By avoiding advice, she told him she believed in him. By listening to his feelings, she told him she cared.

Listening Exercise: Three Yesses

This exercise is especially useful when trying to resolve a disagreement.

The ground rules are that each party will be given a turn to talk without interruption for up to five minutes. At the end of this period, the listener must summarize the main points of what he or she has heard in a *minimum* of three sentences, each of which will be acknowledged with a "yes" if correct. The listener must keep trying until three "yesses" have been received. It is then the listener's turn to talk.

Let's imagine that a mother has been arguing with her teenage son about how little work he does around the house. They have reached an impasse, and have agreed to use Three Yesses. The boy speaks first. After he is finished, Mom attempts to summarize her son's side of the argument as follows:

"You think I don't appreciate how much time it takes to keep on top of schoolwork and sports."

"Yes."

"You believe you already do more around the house than most kids you know."

"Yes."

"You think I'm the meanest mother on the planet."

"Wait a minute! I never said that!"

"Okay. You think I'm a clean freak and my expectations are unrealistic."

"Yes."

It is now Mom's turn to talk, and the boy's turn to listen and respond.

Families who try this exercise often say that listening carefully enough to get three "yesses" can initially be a challenge, but that the effort pays off. Once everyone feels heard and understood, tempers usually cool down, and solving problems often becomes much easier.

LOOK FOR OUTSIDE SUPPORT
WHEN YOU NEED IT

Independence is a virtue that is much admired in America. Although few of us grow our own food or build our own houses these days, many of us do believe we should be able to handle our children without assistance. Some parents are therefore very reluctant to seek outside help for family problems. These adults sometimes find admitting that they cannot manage their own affairs so shameful they deny problems exist, or convince themselves that "it's just a phase—he'll outgrow this behavior any day now."

Experts advise, however, that the ability to turn to others for help and support is a strength that can contribute significantly to quality of life for adults and children alike. For example, several studies have shown that individuals with learning disabilities who build support networks are happier and more successful than those who try to go it alone. For parents, finding appropriate support can make the difference between getting bogged down in unproductive (or counterproductive) habits and managing family matters effectively. Generally speaking, there are three kinds of support available to children with learning disabilities and their families:

Public Services

States provide a variety of services to the families of children with disabilities, in addition to those provided by school districts. For example, states use federal IDEA funds to support free developmental evaluations and services for infants, toddlers, and preschool children who are at risk for substantial developmental delays. Eligibility ages and criteria vary from state to state. Early-intervention services help children with social or emotional development, communication, and/or cognitive-skills issues before they start school. Physical, occupational, and speech therapy can also be provided to preschoolers who need them.

The agencies responsible for screening children and providing services vary from place to place. This information should be available from your school district or state department of education. (For the address and telephone number of your state department of education, as well as other key agencies in your area, request a free "State Resource List" from the National Dissemination Center for Children with Disabilities by calling 1-800-695-0285 (www.nichcy.org/states). NICHCY is a treasure trove of information about disabilities and services; ask them to send you a list of their publications, or access them on the Web.

Under some circumstances, families can get federal support for adaptive technology for a child with disabilities. Under the Technology-Related Assistance for Individuals with Disabilities Act—also known as the Tech Act—support may be provided for devices that enhance personal independence (such as augmentative communication devices), medical equipment, and/or equipment that makes it possible for an individual to participate more fully in school or on the job (such as electronic readers and computers). Training in the uses of adaptive technology can also be provided. Generally speaking, financial support is reserved for individuals with severe disabilities who lack the financial resources to purchase equipment on their own, but information about the uses of adaptive technology is available to all. To find out more, contact your state's Tech Act office. Additional information about locating sources of funds for adaptive technology is available from the National Rehabilitation Information Center (NARIC) by calling 1-800-346-2742 (www.naric.com).

Career-planning and job-training services are available to eligible young adults with learning disabilities under the federal Rehabilitation Act (also known as the Rehab Act) and coordinated state programs. The purpose of the Rehab Act is to maximize employment options for individuals with disabilities and help them become economically independent. Individualized programs are facilitated by a vocational rehabilitation counselor; career exploration, vocational counseling, skills development, work-study opportunities, and help learning independent-living skills can all be provided. In some circumstances, tuition for higher education can also be provided through the Rehab Act. NARIC (see the contact information above) can put you in touch with the agencies that administer rehabilitation programs in your area. Excellent guidance to rehabilitation services is also available through the Higher Education and Adult Training for People with Handicaps (HEATH) Resource Center (www.heath.gwu.edu).

In some communities, federally funded parent training and information programs are available to qualified families. (Help with parenting skills may also be available through schools and other local agencies; contact your school district and department of social services for information.) These programs are designed to help parents learn how to support healthy child development, handle discipline effectively, and access community services that the family needs. More than one hundred Parent Training and Information Centers (PTIs) and Community Parent Resource Centers (CPRCs) exist that use federal IDEA funding to provide training in advocacy and special education issues specifically for parents of children with disabilities. To locate a PTI in your state, contact the Technical Assistance Alliance for Parent Centers (www.taalliance.org) or call 1-888-248-0822. The National Center for Learning Disabilities (NCLD) at 1-888-575-7373 (www.ncld.org) also maintains a "resource locator" to help you find services in your state and community. A private, nonprofit organization, NCLD operates a free information-and-referral service that can help you locate other resources in your area as well.

Note that children identified as economically or educationally disadvantaged (this includes many children with learning disabilities in both urban and rural areas) may be eligible for a much broader range of support services than those listed here from federal, state, and local agencies. Your school district's department of pupil services and local department of social services are good places to start looking for information. Services that provide support to children from birth to age five—as well as to their families—are particularly important. Many experts feel that assistance at this critical stage can prevent many future problems.

Parent Support Groups

Local parent support groups may be chapters of national organizations like the Learning Disabilities Association of America (LDA) (www.ldanatl.org), Children and Adults with Attention Deficit/Hyperactivity Disorder (CHADD) (www.chadd.org), and the International Dyslexia Association (www.interdys.org), or they may be independent organizations. A primary focus of these groups is to introduce families of children with disabilities to one another for the purpose of sharing information and providing mutual support. Some groups offer much more. For example, support groups may provide the following:

- speakers and newsletters;
- resource centers with libraries of books and videos of interest to parents and children;
- access to computers and computer instruction;
- parenting classes;
- professional tutoring;
- summer academic "camps";
- babysitting co-ops and/or respite care;
- social and recreational activities;
- legal guidance;
- help with advocacy at school; and
- information and referrals to other services in the community (everything from vocational rehabilitation services to dentists who are good with children who can't sit still).

Some groups are also involved in political activism and work with legislators and education professionals to improve services for children and adults with learning disabilities, at the local, state, and national levels. Your school district's department of special education should be able to guide you to support groups in your area. For information about reaching the national organizations mentioned above (and a number of other specialized support organizations), turn to Appendix D. Much information and some assistance (e.g., newsletters and other publications, referrals, information about conferences) can be found on these groups' websites.

Individual, Marriage, and Family Counseling

There are times when individuals and families need more assistance than self-help groups and public support systems can provide. The situations described in the checklist on page 393, for example, call for prompt evaluation by a mental-health professional or other qualified counselor (such as an alcohol- or substance-abuse counselor, marriage counselor, or appropriately trained clergy). Families need not wait until matters have become this urgent to take advantage of counseling, however; those who seek help for mild to moderate emotional strain can often prevent these tensions from exploding into major problems. Among the things families can learn from a professional counselor are communication skills, techniques for reducing stress, and methods of resolving conflicts. Counseling can also help individuals resolve persistent feelings of anger, guilt, anxiety, and/or helplessness. Family counselors can help parents identify unproductive or destructive habits, devise systems of rules that work, and improve methods of discipline. Reviewing this list of potential benefits, it is obvious that there are very few families who would *not* benefit from professional help at some point in their lives!

The chief drawback of counseling is that it can be expensive. Many health insurance policies offer benefits that cover some types of counseling, however, and in most communities there are mental health clinics and other counseling agencies that have flexible fee schedules based on family income. Research finds that many problems can be addressed successfully with short-term therapy; no longer does counseling automatically involve a commitment of many months or years. Troubled families without health insurance coverage should therefore not assume that counseling is beyond their reach. Subsidized programs may be found listed under "Mental Health Services" and/or "Clinics" in the yellow pages of your phone book (individual practitioners will be listed under "Counselors," "Social Workers," "Psychologists," and "Psychiatrists"). Free or low-cost counseling may also be available at a local university or hospital; through your synagogue, parish, church, or diocese; or through your child's school.

Two important factors contribute significantly to the success of a counseling experience: willingness of family members to participate, and finding a good "fit" between the family and the counselor. The first factor applies even if counseling is being sought for an individual. As any professional counselor will tell you, it is very difficult to treat a child if parents refuse to become involved. Adolescents or adults dealing with emotional problems or substance abuse can also have a hard

When to Look for Help

It is important to recognize when family problems have worsened beyond the average parents' ability to cope. The following situations are unlikely to improve on their own and call for prompt evaluation by an appropriately qualified professional:

- Parents have become locked into adversarial roles and cannot agree on methods of family management, or family members have lost the ability to communicate without fighting.
- A child persistently ignores or violates all household rules and/or fails to respect the rights of others.
- You are unable to maintain control of your own behavior in confrontations with your child.
- A child exhibits symptoms of severe depression or talks about suicide.
- A child has become excessively or irrationally fearful of particular persons, places, or situations.
- A child has developed a sleep or eating disorder, or other stress-related health problems.
- You suspect a child is abusing or addicted to a drug (including alcohol).
- Your child is unable to stop tormenting or abusing animals or another child, either within or outside of the family.
- A child's school performance is irreversibly deteriorating.
- A child is unable to break a pattern of illegal or antisocial behavior (e.g., lying, stealing, vandalism, truancy).
- A child is repeatedly absent from home or school without explanation, or has attempted to run away from home.
- You are afraid of your child.

It is also wise to seek help if you sense that something is seriously wrong but you're not exactly sure what the problem is. These intuitions are often accurate, and a counselor can help you identify the issues that need to be addressed.

Adapted from Philadelphia Child Guidance Center with Jack Maguire, *Your Child's Emotional Health.*

time addressing these issues in isolation; the support of family members sometimes makes the difference between successful treatment and failure. As we discussed earlier in this chapter, one person's difficulties can eventually entangle other family members in inefficient or destructive patterns of behavior. Addressing individual problems may therefore require everyone to make some changes. If a lot of negativity has built up inside the family, some members may initially decline to become involved in counseling ("Don't ask *me* to waste my time with a headshrinker! I haven't got any problems—*he's* the one who's messed up!"). If this is the case, go ahead and make a start with whoever is willing to participate. You may find the naysayers become interested in joining you when they see others learning improved coping strategies.

Finding the right counselor can sometimes be a challenge. First, there are several different kinds of professionals working in the mental-health field, including psychiatrists, psychologists, and social workers. Some work primarily with individuals, some work with children and families, and some work with groups. Then there is a bewildering array of therapeutic specialties: psychoanalytic therapy, systems therapy, psychodynamic therapy, behavioral therapy, and cognitive therapy, just to name a few (many family counselors draw from more than one type). The kind of professional or brand of therapy you choose, however, will ultimately be less important than finding a counselor with whom you feel comfortable communicating, and whom you feel you can trust. If you regularly come out of a counselor's office feeling demoralized rather than hopeful, you're in the wrong place no matter how many credentials are displayed on the wall. You may have to interview more than one counselor before you find someone who "feels" right. Usually, that will be a professional who

- appears to be genuinely interested in you and your child,
- listens respectfully to your views of your family's situation,
- exhibits knowledge about the types of stress faced by children with learning disabilities and their families,
- listens to and answers questions, and
- offers a coherent intervention plan that addresses your concerns.

Parents at your local support group may be able to recommend counselors who have worked successfully with children with learning disabilities and their families in your community. Your child's school counselor or pediatrician may also be able to refer you to competent professionals. Whatever route you choose, don't be embarrassed about seeking help. There is certainly no shame in wanting to provide a brighter future for your child, or in wanting to improve your own parenting skills.

Family counseling often improves parents' abilities to support and nurture each other as well as to help them care for their children. Enabling Mom and Dad to work together more productively, in fact, is one of the better ways of addressing children's concerns. When parents are divided, young people often invest a lot of energy in manipulative strategies designed to get one parent or the other on their side. So much effort may go into these schemes that children never learn more appropriate and effective ways of getting their needs met. For example, the boy who knows that Mom will ride to the rescue if only he acts helpless and pathetic enough (no matter what Dad says) is not learning tools that will serve him well in the future. Similarly, the girl who counts on Daddy to defend her whenever she fights with Mom about homework or rules may eventually come to feel dependent on male support (and develop questionable ways of getting it). When parents present a united front, manipulative strategies like these become ineffective. Once these bad habits have been broken, more successful methods of dealing with life's challenges can be taught.

Parents who really want to help their children therefore need to find the courage to face their own differences and examine their own roles in the family system. This process may require you to confront control issues or painful memories of your own younger years. Those who are willing to take the risk, however, may be surprised at the benefits in store. "I never thought I'd say I was grateful for my daughter's problems," says a mother who sought family counseling when her rebellious sixteen-year-old refused to return to school, "but helping Sandy compelled everyone in the family to grow. Because we faced that crisis together, our family is closer and stronger than ever before."

Albert Einstein once said, "In the middle of difficulty lies opportunity." Parents who keep looking for those opportunities in hard times teach their children the value of positive thinking and persistence. As we have seen in this chapter, those are qualities that help support both achievement and self-esteem. In the next chapter we will see how a third element—planning—can help young people maximize their opportunities and face the future with confidence and enthusiasm.

12

Looking Forward to the Future

In many families, anxiety mounts as a child nears the age of sixteen. At this point many questions that used to be hypothetical start to become real and pressing. What is the student going to do after high school? How will he or she earn a living? Does the youngster have the academic interests or the intellectual potential to go to college? Is he or she mature enough to live away from home?

Parents of students with learning disabilities often face these questions with an extra measure of concern. In addition to having incomplete academic skills, our adolescents sometimes appear to lack maturity and motivation. They may approach the end of high school without having given much thought to what they want to do in the future. Parents who are becoming increasingly worried about how a child will survive after leaving school sometimes mistake this failure to look ahead as a deficiency of ambition. More often, though, it is lack of experience with planning and decision-making that is the problem. Students who struggle in school (and have many decisions made for them) often develop a survival mentality: what is important to them is getting through each day without humiliation or disaster. Over a period of years, these students become "future impaired"—the concept of next year, or two years from now, has little real meaning for them.

What Is an Individualized Transition Plan?

Federal law requires that students receiving special education be provided with *transition services* to help them make the shift from school to the world of work or higher education and independent living successfully. These services—which are to be individualized according to each student's interests and needs—must be spelled out in an Individualized Transition Plan (ITP). The law requires that an ITP be added to the student's IEP by the end of the student's sixteenth year; however, there is no legal objection to preparing one earlier. Many experts feel that it is wise to initiate an ITP when the student makes the transition from junior high to high school. Like the IEP, the ITP is updated annually.

The ITP lays out a transition curriculum that meets the student's needs in a number of important areas, including career exploration, vocational training and apprenticeships, community-living skills, communication and decision-making skills, self-esteem development, time-management and study skills, academic preparation, appropriate use of accommodations, and more. The most important questions for the team to address include these:

- What are the student's interests and goals for the future? Are additional assessments (such as personal-interest inventories) needed to help identify the student's vocational and educational strengths?

- What courses of study and/or work experiences are needed to help the student prepare to meet stated goals? Are there relationships that should be built with specific business or industry representatives that would be helpful to the student's current program and future education or job opportunities?

Extra support and careful planning may therefore be necessary to help young people with information-processing problems make a successful transition to the world of work or higher education. In recognition of this fact, federal law requires school districts to initiate Individualized Transition Plans for students with learning disabilities no later than age sixteen. Research indicates, however, that the transition plans developed in many high schools offer too little, too late. As a result, too many students with learning disabilities leave school without marketable skills or a coherent, realistic plan for the future.

- What are the goals for independent living, personal/social relationships, and community participation? Does the student need help learning functional skills (such as money management, shopping, or using public transportation) or social/interpersonal skills (such as accepting criticism, knowing how to ask for help, exploring how to develop extracurricular interests and hobbies)?

- Does the student need help with organizational, study, or test-taking skills?

- Does the student need help understanding his or her rights and developing self-advocacy skills? Can the student speak for him- or herself regarding necessary accommodations and services?

- Is the student making adequate use of assistive software or technology, and how can continuing availability of that technology be assured after he or she leaves school?

- What agencies or organizations outside the school district will provide services to support the student after leaving high school? (If outside agencies are identified, representatives of these organizations need to be included in developing the ITP.)

To complete the ITP, the team must develop a statement of measurable goals and a description of specific services (including courses of study) needed to help the student meet those goals. Statements of service should define each program or activity,

continued

Families need to take the lead in the transition planning process rather than leave this important matter entirely to the staff at a child's school. Authorities agree that age sixteen is too late to begin transition planning; most recommend making a start in ninth grade or even earlier. Furthermore, although transition services are improving in many areas, youngsters with learning disabilities are still frequently shortchanged in the postsecondary education and career-guidance process. Guidance counselors are sometimes largely unaware of the needs of individuals with learning disabilities and the programs and including who will provide each service, and the dates when each service will begin and end. It is not enough merely to say, for example, that "Jim wants to be a physical education teacher." A more appropriate statement would be that "Jim will meet with the high school guidance counselor and elect the college preparatory curriculum; Jim will receive instruction in study and test-taking skills from his special education teacher for three 45-minute sessions a week; Jim will complete a summer internship in recreational athletics."

If the student's disabilities are so severe that earning a standard high school diploma is unlikely, it is very important to connect the student with agencies in the community that can continue to provide support after the young adult leaves school, such as the state rehabilitation agency (which can provide interview and job training, job coaching, and placement in mentored jobs in the community). It is the school district's responsibility to help families identify these agencies and involve the agencies in transition planning. If there are organizations you feel should be involved in your child's transition planning, be sure to notify the school district before the ITP meeting.

Before each student with disabilities leaves school, the school district must provide him or her with a Summary of Performance (SOP). The SOP describes the student's levels of academic achievement, functional performance (social and independent-living skills), and recommendations for helping the student meet postsecondary goals, including needed accommodations and supports. It is important to make sure that the SOP includes all the information necessary to help the student access supports, services, or accommodations that may be needed after high school. For example, depending on the

services that are available to assist them. Monitoring and advocacy are therefore more important than ever as children approach graduation in order to make sure that they are exploring a full range of options and receiving help to which they are entitled. Another important objective in high school is to bring the child more actively into the planning and advocacy processes. IDEA requires that students participate in the development of their Individualized Transition Plans, and it is appropriate for students to start attending all their IEP meetings in high school, if they are not doing so already.

In this chapter, we will discuss the three most important questions families must address in order to help young adults with learning disabilities face the future with confidence. We conclude the chapter student's needs, the SOP should include documentation of a disability consistent with the requirements of

- postsecondary institutions, such as colleges and providers of vocational education. (Check with the disabilities office of any school your child is considering about *exactly* what documentation is needed to qualify for accommodations and/or support services.)

- community agencies such as the state rehabilitation agency and the Social Security Administration. (If the student is expected to access services from any agencies after high school, these agencies should be involved in the planning of transition services.)

- Section 504 of the Rehabilitation Act of 1973, which prevents discrimination against qualified people with disabilities in programs or activities that receive or benefit from federal financial assistance, including most colleges and universities.

- the Americans with Disabilities Act, which prevents discrimination in both public and private institutions, such as libraries, restaurants, theaters, transportation, and stores as well as in the workplace.

Although the school district is not required to perform new assessments to complete a Summary of Performance, information on the SOP should be up-to-date. If the student has not had a full evaluation for two years or more, talk to the transition team about completing a new one before the child leaves school.

with a transition-planning timetable that suggests appropriate goals and activities for junior high and each year of high school.

Question One: DOES THE STUDENT HAVE A PLAN FOR CONTINUING EDUCATION OR SPECIFIC JOB TRAINING AFTER HIGH SCHOOL?

Research makes it clear that students who leave school without marketable skills have a hard time finding meaningful work. Some will not even be able to find steady employment. Individuals who do not finish high school face the bleakest economic outlook: not only do dropouts face up to 150 percent higher unemployment rates than those who graduated, but also those who do work earn one-third less than high school graduates. A recent study found that fewer than 25 percent of high school dropouts with learning disabilities earned enough to pay their own living expenses one to four years after leaving school. These young adults were often limited to minimum-wage jobs that offer little in the way of benefits or opportunities for advancement. Employment prospects are particularly grim for dropouts in urban areas, where technical or clerical skills are increasingly required even for entry-level jobs. Young women without skills typically fare even worse than young men when it comes to achieving economic independence. Studies find that female dropouts with learning disabilities usually occupy the lowest rungs on the occupational ladder, are more likely to work at part-time or temporary jobs without benefits, and earn even lower hourly wages than their male counterparts.

When students complete high school and pursue postsecondary education, however, the picture brightens considerably. Studies find that the employment rate of people with learning disabilities who complete vocational education programs compares favorably with that of job-training graduates without disabilities. Students with some postsecondary education earn 20 percent more than high school graduates—250 percent more if they graduate from college. A study of college graduates with learning disabilities found more than 80 percent were employed in professional or managerial positions. Obviously, it is very important to encourage young people to examine their career options and to get as much education as possible to prepare for the jobs of their choice. Young adults who have left school need to be encouraged to explore other means of upgrading their skills and credentials so they can improve their employment opportunities (see box: Getting Back to School).

For many parents, the critical question is whether it is realistic for their child to consider college. The good news is that young people with learning disabilities are attending colleges and universities in record numbers, thanks in part to an explosion of programs and services designed to support them. (Federal law requires all institutions of higher learning to make "reasonable accommodations" for students with learning disabilities; the specific services available vary from school to school.) At some campuses, the number of LD students has increased more than tenfold in recent years. Some authorities feel that the number of students with learning disabilities on college campuses would be even greater if these youngsters were given better guidance in high school. Since many guidance counselors know little about college programs for students with learning disabilities, these students are not always encouraged to consider higher education or to sign up for college-preparatory classes. Students who have uneven academic records and/or standardized test scores may also assume that no college will accept them, and so fail to explore college options. To assess children's potential for success in college, experts suggest applying the following guidelines:

Students who have mild to moderate learning disabilities and average or above-average intelligence should be encouraged to aim for college. Students most likely to succeed are those who can function successfully in regular high school classes with appropriate accommodations; have adequate self-advocacy skills; and do not have serious attention, organizational, or interpersonal problems. Given appropriate academic preparation in high school, a willingness to put forth sustained effort, and resourcefulness in compensating for learning weaknesses, students like these often do well in college with minimal help. Most, however, will need some modifications and accommodations in order to perform successfully. Typical accommodations used by college students with LD are additional time for tests and/or a quiet place to take tests, assistance from note takers, use of books on tape or CD, reduced course loads, priority registration, preferential seating, and access to a writing center for assistance with planning and preparing long papers. Colleges with experiential learning programs (which encourage learning through working in jobs and internships) also expand the opportunities for students with LD to succeed.

Motivated students with moderate to severe disabilities can also succeed in college, but they will require more help. It is important to research educational options carefully and iden-

Getting Back to School

High school dropout rates for students with learning disabilities are alarmingly high, approaching 25 percent nationwide. These young people often leave school before eleventh grade—the point at which vocational education begins at most schools—so many lack both basic skills (reading, writing, and arithmetic) and specific job skills. It is important to encourage individuals who left school before graduation to explore options for improving their skills and continuing their educations. The truth is, a high school diploma is fast becoming a minimum requirement for almost any kind of job: only 5 percent of job opportunities are for unskilled labor today. Two-thirds of available jobs require some postsecondary education. Success in both white- and blue-collar jobs increasingly requires not only literacy but also the ability to handle basic computation and to interpret and integrate many different kinds of information. Basic computer skills are also now required for entry-level jobs in many fields. Here are some suggestions that can dramatically improve employment outlooks.

The General Educational Development (GED) test. The GED program, sponsored by the American Council on Education, gives adults a second chance to obtain a high school credential. In recent years the number of GED applicants with learning disabilities has quadrupled. The test measures reading, writing, mathematics, science, and social studies information. Special testing accommodations (including extended time, help with reading, and alternative recording methods) are allowed for individuals with documented disabilities. For more information about local GED classes and tests, call your school district or Literacy Volunteers of America chapter; you can also find information online on the GED website (www.acenet.edu), or the National Institute for Literacy website (www.literacydirectory.org). More than 17 million people have earned their high school equivalency in this way. Most colleges accept the GED in lieu of the high school diploma, as do employers that require a high school degree. Bill Cosby and Michael J. Fox are two celebrities who earned their high school degrees by means of the GED.

Adult literacy programs. Programs that teach adults to read better, do math, or learn English as a second language—either one-to-one or in small classes—exist in many communities. Most are free. The toll-free National Institute for Literacy Hotline (1-800-228-8813) connects you to a twenty-four-hour bilingual (English/Spanish) service that provides information about literacy programs and other educational opportunities. Ask for their learning-disabilities brochure. ProLiteracy (www.proliteracy.com) is an organization that supports the development of volunteer adult-literacy programs both nationally and internationally. More than 100,000 adults receive tutoring annually—contact them about opportunities in your community.

Adult education courses. Evening courses in keyboarding, basic computer skills, and other vocational subjects are offered by many school districts as well as by community colleges and four-year colleges and universities. Most welcome beginners of all ages. Contact public school districts in your area for information, or call the Learning Resources Network (1-800-678-5376) for help locating providers of adult continuing education (www.lern.org).

Community colleges. Most community colleges offer courses in both basic writing and study skills, which can be lifesavers for adults who hope to enter college eventually. Some also have alternative admissions procedures for adults who do not have high school diplomas and offer extensive support services for students with learning disabilities. Excellent vocational preparation programs and career placement services may also be available. For more information, contact the coordinator of learning disability services at your local community college. In some circumstances, help with tuition can be provided for students with disabilities by the state's rehabilitation services agency (see below).

Job training through state rehabilitation services agencies. The Rehabilitation Act of 1973 (Rehab Act) required each state to establish services to help individuals with disabilities become more employable and independent. The act continues to provide federal support for these services. Eligible individuals can receive career counseling, on-the-job training, and/or financial support for education (technical and trade school or college courses). Help with independent-living skills (such as planning and living on a budget) is also available. For information about services and eligibility, contact your state's vocational rehabilitation agency. If you cannot find this agency under state government listings in your telephone book, you should be able to get the number from your public library or high school guidance office, or call the National Rehabilitation Information Center (NARIC) at 1-800-346-2742 and ask for a state agencies list (www.naric.com).

Note that the student with learning disabilities who moves smoothly through four years of high school followed by four years of college is the exception rather than the rule. It is increasingly common for students to combine part-time work and part-time study. Periodic "breaks" from the stresses of formal education are also to be expected. It is important for both parents and students to avoid becoming discouraged if educational goals are not met "on time." Taking longer to graduate from high school or college should not be viewed as a failure as long as students are willing to keep trying. Taking formal education in small doses can be a sensible strategy for young people with learning disabilities; sometimes, this approach is the most successful route to a diploma or a degree.

tify institutions that can provide the structure and intensity of support that these students need. (Individual tutoring, assistance with study skills, help with advocacy, and specially trained advisors for academic planning and career counseling may all be required, for example.) There are now a number of college guides published especially for students with learning disabilities; these are a good place to start investigating the services and support programs available at different institutions. (If these guides are not available at your high school guidance office, check your public library or local and online bookstores.) Students with multiple or severe disabilities may also want to think about other means of moderating academic pressure, such as attending college part-time. (Check sources of financial aid before making this decision; some apply only to full-time students.) Note that these students may also require extra support and/or extra time in high school to meet college entrance requirements. (Students with disabilities are legally entitled in all states to remain in public school until they receive a standard diploma or reach age twenty-two.)

College will probably not meet the needs of youngsters who have significantly lower-than-average intelligence, major interpersonal problems, and/or very severe language, cognitive-processing, or attention deficits. College is also not the best choice for the student who has developed a strong aversion to formal education. (This may sound obvious, but parents sometimes become so fixed on college as a goal that they fail to consider their children's feelings about the matter. Children who are forced to attend college are rarely successful, regardless of their intellectual potential.) Postsecondary planning for these young people needs to focus on building functional social and vocational skills and/or providing mental-health support. Parents may have to be assertive to make sure that appropriate transition services are provided for these young people, both in high school and afterward. Youngsters with severe learning disabilities—who are often unable to live and work on their own immediately after high school—may be perceived as not disabled *enough* for programs serving adults with disabilities in the community. Without advocates, these young adults are among the most likely to fall between the cracks of the education and social service systems. For these students, staying in high school through age twenty-one may be a better option than racing to graduate, so they can continue to avail themselves of special education, vocational training, and counseling services. When the services of community agencies are needed (for help with finding financial assistance for technology or mentored job placement, for example) it is the responsibility of the student's ITP team to secure the involvement of those agencies; parents should therefore be as thorough and as explicit as possible about their views of the young adult's immediate and long-term needs in ITP meetings.

College Planning

If college has been identified as a goal, it is important to make sure that this is listed on your child's IEP and that the child is enrolled in the most rigorous academic program he or she can handle in high school. Under federal law, colleges cannot refuse to admit students because they have disabilities, but they are under no obligation to admit students who have failed to take an adequate college preparatory program, or whose grades and test scores do not meet their standards (see What About College Entrance Exams? on pages 408–9). It is also wise to start exploring college options early. Success depends on finding a good match between the college and the student, and this process takes time. A thorough college search typically involves reviewing college guides; obtaining information about specific institutions; investigating admissions requirements, academic programs, special services, and financial aid options; and making a personal visit to top-choice campuses. The parent of two college students (one of whom has learning disabilities) advises:

Start in tenth or eleventh grade and avoid making college visits over the summer. You don't learn much about a school from

What About College Entrance Exams?

Colleges do not waive basic admissions requirements for students who have learning disabilities. Youngsters interested in colleges that require SAT or ACT scores must therefore plan to take these examinations. Students with documented disabilities *are* permitted some special accommodations on these tests, including extended time, testing in alternate settings to minimize distractions, use of a computer for written responses, frequent breaks, multiple-day administration, and many more. The accommodations requested must match those the student uses on standardized school-based tests. Note that special test administrations must be arranged in advance; the student cannot simply show up and ask for accommodations on the exam day. The SAT requires up-to-date assessment data to be submitted in support of each accommodation requested (assessments must have been completed within the last five years). The ACT may also request this documentation if it needs verification of the disability and accommodation needs. Information about test accommodations and instructions for documenting disabilities for the SAT and ACT exams should be available at your high school guidance office, or it can be requested directly from

SAT Services for Students with Disabilities
PO Box 8060
Mt. Vernon, IL 62864-0060
(609)771-7137
www.collegeboard.com

ACT Test Administration
301 ACT Drive
P.O. Box 414
Iowa City, IA 52243-0414
(319) 337-1270
www.act.org

Requesting accommodations is wise if your child uses them on a regular basis at school: the College Board finds an approximate 32-point increase on the verbal portion and

touring empty buildings. Visit when classes are in session, and arrange for the student to sit in on an introductory-level class in an area of academic interest. Ask about overnight visits, too. Our sons found that spending a night in a dorm and talking to students informally gave them a much better idea of what went on than the typical campus tour. At one small college that had

26-point increase on the math portion of the SAT, for example, when students receive additional time (additional time for students who do not have disabilities does not show a similar increase in scores). The test-score report sent to colleges does not indicate that accommodations were used.

The more familiar youngsters are with the examination format and with test-taking strategies (such as knowing when it's a good idea to guess at an answer and when it's best to skip a tough question), the better they will do on these tests. Commercial study guides, computer programs, and test preparation courses are all widely available to help young people sharpen their test-taking skills. College-bound students should plan to take required tests more than once if possible; scores often go up the second or third time around. (Colleges usually use the highest scores earned, regardless of when the test was taken.)

Students may find that they are better suited to one exam or the other. Some youngsters with learning disabilities like the ACT, for example, because it is a more straightforward test of knowledge in English, math, and science (students say it is less "tricky" than the SAT, which emphasizes reading and math *reasoning* ability). The ACT's relatively long reading passages, however, can work against youngsters with reading-comprehension problems. Since many colleges accept either test, students may want to take both the SAT and the ACT exams and submit the better set of scores.

Families should be aware that not all colleges require admissions testing. Nearly three hundred two- and four-year institutions—Bard, Bates, City University of New York, Wake Forest University, Smith College, and most community colleges, for example—have made submission of test scores optional. These schools find that the student's high school GPA and subject-area achievement tests (such as the College Board's Advanced Placement exams and subject tests) are better predictors of college success. Applying to institutions that do not require admissions tests may improve the chances of students who have good grades and other credentials but consistently perform poorly on standardized exams.

excellent academic programs, for example, our older son (who has a learning disability) discovered that the "cool" students on campus smoked a lot of pot. That wasn't a social standard he wanted to conform to; we kept looking. He was starting eleventh grade when he found the campus of his dreams, and the impact of that visit was electric: overnight his motivation to do well in

Key Questions for College Applicants

In addition to the usual questions students have about colleges (about admissions requirements, academic programs, internships, recreation, and social opportunities, for example), students with learning disabilities need to make some additional inquiries of college administrators. In most cases you will get the most accurate information from the school's coordinator of services for students with disabilities.

What (if any) special programs and support services are in place here for students who have learning disabilities? While colleges are required by federal law to make "reasonable accommodations" for individuals with disabilities, some do little more. Ask specifically about the types of assistance you are most likely to need. What arrangements are made for students who need help taking notes, for example? Is assistance with writing papers available, and on what basis (a special class, an individual tutor, or a writing lab)? If a book is not available on tape from national recording services, will the college find someone to record it? How long would this take? Is tutoring available in different content areas (math, chemistry, Spanish . . .)?

Are support services included in the tuition, or do they cost extra? Under civil rights law, the college may not charge for providing reasonable accommodations (such as access to recorded books or help from a note taker), but there may be fees for special services such as tutoring or guidance from an LD specialist.

How long has your learning disabilities support program been in existence? Students looking for extensive services should seek out a college with an established track record.

How many students with learning disabilities have received services here in recent years? What percentage of those students graduate? Low numbers may indicate a weak level of support for students who have learning disabilities.

What documentation must I provide in order to obtain services? Documentation must usually be based on an evaluation by a qualified professional and describe specific types of learning disabilities, as well as recommended accommodations. (A letter from your pediatrician stating that you're "dyslexic," for example, won't cut it.) Many colleges will accept a high school IEP or SOP. Others may require a recent psychoeducational evaluation that includes assessment results, and a detailed description of learning strengths and weaknesses.

What is the procedure for negotiating accommodations and modifications with instructors? Are students on their own, or is help with advocacy available? If there is a conflict with a professor, what is the procedure for resolving it?

What is the minimum number of credits per semester required to be considered a full-time student? Limiting one's course load is one key to college success, but some types of financial aid are available only to full-time students.

Are courses available in basic writing and study skills? Do they earn academic credit?

What is the average class size in my areas of academic interest? What is the usual format of these classes (lecture, laboratory, or discussion)? What kind of tests are given most frequently? Do these match my learning style?

Does the college (or the proposed major) have a science, mathematics, or foreign-language requirement? If these subjects present a problem, is it possible to substitute other courses (such as international studies courses, American Sign Language, ethics of science, world health and economics, or computer courses) to satisfy these requirements? Note that colleges and universities are *not* required to waive or change basic requirements to accommodate students with learning disabilities. They may refuse to do so if changing the requirement amounts to altering the nature of the program or relaxing academic standards.

What is available in the way of work-study programs and internships? Can academic credit be granted for these experiences? Many young people with learning disabilities learn best by doing, and so benefit from programs that go beyond the classroom.

Is tutoring and academic and career counseling handled through the learning disabilities support center or through academic departments and general counseling offices? How much experience do advisors and tutors have with students who have learning disabilities?

What kind of technical support is available? How easy is it to get access to a computer? Do you have to walk nearly a mile to the library to get online, or are computers scattered throughout the campus? (A few colleges now provide a laptop computer to any student who needs one.) Where can you find help with special software (such as voice-activated or word-prediction writing programs)?

What grading options are available? Can any courses be taken on a pass/fail basis?

If noise and distraction are a problem, what housing options are available? Are there "quiet dorms" or "quiet floors" (loud music and partying are not allowed after certain hours, or not allowed at all)? Can I get a single room? Do single rooms cost extra?

school skyrocketed. He worked like a demon in all his courses, and he also put a lot of time and effort into preparing for the SATs. His hard work paid off: he applied for early decision and was accepted. In the end, identifying the place he wanted to be had everything to do with his success.

If your child comes across much better in person than on paper (as is often the case with young people who have learning disabilities), also try to arrange for an on-campus interview. This gives your child a chance to impress an admissions officer with his or her intelligence and motivation, as well as an opportunity to explain why that math score or foreign-language grade is so low. If special support for learning disabilities is going to be needed, it is also a good idea to talk to the people in charge of providing these services during your visit. The box on pages 410–11 lists some critical questions to ask before choosing an institution.

If young people are interested in higher education but not yet ready to leave home or attend college full-time, community colleges offer some excellent options. Many have open-admissions policies and offer extensive services for students with academic weaknesses. Most are used to accommodating part-time students, and students who perform well have options for moving on to four-year institutions. Investigating specific support for students with learning disabilities at community colleges, though, is just as important as checking out other institutions. As Barbara Cordoni, a coordinator of special education support services for university students (as well as the mother of two children with learning disabilities), warns in her book *Living with a Learning Disability*, "Do not, repeat, do *not* send him to a community college near home to 'get his feet wet' unless the college has an LD support program. The most difficult time we have at my university is with students who go to community colleges without support programs and who do not do well. They enter the university with poor grades, and by their junior year they are supposed to choose a major. However, most majors require a minimum grade point average, which the student may simply not have because of [low] community college grades that are averaged in." The bottom line? Wherever they go to college, it is important that students with learning disabilities start out with access to all the support they need, and receive informed guidance so they target their goals effectively and do not bite off more than they can chew. Because so many of these college students have time-management issues (plus it's so much more fun to hang out with friends or surf the net than to write a paper for a class one is doing poorly in), connecting with a support person with whom the student can meet weekly to plan how to stay on top of the workload and manage stress can also do wonders for student achievement.

Some students fear that being honest about their learning disabilities during the college-application process will prejudice admissions committees against them and hurt their chances of getting into the school of their choice. This is unlikely, since discrimination against individuals with disabilities is prohibited by federal law. Disclosing a learning disability can, however, help explain discrepancies or weaknesses in the high school record that might otherwise be puzzling. We think being open about a learning disability therefore offers more advantages than disadvantages. (Our experience is that students who are hesitant to disclose their disabilities often hope to make a "fresh start" in college and get by without any special help. While their desire to appear "normal" is understandable, these hopes are also naive. Heavier workloads and harder course content make appropriate support more important than ever in college—another reason why honesty is usually the best policy.)

Career Planning

If students do not intend to go to college, the focus switches to career planning and preparation. In some ways this can be more challenging than locating the right college program. Although public and private career-training opportunities abound, few instructors in vocational education programs are knowledgeable about learning disabilities. (Many have no background in *education*; their experience relates primarily to the skill or trade they are teaching.) Little in the way of formal support may therefore be available for the student who needs help with reading diagrams or manuals, taking notes, or taking timed paper-and-pencil exams, all of which may be required. Vocational education programs designed for special education populations often target the needs of individuals with limited intelligence, or those who have histories of truancy or juvenile delinquency—needs that are quite different from those of a youngster with information-processing problems. Finding a suitable program can be complicated by the fact that young people either have no idea what they want to do or have ideas that are unrealistic (the child may dream of becoming a basketball player or a newscaster, for example, despite lack of athletic or writing ability). Moreover, youngsters' organizational abilities, work habits, or interpersonal skills may be so weak that parents wonder if there is *any* workplace where the child will fit in comfortably.

Because preparation for employment touches on development in so many areas, career planning should be viewed as a long-term process beginning as early as middle school. Career preparation usually involves several phases, discussed below (note that these activities are also appropriate for students who hope to attend college).

Job Awareness and Exploration

Many students' notions of the world of work are very narrow or borrowed largely from the entertainment media. Some young people don't really understand what their parents do at work! Career planning therefore begins with developing youngsters' awareness of the great variety of things people can do to earn a living. Formal career exploration programs (which involve visits to a variety of work sites in the community and events like "career fairs," in which representatives of various trades and professions make presentations) are usually available in junior high and high school to help with this process. Families can also do a lot to improve career awareness on their own. Take children to your workplace and talk about what you do there. Direct children's attention to some of the different things other people do for a living (at the doctor's office, for example, the child may see one or more nurses or physician's assistants, a receptionist, secretaries who make appointments and manage records, a person who handles billing and bookkeeping, and laboratory or X-ray technicians in addition to the doctor). Encourage children to "interview" people in their communities who perform jobs they find interesting. The librarian at your local library (or an online search) can also help you find age-appropriate books about different kinds of work.

As youngsters' interests develop, seek opportunities for hands-on experience. Job-shadow, job-trial, and work-study programs; internships; volunteer work; and summer or part-time jobs can all help students develop realistic expectations for what it takes to make it in fields that appeal to them. Research finds that students who get this kind of experience are most likely to develop good work habits and become responsible employees in their adult years. Furthermore, the more hands-on practice students get in their areas of talent and interest, the more confident they become that their abilities and effort can help them move up the job ladder, particularly if they are comfortable asking for accommodations when necessary.

Remember that it is typical for young people—with and without disabilities—to change their minds frequently during their teenage years about what they want to do. If you expect this, you will not be disappointed or frustrated when your daughter abandons her idea of becoming an astronomer (after you went to great lengths to set up a summer internship at the planetarium for her) or decides midway through her computer keyboarding course that she likes retail sales better after all. Do not be discouraged; experts advise that no education or job experience is ever really wasted. Even if youngsters change career plans several times, their accumulated experience will help expand their understanding of employers' expectations, improve their skills and their ability to work with people, and ultimately enhance their employability.

Vocational Assessment and Career Counseling

If students have reached high school without having developed some ideas about what they might want to do for a living (this is not unusual for students with learning disabilities, whose time and attention may have been occupied with basic academic survival), a formal vocational assessment and/or professional career counseling may help them focus their interests. Vocational assessments also attempt to measure students' aptitudes for different kinds of jobs. If pursuing a vocational assessment, it is important to make sure your child receives a multidisciplinary evaluation coordinated by a psychologist or counselor who is knowledgeable about learning disabilities. Such an assessment would involve interviews, hands-on activities, and observation in simulated job settings, as well as tests to measure the student's aptitudes, interests, dexterity, and academic achievement. Vocational assessments should be available through your school district; if you feel your child would benefit from one, ask for it to be included in the Individualized Transition Plan. For young adults who have left school, assessments and career counseling may be available through the state vocational rehabilitation agency, local community colleges or vocational-technical schools, nonprofit community-based organizations that serve people with disabilities, or private agencies and providers. Since cost and quality of service can vary considerably, it is important to investigate exactly what a vocational assessment will include, the credentials of professionals involved, and the range of services the agency can provide. Look for an agency that works closely with local employers. Career counselors should be up-to-date on the local economy and on "growth occupations" in which employees are needed in your part of the country.

Career Preparation

Career preparation includes both learning the specific skills necessary to perform a certain type of work and also job-search skills such as preparing a résumé, reading and responding to want ads, filling out applications, and conducting job interviews. Sixteen-year-olds who have isolated an area of career interest can often benefit from vocational education programs in high school. (Note that many of these classes require good reading and/or math skills and that instructors may have little experience working with students who have learning disabilities. It is therefore wise to meet in advance with instructors in these programs to review texts and instructional methods and discuss accommodations the student is likely to need.) High schools should also be able to provide guidance in the job-finding process (via the special education department, the guidance department, and/or the department of vocational education), but parents may have to ask for this help. Make sure that specific steps in career preparation—such as preparing a résumé or completing a work-study program—are included among the written objectives in the student's Individualized Transition Plan.

Some youngsters with learning disabilities avoid vocational education in high school because they are not comfortable in these classes (which sometimes have a reputation of being programs for dead-end kids and troublemakers), because they lack the skills needed to compete in these classes, or because they remain undecided about what they want to do. As a result, the challenge for many families is finding appropriate job training *after* high school (several years after, in some cases). Young adults with mild to moderate learning disabilities can often take advantage of industry-sponsored apprenticeships, as well as career education provided by the military; community colleges; and trade, technical, or business schools.* Those whose disabilities are more profound—or are complicated by very poor social skills, severe attention deficits, and/or mental-health problems—need more structure, support, and supervision than these traditional sources of vocational education provide, however. Transition programs (which are designed to help individuals with disabilities make the transition from living at home to living independently) are appropriate choices for some of these young adults. Transition programs may be either residential or day programs; some offer an academic component, while others focus primarily on developing self-care and employment skills. Private, public, and charitably supported transition programs all exist.

Experienced parents caution, though, that quality transition programs often have waiting lists; it is therefore a good idea to begin looking for a transition program as soon as you recognize that one is likely to be needed. Your school district's special education depart-

---

* In some areas, students are permitted to take community-college, university, and business- and technical-school classes for credit while still enrolled in high school— check with your school district for local policies.

Dale

Dale Brown founded the Association of Learning Disabled Adults and served as the first president of the National Network of Learning Disabled Adults. She writes and speaks frequently about learning disabilities and advises on legislative issues related to LD. Her own perceptual deficits were not recognized until she was in college. Here, Dale recalls her first job:

The first day of my senior year in high school, I eagerly applied for jobs. A drugstore manager hired me as a waitress. I was very excited. Minimum wage seemed like a fortune to me! On my first day at work, my first impression was of noise and brightness. Cash registers clattered. Dishes crashed. Silverware clanged. Pam, a slender young woman, explained the system.

"First you take the order," she said, handing me a green pad. "Just watch me." Pam approached a customer and said, "May I take your order, please?" The customer told her, and she wrote it down. "One hamburger!" she shouted to the cook.

"Now we have to make the tuna salad," she said. "Here's the scoop. You put the lettuce on the plate like this, then put the tuna on top. Then you put the tomato here."

We had to lean close to the counter to avoid being hit by a man carrying trays. I tried to watch her as she put the order together, but I could barely follow. "Show me how to make the tuna salad again?" I asked. "I can't until we get another order for it," Pam said. "Now we clean up the counters by putting the dishes down here. . . ." She spent the whole day talking to me and telling me detail after detail. I tried to listen, but the other conversations, the sizzling of the grill, and the rushing of water distracted me. "How do you take an order again?" I asked. "It's *easy,*" Pam replied. "Just write down what they say and look up the prices!"

ment, your state vocational rehabilitation agency, and community mental-health agencies are among the best places to start looking for information about transition programs. The HEATH publication *Young Adults with Learning Disabilities and Other Special Needs*, last updated in 1995, also lists a variety of established transition programs across the country. This publication will alert you to the variety of service models that help young adults transition to independent living. You can access a copy on the internet at www.heath.gwu.edu/files/active/other_special_needs.

The next day, my own section was assigned to me. A man and woman were waiting expectantly. The man asked for a hamburger and a coke. The woman asked for a tuna salad and a root beer. I wrote down the order, but I didn't know the prices.

"How much is a hamburger?" I asked Pam.

"Eighty-five cents."

"How about a coke?"

"Was it large or small?"

"I didn't ask."

"Better find out. Look at the menu next time; it has all the prices."

I went to make the tuna salad. I couldn't find the scoop. The plates had disappeared. I had to interrupt Pam again. . . , Then I couldn't make the lettuce lie flat. I couldn't get the tuna out in a ball. Finally, I spooned the tuna onto the lettuce and hoped it was enough. I gave the woman her salad and got the drinks, using the first paper cups I found. I couldn't easily see the difference between large and small, and I had forgotten to ask which they wanted anyway.

"Where's my hamburger?" asked the man.

I'd forgotten to tell the cook! "I'm sorry," I told him and shouted, "One hamburger!" As I served it to him, two more customers came in. They wanted hot dogs and tea.

"Where's our check?" asked the first customer. I gave it to him.

"How much are we supposed to pay?" he asked. I took the check back. I had forgotten to put on the prices! Panic hit. How much were the cokes? I made up a price, then concentrated on adding everything up right.

continued

Job Placement

Most postsecondary educational institutions (both colleges and vocational schools) offer their graduates some help with job searches and placement. Services may include help with preparing a résumé, practice with job-interview skills, and placement in summer jobs, work/study positions, and internships, as well as referrals to employers who are interested in applicants with particular types of training. Agencies that serve individuals with disabilities can often place young

"Where are our hot dogs?" asked my second customer.

"You overcharged us for the cokes!" said my first customer.

"Sorry!" I said. I approached the huge cash register. I had forgotten how to work it.

"Pam," I said, "please show me how to work the cash register."

"I showed you that yesterday."

"I'm sorry; you need to show me again." Pam rang up my order, without explaining what she was doing. Then I told her, "Wait, I charged them too much for the cokes!"

She glared at me. "Now we have to make up a *void* slip." She turned on a small microphone. "Mr. Connors, please come to the counter. . . . Dale, don't you have other orders to take care of?"

I nodded. But I had lost my order slip. I checked my pad, my pockets, the floor—I would have to ask my customers what they wanted again. But which ones were they? I couldn't remember their faces! How did Pam do this? She moved along efficiently and effortlessly, taking orders, preparing food, and ringing things up. I must have looked as lost as I felt, because Mr. Connors came over and looked at me sympathetically. "You'll catch on soon," he said. "Don't worry; it's only your second day."

But more days passed in a blur of confusion and errors. The other employees were kind at first, but rapidly grew impatient with all my questions. I couldn't memorize the prices—even after taking the menu home—and I kept on forgetting where things were located. Preparing food was difficult, even after being shown several times. (For example, to make a coke you mixed syrup and seltzer, but I couldn't tell the difference between the syrup knob and the seltzer knob on the machine. Each time, I had to squirt a little liquid in the cup and see which one it was.) I could never figure out the sequence of putting an order together. It was not clear to me that you started with the cooked items and worked on the other food while they were cooking (and no one explained it), so I was always giving my customers their food at different times.

adults who have difficulty finding work in the competitive job market in special apprenticeships or mentored employment positions (jobs that provide additional structure and supervision for workers with disabilities) in the community. Families may find, however, that most mentored jobs are designed primarily to meet the needs of individuals with physical handicaps or those with intellectual disabilities. Job coaching (a service in which a government-funded job coach works one-on-one with a new employee at his or her work site until essential

I had trouble working in the confined space between the counter and the food preparation area. I often bumped into other workers and dropped things—once a whole tray of glasses. And because of my difficulty remembering faces, I often confused people's orders. (Sometimes I wrote reminders on my order slips. One customer laughed when she found "blonde hair, blue eyes" on her check.) Gradually I mastered the cash register, although I had a tendency to punch the wrong numbers and end up with $13.80 instead of $1.38. The tax table we used was so small that sometimes I guessed the tax or forgot it altogether.

My favorite job was going to the stock room to get ice. The other waitresses hated it, but I volunteered for it. I would walk downstairs with two buckets. Then I'd sit on a carton for a few minutes and calm myself. Then I'd fill the buckets, and take them upstairs to the ice bin.

Because I was cheerful, reliable about being on time, and conscientious about trying to correct my errors, my boss liked me and kept me on in spite of all my problems. Sometimes he kidded me about all my void slips, but he was very patient. My coworkers, on the other hand, were the ones who had to put up with most of my questions and correct many of my mistakes. Even though I took care of a lot of unpopular jobs, they found me difficult and were undoubtedly glad when a change in bus schedules forced me to leave.

Later, I had many jobs. I was a salesgirl in a department store during Christmas rush. You can imagine the problems! In college, I woke up at six o'clock in the morning to clean the dormitory kitchens. I loved that job, because I worked alone, at my own pace. Later I became a cafeteria worker and served food, washed dishes, and helped the cooks. Each job I did better than the last.

Condensed with permission from D. S. Brown, *Learning to Work: A Story by a Learning Disabled Person*, 1996.

job skills have been mastered) may be a better way to help the young adult with learning disabilities get a solid foothold on the employment ladder. For information about special placements and job coaching, contact your state vocational rehabilitation agency.

Note that self-employment is a career possibility that should not be overlooked. Many individuals with learning disabilities flourish operating their own services or businesses. The appeal of entrepreneurship is that it allows energetic people to maximize their skills and creativity while delegating organizational tasks—as well as those involving math, reading, and/or writing—to others. If your child dreams of becoming his or her own boss, you may therefore want to give some serious consideration to the idea of starting a business. Make sure youngsters understand, of course, that creative people do need business experience and a basic business education (as well as partners or employees who can handle matters such as billing, scheduling, accounting, bookkeeping, inventory, reports, and contracts) in order to succeed. A high level of motivation and sincere interest in the type of work being considered—whether it is fashion merchandising or lawn care—are also helpful for keeping a small business going.

Research finds that substantial numbers of individuals with learning disabilities do not achieve economic independence until they are in their middle to late twenties, and that their education and employment histories can be characterized by wrong turns and false starts. While watching youngsters flounder can be frustrating and sometimes frightening, parents must remember that many of these young people learn best by trial and error; they simply don't know what they like or can do until they try it. As Dale's story reminds us, young people with learning disabilities *do* get better at tasks that are hard for them if they are willing to keep applying themselves. (This story also reminds us that a cheerful countenance and good work habits can help compensate for many problems.) So instead of seeing abandoned jobs or uncompleted educational programs as failures and becoming discouraged, try looking at them as necessary steps in the growth process. Parents who have this perspective are best at helping children maintain the motivation they need to keep trying until they find a niche in which they are truly comfortable.

Question Two: DOES THE YOUNG ADULT UNDERSTAND HIS LEGAL RIGHTS AND ADVOCATE FOR HIMSELF APPROPRIATELY?

Throughout this book, we have referred many times to the Individuals with Disabilities Education Act (IDEA), the package of federal legislation that protects the rights of students who have disabilities in public schools. It is important for young adults with learning disabilities (and their families) to understand that once students leave high school, the protections of IDEA no longer apply. Colleges, vocational schools, and other postsecondary institutions are *not* required to offer special education programs for people who have disabilities. Institutions of higher learning are not obliged to adjust admissions criteria or modify academic standards for these students. Employers cannot be compelled to change basic job descriptions to accommodate individuals with disabilities; nor must employers excuse individuals with disabilities from duties or training activities that are essential to their jobs, even if these assignments are difficult for those workers.

Employers and institutions of higher learning may not *exclude* qualified people who have disabilities, however, or operate programs in a way that makes it unreasonably difficult for these individuals to do their jobs or get an education. People who have disabilities (including learning disabilities) are protected from this kind of discrimination by federal civil rights legislation. It is important for young adults to understand what they can expect under civil rights law, and how to go about getting the modifications and accommodations the law mandates in higher education and job settings.

To begin, students must recognize that once they leave school, a significant shift in responsibility takes place. Under IDEA, schools are responsible for identifying children who need help as well as for initiating services. Under civil rights law, however, assistance is provided *only* to individuals who disclose their disabilities and *ask* for it. (Documentation of the disability may also be required.) Young people who lack understanding of their disabilities—or lack the confidence to explain what they need and ask for assistance—therefore risk losing support to which they are legally entitled. Because schools have traditionally done a very poor job of educating students about their legal rights and obligations, families must take the lead in preparing children to advocate for themselves appropriately in college or the workplace.

Young adults with learning disabilities need to become familiar with the provisions of two particular packages of federal legislation: the Rehabilitation Act of 1973 and the Americans with Disabilities Act (ADA), most recently amended in 2008. Both are civil rights acts that require organizations to provide equal opportunities to people who

Ten Suggestions for Employees with Learning Disabilities

These tips are suggested by Dale Brown.

1. Be prepared to spend extra time learning the job, even if you are not paid extra. Bring price lists home to memorize. Practice filling out forms. If you are working at a chain of restaurants, go to a different restaurant within the chain and watch the workers. If you are slower, be willing to take extra time to finish your fair share of work.

2. Ask for help as you need it. Even though the other employees and supervisors may act impatient, it's better than making errors.

3. On the other hand, never ask for help if you don't need it.

4. In most jobs, accuracy is more important than speed. Take the time to do it correctly, even if people pressure you to go faster.

5. Take full advantage of your first few days on the job. During this "honeymoon period" you can ask questions. Try to find someone who will watch you do the job correctly. Repeat information. Say, "Please listen to me tell you, so I can be sure I understand." Don't let them interrupt you and tell you what to do. Be sure they are listening to you. Some people like helping others. Try to find them.

6. Offer to do tasks which you can handle but that others consider unpopular. Then, you can ask others to assist you with jobs you can't do.

---

have disabilities. Section 504 of the Rehabilitation Act (often referred to simply as Section 504) applies primarily to educational institutions. Specifically, Section 504 states:

> *No otherwise qualified person with a disability in the United States . . . shall, solely by reason of . . . disability, be denied the benefits of, be excluded from participation in, or be subjected to discrimination under any program or activity receiving federal assistance.*

Section 504 broadly defines "person with a disability" as "any person who (i) has a physical or mental impairment which substantially limits one or more of such person's major life activities; (ii) has a record of such an impairment, or (iii) is regarded as having such an impairment." Since learning is a "major life activity," this description has been deter-

7. Develop ways of remembering important facts. Everyone has a particular technique. Write things down, or say them aloud when you are alone. Or ask your friends or parents to drill you.

8. When you make mistakes, apologize and correct them immediately.

9. Report on time. If you have trouble being on time, try to arrive an hour or two early.

10. Try hard and appear to make an effort. Sometimes, when one makes mistake after mistake, it gets tempting to act indifferent or as if you are doing it on purpose. That isn't helpful. Make your effort obvious. That means:

- Appear to pay attention. Look everyone in the eye. Nod your head occasionally as they speak. Respond to what they have said.

- Look at your work as you do it. Don't let your eyes and mind wander when you are on the job. Walk purposefully from place to place.

- Always work, except during lunch or breaks.

- As you improve, tell your supervisors and coworkers. Say, "Thank you for your help. As you can see, I did it correctly this time."

Reprinted with permission of D. S. Brown, 1996.

mined to cover learning disabilities. Under Section 504, colleges and universities that receive federal money may *not* do any of the following:

- limit the number of students with disabilities that they admit,
- make preadmission inquiries about whether or not a student has a disability,
- use admissions tests or other selection criteria that do not make provisions for individuals with disabilities,
- exclude qualified students with disabilities from any course of study,
- limit eligibility for scholarships, financial aid, fellowships, internships, or assistantships on the basis of a disability, or
- use methods of evaluation that adversely affect persons with disabilities.

In addition, Section 504 requires institutions receiving federal funds to provide services and accommodations that enable individuals with disabilities to take full advantage of available programs. Colleges and universities are granted some flexibility in determining how to meet each student's needs. (If a student with learning disabilities needs to use a computer, for example, the college can fulfill this need by providing access to a computer center during certain hours; it does not have to provide a personal computer for the student's use.) Note that colleges need *not* make accommodations that would reduce academic standards or alter essential elements of a program. (A university can legally require students to have a C average to be accepted into a major, for example, or insist on foreign-language mastery for admission to an international-studies program.) If a student with a disability can meet the standards of the institution or perform essential tasks of the program using modifications to compensate for the handicap, however, Section 504 states that the modifications must be provided.

Section 504 also prohibits discrimination in employment practices by employers receiving federal funds (principally federal contractors and the federal government itself). The rights of a much larger number of workers, however, are protected by the Americans with Disabilities Act. This sweeping legislation prohibits any organization with more than fifteen employees from discriminating against people with disabilities (including disabilities affecting learning, reading, concentration, and thinking) in the areas of access, hiring, or promotion. It also requires employers to make "reasonable accommodations" to help workers with disabilities do their jobs. (Religious organizations are exempt from this legislation.) The ADA's provisions also apply to institutions of higher learning, so they expand and reinforce the rights of students set down in Section 504. Among the provisions of the ADA are the following:

- A qualified person cannot be excluded from a program or job on the basis of having a disability.
- Reasonable modifications in policies, practices, and procedures must be made in order to avoid discrimination.
- Employment and program participation should be in the most integrated setting possible.

- Examinations and courses must be accessible.
- Surcharges to cover the costs of accommodations may not be imposed solely on persons with disabilities.
- There may be no harassment or retaliation against individuals who are accessing their rights under the law.

The ADA also requires organizations to actively recruit individuals with disabilities for open positions; to change qualifying examinations, interview procedures, and/or training policies that unnecessarily restrict the rights of these applicants; and to provide technology that will enable employees with disabilities to be fully functional within the employment setting. Under the provisions of the ADA, therefore, it would be reasonable for a worker with a learning disability to request such accommodations as these:

- written directions for work to be performed
- access to word processors with spell-checkers for written tasks
- access to calculators to assist with tasks involving math
- work settings that minimize distractions
- assistance with reading technical or training manuals

Although these laws have been in place for some time, young adults with learning disabilities should not assume that their teachers and job supervisors will understand the provisions of Section 504 and the ADA and comply with them automatically. Research finds that many employers and educators in institutions of higher learning have very limited understanding of these acts. Some don't know that civil rights laws cover individuals with learning disabilities as well as persons with more visible issues (such as vision or hearing impairments or limited physical mobility). Others know next to nothing about learning disabilities themselves. (Some years ago, an Iowa judge ruled that a plaintiff could not have a learning disability because he had a driver's license, normal intelligence, and was capable of responding to questions in court!) Therefore, in addition to knowing what they are entitled to, young people must be prepared to courteously educate teachers and administrators about learning disabilities and the law whenever they ask for accommodations. (Generally speaking, the time to ask for accommodations is at the beginning of a job *before* things go wrong. This prevents problems that can arise when disclosure is "reactive" to a botched assignment. It also avoids the appearance of using a disability to excuse poor performance.) Youngsters who lack self-confidence, lack information about their disabilities, or have personal styles that are less than assertive are at a disadvantage in these situations. Some of these young people will be most successful in programs where the needs of individuals with disabilities are already understood (on college campuses that have well-established LD support programs, for example).

Assertive or not, all individuals with learning disabilities need to know where they can turn for help with advocacy and/or resolving disputes when they need it. Colleges and universities are required to appoint Section 504 compliance officers to help handle complaints. Under the terms of the ADA, employers and educational institutions must also establish a grievance procedure for individuals who believe their rights have been violated, and they must make information about this procedure available to anyone who asks for it. Initiating a formal grievance, however, should be considered an action of last resort. Most disputes can be resolved through informal negotiation. Parents need to be alert, however, since young people sometimes need backup from family, counselors, special-needs support staff, community agencies serving the disabled, and/or legal representatives in order to get a fair hearing.

It must also be acknowledged that there are borderline situations in which the law is not entirely clear on what an individual with learning disabilities is entitled to. For example, does a student with mild disabilities qualify for accommodations, given the language of the law (which refers to "substantial" impairments)? Must employers provide costly equipment to accommodate individuals with disabilities if doing so significantly reduces profit margins? How much writing help can be provided to a graduate student with a Ph.D. dissertation, given that writing a dissertation is an established degree requirement? Can an otherwise qualified individual be denied promotion to a supervisory position on the basis of inability to read or write required reports?

Questions like these are being addressed in America's courtrooms, where new cases involving individuals with learning disabilities are heard each year. While the courts struggle to interpret the finer points of the law, however, individuals must continue to negotiate for what they need as best they can. This usually involves striving for cooperative, mutually respectful relationships (as opposed to adopting an adversarial stance and making blunt demands). Young people who are perceived as hardworking and sincere are most likely to get the support they ask for. If polite negotiation fails, though, families should not hesitate to initiate formal procedures to protect a youngster's legal rights in the classroom or on the job.

Note that many individuals fear that disclosing their learning disabilities in the workplace or at institutions of higher learning will lead to stigmatization and social and/or professional rejection. These fears are not entirely unrealistic. Myths about learning disabilities abound, and ignorant individuals sometimes assume that people with LD are incompetent or irresponsible. Young people who wish to keep their disabilities confidential are of course entitled to do so. (The Family Educational Rights and Privacy Act, sometimes referred to as FERPA or the Buckley Amendment, protects the confidentiality of school records. Information about learning disabilities or participation in special education programs cannot be disclosed to outside parties without a student's written consent.) Under these circumstances, however, special accommodations and modifications cannot be expected. Good compensatory skills and hard work (possibly including many hours of extra unpaid effort) may be required of the individual who wants to succeed.

Try to involve teachers and counselors in the process of preparing students to advocate for themselves after leaving school. A good way to do this is to include the development of self-advocacy skills on the student's Individualized Education Program (IEP) and/or the Individualized Transition Plan, which must be added to the student's IEP no later than age sixteen. Throughout high school, students should also practice self-advocacy by negotiating their own program modifications with teachers whenever possible. (Parents and special education teachers can provide backup if needed.)

Question Three: IS THE YOUNG ADULT READY TO LEAVE HOME?

Concern about children's readiness to live on their own is not limited to the parents of youngsters with learning disabilities. Most parents experience some anxiety when a child prepares to leave home for college or that first apartment. Worries range from simple concerns about the child's health and welfare ("Will she eat balanced meals?" "Will he wear his boots when it snows?") to serious doubts about the child's maturity ("Can he face up to peer pressure?" "Is she savvy enough to conduct herself safely among strangers?"). Apprehensions about our own well-being may also be aroused when a child leaves home ("Am I losing him?" "How lonely I will be without her!"). For many parents (mothers especially), the exit of adult children marks the end of a significant phase of their lives and leaves them wondering, "What will I do now?"

For parents of children who have learning disabilities, all of these feelings may be particularly acute. Since our youngsters are sometimes late to acquire the skills that support independence, they may look less ready than most to leave the nest at age eighteen. In addition, we may find ourselves unusually entangled emotionally with these children. Because parents so often serve as advocates, mentors, teachers, coaches, and cheerleaders for youngsters who have learning disabilities (and sometimes as their best friends as well), involvement with these children can become very intense. Separation may therefore be a painful and difficult process for parent and child alike. This process can be complicated by the fact that young adults with learning disabilities sometimes need extra time to become economically and emotionally self-sufficient. When adult children continue to look to Mom and Dad to get many of their needs met, parents often find their feelings ping-ponging between "How will this kid ever survive without me?" and "It's time for this child to go!"

To assess a child's readiness for independence, it is important to realistically evaluate general maturity as well as academic and occupational skills. The checklist on pages 432–33 presents some important indicators of maturity. While few children will be performing well in all these areas at age eighteen (indeed, many of us continue to struggle with some of these skills as adults), difficulties in many areas suggests that a young person still needs a protected environment, regardless of his or her age. Giving such children an extra year or two to grow up and improve their abilities to meet the challenges of daily living makes much more sense than propelling them into a job or educational program for which they are not ready. As they become better able to take care of themselves and communicate with others, young adults' pride in their own competence and self-esteem usually grows. This growth in confidence will eventually help support success in everything they do. Some skills on the checklist are likely to improve as the child grows older, broadens his or her experience, and completes stages of development that have been delayed. For others (shopping and meal preparation, for example), the child will need explicit instruction. Remember that the best favor a parent can do for a child is to slowly reduce supports, so that their son or daughter steps up to the plate and starts to take personal responsibility. No employer will be happy with an employee who doesn't trust his own judgment and needs continual hand-holding.

Determining where a young adult should receive continuing support, however, can be a thorny problem. Although research indicates that many young people with learning disabilities continue to live at home into their twenties, availing themselves of parental assistance while completing their educations and/or settling into a job, this is not the best option for every family. Parents may doubt their ability to provide children with the guidance they need, or may themselves be in need of a respite from the responsibilities of child rearing. Children may *want* to leave home and try their wings (a normal desire for those approaching the end of adolescence). Children who have become overdependent on parents may need to leave home in order to develop some confidence in their ability to care for themselves. These are only a few of the considerations that can have parents looking for a supportive environment away from home.

For young people who have adequate academic preparation, college can provide the transitional setting they need if the program is carefully selected. (Immature children need more structure and supervision than others, and social as well as academic support is often

Is Your Child Ready to Leave Home?

The checklist below presents some important indicators of maturity. Young adults whose self-management skills are good in most of these areas are probably ready for independent living. (Note that even the best-prepared youngsters will not start out functioning well in *all* areas.) Those who lack ability in many areas, however, may need to live at home or in another supervised environment until their skills improve.

Mature Young Adults
- can set reasonable short-term goals and make plans to achieve them (can plan a social engagement or make a realistic list of priorities for the day, for example)
- can stick to their principles and stand up to peer pressure
- have reasonable impulse control; can delay gratification when appropriate (they can balance "what I want to do" and "what I need to do" most of the time, for example)
- understand their own strengths and limitations; can identify situations/settings/ modifications that make it possible for them to do their best
- can manage day-to-day personal finances (make deposits, pay bills, keep simple accounts, keep spending within budget guidelines)
- can stick to a schedule (get up and go to bed at reasonable hours; get to work/ meals/class on time)
- have developed "memory methods" for keeping track of appointments, assignments, chores, and other obligations
- can shop for and prepare simple meals

needed. This kind of support is most often found at colleges with well-established programs for students with learning disabilities.) For young people who are not ready for college, parents may wish to consider such options as boarding schools (some "prep" schools specialize in assisting older adolescents who want to improve their academic skills and go to college eventually; others focus more on vocational and independent living skills) and residential transition programs (including group homes). Arrangements in which the child lives with another relative—such as a grandparent or an older sibling—or moves into an apartment but continues to receive some income and assistance from parents (with shopping and bill paying, for example) may

- have good health and grooming habits: dress appropriately for the weather; know how to keep selves, clothing, and living spaces clean; are reliable about following doctors' orders (including taking medications on time); understand the consequences of drug and alcohol abuse and the importance of practicing safe sex
- can drive or use public transportation safely
- can monitor their own behavior (are usually aware of the impact their behavior has on others; can identify when their behavior has been irresponsible, inappropriate, or offensive)
- are accountable for their own actions; take pride in their successes and responsibility for their mistakes
- can respond appropriately to emergencies (know what to do in case of injury or medical emergency, fire, power failure, etc.)
- can ask for help and locate appropriate sources of support when needed, can accept supervision and constructive criticism
- can follow directions and work independently for reasonable periods of time (do not have an excessive need for praise, monitoring, or other forms of attention)
- usually interact courteously with supervisors, teachers, coworkers, and service providers
- can initiate and maintain appropriate social relationships with peers
- know and practice healthy methods of reducing stress (such as exercise, talking problems over with others, meditation, hobbies, sports, and other recreational activities)

also meet the young adult's need for increased independence while providing some continuing support. Experienced parents advise that several arrangements like these may have to be employed before a young adult is ready to live on his or her own. It is important to avoid becoming discouraged during this extended separation process (the great majority of young people with learning disabilities *do* become able to take care of themselves eventually) and to be persistent about seeking placements that respect the child's dignity and status as an emerging adult while offering adequate protection.

What if it appears that a child will never be able to become fully independent? This may be the case if a child's learning disabilities are

Estate Planning for a Child with Disabilities

Parents who want to provide for a child's housing, health care, or education in the future, or who hope to supply long-term support for a child with severe disabilities, need to plan their estates carefully. If a child is receiving government benefits—or is expected to need them in the future—it is important to pass on assets in a way that does not affect his or her continuing eligibility for government assistance. The child's level of maturity and ability to manage money must also be considered. When preparing wills, parents have four basic options, outlined below.

Disinherit the child: No state *requires* parents to leave money to a child, disabled or not. If your resources are limited and your child's needs are great, it may be wisest to disinherit your child so that he or she will be eligible for federal and state benefits after your death. Instead of complete disinheritance, you may want to leave your child a gift of modest but sentimental value, such as his or her bedroom furniture. The value of this gift will be small enough not to affect government benefits but will indicate your love and concern.

Leave the child an outright gift: For example, your will might read, "I leave my son Tom $10,000," or "I leave half of my estate to my daughter Susan." If the child is not expected to need government benefits, this may be the most desirable course. If you question a child's competence or ability to handle financial responsibility, however, an outright gift is not a good choice. A trust is a better means of providing for the child's future.

Leave a morally obligated gift to another of your children: Suppose parents have two children: James (who has severe learning disabilities) and Mary. The parents leave all their assets to Mary. But they also instruct Mary before their deaths that half of this money is to be used for James's benefit in whatever way she thinks best. The money has been left to Mary so that James will not lose his government benefits, and because Mary can be trusted to think of appropriate ways to help her brother (such as taking him on vacation trips, or paying for health care not covered by his benefits). This arrangement is a *moral* obligation because it has no legal force; once she has the money, Mary can do whatever she wants with it. There is therefore some risk that the parents' wishes will not be implemented. (Even if Mary is honest, unforeseen circumstances could make it difficult for her to carry out her parents' plan. If one of Mary's children falls gravely ill, for example, she might feel a greater obligation to save her child than to support her brother. Or the money might be lost in a settlement if Mary divorces.) Morally obligated gifts can be a reasonable solution, however, if parents have a modest amount of money to distribute and do not expect to provide lifetime care for a child with disabilities. Be sure to seek input and approval from the obligated sibling before committing to this plan.

Establish a Special Needs Trust. The purpose of a Special Needs Trust is to manage assets in a way that provides limited income over a long period of time, preserving a child's eligibility for government benefits. Assets are managed by a trustee, who is given authority to determine how and when funds will be distributed to the trust's beneficiary. There are two kinds of trusts: the *testamentary trust,* which goes into effect when parents die, and the *intervivos trust,* which is activated when parents are still living (parents may serve as trustees during their lifetimes). Each offers distinct advantages and disadvantages that should be discussed with an attorney experienced in estate planning for individuals with disabilities. The services of a financial planner may also be needed to help families examine their resources and determine how best to fund trusts. Again, it is essential to find a professional who is familiar with Special Needs Trusts, which are quite different from Family Living Trusts and other modern estate-planning tools. Although they are more difficult to set up, Special Needs Trusts are regarded as the most secure way of providing for the long-term needs of a child who has disabilities.

All of the above considerations must take into account the best way to maximize the assets you have to live on, while also securing the future of your child. You will need to seek expert financial and legal advice on secure investments, tax planning for retirement, annuities, and insurance policies, as well as preparing a will. Experts advise that, in addition to preparing a will, parents should prepare a *Letter of Intent* that summarizes their wishes for their child's future in such areas as housing, education, religious upbringing, employment, social environment, behavior management, and medical care. This information will help guide your child's advocates when you are no longer there. This letter (write it *now* and update it periodically) has no legal status, but it can give people who may not know your child well valuable insight into his or her history, values, personality, goals, and needs.

Adapted from "Estate Planning," *NICHCY News Digest,* a publication of the National Dissemination Center for Children with Disabilities, www.nichcy.org/informationresources/documents.

very severe or complicated by mental-health problems. Since these young adults may find it difficult to work steadily or to find jobs that provide health-care benefits, it is of urgent importance for parents to help them explore what government assistance may be available. Individuals with documented disabilities may be eligible for Supplementary Security Income (SSI) or Social Security Disability Insurance (SSDI) benefits from the Social Security Administration. Note that parents' income or job status does not necessarily affect eligibility for federal assistance (parental income is not considered for SSI applicants over the age of eighteen, for example). Recipients of these benefits are permitted to work and earn money within limits, as well as allowed to receive some money from their families. In some states, individuals receiving SSI are automatically eligible for additional benefits such as health insurance (Medicaid) and food stamps; in others, a separate application has to be made for these and other services (such as job counseling, support for education, and subsidized housing). Your local Social Security Administration office and the state department of social services are the places to start gathering information about the support available for adults with disabilities in your community.

Parents may also wish to arrange their affairs so that continuing provisions are made for a child with disabilities after the parents die. The box on pages 434–35 outlines some estate-planning options. If a child receives government benefits (or is expected to need them in the future), it is very important to pass on assets in a way that does not affect his or her continuing eligibility for assistance. The guidance of an expert in estate planning for persons with disabilities should be sought when making a will. The National Dissemination Center for Children with Disabilities (NICHCY) has produced an excellent publication for parents covering this and other aspects of making long-term provisions for the support of an adult child. For a free copy of the "Estate Planning" issue of their *News Digest,* go to www.nichcy. org/informationresources/documents.

Ultimately, our ability to provide appropriate support for our sons and daughters as they make the transition to adulthood depends on our ability to find the support—and the courage—we need to enter into a new phase of our own lives. We cannot do a good job of helping our children leave the nest if we feel we have little to look forward to after they have gone! Similarly, if we are afraid of relinquishing control, fearful of facing up to difficult issues in our own lives, anxious about being alone, or insecure about our value if nobody needs us anymore, we can find ourselves holding on to our children a little too tightly and a little too long.

Because it is so easy to confuse the legitimate needs of a child who has disabilities with the needs of a mother or father who has difficulty letting go, it is important for parents to put some thought and effort into mapping their own transitions to the future as children get older. What new opportunities will relief from the day-to-day responsibilities of child care open up for you? What obstacles to your happiness exist, and how can you go about overcoming them? What support will you need to accomplish your goals and cope with new challenges? Where can you find that support?

Parents who seek answers to questions like these will be in the best position to deal with the feelings of loss that inevitably accompany a child's departure from home. These parents also teach, by example, that growth is a lifelong process. Among the many lessons we teach our children, this is possibly the most important. All young people—not just those with learning disabilities—need to know that there is no time limit on learning or achievement. If we haven't met our goals by age eighteen (or thirty, or fifty), we get not only second chances, but also third, fourth, and fifth chances—as many chances as we need.

As our children spread their wings and prepare to fly, then, we must look to our own paths and practice what we preach. We must trust that it is never too late to learn, to ask for help, or to reach for dreams. And as we move forward, we need to remember this Chinese proverb as well as teach it to our children:

> *Be not afraid of growing slowly;*
> *Be afraid only of standing still.*

Timetable for Transition Planning

Junior High School

- *Take advantage of career-exploration programs and activities.* Expose students to as many different career options as possible. Improve career awareness by visiting different kinds of work sites and encouraging children to talk to people with different occupations about what they do.

- *Make a list of the student's personal strengths and interests.* Use it to make some preliminary choices about career paths (a student who is outgoing, enjoys working with people, and has good math skills might be encouraged to look into business careers, for example).

- *Identify what kind of educational preparation is necessary for top career choices.* Will the student need college? Vocational education? On-the-job training? A combination of these approaches?

- *Make a list of challenges that will have to be met.* The student interested in becoming a police officer will probably need to take some college-level courses, for example. A would-be boutique owner will need sales experience as well as a basic business education. Start to rule out choices that are hopelessly inappropriate. (The youngster who frequently transposes numbers and letters, for example, would probably not succeed at computer data entry.)

- *Meet with the guidance counselor to discuss high school course selection.* Students hoping to go to college should take as many college preparatory classes as they can, using accommodations as necessary. Research finds that ability to achieve in regular high school classes is a strong predictor of college success. Instruction in study skills, time management, and test preparation should also be sought now if it has not been already provided. Students not planning on attending college need to ask about options for career education. Note that many vocational education classes require relatively high functional abilities in reading and math; if students' skills in these areas are below the fifth- or sixth-grade level, continuing remedial instruction needs to be provided in high school. Students in college preparatory and vocational educational programs both need to become computer literate.

- *Promote independence and decision-making at home.* Gradually begin to decrease the level of guidance and supervision you are providing in areas like homework and recreation, and encourage children to rely more on their own initiative. (Continue this process through high school.) Living away from home for short periods—visiting out-of-town relatives, traveling with youth groups, or going to overnight camp—can help boost youngsters' confidence and self-reliance.

Ninth Grade

- **Develop a written Individualized Transition Plan.** Federal law requires schools to initiate Individualized Transition Plans for students with disabilities no later than age sixteen, but there is no rule that says an ITP can't be written earlier. Doing so can help improve the focus of both the student and school personnel on important issues related to college preparation, job-skill development, and independent living. It is important for students to participate in developing the ITP. The job of the transition team is to help students figure out how to meet their own goals, not tell students what they should do. If the student doesn't attend the ITP meeting, the school must take other steps to ensure that the child's preferences and interests are considered.

- **Work on self-advocacy skills.** Students need to develop an understanding of learning disabilities in general, and the nature of their own disabilities in particular. (One way to do this is to ask the special education teacher or school psychologist to review the most recent evaluation with a student, explaining strengths and weaknesses in nontechnical language.) Youngsters should learn to describe their preferred methods of working, their specific learning disabilities, and the settings, instructional methods, and accommodations that make it possible for them to do their best. Students should start participating in IEP meetings and academic planning sessions with guidance counselors now if they are not already doing so.

- **Explore recreational opportunities.** Look for leisure-time activities at school and in the community that will put youngsters in touch with others who have similar interests. Spectator sports, community volunteer work, church activities, recreational athletics, crafts and exercise classes, and special-interest clubs (like gardening, bowling, or bird-watching) can all provide a basis for rewarding relationships as well as help youngsters make productive use of their free time.

continued

Note that the more developed students' interests become, the easier it will be for them to make friends after leaving school. For example, a youngster who is a competent chess player, sings with the church choir, knows his way around political election campaigns, and is a pro football fan has a basis for meeting people almost anywhere he goes.

- *Look for ways of getting work experience.* Research shows that work experience during high school is closely associated with future job success. Internships, job-shadow and work-study programs, volunteer work, and part-time or summer jobs are all good ways of gaining work experience. These activities can help students explore their career interests, develop realistic job expectations, improve their skills, and boost their levels of self-esteem, responsibility, and independence. Students with demanding academic schedules, though, must be careful to avoid becoming overloaded. (For them, summer employment is often the wisest option.)

- *Continue to refine career options.* Throughout high school (and college), students change their minds frequently about what career paths they want to follow. This is normal, and continuing career exploration should be encouraged. The high school curriculum needs to be planned in a way that preserves the greatest possible range of choices. (If students have the potential for success in college, for example, college preparatory courses should be taken even if the child does not presently plan to go.)

Tenth Grade

- *Refine or revise goals based on work and school experience.* The student who thought she was interested in health sciences may feel differently after volunteering at the local hospital for six months. The student who hoped to be a high school athletic coach may be brought up short by low grades in college preparatory classes. As youngsters' interests and aptitudes become clearer, goals need to be redefined and plans adjusted.

- *Begin to explore postsecondary education opportunities.* As students' goals become more focused, start to gather information about institutions that provide education in careers of interest (two- and four-year colleges, apprenticeship programs, trade schools, working one's way up within a corporation, and the military may all be options). Identify admissions requirements, including tests that may have to be taken (such as the SAT and ACT exams for college). Review high school course selections with the high school guidance counselor in light of these requirements and make necessary adjustments.

- *Learn about the legal rights of individuals with disabilities.* Many teachers and employers—and many students—do not fully understand that accommodations for people with disabilities in public school, in the workplace, and in institutions of higher learning are required by federal law. Students need to learn about how the Individuals with Disabilities Education Act (IDEA) and civil rights laws (particularly Section 504 of the Rehabilitation Act, and the Americans with Disabilities Act) apply to them.

- *Practice self-advocacy skills.* Students should take over the process of explaining their learning disabilities and negotiating for accommodations or modifications with their teachers and employers as much as possible (parents and special education teachers can provide backup if needed). Young adults who are most successful in college and on the job are those who can clearly articulate their own interests, abilities, and needs.

- *Increase the student's level of responsibility for self-care at home.* Has the child learned to keep track of appointments and take medications without prompting? To do laundry? To use public transportation? To budget money? If not, now is the time to start encouraging him or her to take on these and other tasks essential for independent living. Research indicates that this is one of the most neglected aspects of transition planning.

Eleventh Grade
- *Seek out vocational assessment and education opportunities.* Students who have not yet identified career goals may benefit from a formal vocational assessment (which can help pinpoint occupational strengths and interests) and/or the assistance of a career counselor. Ask that these services be included in the student's ITP. Students who have targeted an area of career interest may be eligible to begin taking technical or other vocational courses now. Since few vocational education teachers are knowledgeable about the needs of students with learning disabilities, check out these courses carefully in advance and discuss accommodations that a student might need with instructors.

- *Prepare a "short list" of colleges or other educational institutions.* Students should begin to narrow their choices of colleges or other postsecondary institutions, using criteria such as size, location, cost, quality of programs in areas of interest, social atmosphere, and availability of support services for

continued

students with learning disabilities. Commercial college guides (available at bookstores, public libraries, and many high school guidance offices) can be very helpful in this process; there are now guides published specifically for college applicants with learning disabilities. You may want to search out colleges that value "experiential learning" (work/study programs, internships, co-op programs) as well as traditional "book learning." Use the Web to explore or write to request catalogs and applications, and make plans to visit and interview at top-choice institutions. Overnight visits that include sitting in on one or more classes, a chance to talk informally with students, and an opportunity to sample campus social life are highly recommended.

- *Take the SAT and/or ACT exams (if the student is applying to colleges that require them).* Preliminary college aptitude tests (the College Board's PSAT and the ACT's PLAN) are administered early in the junior year. (The results of these tests are not reported to colleges, but scores do determine eligibility for some academic scholarships.) If preliminary test results are less than satisfactory, make a plan for improving test-taking strategies by means of review books, computer programs, classes, or tutors. Many students take college entrance exams in both their junior and senior years. Test modifications are available to students with learning disabilities, but nonstandard testing must be arranged in advance and documentation of the disability provided. Careful attention to test schedules is therefore required. Schedules and forms for signing up for the SAT and ACT exams will be available from the high school guidance office and online.

- *Begin to assemble a personal transition file.* To receive accommodations after leaving high school (in college or the workplace), young adults will have to request them—they will *not* be offered automatically—and in some cases document their eligibility (that is, prove that a learning disability exists). Families should start gathering this documentation now. Contents of the file should include the most recent diagnostic assessment results and evaluation reports, medical records (if applicable), a copy of the student's most recent IEP (which should include a description of all modifications and accommodations used or allowed), and a copy of the student's Individualized Transition Plan. High school transcripts, ACT or SAT scores, employment evaluations, awards, letters of recommendation, and information about extracurricular activities and other outside interests may also be useful to counselors attempting to help students select an appropriate program. If the student's most recent evaluation is more than two years old, ask the school district to complete a new one in the child's final school year. Some institutions will not grant accommodations without an up-to-date assessment.

- ***Explore summer opportunities.*** Some colleges (and some boarding schools for students with learning disabilities) offer summer programs that combine improving academic skills with an introduction to living away from home. For a current list of precollege programs for students with learning disabilities contact the HEATH Resource Center's Clearinghouse on Postsecondary Education for Individuals with Disabilities at 1-800-544-3284 (www.heath.gwu.edu) or your local Learning Disabilities Association. Students not attending summer school programs should seek summer jobs or internships in areas related to their career interests If at all possible.

Twelfth Grade

- ***College-bound students need to start writing college application essays, securing letters of recommendation, and filling out application forms as early in the school year as possible.*** Pay careful attention to deadlines. It is a good idea for students to ask their guidance counselors to review applications for completeness and accuracy two to four weeks before they are due (neatness counts, too). Use of the Common Application Form can save students a great deal of time and essay writing. Copies of the Common Application (and a list of the nearly four hundred institutions accepting it) should be available in the high school guidance office, or find it online (www.commonapp.org).

- ***Investigate technical and trade schools that offer instruction in areas of interest.*** While some of these institutions provide excellent training, commercial career education is also a field that is rife with scams, so programs have to be checked out carefully. Ask your Better Business Bureau and local vocational rehabilitation agency about any programs you are seriously considering. Beware of "counselors" who are salespeople in disguise (they recruit students on commission rather than on the basis of ability or aptitude), of promotions featuring "talent tests" or celebrity instructors, and of "bait and switch" lures (students answer a help-wanted ad, only to be told certain courses must be taken to "qualify" them for the job, or they are told that the free or discounted course they applied for is full, but they are eligible for others). Ask about the length and costs of training and how the curriculum addresses the specific needs of local

continued

employers—there is not much point in preparing practical nurses or computer programmers if the local job market is oversaturated with them. Do instructors have experience working with students who have learning disabilities? If tutoring in math, reading, or writing is needed, is it available? Read all contracts carefully (or have a lawyer review them) before signing.

- *Job seekers need to prepare a résumé, obtain letters of recommendation, practice job interview skills, and learn how to complete applications.* These objectives should be included on students' ITPs. A summary of the information typically called for on job applications (including dates of previous employment, Social Security number, and names and addresses of references) should be prepared to take along when students visit prospective employers, since many will want applications filled out on the spot.

- *Identify sources of financial support.* High school guidance counselors can provide assistance with college financial aid forms. If families intend to explore resources available through the state vocational rehabilitation system or the Social Security Administration, intake interviews to establish eligibility should be arranged with those agencies.

- *Identify options for children who are not yet ready for work or higher education.* For students who lack the skills or the maturity to attend college or hold down full-time jobs, a transition program may be the answer. These range from boarding schools that provide an extra year of high school for students who want to improve their chances of getting into college to group homes that help young adults with severe learning disabilities learn self-care, social, and employment skills. Some transition programs are private and tuition based; others are supported by public funds or charitable organizations—your school district's department of special education, local support groups, and the state vocational rehabilitation agency are good places to start looking for information. Remember also that students with special education needs are entitled to remain in public school until they reach age twenty-two. Students aren't usually crazy about this option, but willingness to commit an extra year or two to high school can sometimes make the difference between completing a college-preparatory high school program and leaving school with a special education certificate or other nonstandard diploma.

- *Review the student's SOP.* The school district must provide each special education student with a Statement of Performance as he or she approaches graduation, which outlines the students' achievement levels, assessment findings, and special needs. Make sure the information included in the SOP matches the requirements of institutions and/or agencies the student is expected to deal with in the future.

After High School

- *Continue to monitor youngsters' progress.* Young people with learning disabilities frequently have difficulty adjusting to new environments. The increased freedoms and responsibilities that come with leaving high school can make the transition to college or the workplace particularly rocky. While it is important to avoid being overprotective (students must try their wings and make some mistakes in order to learn), be alert for signs of excessive stress, anxiety, or depression. These are signals that some changes need to be made, or additional supports provided.

- *Help young adults build a personal support network.* Young people with learning disabilities who make successful transitions to independent living often rely on the guidance and encouragement of mentors and "coaches." It is therefore important to urge youngsters to make positive connections with teachers, tutors, counselors, academic advisors, and job supervisors and take advantage of help that is available from these quarters. Parents and other family members can be effective mentors (and often continue to coordinate different aspects of children's programs for several years after high school), but it is important for young adults to explore sources of support beyond the home as well.

- *Provide loving acceptance and encouragement.* In studies, young people with learning disabilities frequently say that the emotional support and encouragement of family members was indispensable for helping them maintain their motivation, especially when things were not going well or their lives were not proceeding as planned. The road to success for a young person with learning disabilities often looks more like a zigzag path (interrupted here and there by landslides, swamps, and bogs) than a straight route to the top. A parent's most important job as children negotiate this course is to prevent them from becoming discouraged, losing faith in themselves, and giving up. In this way, parents graduate from serving as their children's physical guardians to becoming the protectors of their children's hopes and dreams.

Appendix A

Common Assessment Measures

Dr. Michelle Storie

Following are brief descriptions of the most commonly used measures of achievement, memory and learning, cognitive abilities, and socio-emotional functioning. While test specifics vary from one another, there are some commonalities that exist among the tests.

In general, if a test contains a verbal-comprehension measure, tasks will consist of defining words, providing synonyms of terms, answering comprehension questions or questions assessing general knowledge base, or remembering the content of a story. Nonverbal tasks will measure a child's visual-spatial skills, and may involve the child copying designs, putting blocks together to create a pattern, identifying items that come next in a pattern, and pointing to designs that are related to one another. Processing-speed problems are timed, and may involve simple copying tasks or a child identifying whether a symbol is presented in another line of symbols. Memory tasks present a child with lists of words or images to memorize. Many memory tests involve a delayed component, in which the child is asked to remember information after a period of time has passed.

Be sure to ask the school team what tests are being used with your child. If you ask to be shown examples of the tasks that gave your child the most trouble (as well as those on which he or she excelled) you can gain a better sense of your child's strengths and weaknesses.

ACHIEVEMENT MEASURES

General Achievement Batteries Used for Screening Purposes

Woodcock-Johnson, Third Edition (WJ-III/NU) (ages 2–90+ years)

The **WJ-III/NU** is a comprehensive achievement test which measures the ability to read isolated letters and words, the ability to read nonsense words that follow English structural and phonetic patterns, reading comprehension, knowledge of synonyms and antonyms, calculation ability, the ability to solve practical mathematical problems, mathematical conceptual understanding, spelling, punctuation, capitalization, written expression, and knowledge in science, social studies, and the humanities. The reading disabilities of children who don't recognize words rapidly but can sound out words if given time may not be evident on the WJ-III/NU, because the child can take as long as necessary during the test to figure out a word. In addition, little information is gained on reading fluency because the examiner listens only to how a child reads single words, not sentences or paragraphs, and the Reading Fluency subtest is completed on paper, with students answering questions about brief sentences. Many older students can read the sentences easily, not reflecting true age-appropriate reading-fluency abilities. On the WJ-III, the reading-comprehension task is unlike real-life comprehension demands (the child is asked to fill in a missing word in a sentence that is read silently). Writing ability is also judged by limited information (the quality of individual sentences that are produced, rather than the quality of paragraphs).

Wechsler Individual Achievement Test, Third Edition (WIAT-III) (ages 4–85 years)

The **WIAT-III** measures achievement in all areas specified in the federal law's definition of learning disabilities: oral expression (while looking at pictures, children name words, produce as many words in a category as they can within a 60-second period, and repeat sentences); listening comprehension (children identify the picture that corresponds to an orally presented word and respond aloud to questions about orally presented passages); early reading skills (children name letters, identify rhyming words, blend phonemes, and recognize words); basic reading skills (children read sight words and nonsense words on separate word lists); reading comprehension (children read passages and respond to oral questions); reading fluency (children read passages and are timed on their speed and accuracy); written expression (children write letters in a 30-second period, produce dictated spelling words, create sentences using different terms, combine sentences, and write a brief essay in a 10-minute period); mathematics calculation (children work math problems); mathematics fluency (children complete addition, subtraction, and multiplication problems in 60-second periods); and mathematical problem-solving (children respond to practical questions involving math reasoning). Reading comprehension more closely resembles what students are asked to do in the classroom (students read passages and answer comprehension questions) than on some of the other broad achievement measures.

Kaufman Test of Educational Achievement, Second Edition (K-TEA-II) (ages 4 years, 6 months–25 years for the comprehensive form; ages 4 years, 6 months–90 years for the brief form)

The **K-TEA-II** comprehensive battery measures decoding of letters and individual words, spelling, reading comprehension (children answer questions orally after silently reading short passages), mathematics computation, and the ability to answer math conceptual and reasoning questions. Subtests were designed to cover sections mandated by IDEA and Reading First. There is also a brief form, which only assesses reading (both decoding and reading comprehension), math, and writing. The comprehensive and brief batteries provide alternate forms, so that progress and/or response to interventions can be ascertained. The K-TEA-II also measures phonological awareness and has a listening-comprehension subtest involving a student listening to paragraphs and then answering questions. On the reading-comprehension subtest, students have to read passages and comprehension questions independently, a component that differs from other testing measures.

Peabody Individual Achievement Test, Revised (PIAT-R/NU) (ages 5–22 years, 11 months)

The **PIAT-R/NU** measures knowledge of general information, decoding of individual words, reading comprehension (children choose which of four pictures depict the content of a sentence they have read), mathematics (children choose which of four answers is correct), spelling (children choose the correct spelling from four choices), and written expression (children copy letters, write from dictation, compose a story). Due to the multiple-choice format on three subtests, the PIAT-R/NU is attractive for use with students with speech and fine-motor weaknesses. The scores gained from the multiple-choice format can be misleading, however, as they are not comparable to classroom tasks that require students to produce, rather than simply recognize, information. In addition, the writing subtest is to be used with caution because of low reliability.

Wide Range Achievement Test, Fourth Edition (WRAT-4) (ages 5–94 years)

The **WRAT-4** measures the ability to read individual letters and words, spell from dictation, and work math calculations. There is a Sentence Comprehension subtest as well, which uses fill-in-the-blank sentences to determine if a student understands the meaning of a sentence. The test has two forms, so that progress and response to interventions can be measured. In contrast to tests that allow unlimited time to decode words, the WRAT-4 allows only 10 seconds. Therefore, the WRAT-4 is likely to identify children with reading disabilities who take a long time to recognize or sound out words. A disadvantage of the WRAT-4 is the absence of full reading-comprehension and math-concept subtests.

Woodcock Reading Mastery Tests, Revised (WRMT-R/NU) (ages 5–75+ years)

The **WRMT-R/NU** measures word identification, pronunciation of nonsense words that follow English structural and phonetic patterns, word comprehension (the child completes antonyms, synonyms, and analogies), and reading comprehension (the child reads a passage silently and supplies a key word that is missing). Form G of the test also includes a subtest that measures the child's ability to identify letters presented in common and uncommon type styles, and a subtest that measures ability to associate abstract visual symbols with familiar words and then "translate" sentences built from these symbols. Criticisms mentioned earlier for the WJ-III/NU (page 448) regarding reading-comprehension procedures pertain here as well. The WRMT-R/NU does impose a 5-second limit for decoding words on the word list. The weaknesses of children who are slow yet accurate decoders will therefore be reflected in the test score. The two forms of the test allow for progress or response to interventions to be assessed.

Diagnostic Achievement Tests Used for Instructional Planning

Gray Oral Reading Test, Fourth Edition (GORT-4) (ages 6–18 years, 11 months)

The **GORT-4** measures a child's speed and accuracy when reading paragraphs aloud and ability to respond to comprehension questions about these paragraphs. It measures reading fluency, since the passages are timed. One of the weaknesses of the test is that the questions are multiple choice, which may not reflect expectations of reading comprehension within the classroom. Still, the measure provides information about reading under timed circumstances, so students with slower rates of reading will perform more weakly on this test than on untimed measures of reading ability.

The Comprehensive Test of Phonological Processing (CTOPP) (ages 5–24 years, 11 months)

The **CTOPP** measures phonological skills, which are a precursor to reading fluency. The test assesses phonological awareness (the ability to recognize that words are broken down into individual phonemes or sounds), phonological memory (the ability to hold phonological information in memory), and rapid naming (the retrieval of phonological information from memory and the ability to follow a sequence quickly and fluidly). The test can provide good information about instructional activities that can build phonological-awareness skills.

Test of Word Reading Efficiency (TOWRE) (ages 6–24 years, 11 months)

The **TOWRE** measures reading accuracy and fluency. Students are asked to read a list of recognizable sight words and a list of nonsense words as quickly as they can in a 45-second period. As on other test measures, there are two forms, so progress from instruction can be determined. The test is very brief but can provide information that can drive instruction and special interventions. Due to the time component, students with slower rates of reading may perform more weakly on this test than on untimed measures of reading performance.

Test of Written Spelling, Fourth Edition (TWS-4)
(grades 1–12)

In the **TWS-4,** spelling words of various levels of difficulty are dictated to the student. There are two forms so that progress and response to intervention can be measured. Information is not broken down regarding spelling patterns, so an error analysis would be necessary to determine what type of spelling errors are occurring.

Test of Written Language, Fourth Edition (TOWL-4)
(ages 9–17 years, 11 months)

The **TOWL-4** measures strengths and weaknesses in written language by having the student write a story in response to a picture. The child's story development, vocabulary level, accuracy of grammatical structure, spelling, punctuation, and capitalization are measured. In addition, the child is asked to write sentences using specific words, spell words accurately, punctuate and capitalize, rewrite illogical sentences, and combine several sentences into one. Performance on the section of this test that doesn't require writing a story may be confounded by poor reading performance, since the child has to read the items independently. Additionally, the pictures that the student has to write stories about may not capture the student's interest. There are two versions of this test, so writing progress and response to intervention can be measured.

Key Math 3 Diagnostic Assessment
(ages 4 years, 6 months–21 years, 11 months)

The **Key Math 3 Diagnostic Assessment** assesses the student's knowledge of basic mathematical concepts (number knowledge, fractions, decimals, percentages, geometric shapes, and principles), operations (addition, subtraction, multiplication, division, mental computation), and applications (measurement, time, money, estimation, interpreting data, and problem-solving). The test is untimed, so students who require additional time for processing math information are provided with unlimited time to do so. However, because of this format, math fluency is not measured. Two formats of the test are provided, so that progress from intervention can be measured.

Dynamic Indicators of Basic Early Literacy Skills (DIBELS)
(grades K–6)

The **DIBELS** is a quick way of measuring early literacy skills, which have been found to be predictors of later reading ability. These include phonological awareness, knowledge of the alphabet, reading fluency, vocabulary, and comprehension. Measures of phonological awareness involve a student identifying and providing the initial sound in a word and generating different sounds in words. Knowledge of the alphabet is determined by having students identify letters and blend sounds together to create nonsense words. Reading fluency is assessed by having students read a passage for a 1-minute period, and tracking the number of errors committed. While the test purports to measure reading comprehension, the manner of doing this is to have students retell the passage read, and the number of words retold is counted. The number of words provided may not reflect a solid understanding of the story; therefore, the use of the DIBELS as a measure of reading comprehension is questionable. There is also a word-use fluency task, which provides a measure of vocabulary and oral language. One of the benefits to this measure is that there are many versions of this test, and it is intended to monitor progress. The brief nature makes it ideal for repeating on a frequent basis to determine whether students respond to intervention.

Informal Reading Inventories (vary from grades 1–12)

These reading inventories ask the student to read aloud word lists and passages of increasing difficulty. The child's reading rate and accuracy are measured, and reading errors are analyzed. Following each passage, comprehension questions are asked that require identification of the main idea in the passage, facts, sequence of events, vocabulary definitions, ability to make inferences from the passage, and critical-thinking ability. Scores may be used to indicate the child's independent reading level (the child is able to read this material without aid and with good comprehension), instructional level (material is challenging but not overly difficult), and frustration level (the child has difficulty recognizing words or comprehending much of what is read). Some inventories, in addition, measure comprehension after students read silently or listen to material being read to them. Contrasting oral-reading comprehension with silent-reading and listening comprehension is helpful in terms of suggesting classroom interventions. (Parents should be cautioned that grade-level scores are not necessarily accurate.) Examples include Analytical Reading Inventory, Bader Reading and Language Inventory, Basic Reading Inventory, Classroom Reading Inventory, Comprehensive Reading Inventory, Informal Reading Inventory, Qualitative Reading Inventory-4, and the Critical Reading Inventory.

MEMORY AND LEARNING MEASURES

Test of Memory and Learning, Second Edition (TOMAL-2) (ages 5–59 years, 11 months)

The **TOMAL-2** measures memory of information presented in both verbal and visual formats. For verbal tasks, a child is asked to remember a list of words, recite stories read aloud, recall word pairs, and remember a list of objects presented both visually and verbally. For nonverbal tasks, the child is asked to recall faces, identify designs when similar-looking items are presented, remember designs in order, and recall dots on a grid. The test also includes a delayed-recall index, which is supposed to measure more delayed retention of information. However, the delayed-recall subtests only measure verbally presented information and are administered after only 30 minutes from initial presentation, so the tasks do not mimic classroom learning very realistically. The measure also provides information regarding the ability to concentrate/sustain attention to testing tasks, the ability to remember information presented in sequence, and whether learning increases with repetition of information. Additional measures look at whether a student remembers associated or related information better than when given no cues to recall (associative recall versus free recall). It can provide good information regarding instructional strategies to be used in the classroom and how a student can study most effectively. Although the measure is normed for five-year-olds, the tasks may be difficult for a five-year- and possibly six-year-old to understand, confounding the test results.

Wide Range Assessment of Memory and Learning, Second Edition (WRAML-2)
(ages 5–90 years)

The **WRAML-2** assesses memory of verbal and nonverbal information, and also has a section measuring attention and concentration. Subtests include story memory (remembering a story read aloud by the examiner), verbal learning (recalling a list of words), design memory (reproducing a design using paper and pencil), picture memory (recalling objects that changed within a picture), finger windows (remembering a sequence of pencil taps among different openings on a card), and number/letter sequencing (recalling a string of letters and numbers). The WRAML-2 can provide information on working memory abilities, and also has a section that looks at recognition of information as opposed to straight recall (generating the information yourself). There is also a delayed measure, which provides information about rapid memory decline, which occurs 15 minutes after initial presentation of testing tasks. As with the TOMAL-2, this time delay does not reflect classroom expectations. There is a memory-screening form as well, but for a thorough investigation of memory abilities, the full test measure is best. Again, caution should be used when administering this test to younger students, as the test is lengthy and may be difficult to understand.

Children's Memory Scale (CMS)
(ages 5–16 years)

Similar to the other memory test measures, the **CMS** assesses verbal and visual memory, in addition to attention and concentration. Students are asked to remember locations of dots, recall stories, remember word pairs, recall number strings, and remember sequences. One aspect of this test that is unique is its provision of short- and long-delay memory tasks. Students are given several opportunities to return to information presented originally, which can provide additional insights about retention of information. It may not be beneficial to give this test to younger students for the same reasons as the other memory measures. Similarly, delayed-recall tasks occur within 30 minutes following initial presentation of information, limiting the assessment of long-term memory.

Wechsler Memory Scale, Fourth Edition (WMS-IV)
(ages 16–90 years, 11 months)

The **WMS-IV** provides a measure of adult memory and learning, similar to the other tests. The test gives information regarding auditory memory (remembering word pairs and stories), visual memory (reproducing designs, recalling design locations), visual working memory (remembering dot overlap among two different stimulus pictures, identifying sequences of symbols), immediate memory, and delayed memory. As with the other test measures, the delayed-memory tasks are administered within 30 minutes from initial time of presentation.

NEUROPSYCHOLOGICAL MEASURES

Conners' Continuous Performance Task, Second Edition (CPT-II) (ages 6 years–adult)

The **CPT-II** is a computerized task that measures attention. There is a brief practice task to ensure that the child understands what he/she is being asked to do. Students are asked to press the computer's space bar or mouse whenever a letter other than X appears on the computer screen. The test measures reaction time, perseveration, consistency in responding, and number of errors committed. The full test takes 14 minutes to administer. Because reliability information is limited for the test, the results should be interpreted cautiously. Additionally, the tedious nature of the task may be viewed as boring to some participants, which may result in inaccurate findings.

NEPSY-II (ages 3–16 years, 11 months)

The **NEPSY-II** is a neuropsychological battery that measures executive functioning and attention (e.g., point to colors when named on tape, then point to the opposite color for response set section, name items as quickly as possible while changing response depending on whether the object is shaded or solid), language abilities (e.g., name a series of letters, colors, and numbers as quickly as possible; determines ability to understand increasing complex directions, ability to process phonological information), memory skills (ability to remember names, faces, and stories), processing of visual-spatial information (copying designs, identifying puzzles within a geometric frame), sensory processing (speed of performing various motor tasks, ability to imitate hand movements, accuracy and speed of maze completion), and social-perception abilities (tests ability to recognize affect of people in photos, ability to understand the fact that others have their own beliefs and how emotions relate to social context). The NEPSY-II directly relates to how a child is functioning in preschool or school and contains thirty-two different testing tasks, although not every subtest needs to be administered. To fully assess all testing areas, the test can take a long time to complete (close to 3 hours). Additional scores provide information on completion time, tendency to respond to items in a similar fashion, delayed versus immediate recall, and free recall compared to cued recall.

INTELLIGENCE MEASURES

Wechsler Intelligence Scale for Children, Fourth Edition (WISC-IV) (ages 6–16 years, 11 months)

The **WISC-IV** is one of the most common intelligence measures administered. It assesses four components of cognitive functioning: verbal comprehension (providing definitions, answering comprehension questions, naming similarities between two concepts), nonverbal reasoning (creating designs with blocks, completing patterns, identifying nonverbal pictures that are related), working memory (stating digits forward and backward, remembering strings of numbers and letters in a specified order), and processing speed (completing a coding task, identifying symbols in an array). The Full Scale IQ score is a composite score, representing performance across all four domains. On this measure, a child has opportunities to demonstrate strengths and weaknesses in several areas: interpretation and problem-solving with words or visual images, speed of information processing, planning and organization, attention, and short-term and long-term memory. The WISC-IV adequately assesses verbal and visual processing of information. Students with slower rates of processing may struggle on this measure, as several of the subtests are timed. There are also heavy language demands, even among some of the nonverbal subtests, and some test items have a cultural bias. As a result, caution should be exercised when the test is administered to students from other cultures and/or students with language difficulties.

Wechsler Preschool and Primary Scale of Intelligence, Third Edition (WPPSI-III) (ages 2 years, 6 months–7 years, 3 months)

The **WPPSI-III** is an easier version of the WISC-IV, designed for younger children. The subtests are briefer and more gamelike, to capture the attention of younger examinees. The test measures verbal comprehension (defining vocabulary terms, answering general-knowledge questions, describing objects/concepts from clues), nonverbal reasoning (creating designs with blocks, identifying the next item in a pattern, and forming groups with common organizational concepts), and processing speed (copying a code pairing symbols and shapes, identifying whether a target symbol appears in a group of shapes). This latter component is assessed in students four years of age and older. Six- and seven-year-olds generally score higher on the WISC-IV. Six- and seven-year-olds who are below average intellectually, however, have more of an opportunity to demonstrate their range of problem-solving skills on the WPPSI-III than on the WISC-IV. As with the WISC-IV, the full-scale score of a student with slow processing speed may be artificially lower due to the timing constraints of some of the subtests.

Wechsler Adult Intelligence Scale, Fourth Edition (WAIS-IV) (ages 16–90 years, 11 months)

The **WAIS-IV,** designed for older teenagers and adults, is a more challenging version of the WISC-IV. It, too, follows the structure of the WISC-IV and the WPPSI-III, measuring verbal comprehension (defining vocabulary words, answering comprehension questions, and providing answers to questions assessing general fund of information), nonverbal reasoning (creating designs from blocks, viewing a completed puzzle and selecting three options that reconstruct the puzzle when combined, looking at a matrix and identifying which item comes next), processing speed (completing a code pairing symbols and numbers, identifying whether a symbol is present in a set of symbols), and working memory (repeating a sequence of digits forward and backward, answering arithmetic problems without paper and pencil). Again, as on the WISC-IV, there are heavy time demands on many subtests, so the test may not provide an accurate reflection of functioning for students with slower rates of processing.

Stanford-Binet Intelligence Scale: Fifth Edition (SB5) (ages 2–85+ years)

The **SB5** is another popular measure of cognitive functioning, with a different breakdown of skills. The SB5 measures fluid reasoning (identifying which items comes next in a pattern or matrix, identifying absurdities in pictures or statements, categorizing common objects, solving verbal analogies), quantitative reasoning (solving math problems), knowledge (answering questions pertaining to general fund of information), defining vocabulary terms, visual-spatial processing (identifying directional terms, including cardinal directions, answering questions involving directionality, creating designs containing form patterns), and working memory abilities (tapping blocks in two different formats, repeating sentences, repeating the last words in multiple questions). The SB5 is a good measure for children who are slow information processors because it contains only one timed subtest. This lack of timing, however, may make the testing session exceedingly long. The SB5 contains a number of manipulatives, which hold the interest of students, and the testing activities are varied and ever changing. Language demands are also minimized on this test measure. It should be noted that this test is less reliable for very young children and those with low cognitive abilities.

Differential Ability Scales, Second Edition (DAS-II) (ages 2 years, 6 months—17 years, 11 months)

The **DAS-II** provides yet another measure of verbal and visual reasoning, but also measures working memory, processing speed, and school readiness in younger students. Subtests require students to copy drawings, identify which item comes next in a matrix, copy block patterns (nonverbal reasoning), name objects, manipulate sounds, match pictures with a common element, define words, understand oral directions (verbal reasoning), remember digits forward and backward, recall designs and pictures, and perform simple mental operations (working memory); it also measures knowledge of prenumerical and numerical concepts (readiness). The DAS-II is generally deemed a more culturally fair measure than other intelligence tests. It contains a number of manipulatives and is a child-friendly test as a result.

Woodcock Johnson Tests of Cognitive Ability (WJ-III) (ages 2–90+ years)

The **WJ-III Tests of Cognitive Ability** measure cognitive abilities in the following areas: comprehension/knowledge, long-term retrieval, visual processing, auditory processing, fluid reasoning, processing speed, and short-term memory. The WJ-III Tests of Cognitive Ability examines fluid reasoning abilities (problem-solving skills) in more detail than the WISC-IV. The verbal-comprehension section involves more than a student defining words (as on the WISC-IV); it contains sections measuring synonyms, antonyms, and analogies. The test also measures the following areas: Efficiency, General Information, Retrieval Fluency, Decision Speed, Planning, Fluid Reasoning, Comprehensive Knowledge, Visual-Spatial Thinking, Processing Speed, Short-Term Memory, and Broad Attention Knowledge. Test results should be interpreted cautiously for preschool-age children, as other test measures may provide more reliable and valid results.

Kaufman Assessment Battery for Children, Second Edition (KABC-II) (ages 3–18 years)

The **KABC-II** measures problem-solving ability using a variety of tasks requiring sequential processing (arrangement of stimuli in serial order) or simultaneous processing (spatial and organizational problems that require the processing of many stimuli at once). Additional tasks measure planning, learning, and general fund of knowledge. Mental Processing Composite subtests minimize reliance on verbal ability or previously learned information. The KABC-II should not be the primary instrument used to measure intelligence for several reasons: it puts too much weight on simultaneous processing; it is not challenging enough to validly assess gifted children; it does not tabulate language skills (a significant predictor of achievement) into the Mental Processing Composite; and it can yield a significant discrepancy between mental processing and achievement scores that is entirely caused by test construction rather than the child's learning patterns. However, the measure is less culturally loaded than other test measures, as the subtests were created to minimize verbal cues and language, and the test contains limited cultural content. A nonverbal score can be computed for students whose verbal skills are significantly delayed.

SOCIAL AND EMOTIONAL ADJUSTMENT MEASURES
Adaptive Behavior

Vineland Adaptive Behavior Scales, Second Edition (Vineland-II) Interview Edition (ages birth–90 years) Teacher Edition (ages 3–21 years, 11 months)

The **Vineland-II** assesses social competence by interviewing a parent or having a teacher complete a rating scale regarding the behavior of the student. Adaptive behavior is measured in four areas: spoken and written communication, daily living skills and behavior in the community, sensitivity to and socialization with others, and gross- and fine-motor coordination skills. A Maladaptive Behavior section score is also provided. The Expanded Form of the Vineland has sufficient numbers of items to assist in specific intervention planning.

Scales of Independent Behavior, Revised (SIB-R) (ages infancy–80+ years)

The **SIB-R** is an interview instrument that asks the parent very specific questions about the child's development in several areas: gross- and fine-motor skills, social interaction, language comprehension, language expression, eating, toileting, dressing, personal self-care, domestic skills, time and punctuality, money and value, work skills, and home/community functioning. The test contains a short form and an early-development form. A support score predicts the amount of support needed based on adaptive-behavior ratings. Additionally, an individual plan recommendation form allows individuals to plan for and monitor supports and needs.

AAMR Adaptive Behavior Scale-School, Second Edition (ABS-S:2) (ages 3–21 years)

The **ABS-S:2** is a rating scale completed by a teacher. The test is divided into two sections: coping skills important for independent functioning, and personality and behavior disorders. The test measures behavior and social adjustment of children.

Behavioral Questionnaires

Behavior Assessment System for Children, Second Edition (BASC-2) Teacher & Parent Rating Scale (ages 2–21 years) Self-Report Rating Scale (ages 8–25 years)

The **BASC-2** is a set of rating scales examining the social and emotional functioning of students. There are three versions of the test: a parent rating scale, a teacher rating scale, and a student self-report rating scale. The measure assesses behavior (activity level, aggression, tendency to follow rules), emotionality (display of anxious and depressive symptoms, reports of physical problems), learning and attention span, social skills, display of atypical behaviors, and adaptive skills (adaptability, leadership, communication skills, study skills). On the self-report scale, additional measures examine interpersonal relations, self-esteem, and relations with parents. Individuals respond to True/False statements, and rate statements on the frequency of occurrence ("Never," "Sometimes," "Often," or "Almost Always"). The test includes validity indexes to check to see if students, teachers, and parents are answering honestly and consistently. There is also an observation component and an interview to gather information about the student, which can be conducted in addition to the rating scales. Results may be helpful for identifying problematic behavior and difficulties that may be interfering with academic success.

Child Behavior Checklist (CBCL)
Preschool Forms (ages 1 year, 6 months–5 years)
School-Age Forms (ages 6–18 years)
Adult Forms (ages 18–59 years)

The **CBCL** contains a list of behavioral problems that are rated by the parent as not true, somewhat true, or very true. Children are compared with same-age peers on areas such as anxiety, depression, lack of communication, obsessive-compulsive behavior, somatic complaints, social withdrawal, hyperactivity, aggression, and delinquent behavior. Self-report and teacher report forms are also available. As with any behavior checklist, it is helpful to obtain input from both parents and several teachers. Behavior, as measured by these scales, is in the eye of the beholder—that is, each parent and teacher is likely to view the student differently. Therefore, the best perspective on the child's usual behavioral tendencies is gained by comparing multiple viewpoints. Observations and a clinical interview for children and adolescents are also part of the information-gathering process. There are six scales that relate to disorders listed in the *Diagnostic Statistical Manual* (anxiety problems, attention-deficit/hyperactivity disorder, conduct problems, oppositional defiant problems, somatic problems, and affective problems), which can give insight into mental-health difficulties a child may be experiencing.

Conners' Teacher & Parent Rating Scale, Revised
(ages 3–17 years)
Conners-Wells' Adolescent Self-Report Scale
(ages 12–17 years)

The **Conners' Scales** are checklists on which parents and teachers rate a variety of behavior problems on a four-point scale. Behavioral characteristics include oppositional, cognitive problems, inattention, hyperactivity, anxiety, perfectionism, shyness, social problems, and psychosomatic concerns. Additionally, all rating scales produce an ADHD Index, which identifies symptoms of ADHD, and a DSM-IV Symptom Checklist, which may identify other disorders which could be interfering with successful functioning. Both long and short forms of these scales are available. As many of the items on the hyperactivity scale involve acting out and annoying behaviors, this scale may not identify the child with an attention deficit who is well socialized.

Personality Inventory for Children, Second Edition (PIC-2)
(ages 5–19 years)

The **PIC-2** uses a true/false format and asks the parent to rate 275 items pertaining to the child's adjustment, achievement, intelligence, developmental skills, psychosomatic complaints, depression, family relations, delinquency, withdrawal, anxiety, psychosis, hyperactivity, and social skills. A shorter behavioral summary can be completed as well.

Projective Measures

Roberts Apperception Test for Children, Second Edition (RATC-2) (ages 6–15 years)
Thematic Apperception Test (TAT)
Children's Apperception Test (CAT) (ages 3–10 years)
Sentence Completions
Human Figure Drawings
Kinetic Family Drawings

Projective tests are designed to measure emotions that the child projects into stories told in response to pictures on "apperception" cards, words used to fill in blanks in sentences (such as "Mothers should ____"), or pictures drawn about the family and classroom. Validity is poor because evaluation of the child's responses involves a great deal of subjective interpretation by the examiner, and interpretations will differ from examiner to examiner. (When results from these measures are shared with you, ask to see your child's responses so you can add your own interpretations.)

Self-Concept Measures

Piers-Harris Children's Self-Concept Scale, Second Edition (Piers-Harris 2) (ages 7–18 years)
Multidimensional Self-Concept Scale (ages 9–19 years)
Tennessee Self-Concept Scale, Second Edition (TSCS-2) (ages 7–90 years)
Coopersmith Self-Esteem Inventory (ages 8–15 years)
Self-Esteem Index (ages 7–18 years)

Self-concept measures generally ask children to read a statement (such as, "I am an unhappy person") and indicate whether they agree or disagree with that statement. Sometimes open-ended sentence stems also are completed, and the child may be asked to list his or her strengths and weaknesses. While useful information can be derived from these scales, the positive and negative intent is obvious to children, and often they will respond the way they think others expect them to respond. This is accounted for on the Piers-Harris 2, as two validity indexes are included, one examining the tendency to respond randomly and the other measuring biased responding. Scores on the Piers-Harris 2 can be derived for overall self-esteem or subareas of self-esteem such as appearance, athletic skills, intelligence, academic skills, or social skills.

DEVELOPMENTAL MEASURES
Tests of Language Development

Peabody Picture Vocabulary Test, Fourth Edition (PPVT-4)
(ages 2 years, 6 months–90+years)

The **PPVT-4** measures vocabulary by having the student point to the correct picture (from among four) that depicts a dictated word. Children who have poor visual comprehension of pictures, or who tend to respond impulsively, may earn low scores on the PPVT-4 despite adequate language skills. Because the PPVT-4 assesses only one aspect of language development, it should be used in conjunction with tests that measure other aspects of language ability, such as comprehension of grammatical structure and oral communication skills. There are two forms so that progress and/or response to intervention can be ascertained.

Clinical Evaluation of Language Fundamentals, Fourth Edition (CELF-4)
(ages 5–21 years)

The **CELF-4** assesses overall language abilities, including receptive understanding, expressive language, language structure, language content, and working memory. The test also gives information about the impact of the student's language abilities on classroom performance and social functioning.

Goldman Fristoe Test of Articulation, Second Edition (GFTA-2)
(ages 2–21 years)

The **GFTA-2** assesses speech-sound production using both spontaneous and imitative formats for words and within conversations. Thirty-nine consonant sounds and blends are used to identify articulation difficulties in the beginning, middle, or ending of words. The test measures the test taker's ability to produce the sounds in words, not in conversation, so scores might not accurately reflect a child's struggles with conversational speech.

Test of Auditory Comprehension of Language, Third Edition (TACL-3)
(ages 3–9 years, 11 months)

The **TACL-3** tests auditory comprehension by having children point to the correct picture (from among three choices) when the examiner dictates single words, words with modifiers, short sentences that vary in grammatical form, and complex sentences. As on the PPVT-4 (above), weak perceptual discrimination in analyzing the pictures and impulsivity may reduce a child's score, even if language comprehension is good. The TACL-3 should be supplemented with tasks that measure the child's expressive language abilities.

Test of Language Development: Primary, Fourth Edition (TOLD:P-4)
(ages 4–8 years, 11 months)

The **TOLD: P-4** measures the younger child's semantic abilities (picture vocabulary and oral vocabulary), syntax (understanding sentence structure, repeating dictated sentences, and using appropriate grammatical forms), and phonology (word discrimination and articulation) through both receptive and expressive channels.

Test of Language Development: Intermediate, Fourth Edition (TOLD: I-4) (ages 8–17 years)

The **TOLD: I-4** measures semantic ability and syntax by means of combining sentences, oral vocabulary, ordering words within sentences, understanding of abstract relationships, recognition of grammatical sentences, and identifying multiple meanings of words.

Test of Adolescent and Adult Language, Fourth Edition (TOAL-4) (ages 12–24 years, 11 months)

The **TOAL-4** helps determine areas of relative strength and weakness in language abilities by means of several tasks: naming a word that matches a definition, providing a word at the end of a sentence that makes sense, completing an analogy, writing words with the same meanings as other words, combining two sentences into one when writing, and dictating sentences, including appropriate punctuation. The test produces scores in three areas: Spoken Language, Written Language, and General Language.

Test of Language Competence, Expanded Edition (TLC) (ages 5–18 years)

The **TLC** measures sophisticated semantics, syntax, and conversational skill by means of several tasks: the student reads a sentence that could mean more than one thing and identifies both meanings; the student reads two related statements and then chooses inferences that are appropriate; the student creates a sentence given three words and a picture; the student must explain the meaning of sentences with metaphors.

Tests of Visual-Perceptual and Motor Development

Bender Visual-Motor Gestalt Test (Bender-Gestalt II) (ages 3+ years)

The **Bender-Gestalt II** measures visual-motor ability by presenting fourteen geometric figures for the child to copy, one at a time. The products are scored for distortions of shape, rotations, integration difficulties, and perseveration (for example, extra lines or too many dots). Because most eight- to nine-year-old children can reproduce all the designs perfectly, beyond age eight the test is useful only for distinguishing whether a child's perceptual-motor maturity is below that of an eight-year-old's. A component assessing visual-motor memory is also included. Additional tests measure motor and perceptual skills to help identify visual-motor deficits.

Beery-Buktenica Developmental Test of Visual-Motor Integration, Fifth Edition (VMI 5)
(ages 2–100 years)

The **VMI 5** measures perceptual-motor ability by having the child copy up to twenty-seven geometric forms within a drawing booklet. There are both long and short forms of the test. The VMI tends to produce higher scores than the Bender-Gestalt II, perhaps because performance is facilitated by VMI designs being presented within a structured space with the child copying designs in adjacent areas. Supplemental visual-perception and motor-coordination tasks may also be included to identify the cause of difficulties on the VMI 5.

Test of Visual Perceptual Skills, Third Edition (TVPS-3)
(ages 4–18 years)

The **TVPS-3** assesses a child's ability to make sense out of what is seen (visual-perceptual skills), with tasks measuring visual discrimination (the ability to differentiate one item from another), visual memory (the ability to hold nonverbal information in memory for a brief period), visual-spatial relationships, form constancy, visual-sequential memory (the ability to remember a sequence of nonverbal information), visual figure-ground, and visual closure. Items are presented in multiple-choice format, and children can respond either by pointing or using words, making the test appropriate for students with speech/language or motor difficulties. The test can be given individually or to a group.

Developmental Test of Visual Perception, Second Edition (DTVP-2)
(ages 4–9 years)

Subtests on the **DTVP-2** examine eye-hand coordination, spatial relations, figure-ground, copying information without an academic component, visual motor speed, visual closure, and form constancy. It allows you to examine "pure" visual perception without motor-response and visual-motor integration skills.

Motor-Free Visual Perception Test, Third Edition (MVPT-3)
(ages 4–70 years)

The **MVPT-3** measures visual perception by having the child select the correct figure during five types of tasks: spatial relationships, visual discrimination, figure-ground relationships, visual closure, and visual memory. The MVPT-3 has questionable validity but may yield some information of value when used in combination with a copying measure such as those described above.

Peabody Developmental Motor Scales, Second Edition (PDMS-2)
(ages birth–5 years)

The **PDMS-2** assesses fine-motor and gross-motor development in young children. Subtests assess motor skills that develop early in life, including reflexes, body control, locomotion, object manipulation, grasping, and hand-eye coordination. The test helps identify areas for remediation.

Bruininks-Oseretsky Test of Motor Proficiency, Second Edition (BOT-2) (ages 4–21 years)

The **BOT-2** measures large- and fine-motor functioning on subtests that sample running speed, balance, coordination of limbs, muscle strength, speed of motor response, coordination of eye and hand movements, precision of eye and hand movements, and hand and finger dexterity. Information is compiled regarding fine-motor control, hand coordination, body coordination, strength, and overall motor functioning.

Appendix B

The Development of Reading, Writing, Mathematics, and Learning Strategies

This section describes the sequence in which children typically acquire skills in reading, writing, mathematics, and thinking and memory. Significant delays in any of these areas should be investigated promptly, so that your child's needs can be appropriately addressed in school. Note that children who are not meeting grade expectations are at increased risk for performing poorly on standardized tests, which may affect decisions about promotion (and ultimately graduation). Ask the school to keep you informed about both your child's individual progress *and* where he or she stands with regard to grade-level performance standards.

THE DEVELOPMENT OF READING SKILLS

Kindergarten
Decoding. A kindergarten child can typically sing the alphabet song; point to/name uppercase and lowercase alphabet letters; recognize some commonly seen words (e.g., *stop,* McDonald's, Sesame Street, own name). Children have begun to associate letters with their sounds, match simple words to corresponding pictures, and make rhymes. There is growing awareness of whether words begin or end with the same sound; of developing an ability to break spoken words into syllables and blend a dictated sound with a stem to make a word (d og); and there is recognition that reading proceeds from left to right and from top to bottom on a page. Children have an easier time "cracking the code" when introduced to fewer letters at a time, especially "sustainable" sounds (sounds that can be stretched out . . . ssss, mmmm . . . versus "stop consonants" . . . t or b . . . that don't persist long enough to be easily processed). Children also respond better

to working on larger sound units in "linguistic" (rhyming; h-*at*, m-*at*; *sa*-t, *sa*-d) patterns; these don't require the child to break down, remember, and organize every sound in a word, avoid vowel confusion, and require less blending skill.

Comprehension. Children can interpret picture stories; recognize/compare/ contrast facts in a story; are aware of time sequence in a story and predict outcome; recognize poetry; distinguish reality from fantasy.

First Grade

Decoding. Most children can identify consonant sounds and the sound heard in the middle of a dictated word; read long and short vowels and some vowel teams (e.g., *ee, ea*) and consonant diagraphs (e.g., *ch, sh, th*). Growing ability to break dictated words into individual sounds; can read word families (e.g., c-*at*, h-*at*, r-*at*). Growing sight vocabulary; begin to divide words into syllables by recognizing grammar cues (*ing, ed*), prefixes (*un, dis*), suffixes (*ly, er*), root words (*big, slow*), irregular spelling patterns (*ight, kn*), and syllable types (*it, ite*). Children need to see a word approximately thirty-five times before it will be automatically recognized. They learn concrete words (e.g., *table* versus *about*) and words that are phonetically regular and presented in context faster. Aware of root words, endings, compound words, and contractions; typically scan the word twice before reading it. Over the year students progress from reading an average of five words per minute to 40 to 60 words per minute. Ten errors per minute is common.

Comprehension. Children can recognize main idea and cause/effect in a story; draw conclusions; follow simple written directions; are aware of author, title, table of contents, alphabetical order; recognize a play; interpret maps and globes.

Second Grade

Decoding. Children show growing mastery of harder phonetic skills (e.g., *kn, wr, gh, ck, lk, ir, ur, oi, au, oa*); sound out unfamiliar words based on individual letter sounds, familiar spelling patterns (e.g., *tion*), root words, endings. They can identify words from contextual clues; experience less confusion with reversible letters (*b–d*); read new words by analogy (*cup-pup, mother-brother*); find it easy to substitute one consonant for another in a word. They vary pitch, stress, volume when reading aloud; are aware of syllabication rules, prefixes/suffixes, changing *y* to *i* or *f/fe* to *v* before adding ending; are more stable in visual fixations (additional letters within sight while fixating on a word aren't "dancing" or confusing). Reading rate increases to 80 to 100 words per minute.

Comprehension. Students compare/evaluate information; recognize character, setting, motive, resolution of a story; predict; use library for simple research purposes; interpret graphs; use dictionary.

Third Grade

Decoding. Increasing sight vocabulary (little letter-by-letter sounding out required); reading focus shifts from decoding to comprehension; rapid extension of sight vocabulary and word-analysis skills (e.g., *igh, eight*). Students interpret homophones (e.g., *way, weigh*) and homographs (e.g., grizzly *bear*, *bear* arms); use comprehension skills to read word parts with inconsistent pronunciations (e.g., s-*aid*, m-*aid*; l-*ove*, st-*ove*). Reversals of letters and words generally disappear (*saw-was*); reading speed increases with development of silent-reading skills. It is common to subvocalize when reading silently.

Comprehension. Children read selectively to locate information; distinguish fiction/nonfiction, fact/opinion, synonym/antonym; recall prior knowledge and relate it to new content; recognize author's bias and purpose; use index, captions, subheadings, margin notes; use encyclopedia, telephone directory; interpret diagrams; read for both knowledge and recreation. When comprehension breaks down, children employ strategies such as rereading, slowing down, scanning ahead for clarification, looking at visuals, looking up new vocabulary words, connecting what is read to one's prior knowledge, rephrasing and thinking about what was just read, picturing what was just read in one's head. Most can follow modeled self-questioning strategies to aid comprehension (e.g., CAPS for the basic questions: Who are the *c*haracters? What is the *a*im or purpose? What *p*roblem occurs in the story? How is the problem *s*olved?).

Fourth Grade

Decoding. Students begin to develop different reading styles/rates for different purposes (e.g., skimming); increase silent reading rate; expand vocabulary; need only one visual fixation per word (lasts about 1/4 second). Reading rate reaches 100 to 180 words per minute.

Comprehension. Students learn to locate and use references; recognize plot and implied main idea; understand idioms/multiple meanings. Can paraphrase or summarize a story or article; select/evaluate/organize study materials; discriminate different forms of writing (e.g., folk tale, science fiction, biography); appreciate author's point of view; considerable independent reading expected in school; can read newspaper, restaurant menu.

Fifth Grade

Comprehension. Most children can make generalizations; recognize theme. Students learn to use copyright page, preface, cross-references; become familiar with more literary forms (e.g., autobiography, fable, legend); reason using syllogisms (e.g., if a = b and b = c, then a = c); can read many popular magazines. Reading errors are reduced to one or two per minute.

Middle School

Reading. Can read many adult-level books. The average reading rate remains about 140 to 150 words per minute; highly skilled readers may read as fast as 300 words per minute.

Comprehension. Students increasingly understand paradoxes; appreciate elements of style (e.g., imagery/foreshadowing/flashback/symbolism/irony/mood); recognize biased writing and propaganda; use appendices, atlas, almanac, appropriate reference sources; recognize figures of speech such as personification (e.g., *the computer yawned and spit out the dish*), hyperbole (intentional exaggeration, e.g., *I waited an eternity*), onomatopoeia (words that imitate sounds, e.g., *cuckoo*). They can independently follow internalized questioning strategies to aid comprehension (e.g., RAM: *r*ead the passage, *a*sk the "wh" questions, *m*ark the answers as I come across them in the passage).

THE DEVELOPMENT OF WRITING SKILLS

Kindergarten

Children develop ability to hold and use pencils in three-finger grasp; trace/copy/write letters, their name, and simple sight words; print letters from memory; write short "stories" using dashes for words or invented spellings. Forming letters with vertical and horizontal strokes (*T, L, F*) is easier than writing those containing diagonals (*K*) or curves that meet lines (*R*).

First Grade

Students typically use traditional as well as invented spellings; work on copying letters and words; write simple sentences; begin to write short poems, invitations, and compositions. Children try to use words that describe what they see, hear, and feel as well as how things look, act, feel; capitalize the first word of a sentence, first and last names, names of streets/towns/the school, and *I*; add a period at the end of sentences and after numbers in a list; print from left to right and stay reasonably close to the line. Letters vary in size, spacing, alignment, proportion, slant, pencil pressure, and form. Letter reversals and reversals of sequence of letters in a word are common. Children can dictate a simple story far better than write it themselves.

Second Grade

Most students write letters legibly and use appropriate size; understand how writing should be laid out (e.g., margins); and can combine short sentences into paragraphs. Spelling and grammatical expression continue to improve. Students use words with similar and opposite meanings in writing; alphabetize; capitalize important words in book titles, proper names, Mr./Mrs./Miss/Ms.; add question mark at the end of a question; add commas after salutation and closing of a letter; add comma between the month/year and city/state; avoid running sentences together with *and*; begin to use cursive; begin to develop proofreading skills. Number reversals are resolved before letter reversals.

Third Grade

Children use both printing and cursive writing; write short passages expressing a central idea; sequence ideas well and use expanded vocabulary; identify/use various sentence forms (e.g., declarative, interrogative/exclamatory); combine short, choppy sentences into longer ones; use interesting beginning and ending sentences; avoid run-on sentences; use synonyms; distinguish meaning and spelling of homonyms; use the prefix *un* and the suffix *less*; capitalize month/day/common holidays/first word in a line of verse/*Dear/Sincerely*; add periods after abbreviations/initials; use apostrophes in common contractions (e.g., isn't); add commas in a list; indent; spell many words in sight vocabulary (including irregular words such as *eight*). Most students don't engage in much planning; can proofread their own and others' work; copy accurately from the book or blackboard; can fill out simple forms. Letter reversals disappear. The average number of words written about a picture is 85.

Fourth Grade

The majority of children write in cursive; develop interesting paragraphs and a sense of the writing process (outline first, write, proofread); choose words that appeal to the senses or that precisely explain a point; capitalize names of cities/ states/organizations; use apostrophe to show possession, hyphen to divide word at the end of a line, exclamation point, colon after salutation, quotation marks, comma before quotation in a sentence, period after outline items or Roman numerals; use command sentences; avoid sentence fragments; select appropriate titles; make simple outlines; write/tell stories that have characters and plot, including information related to time, setting, action, goals, motives, feelings, thoughts of characters, relationships, and an ending. Most can spell approximately 80 percent of their sight vocabulary correctly.

Fifth Grade

Students start to vary their type of sentences, including the imperative. Subjects and verbs agree; ideas are clearly stated in more than one paragraph. Most can keep to the topic; use compound subjects and predicates, antonyms/prefixes/ suffixes/contractions/compound words/words with sensory images/rhyme and rhythm; and have greater precision in choice of words. Students use the dictionary for definitions/syllables/pronunciation; capitalize names of streets/places/ persons/countries/oceans/trade names/beginning items in outlines/titles with a name (e.g., President Roosevelt); use quotation marks or underlining for titles; classify words by parts of speech; use subheads in outlines; write from an outline; write dialogue; recognize topic sentences; enjoy writing/receiving letters, e-mail; enjoy keeping diaries or journals.

Middle School

Students typically plan and revise using notes; develop increasing sophistication in ideas and expression, including themes such as morality and causation; choose accurate/effective/appropriate words and phrases. They increasingly edit to improve style and effect; avoid wordiness and unnecessary repetition; use complex sentences; avoid vagueness and omissions; develop paragraphs with details/ reasons/examples/comparisons; check for accuracy of statements; use logical transitions between sentences, ideas, and events; connect ideas with transition words that signal relationships (*although, however, first, finally, most important*); develop paragraphs with topic sentences; add introductions and conclusions; check reasoning; elaborate ideas; and are creative. Typically they can proofread work critically and make modifications that affect meaning (reorganize, improve beginnings and endings, delete insignificant details). Stories are believable, even if fantasy; unique style is developing (tone, choice of vocabulary, different sentence forms); may begin to use plays on words and metaphors. Students learn to use several sources to prepare a report; make a bibliography; capitalize the first word of a quote and adjectives of race and nationality; punctuate appropriately; uses footnotes; learn note-taking skills. The average number of words written about a picture jumps to 200. A unique handwriting style has developed in most students, especially in girls, that persists through life. On average children write 70 characters per minute.

THE DEVELOPMENT OF MATHEMATICS SKILLS

Kindergarten

Children typically match/sort/name objects by size, color and shape; count/add up to nine objects (even if adding a set of two objects and a set of one, the child will recount all objects); recognize that the last number "word" counted indicates the total number of items in the set; evaluate objects by quantity, dimensions, size (e.g., more/less, longer/shorter, tall/tallest, bigger/same); recite and recognize numbers 1–20; write numbers 1–10; understand concepts of addition and subtraction; know symbols +, -, =; recognize whole versus half; understand ordinals (first, 5th); learn beginning concepts of weight, time (e.g., before/after; understand lunch is at 12:00; tell time to the hour), money (know value of pennies, nickels, dimes), and temperature (hotter/colder); aware of locations (e.g., above/below, left/right, nearest/farthest); interpret simple maps, graphs and tallies.

First Grade

Students learn to count/read/write/order numbers to 99; begin learning addition and subtraction facts; "counting up" (on fingers, objects) speeds up memorization of number facts. Children perform simple addition/subtraction problems (e.g., 23+11); understand multiplication as repeated addition; count by 2s, 5s and 10s; identify odd/even numbers; estimate answers; understand 1/2, 1/3, 1/4; flexibly reason that things can look different but be the same (2+4 and 3+3) or appear the same but be different (the 4 in 1/4, 40, 400); gain elementary knowledge of the calendar (e.g., count how many days to my birthday), time (tell time to half hour; understand schedules; read digital clock), measurement (cup, pint, quart, liter, inch, centimeter, kilogram, pound), and money (know value of a quarter; compare prices); solve simple number-story problems; read bar graphs and charts. Adding with objects is far superior to adding with numerals.

Second Grade

Children can identify/write numbers to 999; add/subtract two- and-three digit numbers with and without regrouping (e.g., 223+88, 124-16); multiply by 2, 3, 4, 5; count by 3s, 5s, 10s, 100s; can add mentally by starting with the number in one set (5), and counting on as many numbers as are in the second set (5+3 = 5 . . . 6, 7, 8); read/write Roman numerals to XII; count money and make change up to $10.00; recognize days of the week, months, and seasons of the year on a calendar; tell time to five minutes on a clock with hands; learn basic measurements (inch, foot, pint, pound); recognize equivalents (e.g., two quarters = one half; four quarts = one gallon); divide area into 2/3, 3/4, 10ths; graph simple data.

Third Grade

Students understand place value to thousands; subtract mentally by counting up from the number in the smaller set, or counting down from the number in the larger set; add and subtract four-digit numbers (e.g., 1017-978); learn multiplication facts to 9 x 9; solve simple multiplication and division problems (642 x or ÷ 2); relate multiplication to repeated addition, and division to repeated subtraction; learn harder Roman numerals. Students are introduced to fractions (can add/estimate/order simple fractions; understand mixed numbers; read fractions of an inch) and geometry (can identify hexagon, pentagon; understand diameter, radius, volume, area); can understand decimals; begin to learn about negative numbers, probability, percentage, ratio; can solve harder number-story problems. Half of children "count up" and half recall number facts.

Fourth Grade
Children learn to add columns of three or more numbers; multiply three-digit by two-digit numbers (348x34); perform simple division (44÷22); reduce fractions to lowest terms; add/subtract fractions with different denominators (3/4+2/3); add/subtract decimals; convert decimals to percents; count/make change for up to $20.00; estimate time (can measure time in hours, minutes, seconds); compute area of rectangles; identify parallel, perpendicular, intersecting lines; calculate weight in tons, length in meters, volume in cubic centimeters. Children can ignore extraneous information in word problems and interpret word problems where the language implies a decrease (suggests subtraction) but the opposite is true (must add).

Fifth Grade
By the end of the year most children can multiply three-digit numbers (962x334); do harder division problems (102÷32); add, subtract, multiply mixed numbers; divide a whole number by a fraction; represent fractions as decimals, ratios, percents; add, subtract, multiply with decimals; divide a decimal by a whole number; understand use of equations, formulas, "working backward"; estimate products/quotients. Students begin to learn about exponents, greatest common factors, bases, prime factors, composite numbers, integers; understand percent, ratios; understand mean, median, mode; measure area/circumference of a circle, perimeter/areas of triangles and parallelograms; perform metric conversions; use compass, protractor; read scale drawings. Math-fact retrieval becomes equal to that of adults, which facilitates mental calculation.

Middle School
Students master order of operations in complex problems; learn to multiply/divide two fractions; add, subtract, multiply, divide decimals to the thousandth; convert decimals to fractions, percents, ratios; understand real, rational, irrational numbers and different number bases; calculate square and cube roots; estimate percentages/proportions; calculate discount, sales tax, restaurant tip; understand markup, commission, simple interest, compound interest, percent increase/decrease; understand angles (complementary, supplementary, adjacent, straight, congruent . . .); calculate volume of a cylinder; calculate area of a circle; understand equilateral, isosceles, scalene, obtuse figures; organize sets of data; graph coordinates, transformations, reflections, rotations, equations with two variables; solve equations by substitution; begin to learn about conditional probability, permutations, factorial notation, relative frequency, normal curve, Pythagorean theorem; deepen understanding of previously taught skills and concepts.

THE DEVELOPMENT OF LEARNING
AND MEMORY STRATEGIES

Kindergarten

The attention of kindergarten children is drawn more to familiar than novel objects; color and shape attributes of tasks attract attention and increase recall, as does handling three-dimensional objects. Pointing out important features also increases attention and recall. Most do better with recognition than recall (point to a *cow* versus *name this animal*); can attend to a single activity for about 7 minutes. Children may set a goal to remember but don't know how to go about remembering unless instructed; do not spontaneously rehearse information in order to aid recall; can pay attention to categories to increase recall (*animals, foods*), but only when directed to do so; tend to ignore obvious cues that would stimulate recall. Most can distinguish the most important material in an age-appropriate story; recognize that noise, disinterest, and a wandering mind hinder attentiveness and learning; recognize that looking at information isn't sufficient to remember it (one must "work" on it). Children remember much better if instructed to verbalize what is being observed and realize that the more information to be remembered, the harder the task; most can generate one strategy to help remember, but they seldom apply it; they tend to retrieve information through simple strategies such as association cues ("*I'm hungry; I stopped at the principal's office when I came to school; did I leave my lunch there?*").

First Grade

Most students need to literally see or be shown the similarities between new and old objects/information to have the old information help them understand and store the new; can be guided to use a memory strategy (e.g., repetition) but won't seek out the best strategy on their own; have immediate memory spans of about seven items (increases with the use of a memory strategy). Attention and recall increase dramatically when teachers model a task and students repeat the teachers' verbal prompts ("*to add, first I . . . then I . . .*"); when students are instructed to rehearse and name information aloud memorization improves. Repetition aids recall; children can generate images to aid recall but are inefficient at using them to memorize information. Most recognize that remembering is easier the more familiar a task, the more time is available to study, and when pointing or answering "yes-no" is required (versus verbal or written recall); realize that categorization assists recall of random material. Children tend to see themselves as people who remember well and never forget (hence, using strategies to assist learning doesn't automatically come to mind); a child can be helped to remember if given a cue at the time of memorizing, and cued again at the time of recall (e.g., "*To remember where <u>Florida</u> is, let's draw <u>a sun and beach</u> on the U.S. map*"). Encouragement of self-verbalization (talking oneself through a task) markedly increases success, even in behavior ("*I'm not going to walk past Charlie's desk, because he'll poke me and get me in trouble*").

Second Grade

Children become more selective and thorough in attending to relevant features of a task without being guided; reason and remember more effectively because information is interpreted in relation to similar information learned in the past (the more new material can be linked to familiar information, the more memorable it becomes); use different strategies on successive problems of the same type (so they are inconsistent). Immediate recall ability begins to improve due to increasing knowledge base; information processing becomes more rapid; and we see growing strategy use. Children spontaneously rehearse information in order to remember it, but need a list to work from (e.g., number facts; gifts to shop for); categorizing helps more than repetition when learning lists of information. Most children don't judge whether directions have been understood (need to try the task to see if it was understood). They begin to attend to the context to increase understanding, but can't self-generate images to help with recall—they need visual cues (can remember to take sneakers to school if the sneakers are left by the door, but won't remember if they go to bed and simply "imagine" taking the sneakers the next day).

Third Grade
Activity level typically declines in active children, and is often replaced by finger/pencil tapping, leg wagging, chair rocking, and intermittent attention. Children have more past knowledge to connect with new information to aid recall; more automatically find prior knowledge in memory and connect it with new information; begin to discover memory strategies without needing them to be modeled or suggested by the teacher. Students start to think categorically about information, which then increases recall (*"What sports equipment must I remember to take on vacation? Which books?"*); inclination is to use functional associations as memory aids (e.g., linking *bathing suit* with remembering to pack the *sand shovel*); can self-generate images to represent a story line, and this augments recall; can use mnemonics made up by the teacher to increase recall (HOMES = the Great Lakes).

Fourth Grade
Memory improves as children get better at inferring deeply about and elaborating on meaning (*describing, interpreting, differentiating, questioning, hypothesizing, comparing and contrasting, making judgments, analyzing, explaining, predicting, evaluating, generalizing*), and there is an improving sense of how to get organized and when one has studied well enough to remember—a greater awareness that one can remember unrelated items best if the items are linked through a story, through opposites, or through categorization (memorize the South American countries as a group, and then the Central American countries); increasing recognition that it's easier to recall information if translated into one's own words, and that information that is too similar will be confused and less memorable (memorize *one* word in a homonym pair until it is well known, then the other word); ability to decide on multiple strategies to remember, relying more on oneself than on an external prompt (such as Mom); recognition that memorization skills vary from person to person and situation to situation; recognition that one doesn't have an equally good memory in all situations (math facts versus story).

Fifth Grade
Most students can detect inconsistencies in text and errors in their own work; study longer when the work is more difficult; consider different perspectives on an issue; use memory strategies on their own without prompting. More sophisti-

cated strategies replace older ones, but the old persist as well (e.g., counting on fingers while also using memorized number facts). Children verbalize (rehearse) information even when not visible (e.g., list of children coming to the birthday party); tend to rehearse one item at a time versus a small group of items. Many don't reinspect the text when they don't remember it; need to be given mnemonic aids, self-questioning techniques, and told to use verbal self-instruction if this hasn't yet become automatic; most recognize how much studying is necessary in order to do well.

Middle School

Increasingly, students can set a goal, make decisions about what to attend to, avoid responding to distractions, try new strategies when old one's don't work; ask for clarification; overview reading material from headings, captions, and summaries; reread material when it is not understood; locate related sources of information for a project; use table of contents and index; sort relevant from irrelevant details in passages; underline and take notes; keep an open mind about additional information that can modify the solution to a problem. Learning strategies become more automatic and elaborate; students discover new learning strategies due to their growing conceptual abilities and try new strategies when the old ones do not lead to success. As strategies become more automatic and effortless, cognitive energy is freed for understanding and storing information. Students' internalized sense of story structure aids comprehension; rehearsing terms several times and grouping them aids recall. Students spontaneously elaborate on information, which increases memory . . . the richer the associations the more ways memory can be cued.

Mental imagery reaches peak effectiveness in assisting recall. Most students still don't recognize inconsistencies in a text unless forewarned. They will reduce reading speed and look back if the material is unclear, and they become better at keeping attention from being drawn to irrelevant aspects of tasks. Students are paraphrasing and reorganizing text while taking notes, which assists comprehension and recall; students begin to record past problem-solving attempts in order to remember what worked and what did not; most understand that categorization is superior to other memory strategies (such as rehearsal, naming items) and have a more realistic and accurate picture of their own memory abilities and limitations. Students become more aware of and sensitive to the need to memorize (e.g., to study longer and enlist a memory strategy); can exhaustively search their memories and evaluate/reorganize information to aid memory.

Youngsters start to become savvy about what a teacher wants and plan their study time and strategy accordingly (e.g., study details or only the main ideas: *"Will I need recall for an essay?"* or, *"Is recognition good enough for a multiple-choice exam?"*); they study difficult material differently; break down large tasks; accept or reject information, depending on how it fits in with what they already know; recognize when note taking is useful and when it is not worth it; think about all alternatives before choosing an answer. Most can follow instructions for self-questioning techniques to aid comprehension and recall; self-evaluate performance and take corrective action (*"I ran out of time because I did the hard questions first, instead of the easy ones"*); benefit from silent "self-verbalization" that walks the student through the task step by step (*"Have I stated the main idea . . . used topic sentences . . . stated my conclusion . . . corrected spelling and punctuation . . . ?"*).

Sophistication develops for constructing mnemonics or clever associations to augment memory (*"Mom told me to buy PEAR at the grocery, **p**opcorn, **e**ggs, **a**pplesauce, **r**aisins"; "I can remember that Concord is the capital of New Hampshire by imagining me walking a hamster with a cord around its neck"*).

Memory for details fades over time, so that only a "fuzzy trace" (vague gist), remains; however, children recognize the similarities between these fuzzy traces and new ideas they encounter, so they problem-solve at higher levels.

Appendix C

Using Assistive Technologies

Dr. Jitka Sinecka

Many people are confused by the word *technology*. When they hear "assistive technology," they first think of computers. Assistive technologies certainly do include computers, but the term refers to a huge array of accommodations and adaptations which enable people with disabilities to function with greater ease and independence. These include very nontechnical and low-cost items such as colored highlighters, sticky notes, Wiki Stix, an office binder that serves as a slant board for a keyboard, or soft-cushioned seating in a quiet corner with good lighting. As Simone's story on page 478 illustrates, the refrigerator at home becomes an assistive technology when it is used as a bulletin board to help a student remember what he or she needs to do.

Computers are an important type of assistive technology, though, because they open up so many exciting possibilities for communication, writing and reading, finding information, organizing ideas, or controlling one's environment. Their value to people with disabilities is reflected by the growing means we have of operating computers: in addition to the mouse, trackballs, touch screens, and alternative keyboards, there are computers that respond to voice commands, head pointers, eye blinks, and/or movement of almost any functioning body part. Computers can assist communication by converting text to speech or speech to text; they can assist literacy and access to information by scanning and reading text aloud; they can assist individuals with organization of tasks and schedules, and even with recreation.

A great many assistive technologies have been developed for people with learning disabilities. Although it is impossible to produce a complete list, this appendix will give you ideas about what kinds of support to look for in areas in which children with learning disabilities are most likely to need help. At the end of this appendix, you will find a resource list that will help you keep up with this rapidly evolving field.

Simone

Ten-year-old Simone is a bright, eager child with many friends. She does well in school when she is organized, but she needs a tremendous amount of help to structure her thoughts and ideas, which are often all over the place. Simone remembers what she learns, but cannot distinguish what is important from what is not. At home, she is often so immersed in her thoughts that she forgets to brush her teeth in the evening or feed the fish that she wanted so much for her tenth birthday. Increased demands for independent written work in fifth grade left Simone floundering and earning grades much lower than her parents and teachers knew she was capable of. Midway through this unhappy school year, a learning specialist recommended that Simone's teachers and her family consider some strategies that address this issue.

One idea was to use a computer software program to help Simone organize her thoughts. When Simone writes papers and prepares assignments, she can now "throw" or "dump" all her ideas on one page on the computer screen; later she can link them to related material as necessary without fear of "losing" her key points. The program also enables her to organize her thoughts into subgroups, enclose them in smaller and bigger bubbles, add notes to the bubbles, and connect ideas to pictures and internet links. Using this program, which also guides students through the writing process, Simone quickly began to produce written work that was above average for her grade.

Simone's teachers now help her with her class work by breaking down tasks for her and giving her step-by-step instructions. Simone checks boxes on a simple checklist as each task is done. This prevents her from becoming "lost" among details of a project and helps her complete her work on time.

At home, Simone uses new scheduling tools such as magnetic pictures that can be easily moved around on the fridge to remind her of her daily responsibilities. Simone now sees pictures of toothbrushing on the mirror when she gets up and before she goes to bed and does not forget. Recently, Simone has begun using a "smart phone" to help her plan, organize, store, and retrieve her calendar, task list, contact data, and other information. Her increasing comfort level with these tools is reflected in greater confidence and improved performance both at home and at school.

Literacy

Writing as a Physical Act

There are two types of writing: writing as a physical activity and writing as a creative process. There is also the aspect of writing that calls for organizing ideas that result in a paper or written homework assignment. To assist with the motor aspect of writing, low-tech supports such as pencil grips, raised-line paper that helps students keep handwriting straight, interestingly shaped pencils that build enthusiasm for writing, or a pencil with a little stand that does not need to be held in the hand can all be valuable. More advanced tools include a variety of keyboards. Portable keyboards are very light and run for hundreds of hours on batteries. After typing, they can be connected to a computer to transfer text to a word-processing program. Keyboards with speech output can say out loud every letter that is typed and/or pronounce whole words or sentences as they are completed. This helps students quickly recognize and correct spelling and grammar mistakes. These programs may also have both visual and audible spell-checkers (when a word is spelled wrong, a list of plausible words pops up to select from) and customizable word prediction (once accustomed to your child's vocabulary, the computer guesses and completes the word your child is typing from the first few letters).

Keyboards with large, colorful keys, or alternative key setups such as "abcd . . ." can help with distinguishing letters, numbers, and other function keys on the board. Onscreen keyboards, used with a touch-screen window, can eliminate the need to type, and can also enable people with disabilities to type with the slightest move of an eyebrow (or other body part) while a camera connected to the computer watches for these tiny movements. You can also find speech-to-text programs that type words as you speak them into a microphone. Note that these programs often require some training so the computer understands the individual user's pronunciation, speech patterns, and phrasing.

Writing as a Creative and Learning Process

To organize ideas in order to compose a paper, graphic organizers and outlining programs allow the author to "dump" unorganized information onto one page, and later add notes and short paragraphs that create a base for structuring a project. These programs offer step-by-step instructions: they start with gathering known information and facts; move on to doing new research to expand ideas; and then guide the student through typing the paper, which is later checked by the computer for spelling errors and grammar mistakes. The finished result can be printed out or published online.

Word-prediction software helps the writing process flow easier by "predicting" from the first few letters what word the user intends to type. Predictions are based on how American sentences get created, so after a noun there is a verb and so on. It also predicts based on spelling, meaning and grammar, and frequent/recent use. As a word is typed, a list of up to ten choices comes up; the student then chooses the correct word. Your child can hear how each word sounds by pointing at it with the mouse cursor or using the arrows, which is very helpful to children who recognize a word when they hear it but would not necessarily recognize it when it is written. A neat feature of many of these programs is that they detect commonly misspelled words, so when a child starts typing *b-l-*, the word *balloon* comes up because it is known that that is how children often write it.

Some new technologies extend the possibilities of writing even further. A paper-based computer pen, for example, records and links audio to what a person writes using the pen and special paper. Your child can take notes, for example, while simultaneously recording the teacher speaking. She can later listen to any section of the lecture by touching the pen to the corresponding notes. Another feature of this pen is that whatever is written on the special paper can be sent to a screen and appears as typed text that can be further edited. It also has a lot of fun features, such as setting up talking calendars, solving math problems on a talking calculator, even playing music on a special paper that has drawn on it a piano keyboard or a drum set.

The Mechanics of Writing
Any word-processing program will likely have built-in spelling and grammar checks and a thesaurus. Spell checks alert you by underlining in color a word that was not correctly spelled. When you right-click on the word, several options are offered regarding how to spell the word. Grammar checks provide alerts when a sentence is not grammatically correct by underlining the phrase in another color. A right-click suggests alternative phrasing. The thesaurus looks up the definition of any word and suggests its use in sentences, as well as offering synonyms and antonyms. Abbreviation programs allow a user to create, store, and reuse abbreviations for frequently used words or phrases. This can save the user keystrokes and ensure proper spelling of words and phrases that were coded as abbreviations. For example, typing *Syr* would signal the computer to type *Syracuse*.

To get remedial help with spelling, look for programs that flash a word at the student; when the word disappears from the screen, the student types the word he or she remembers seeing. The word flashes for less and less time as the program continues. There are also programs that slowly sound out and add each successive letter to create a correctly spelled word. Then, the student is required to follow only the voice of the computer to type each successive letter. When the word disappears, the student types from memory. Other programs play verbal games with you: for example, the first, or the first and the last letters of a three-letter word appear on the screen and the student is directed to fill in the blank after the computer says the word aloud. The student sees *r_t* and types in *a* for a *rat*, or sees *r_* and types *ed* when he hears *red*.

Reading
Simple technologies to help with reading include positioning a book on a stand or a slanted board for easier viewing, and cutting a rectangle from black paper to separate the one line on a page that is being read (or one paragraph if the cut-out piece is larger) to eliminate distracting elements on the page and help students focus on one area of print at a time. Sticky notes and colored highlighter pens help children find and note important information and vocabulary. Recorded publications allow users to listen to text; recordings are available in a variety of formats, such as CDs and MP3 downloads (less and less on tape). You can subscribe to a library or an online service to choose from hundreds of available

titles. Special playback units allow users to search and bookmark pages and chapters. A new product on the technology market, Kindle 2, is a slim tablet that reads out loud any newspaper, magazine, or book that can be downloaded from the internet; in many cases, the download process takes less than a minute. The text on the screen can be enlarged for easier reading. All these technologies give students access to high-level reading materials they might find difficult to read on their own.

A reading pen that looks like an ordinary pen, but has a scanning and computer mechanism inside, can scan an unknown word, pronounce it out loud, and look up the definition in a vast internal dictionary. Software programs today can do such miracles as reading aloud and highlighting each word that your child types. In this way the writer gets both visual and auditory feedback as he goes along. Other programs—called speech synthesizers or screen readers—are able to display and read aloud any text on a computer screen, including text typed by the user, text scanned in from printed pages (e.g., books, letters), or text appearing on the internet. Reading can also be fun with electronic books that are accessible online. Those books read the text aloud from a web page that is designed to look like a real book (you can even hear the flipping pages). Actors with appealing voices read the stories, which helps maintain interest. At the end you can test your comprehension and what you learned from each chapter.

Some software programs are designed specifically for the child with reading and other literacy-related difficulties. For example, *Wynn Literacy, Read & Write Gold*, and *Kurzweil 3000*, all read aloud any kind of text on a computer screen and highlight it simultaneously. They also take "voice notes" and include word-processing tools that assist with such aspects of writing as outlining papers, planning paragraphs, editing documents, and spelling. Other features include "talking dictionaries" and guidelines for finding facts and organizing them for an assignment. Programs that highlight words as they are read aloud by the computer can help students learn whole-word recognition and improve reading fluency. Look also for programs that introduce readings at different levels (from kindergarten to high school), and that offer multiple formats (such as a real paper book, a CD, and software that provides an electronic version of the book with illustrations and quizzes). You can also find online books that check comprehension at the end of each page or chapter by asking multiple-choice questions. In some, interaction is encouraged by a voice reading and asking the questions, as well as fun sound features and animation.

Listening
Some children benefit more from hearing information than from seeing it or writing it down. For them, tape recorders and digital recorders are very useful and affordable. The student can listen to a lecture or recorded text as often as necessary to remember it. On modern equipment it is possible to slow down the tape or speed it up without distorting the speaker's voice. For students who have trouble screening out background noise, or are slow auditory processors, assistive listening devices can transmit the teacher's voice directly to the user's ear. These units consist of a wireless transmitter with microphone worn by the speaker and a receiver with earphones worn by the listener.

Math

Technology solutions for math provide visual and audio support so that users can better set up and calculate basic math problems. Starting with low-tech solutions, try using a piece of graph paper turned sideways to help children keep their math problems lined up, or place a piece of paper or cardboard under the line being worked to keep a child's eyes from straying. Electronic math worksheets are software programs that help the user organize, align, and work through math problems on a computer screen. Numbers that appear onscreen can also be heard aloud via a speech synthesizer. This may be helpful to students who have trouble aligning math problems with pencil and paper. "Talking calculators" also have built-in speech synthesizers that read aloud numbers, symbols, and operation keys that the user presses; they also vocalize the answers to each problem (headsets can be used in class to avoid distracting other students). This auditory feedback can help a student learn math facts and verify the answers to problems before they are transferred to paper.

Some software programs teach basic mathematical concepts in the form of games. For example, the student participates in a horse or car race, trying to solve math problems (chosen according to topic and grade level) as fast as possible. For each correct answer, the horse or car speeds up while other horses/ cars are catching up. The student races against her own five best results, which are established during the first game. There are also programs that are very visual and teach math through pictures or music. One program asks "How many do you see?" while displaying three apples and gives a choice of the number 2 or 3, or asks the child to sort apples and pears and then count them. When a program teaches you a song about number 4 and uses repetition, music output, and pictures, it becomes easy to remember!

Organization, Attention and Memory

Assistive-technology tools like "smart phones" and Personal Digital Assistants (PDAs) can help your child to plan, organize, and keep track of his calendar, schedule, task list, contact information, and miscellaneous notes. Some of these devices can transfer information to a computer. These handheld machines often include alarms, so that when it is time to attend a meeting, for example, the device beeps and shows a message to remind you about it. (Computers can also be programmed so that a reminder "jumps out" at you on your computer screen.) By entering appropriate notes into a PDA, you can "ping" yourself reminders of anything from when to buy a card for your best friend's birthday to when to walk your dog.

Before You Buy

Before you buy any special device or software, make sure you don't have something similar in your home already. You may not be aware of the extent to which the computer hardware and software you already own may include features and functions that can improve your child's academic performance. For example,

Microsoft Word has an option for changing contrast between the text and background. It provides a dark blue background with white, yellow, or light yellow print. This enables some children to focus more clearly. You can also enlarge the font or the entire screen to make text easier to read. Many computers come with text-to-speech programs that read any text aloud, and also speech-to-text programs, which allow you to dictate what you want to type into a microphone while the computer converts it into text. Many computers also have an on-screen keyboard that can be navigated via a switch or touch-screen window. You can also usually zoom in and out on anything on the screen, highlight it, look up definitions of unknown words in a dictionary, and so on. Macintosh computers allow you to adjust keyboard, color, and mouse options to your needs (for example the computer can be instructed to read anything to which you move the mouse, such as task commands). Books can be downloaded onto most computers from some websites, and you can also download free and amazing programs, such as Dasher, that enable you to type with a slight move of an eye or any part of your body in any language you can imagine.

If you need hardware or software in addition to those typically available on a home computer, the rule is *try it before you buy it*. Many companies and vendors are willing to demonstrate their products and try them out with your child; go to the company website and look for information about free trials of their products. You may also be able to "test drive" technologies at your school's assistive-technology center, at your local library, or at a local chapter of parent-professional support groups such as the Learning Disabilities Association of America.

It is also wise to think of assistive technologies as a continuum: start out with simple low-tech (or no-tech!) solutions and move on to more sophisticated and high-tech devices only if they become necessary. This can save you hundreds—if not thousands—of dollars.

Selected List of AT Resources

Companies, Producers, Vendors

- Don Johnston, Inc., http://www.donjohnston.com/ Producer of writing, reading, phonics, and assistive-technology software and hardware.
- Enablemart, http://www.enablemart.com/ Large variety of products for children and adults with special needs including vision, hearing, learning, environmental controls, keyboarding, and computer equipment.
- Enabling Devices, http://www.enablingdevices.com/ Dedicated to developing affordable learning and assistive-technology devices to help people of all ages. Focus on adapted toys, mobility, sensory items, communicators, switches, computer aids, etc.
- Mayer-Johnson, http://www.mayer-johnson.com/ Producer of Boardmaker and related picture-based communication and organizational tools. Links to other agencies, associations, organizations; searchable databases.
- AbleData, http://www.abledata.com/ Compiles AT in 20 categories

of disabilities, including learning disability, and compares them. Includes searchable database of more than 23,000 products.

- Alliance for Technology Access, http://www.ataccess.org/ A national network of community-based resource centers, product developers, vendors, service providers, and individuals. Provides information and support services to children and adults with disabilities, and works to increase their use of technology.
- Assistive Technology, Inc., http://www.assistivetech.com/ Specializes in eye tracking and communication solutions.
- Center for Applied Special Technology (CAST), http://www.cast.org/ A framework for designing curricula that enable all individuals to gain knowledge, skills, and enthusiasm for learning (universal design for learning).
- Center for Universal Design, http://design.ncsu.edu/cud/ A national information, technical-assistance, and research center that evaluates, develops, and promotes accessible and universal design in housing, commercial and public facilities, outdoor environments, and products. The mission is to improve environments and products through design innovation, research, education, and design assistance.
- Closing the Gap, http://www.closingthegap.com/ Provides parents and educators with the information and training necessary to locate, compare, and implement assistive technology. Provides the latest information and training available for individuals with disabilities and those who work with them through an annual international conference on AT, magazine, and website that includes searchable databases of thousands of products on the market.
- Edutopia, http://www.edutopia.org/ Innovative resources and ideas on what works in public education, including technology integration among other topics. Technology planning must support four key components of learning: active engagement, participation in groups, frequent interaction and feedback, and connection to real-world experts.
- National Public Website on Assistive Technology, http://www.assistivetech.net/ Provides access to information on AT devices and services as well as other community resources for people with disabilities and the general public. Searchable database and online information on assistive technologies, adaptive environments, and community resources.
- Trace Center, University of Wisconsin–Madison, http://trace.wisc.edu/
- Wisconsin Assistive Technology Initiative (WATI), http://wati.org/ State-funded project to help schools improve their assistive-technology services. Includes comprehensive assessment package, resources, lending library information, and related links.

AT Services

- Quality Indicators for Assistive Technology Services, http://www.qiat.org/ Guides the development and delivery of quality assistive-technology services in a way that provides users with a gateway to quality indicators, matrices, shared resources, and a searchable database.

Parental and Family Guides

- Parents, Let's Unite for Kids (PLUK), http://www.pluk.org/AT1.html/ Helps parents learn more about assistive technology and how it can help their children. This guide includes tips for getting started, ideas about where to look for money, and suggestions for what to do when applying for funding. Suggests places to contact for more information or to find software and equipment.
- STAR Center, http://www.starcenter.tn.org/ A model demonstration, resource and training center dedicated to ensuring that all individuals with disabilities or other special needs maximize their potential for independence and achieve their personal goals of employment, effective learning, and independent living through assistive technology, assistive aids, and support services.
- Family Center on Technology and Disability, http://www.fctd.info/ resources/ Supports organizations and programs that work with families of children and youth with disabilities through a range of information and services on assistive technologies.
- Project KITE, Pacer Center, http://www.pacer.org/stc/kite/index/htm/ Provides a training curriculum for parents and teachers of young children with disabilities used to promote inclusion through the use of technology.
- Let's Play Projects, Center for Assistive Technology, http://www .letsplay.buffalo.edu/ These projects provide ideas and strategies to promote play through better access to play materials, and use assistive technology to give children this access.
- Council for Exceptional Children, Division for Early Childhood, http://www.dec-sped.org/ Professionals and parents look to the Council for information, resources, advocacy, and the opportunity to network. Members have access to five journals, an international conference, regional training events, a policy and advocacy network, listservs, and publications.
- Schwab Learning, http://www.schwablearning.org/ Serves families by providing information, guidance, and support that address the emotional, social, practical, and academic needs and concerns of kids with learning and attention difficulties, and their parents.

Computer Accessibility

- Apple Accessibility, http://www.apple.com/accessibility/
- Microsoft Accessibility, http://www.microsoft.com/enable/

Legal Resources on AT

- IDEA Legislation Information, http://www2.ed.gov/policy/speced/ guid/idea/idea2004.html
- U.S. Department of Justice Americans with Disabilities Act (ADA), http://www.ada.gov/adahom1.htm

Funding

Funding is often a major issue for families, as assistive technology can get pricey. If the AT is needed for use in school, the school district must pay for it, but it belongs to the school and the child sometimes cannot take it home. Parents who cannot afford technologies needed for use at home may be able to get support from Medicaid, private insurance, disability agencies, or charities. Another way for families to obtain assistive-technology programs is to search for "shareware." Shareware is software that is sold for a very minimal price or given away for free. Several websites gather information on this kind of software and list available products, including on-screen keyboards that can appear in various sizes, letter layouts, or colors; typing programs with word prediction; switches and alternative mouse setups; text-to-speech readers; and programs that make websites more accessible by enlarging them, viewing them only as text, or reading them out loud. Two rich resources for free or cheap software programs are One Stop for Free Assistive Technology (http://www.onlineconferencingsystems.com) and AssistiveWare (http://www.assistiveware.com).

Appendix D

Resource List

Learning Disabilities Organizations

Attention Deficit Information Network (AD-IN)
475 Hillside Avenue, Needham, MA 02194
Phone: (617) 455-9895
Website: www.addinfonetwork.com
Email: adin@gis.net

Offers support and information to families of children with attention deficit disorder (ADD), adults with ADD, and professionals through a network of AD-IN support group chapters throughout the country. Community resource for training programs and speakers on ADD. Presents conferences and workshops for parents and professionals on current issues, research, and treatments for ADD.

Children and Adults with Attention-Deficit/Hyperactivity Disorder (CHADD)
8181 Professional Place, Suite 150, Landover, MD 20785
Phone: (301) 306-7070
Website: www.chadd.org

Serves children and adults with ADHD and their families through education, advocacy, publications, support groups, and annual and regional conferences. Helps parents locate local CHADD chapters and also administers the National Resource Center on ADHD (800-233-4050; www.help4adhd.org), a clearinghouse for science-based information about ADHD, and the Parent-to-Parent educational forum (parent2parent@chadd.org).

International Dyslexia Association
40 York Road, 4th Floor, Baltimore, MD 21204
Phone: (410) 296-0232
Website: www.interdys.org
Email: info@interdys.org

The leading literacy organization dealing with scholarly issues in remediation of reading disorders. Free information, referral services for assessment and tutoring, excellent online bookstore. Sponsors annual conference and distributes publications relating to dyslexia. Membership includes parents, researchers, and other professionals.

LDonline
WETA Public Television
2775 S. Quincy Street, Arlington, VA 22206
Website: www.ldonline.org

A national educational service of WETA-TV, the PBS station in Washington, D.C. Provides information and advice about learning disabilities and ADHD. The site features hundreds of helpful articles, multimedia, monthly columns by noted experts, first-person essays, children's writing and artwork, a comprehensive resource guide, very active forums, and a yellow pages referral directory of professionals, schools, and products.

Learning Disabilities Association of America (LDA)
4156 Library Road, Pittsburgh, PA 15234-1349
Phone: (412) 341-1515
Website: www.ldanatl.org

Provides information and advocacy-related resources. Conducts an annual conference for parents and professionals. Numerous state and local affiliates.

Learning Disabilities Association of Canada (LDAC)
250 City Centre, #616, Ottawa, ON KIR 6K7
Phone: (613) 238-5721
Website: www.ldac-taac.ca
Email: information@ldac-taac.ca

Conducts programs and provides information for children and adults with learning disabilities in Canada. Sponsors the forum "youth2youth.ca" where individuals can ask questions and share information and concerns.

National Center for Learning Disabilities (NCLD)
381 Park Avenue, Suite 1401, New York, NY 10016
Phone: (212) 545-7510 or (888) 575-7373
Website: www.ncld.org

Maintains an extensive informational website; offers many excellent free publications; provides referral services through a Resource Locator. Conducts educational summits and programs around the country. Membership open to parents and professionals.

Other Relevant Organizations

American College Test (ACT): Act Universal Testing Special Testing
301 ACT Drive, PO Box 4028, Iowa City, IA 52243-4028
Phone: (319) 337-1332
Website: www.act.org

Provides information on the ACT and accommodations processes.

The College Board: Services for Students with Disabilities
PO Box 6226 Princeton, NJ 08541-6226
Phone: (609) 771-7137
Website: www.collegeboard.com
Email: ssd@info-collegeboard.org

Provides information on the SAT and special accommodations available to students with disabilities. Also offers programs and services related to college admissions, guidance, assessment, financial aid, enrollment, and teaching and learning.

Educational Resources Information Center (ERIC)
ERIC Project
c/o Computer Sciences Corporation
655 15th Street, NW, Suite 500, Washington, DC 20005
Website: www.eric.ed.gov

An online digital library of education research and information sponsored by the Institute of Education Sciences (IES) of the U.S. Department of Education. Provides online access to research publications in education.

Educational Testing Service (ETS)
Rosedale Road, Princeton, NJ 08541
Phone: (609) 921-9000
Website: www.ets.org

Information on special accommodations available to students with disabilities on the Graduate Record Exam (GRE) and Graduate Management Admission Test (GMAT).

Family and Advocates Partnership for Education (FAPE)
PACER Center
8161 Normandale Boulevard, Minneapolis, MN 55437-1044
Phone: (952) 838-9000
Website: www.fape.org
Email: fape@fape.org

Links families, advocates, and self-advocates to information about the Individuals with Disabilities Education Act and other pertinent legislation.

HEATH Resource Center: Clearinghouse on Postsecondary Education for Individuals with Disabilities (Higher Education and Adult Training for People with Handicaps)
2134 G Street NW, Washington, DC 20052-0001
Phone: (800) 544-3284
Website: www.heath.gwu.edu
Email: askHEATH@gwu.edu

Online clearinghouse on postsecondary education for individuals with disabilities. Resource Center offers information on support services, policies, procedures, adaptations, and accessing college or university campuses, career-technical schools, and other postsecondary training entities. Information on financial assistance, scholarships, and materials that help students with disabilities transition into college, university, career-technical schools, or other post-secondary programs is also available. Many excellent publications, including *Getting Ready for College*.

National Association of Private Special Education Centers (NAPSEC)
1522 K Street NW, Suite 1032, Washington, DC 20005-1202
Phone: (202) 408-3338
Website: www.napsec.org
Email: napsec@aol.com

Provides information on private early-intervention services, schools, residential therapeutic centers, postsecondary services, adult-living programs, and vocational rehabilitation services. Publishes online *Exceptional Parent* magazine.

National Dissemination Center for Children with Disabilities (NICHCY)
1825 Connecticut Avenue, NW, Suite 700, Washington, DC 20009
Phone: (800) 695-0285
Website: www.nichcy.org
Email: nichcy@aed.org

Information clearinghouse that provides information on a wide variety of disability-related issues for children and youth up to age 22. Excellent free publications on disability law, resources, and research.

Parents Helping Parents (PHP)
Sobrato Center for Nonprofits—San Jose
1400 Parkmoor Avenue, Suite 100, San Jose, CA 95126
Phone: (408) 727-5775
Website: www.php.com

Provides referral sources, workshops, training sessions, and support meetings for parents of children with a wide range of special needs. Resource library.

Technical Assistance ALLIANCE for Parent Centers (the ALLIANCE)
8161 Normandale Boulevard, Minneapolis, MN 55437-1044
Phone: (952) 383-9000 or (888) 248-0822
Website: www.taalliance.org
Email: alliance@taalliance.org

A partnership of national and regional parent technical-assistance centers funded by the U.S. Department of Education's Office of Special Education Programs. Projects aim to improve outcomes for children ages birth–26 years with all types of disabilities by developing, assisting, and coordinating Parent Training and Information Centers and Community Parent Resource Centers. Centers are found in all states.

Summer Camps

American Camp Association (ACA)
5000 State Road, 67 N. Martinsdale, IN 46151-7902
Phone: (765) 342-8456 or (800) 428-CAMP
Website: www.ACAcamps.org
Email: parents@ACAcamps.org

Provides listings of summer camps for children with special needs. CampParents.org is a comprehensive summer-camp resource for families, offering advice on camp selection, readiness, child and youth development.

Books on Tape

Bookshare
480 California Avenue, Suite 201, Palo Alto, CA 94306-1609
Phone: (650) 644-3404
Website: www.bookshare.org

Online library of digital books for people with print disabilities, supported by the U.S. Department of Education; offers downloads of books, textbooks, and newspapers. Users read the material using adaptive technology, typically software that reads the book aloud (text-to-speech) and/or displays the text of the book on a computer screen.

Library of Congress: National Library Service for the Blind and Physically Handicapped (NLS)
1291 Taylor Street NW, Washington, DC 20011
Phone: (202) 707-5100 or (888) 657-7323
Website: www.loc.gov/nls
Email: NLS@loc.gov

Provides taped and digital books, magazines, and other resources free for youth and adults with special needs.

Recording for the Blind & Dyslexic (RFB&D)
20 Rozel Road, Princeton, NJ 08540
Phone: (800) 221-4792
Website: www.rfbd.org
Email: custserv@rfbd.org

Provides taped educational books and books on diskette free on loan. More than 109,000 scanned titles.

Government Offices

Federal Student Aid Information
U.S. Department of Education
400 Maryland Avenue SW, Washington, DC 20202
Phone: (800) 872-5327
Website: www.ed.gov

Provides information for students about loan programs to assist in funding higher education.

Office for Civil Rights (OCR)
U.S. Department of Education
Office for Civil Rights, Customer Service Team
400 Maryland Avenue SW, Washington, DC 20202-1100
Phone: (800) 421-3481
Website: www.ed.gov

Maintains offices for inquiring about and filing formal civil rights discrimination complaints (both Section 504 and ADA complaints).

Office of Disability Employment Policy (ODEP)
U.S. Department of Labor
200 Constitution Avenue, Washington, DC 20210
Phone: (866) 633-7365
Website: www.dol.gov/odep

Provides information and assistance with employment issues for individuals with disabilities.

Social Security Administration
Office of Public Inquiries
Windsor Park Building, 6401 Security Boulevard, Baltimore, MD 21235
Phone: (800) 772-1213
Website: www.ssaonline.us

Provides information on SSI benefits and how children who meet disability-eligibility requirements can access SSI support.

U.S. Department of Education
400 Maryland Avenue SW, Washington, DC 20202-1100
Phone: (800) 421-3481
Website: www.ed.gov

Provides information on education initiatives and loans. Free publications.

Employment

ADA Information Line
U.S. Department of Justice, Civil Rights Division
Disability Rights Section
950 Pennsylvania Avenue, NW, Washington, DC 20530
Phone: (800) 514-0301
Website: www.ada.gov/infoline.htm

Answers questions about the Americans with Disabilities Act (ADA) and provides guidance for related legal, technical, and informational services.

Job Accommodation Network (JAN)
West Virginia University, PO Box 6080, Morgantown, WV 26506-6080
Phone: (800) 526-7234
Website: www.jan.wvu.edu
Email: jan@an.wvu.edu

Service provided by the U.S. Department of Labor's Office of Disability Employment Policy to facilitate the employment and retention of workers with disabilities. Offers employment providers, people with disabilities, and their family members with information on job accommodations, entrepreneurship, and related subjects.

Adult Education

Attention Deficit Disorder Association (ADDA)
PO Box 7557, Wilmington, DE 19803-9997
Phone: (800) 939-1019
Website: www.add.org
Email: info@add.org

Dedicated to providing information, resources, and networking opportunities to adults with attention-deficit/hyperactivity disorder (ADHD), their families, and the professionals who serve them. Source for information and resources exclusively for and about the adult ADHD community.

Commission on Adult Basic Education (COABE)
PO Box 620, Syracuse, New York 13206
Phone: (888) 442-6223
Website: www.coabe.org
Email: info@coabe.org

Promotes adult education and literacy programs, including Adult Basic Education, Adult Secondary Education, English for Speakers of Other Languages,

Family Literacy, Skills Development, and Workforce Development. Provides information about state, federal, and private programs that assist undereducated and/or disadvantaged adults to function more effectively in society.

The General Educational Development Testing Service (GEDTS)
American Council on Education
1 Dupont Circle, Washington, DC 20036-1193
Phone: (202) 939-9300
Website: www.acenet.edu
Email: ged@ace.nche.edu

Administers the General Education Degree (GED) Test (high school equivalency exam) and provides information on disability-related adaptations and accomodations.

National Rehabilitation Information Center (NARIC)
8201 Corporate Drive, Suite 600, Landover, MD 20785
Phone: (800) 346-2742
Website: www.naric.com
Email: naricinfo@heitechservices.com

Extensive resource on education and job training for adults with disabilities, and about obtaining and using adaptive technology.

ProLiteracy
1320 Jamesville Avenue, Syracuse, NY 13210
Phone: (315) 422-9121 or (888) 528-2224
Website: www.proliteracy.org
Email: info@proliteracy.org

Links adults seeking literacy instruction to local resources. Volunteers in local affiliates provide tutoring for more than 100,000 adults a year.

Independent Living

National Council on Independent Living
1710 Rhode Island Avenue NW, 5th Floor, Washington, DC 20036
Phone: (202) 207-0334 or (877) 525-3400
Website: www.ncil.org
Email: ncil@ncil.org

Works on a wide array of disability-rights issues to provide people with disabilities the opportunity to choose where and how they receive personal-assistance services in their homes and communities. Referral source for local and regional independent-living facilities.

Index

A

absentmindedness, 8
academic support, 146–50
accommodations, *see* modifications
    and accommodations
achievement tests, 113
  description of specific,
    448–54
  in severe discrepancy formula,
    109, 110
ACT, *see* American College Test
activity level, 297
ADA Information Hotline, 493
Adderall, 27
adolescents:
  depression in, 98
  moral development in,
    333–35
  peer relationships and, 289,
    307–10, 312
  social and emotional growth in,
    306–14
  television viewing and, 355
adult education, 405, 493–94
adult literacy programs, 404
advocacy, 174, 400
  see also self-advocacy
allergies, 14
allowances, 341–43

American College Test (ACT),
    122, 194
  retaking, 442
  sources of information on,
    408–9, 489
Americans with Disabilities Act
    (ADA), 401, 423, 426–27
anger:
  at learning disability diagnosis,
    127, 129
  as a warning sign, 97
animal studies:
  on environmental influences,
    32
  of learned helplessness, 100
antidepressants, 206
antisocial/oppositional behavior,
    99–100
anxiety, 97
appearance, 350
arithmetic, *see* math
artistic ability, 134–35, 232
assessment measures, 447–64
  see also tests, in learning
    disabilities evaluations
assignments, keeping track of,
    237
assistive technology, 47, 208,
    477–86

attention-deficit/hyperactivity
    disorder (ADHD), 42–49, 75,
    104, 285
  in adolescents, 312
  behavior and emotional
    problems in, 96
  checklist for, 44
  diagnostic criteria for, 46–47
  driving and, 345
  in elementary school children,
    304
  emotional support and, 155
  heredity in, 28
  importance of early
    identification, 48–49
  medication for, 26–28, 48, 203,
    204–7
  neurochemical imbalances in,
    25–28
  with other disabilities, 74
  positive side of, 325
  social support and, 151
  substance abuse and, 308–9
  technology support and, 47
  see also attention deficits
Attention Deficit Information
    Network (AD-IN), 487
attention deficits, 7–8, 40,
    141
  without hyperactivity, 42
  learning style affected by,
    243
  see also attention-deficit/
    hyperactivity disorder
audiologists, 209
auditory approach to learning,
    239
auditory processing disabilities, 63,
    182, 186, 274, 283, 302
authoritative parents, 364, 367

B
basic academic skills, 254–63
  Individualized Education
    Program and, 190–92,
    216–17
  monitoring progress in, 255

normal order of teaching,
    465–75
parent-teacher communication
    on, 257–60
reinforcement at home,
    260–63
behavioral questionnaires,
    458–59
behavior modification, 27–28
behavior problems:
  Individualized Education
    Program assistance for,
    201–3
  as a warning sign, 96–99
biological factors, 16
blame, 127, 378–79
books, keeping track of, 237
books on tape, 491–92
boredom, 91–92
brain-development errors, 16,
    20–25
brain injuries, 16–20
Buckley Amendment (Family
    Educational Rights and
    Privacy Act), 429

C
calculators, 250, 270
career awareness, 414–15
career counseling, 415–16
career exploration, 414–15, 438
career planning, 413–14
career planning services, 389–90
career preparation, 413–14,
    416–18
case histories:
  Alexander (poor motor planning
    and overly analytic style),
    94–95
  Ben (extracurricular activities),
    360–61
  Casandra (feelings of shame),
    10
  Casey (visual-perception
    weaknesses), 124
  Chad (incompatible teaching
    and learning styles), 292–93

Dale (job stresses), 418–20
David (artistic talent), 232
Eden (self-concept), 299
Eli (brother's learning disability),
    376–77
Jason (business success), 69
Jeff (patronizing behavior),
    220–21
Jeff (self-confidence), 316–17
Jessica (learning disabilities
    evaluation), 108
Jimmy (hereditary factors),
    30–31
Joe (emotional problems),
    98–99
Julie (decision-making), 348–49
Mancele (poor teaching), 37
Maria (learning disabilities
    evaluation), 116
Martin (substance abuse),
    308–9
Matthew (moral development),
    334–35
When Nathan Colors (fine-
    motor weakness), 73
Nick (unsympathetic teacher),
    154
Norman (parental rejection),
    330
Rachel (ask the child),
    119
Rebecca (family concerns),
    301
Sarah (musical talent), 283
Simone (thought organization),
    478
Teddy (brain damage), 18–19
cell phones, 274
cerebral cortex, 20, 21
    fine-motor disabilities and, 72
    language-processing disabilities
        and, 66
    visual-perception disabilities
        and, 55–58
cheat sheets, 270
child development, *see* social and
    emotional growth
Chess, Stella, 330

Children and Adults with
    Attention Deficit Disorder
    (CHADD), 325, 390, 487
chores, 198, 368
    appropriate division of, 382–83
    responsibility for, 340–41
clonodine, 206
clumsiness, 8–9, 53
college, 402–13
    emphasizing, 327–28
    factors contributing to success
        in, 403–7
    final steps in applying to, 443
    grievance procedures in, 428
    key questions for applicants,
        410–11
    legal rights in, 402–3, 407, 413,
        422–23, 425–26
    preparatory classes for, 438
    preparing short list, 441–42
    social support in, 432
    summer programs in, 443
College Board, The: Services for
    Students with Disabilities,
    489
college entrance examinations,
    408–9
    modifications and
        accommodations in, 194
    retaking and accommodations,
        442
    sources of information on,
        409
    *see also preliminary college
        aptitude tests, ACT, SAT*
Common Application Form, 443
community colleges, 405, 412
community service, 357
compensatory skills, 191
competition, 215–16, 363
computers, 249
    applications of, 266–69
    language-processing disabilities
        and, 68–69
    laptops, 275
    visual-perception disabilities
        and, 58
confidence, *see* self-confidence

confidentiality of school records, 429
consistency, 363–72
conversation difficulties, 8
counseling, 391–96
criminal behavior, 9, 312
culturally biased tests, 113, 114–15, 116
current events, 357
curriculum:
    keeping on top of, 245–49
    sequence of, 465–75
    shortcomings in, 147
curriculum-based measurement (CBM), 117, 218–19, 255
Cylert, 204, 205

D
debriefing, 384, 385
decision-making skills, 149, 347–49, 438–39
denial, 127, 375
depression, 97–98, 205
    see also anxiety; emotional problems; social and emotional growth
developmental delays, 80–85, 104
developmental measures, 461–64
development of learning and memory strategies, 473–75
Dexedrine, 204, 205
diet, *see* nutrition
digital recorders, 271–73
direction, poor sense of, 55
directions, difficulty following, 8
discipline, 202, 203, 363–72
distractibility, 297
distractions, 187, 215
documentation:
    for college and workplace, 423, 442–43
    of learning disabilities evaluations, 122–25
driving, 344–45, 346
drug abuse, *see* substance abuse

due-process hearings, 131, 223
dyslexia, 14, 140, 220–21
    see also language-processing disabilities; reading disabilities

E
E-books, 273–74
Educational Resource Information Center (ERIC), 489
Educational Testing Service (ETS), 489
Education of All Handicapped Children Act, 167
    see also Individuals with Disabilities Education Act
egocentricity, 306
electronic notebooks, 273–74, 275
electronic spellers, 274
elementary school-aged children:
    moral development in, 332–33
    social and emotional growth in, 302–6
emotional problems, 96–99
    see also antisocial/oppositional behavior; anxiety; depression
emotional support, 153–60
emotions:
    ability to express, 350–52
    listening to, 386–87
employment:
    discrimination in, 426–27
    gaining experience in, 440
    legal rights in, 422–29
    sheltered, 419–20
    ten suggestions for success in, 424
    see also entries under career; job
enrichment programs, 81–84, 216, 251
environmental influences, 30–38
    at home, 31–35
    at school, 35–38
escapist behavior, 98–99
estate planning, 434–35, 436

evaluation, *see* assessment
measures; tests, in learning
disabilities evaluations
expulsion, from school, 202

F

failure, perspective on, 326–27
fairness, 172–73
families, 372–87
blame in, 378–79
denial in, 375
giving siblings an even break in,
380–83
listening in, 383–87
roles in, 373–74
scapegoating in, 374
secrets in, 379–80
slighting sibling interests in,
375–77
support for, 388–96
see also parents
Family and Advocates Partnership
for Education (FAPE), 489
family counseling, 48, 391–96
Family Educational Rights
and Privacy Act (Buckley
Amendment), 429
fear, 127
see also anxiety
federal law, *see* legal rights
feelings, *see* emotions
fine-motor disabilities, 7, 40,
70–74, 75, 141, 249, 270
checklist for, 71
handwriting and, 249
with other disabilities, 74
flexibility, 217
friends, 363
see also peer relationships
frontal lobes, 22, 44

G

gender, 42
General Educational Development
(GED) test, 404
gifted children, 44, 137

global processing, 22, 242–43
goal setting, 351
grief and loss, 129–30
guidance counselors, 365,
399–400, 403, 438
guilt, 127

H

handwriting, 27, 249
see also writing
health insurance:
counseling and, 392
learning disabilities evaluations
and, 112
health problems, 136–37
hearing impairments, 136, 177
heredity:
in learning disabilities, 13, 16,
28–29, 30–31
in temperament, 294, 296–97,
329–31
high school dropouts, 402,
404–5
hobbies, *see* recreational activities
home:
ability to leave, 430–37
basic skills reinforcement in,
260–63
environmental influences in,
31–35
providing appropriate support
in, 181–87
home schooling, 211, 212–13
home visits, 107, 108
homework, 217
avoiding traps, 275–82
emotional issues in, 282
excessive, 164
keeping track of, 237–38
modifications and
accommodations in,
196–97
providing assistance with,
181–82, 279–82
reasonable standards for,
277–78
regular time for, 278–79

hostility, 97
humor, sense of, 305, 325
hyperactivity, 8, 44, 45
　attention deficits without, 42
　myths and, 14–15
　in preschoolers, 300
　in young adults, 314
　see also attention-deficit/
　　hyperactivity disorder
hypoactivity, 26

I
imipramine, 206
impulse control difficulties, 9, 45,
　304
　see also attention-deficit/
　　hyperactivity disorder
impulsive learners, 147
inattention, 44–45
　see also attention deficits
inclusion policies, 172
inconsistent performance,
　|85–88
independence, 438–39
Independent Educational
　Evaluation, 130–31
Individualized Education Program
　(IEP), 188–228, 429
　basic skills focus in, 190–92,
　　216–17
　behavior problems addressed in,
　　201–3
　class size in, 215
　distraction limitation in, 215
　due-process hearings and, 131,
　　223
　effective guidance in, 215
　initial reactions to, 125–26
　instructional flexibility in, 217
　keeping up with class content
　　in, 192–93
　monitoring student progress in,
　　177–81, 218–19
　noncompetitive atmosphere in,
　　215–16
　obtaining placement in,
　　221–23

orderly approach to learning in,
　216
parental consent needed for,
　125–26, 175, 222
positive feedback in, 220
preparing, 175–77
special services in, 208–9
student resistance to, 177
teaching appropriate educational
　strategies in, 194–200
types of classes available in,
　210–14
　see also special education
Individualized Education Program
　(IEP) document, 190, 208
Individualized Education Program
　(IEP) meetings, 175
addressing specific needs in,
　203–8
decisions to be made at,
　189–90
preparing for, 189–90, 225–28
student attendance at, 200
Individuals with Disabilities
　Education Act (IDEA),
　86–87, 104–5, 111, 167–69,
　214, 422–23
Individual Transition Plan,
　398–401, 407, 417, 429, 439,
　441
　see also transition planning
inflexibility, 8
information processing disabilities,
　24, 182, 183, 186
information processing speed, 24,
　244
information processing styles,
　21–22, 148–49, 238–45
intelligence, 137–40
　multiple types of, 138–39,
　　140
intelligence (IQ) tests (or
　measures), 113, 138,
　455–57
　limitations of, 137–40
　in severe discrepancy formula,
　　109, 110
intensity, 296

International Dyslexia Association, 390–91, 488
interpreters, 177

J
job coaching, 420–22
job placement, 419–22
job training, 389–90, 401–22

K
kindergarten, 81–84

L
language development, tests of, 461–62
language (English) difficulties, 113, 115, 177
language-processing disabilities, 7, 15, 40, 59–70, 75, 141, 163
  basic-skills instruction and, 191
  behavior and emotional problems in, 94–95
  checklist for, 60–61
  in elementary school children, 304–5
  heredity in, 28
  inconsistent performance and, 85–86
  with other disabilities, 74
  phonics vs. whole-word method and, 246–47
  in young adults, 314
LDonline, 488
learned helplessness, 100–101
learning disabilities, myths about, 14–15
Learning Disabilities Association of America (LDA), 126–27, 174, 187, 390, 488
learning disabilities evaluations, 79–80, 85, 104–33
  criteria for learning disabilities in, 104–6

dealing with results of, 125–30
documentation of, 122–25
elements of, 106
evaluations in, 111–13
factors affecting quality of, 107, 109
home visits in, 107, 108
information collected in, 118–21
information on legal rights, 110, 111
preparing the child for, 121–22
private, 112–13
in public schools, 111–12
second opinions in, 130–33
tests used in, 113–18
see also assessment measures; tests
learning disabilities organizations, 487–91
learning measures, memory and, 452–54
learning potential, 137–40
learning specialists, 209–10
learning strategies, development of memory and, 472–75
learning styles, 147, 238–45
  realistic expectations for, 336–39
  sensory modes in, 239
  see also metacognitive skills
least restrictive environment criteria, 125, 164
  interpretation of, 168
left-handedness, 15
left hemisphere of brain, 21–22
left/right, problems in distinguishing, 55
legal rights, 80, 81–82, 111, 406
  in college, 402–3, 407, 413, 422–23, 425–26
  differing interpretations of, 107
  in employment, 422–29
  to family services, 388–90
  in Individualized Education Program, 190
  in Individual Transition Plan, 398

legal rights (*cont.*)
  learning disabilities criteria and,
    104–5
  obtaining information on, 110,
    111
limits, consistency in, 363–72
listening, 383–87, 481
literacy, 479–81
Literacy Volunteers of America
  (LVA), 402
loss of interest in learning,
  88–92

M
mainstreaming, 169, 213
marriage counseling, 391–96
math:
  in curriculum-based
    measurement, 219
  language-processing disabilities
    and, 61
  by rote, 249–54
  technology solutions in, 482
  visual-perception disabilities
    and, 51, 54, 55
math skills development,
  470–71
math specialists, 208
maturational lag, 23
measurable goals/objectives,
  207
  see also Individualized Education
  Program
mediators, 373
Medicaid, 436
medication, 26–28, 48, 203,
  204–7
  side effects of, 136, 204–7
memory and learning measures,
  452–54
memory deficits, 24, 85, 90
memory skills, 149
memory strategies, 338–39,
  472–75
mental exercise, 260
mental retardation, 104, 110,
  137

mentors, 217, 282
metacognitive skills, 146, 148–49,
  196–97, 198
  see also learning styles
methylphenidate, *see* Ritalin
modifications and
    accommodations, 192–93,
    408–9
  documenting, 208
  examples, 194–97
money management, 261,
  341–44
monitoring progress, 177–81,
  218–19, 255–59
mood, 297
moral development, 331–35
motivational techniques, 121
multidisciplinary evaluation, 416
multiple disabilities, 74, 75–76
multiple intelligences, 138–39,
  140
multisensory approach to learning,
  186, 239, 247
muscle-coordination disabilities,
  see fine-motor disabilities
music, 234
musical ability, 283

N
National Institute for Literacy
  Hotline, 402
negotiation, 366–67
neural "networking," 66
neurochemical imbalances, 16,
  25–28
neuropsychological measures, 454
neurotransmitters, 25
No Child Left Behind Act (2001),
  198–200, 252, 254
nutrition, 17, 45

O
occupational therapists, 209
organizational skills, 8, 57, 148,
  185–86, 231–38, 279, 482
overprotectiveness, 323

P

parental consent, 106, 125–26,
175, 222
parents:
authoritative, 364, 367
instincts of, 102–3
overemphasis on academic
performance, 284–86
permissive, 364, 365
sharing by, 168, 171, 176, 182
strict, 364, 365
support for, 128, 388–96
support groups for, 47–48,
390–91
teachers and, 178–81, 257–60
see also families
*Parent's Notice of Procedural
Safeguards,* 111, 225
peer relationships:
adolescents and, 289, 307–10,
312
elementary and school children
and, 153, 303
moral development and, 332
preschoolers and, 300
understanding, 354
pemoline, *see* Cylert
perfectionism, 339
permissive parents, 364, 365
perseverance, 231
persistence, 296
personal digital assistants (PDAs),
274
personality, *see* temperament
phonics, 120, 147, 191, 246–47
physical therapists, 209
planning skills, 8, 57, 352
positive attitude, 315, 325–26
positive reinforcement, 201
guidelines for, 368–72
positive vocabulary, 323–24
poverty, 34
praise, 369
fifty examples of, 371
pregnancy:
risk factors for brain damage to
fetus, 17
teenage, 310, 312

preliminary college aptitude tests,
442
see also college entrance
examinations
premature infants, 17
preschool children:
moral development in, 331–32
social and emotional growth in,
295–302
private schools, 170, 188*n*,
211
problem-based curricula, 250–51
problem-solving skills, 149
ProLiteracy, 402
psychologists, 208
Public Law 94–142, *see* Education
of All Handicapped Children
Act
public services, 388–90
pull-out service model, 169,
211
push-in service model, 169,
210

R

reading, 144, 262–65, 480–81
to children, 260–61, 262, 280
comprehension skills and, 15,
247, 264–65
in curriculum-based
measurement, 218–19
fluency skills and, 247
language-processing disabilities
and, 60–61, 68, 70, 72
modifications and
accommodations for teaching,
193
parental guidelines for aiding
with, 262–65
phonics in, 120, 147, 191,
246–47
visual-perception disabilities
and, 51, 54–55
whole-language method of, 147,
150, 246–48
reading skills development,
247–48, 465–67

reading specialists, 208
realistic expectations, 328–39
realistic goals/objectives, 205–6
Recording for the Blind and
    Dyslexic, 273, 492
record keeping, 122–25
recreational activities, 358–63,
    439–40
Rehabilitation Act of 1973 (Rehab
    Act), 389, 405
    Section 504 of, 401, 424–27,
    428
Reliability of tests, 114
rescuing, 367
residential institutions, 211
resource rooms, 211
Response-to-Intervention (RTI),
    86–89, 105, 109
responsibility, 339–49
    for chores, 340–41
    for decision-making, 347–49
    for transportation, 344–47
retention, 256–57
rewards, *see* positive reinforcement
right hemisphere of brain, 21–22,
    55–58
Ritalin, 26, 203, 204, 205
role-playing, 352–54
rote learning, 249–54
routine, 234–35
rules, consistency in, 363–72

S
scapegoating, 374
Scholastic Aptitude Test (SAT),
    194, 270, 412, 442
    sources of information on, 409
school, 229–86
    behavior and emotional
        problems in, 96
    changing of, 252–53
    environmental influences at,
        35–38
    failure to meet AYP standards
        by, 252–53
    impact of positive experience on
        later success, 318

keeping on top of the
    curriculum, 245–49
learning styles in, 238–45
organizational skills and, 231–38
technology uses in, 208, 264–75
school readiness, 81–84
schoolwork:
    complaints about difficulty of,
        91
    keeping track of, 236–38
    loss of pride in, 92
scope and sequence charts,
    245–46, 465–75
Section 504, 424–27, 428
    see also Rehabilitation Act
seizure disorders, 18–19, 20,
    136
self-advocacy, 199, 422–29, 439,
    441
self-awareness, 315
self-confidence, 100–102, 144,
    315, 316–17
    declining, 100–102
self-determination, 200
self-employment, 421–22
sensitivity to environment, 296
severe discrepancy criteria:
    differing interpretations of,
        109
    formula for, 109, 110
sexual activity, 98, 310–12, 354,
    355, 358
    survival skills for, 358
sexually transmitted diseases,
    310–11
sheltered employment, 419–20
siblings, 324
    chores and, 341
    giving an even break to, 380–83
    slighting interests of, 375–77
sociability, 244
social and emotional growth,
    289–319
    in adolescents, 306–14
    in elementary school children,
        302–6
    language-processing disabilities
        and, 66

in preschool children, 295–302
in young adults, 314–19
social awareness, 356–58
social conscience, 333
social immaturity, 8
Social Security Disability
Insurance (SSDI), 436
social skills, 28, 32, 151–53, 203
social awareness in, 356–58
strategies for improving, 349–63
television as hindrance to,
355–56
types of, 353
social support, 151–53
social workers, 209
spatial relationships, 55–56
special education:
for attention-deficit/
hyperactivity disorder, 47
cost-containment and, 109
evolution of, 167–71
full-time attendance in, 210,
211
for language-processing
disabilities, 67
shortcomings of, 163–66
social and emotional
development and, 305
see also Individualized Education
Program; learning disabilities
evaluations
Special Needs Trusts, 435
specific goals/objectives, 206–7
speech disorders, 60
speech-language pathologists,
208
spelling, 55, 56, 65, 219
standard deviations, 109, 110
standardized tests, 198–201
state rehabilitation services
agencies, 405
stigma, 133, 169, 210
stimulants, 26, 204–6
Strattera, 206
strict parents, 364, 365
study buddies, 217, 237, 281–82
study skills, 148
see also metacognitive skills

substance abuse, 9, 98, 206, 355
in adolescents, 310, 311, 312
attention-deficit/hyperactivity
disorder and, 308–9
pregnancy and, 17
success, defining, 231
sugar, 14–15
suicide, 9, 98
Summary of Performance (SOP),
400–401, 444–45
summer camps, 491
Supplemental Education Services
(SES), 253
Supplemental Security Insurance
(SSI), 436
support:
academic, 146–50
emotional, 153–60
for parents and families, 128,
388–96
social, 151–53
for young adults, 315, 318
support groups, 47–48, 390–91
suspension, from school, 202

T
tactile approach to learning, 240
tardiness, 56, 304
task restructuring, 235–36
teachers:
effective guidance provided by,
215
expectations for, 156–59
Individualized Education
Program and, 181
parents and, 178–81, 257–60
unsympathetic, 154
technical schools, 443–44
technology:
assistive, 47, 208, 477–86
description of types, 264–75
federal support for, 389
language-processing disabilities
and, 68–69
Technology-Related Assistance for
Individuals with Disabilities
Act (Tech Act), 389

teenagers, *see* adolescents
television, 355–56
temperament, 294
  areas resistant to change,
    296–97
  realistic expectations for,
    329–32
tests:
  assessment measuring,
    447–64
  culturally biased, 113, 114–15,
    116
  in learning disabilities
    evaluations, 113–18
  modifications and
    accommodations in, 195–96,
    200, 408–9
  reliability of, 114
  standardized, high-stakes,
    198–201
  validity of, 114
test-taking skills, 148–49
thrill-seeking behavior, 99,
    312
time limits, 121, 217
time-management skills, 148,
    234–35, 279–80, 413
time out, 352
Tourette's syndrome, 205,
    206
toxins, exposure to, 17
trade schools, 443–44
transition planning, 398–401,
    438–39
  see also Individual Transition
    Plan
transition programs, 418
transportation, 344–47
trial teaching, 118
trusts, *see* estate planning
tutoring, 170
typing, 249

U
underachievement, 92–93
Universal Design for Learning
    (UDL), 173, 185–87

V
validity of tests, 114
visual approach to learning, 35,
    239
visual-perception disabilities, 7,
    24, 40, 49–59, 75, 141
  behavior and emotional
    problems in, 94–95
  checklist for, 52–53
  handwriting and, 249
  homework and, 280–81
  phonics vs. whole-word method
    and, 147, 150, 246–47
  in preschoolers, 300
  social support and, 151
visual-perception tests, 462–64
visual prompts, 235
vocational assessment, 415–16
vocational education, 416–18,
    438
vocational educators, 209

W
warning signs, 79–80
  behavior or emotional problems,
    96–99
  declining confidence and self-
    esteem, 100–102
  developmental delays, 80–85
  inconsistent performance,
    85–88
  loss of interest in learning,
    88–92
  unexpected underachievement,
    92–93
watches, 271
weekly progress reports, 255–56,
    258
whole-language method of reading,
    147, 150, 246–48
word processors, 248, 267–68,
    269
work ethic, 315
work space, organizing, 233–34
writing:
  as creative and learning process,
    479–80

in curriculum-based
measurement, 219
fine-motor disabilities and,
70–74
language-processing disabilities
and, 61, 68
mechanics of, 480
modifications and
accommodations for teaching,
192

overemphasis on mechanics of,
248–49
as physical act, 479
visual-perception disabilities
and, 51, 54–55
see also handwriting
writing-process curricula,
248
writing-skills development,
468–69

Acknowledgments

We would like to express our gratitude to the Learning Disabilities Association of Central New York and to the many students, parents, and teachers whose reflections have taught us and led us. Their stories have enriched our own perspectives, and we applaud their wisdom and their courage. In particular, we would like to thank Lesley Bogad, Aggie Glavin, Sarah Dewan Litchfield, Sue Loveland, Rebecca Moldover, Paul DeJong, Margie Boudreau, Mary Aitcheson, Teri Hubler, Jennifer Shulman, and Tom Haley.

Producing a book like this one involves the assistance of many people. We are indebted to our editor, Sydney Tanigawa, for guiding this revision.